NONE IS TOO MANY

Canada and the Jews of Europe 1933–1948

[This] is a story best summed up in the words of an anonymous senior Canadian official who, in the midst of a rambling, off-the-record discussion with journalists in 1945, was asked how many Jews would be allowed into Canada after the war ... "None," he said, "is too many."
From the Preface

One of the most significant studies of Canadian history ever written, *None Is Too Many* conclusively lays to rest the comfortable notion that Canada has always been an accepting and welcoming society. Detailing the country's refusal to offer aid, let alone sanctuary, to Jews fleeing Nazi persecution between 1933 and 1948, it is an immensely bleak and discomfiting story – and one that was largely unknown before the book's publication.

Irving Abella and Harold Troper's retelling of this episode is a harrowing read not easily forgotten: its power is such that, "a manuscript copy helped convince Ron Atkey, Minister of Employment and Immigration in Joe Clark's government, to grant 50,000 'boat people' asylum in Canada in 1979, during the Southeast Asian refugee crisis" (Robin Roger, *The Literary Review of Canada*). *None Is Too Many* will undoubtedly continue to serve as a potent reminder of the fragility of tolerance, even in a country where it is held as one of our highest values.

IRVING ABELLA is the J. Richard Shiff Chair for the Study of Canadian Jewry and a professor in the Department of History at York University.

HAROLD TROPER is a professor at the Ontario Institute for Studies in Education at the University of Toronto and author of *The Defining Decade* (UTP), winner of the Vine Canadian Jewish Book Award for Scholarship.

NONE IS TOO MANY

Canada and the Jews of Europe
1933–1948

IRVING ABELLA & HAROLD TROPER

UNIVERSITY OF TORONTO PRESS
Toronto Buffalo London

Toronto Buffalo London
www.utppublishing.com
Printed in the U.S.A.

Reprinted 2013

ISBN 978-1-4426-1407-9

Printed on acid-free paper

Library and Archives Canada Cataloguing in Publication

Abella, Irving, 1940–
None is too many : Canada and the Jews of Europe, 1933–1948 /
Irving Abella & Harold Troper.

Includes bibliographical references and index.
ISBN 978-1-4426-1407-9

1. Jewish refugees – Government policy – Canada. 2. Holocaust, Jewish (1939-1945). 3. Canada – Emigration and immigration – History – 20th century. 4. Antisemitism – Canada
I. Troper, Harold, 1942– II. Title.

D810.J4A23 2012 940.53′181420971 C2012-904760-0

University of Toronto Press acknowledges the financial assistance to its publishing program of the Canada Council for the Arts and the Ontario Arts Council.

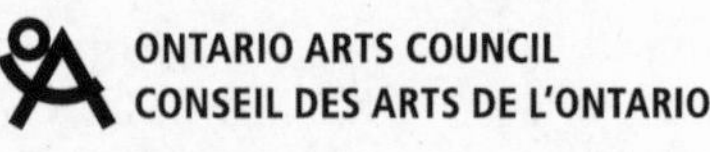

University of Toronto Press acknowledges the financial support of the Government of Canada through the Canada Book Fund for its publishing activities.

To the memory of Saul Hayes and all those who attempted to open Canada's doors, but failed.

CONTENTS

INTRODUCTION

(Revised for the 2012 edition)

None Is Too Many was first published thirty years ago. With the release of this 2012 edition, *None Is Too Many* becomes available to readers for a fourth consecutive decade. Defying expectations, including those of the book's two authors, *None Is Too Many* continues to engage readers and have an impact on the public discussion of ethics and morality in government, the righting of historical wrongs, the shaping of Canadian immigration and refugee policies, the responsibility of the bystander in history, and the role of the historian as witness. And, several years ago, when *The Literary Review of Canada* honoured *None Is Too Many* as one of Canada's 100 Most Important Books, books that "may be viewed as having made us what we are today," it commented that the book "forced a reckoning of the Canadian conscience and policy."

None Is Too Many is first and foremost a work of history, a history of Canada's encounter with the Holocaust as filtered through the prism of Canadian immigration policy of the day and its crushing impact on European Jews. It is a sad tale of a Canada which, faced with a humanitarian crisis of unprecedented proportions, refused to offer support let along sanctuary to those in greatest need. It is the tale of a Canada awash in homegrown racism and anti-Semitism. It is a tale in which those who swam against the xenophobic tide were few, far outnumbered by those who decried Canada's intake of foreigners as a threat to the nation's economic and social stability.

Following the First World War, there were widespread calls for cutbacks and increased origin selectivity in immigration. And as Canadian politicians and immigration officials responded to the clamour of those favouring immigration restriction, no European group caught their eye the way Jews did. Keepers of the Canadian gate warned their political masters that something had to be done about European Jewish immigrants piling up in Canadian cities in contradiction to the goals of the country's immigration policy.

In Quebec – then a rural and inward looking French-speaking Catholic society wedged into a larger English-speaking Protestant North America – the powerful Church regarded it a sacred trust to defend both the faith and the faithful from alien corruption; and for the Church, the Jews, portrayed as money grubbing, rootless, and contemptuous deniers of Christ's divinity, were prime purveyors of that corruption. From the pulpit Jews were denounced as Christ-killers, as exploiters who would cheat the innocent *habitant*, and as parasites spreading alien ideologies and an insidious modernism, which left unchecked would undermine French Canada's moral fiber. Popular French-language journals portrayed Jews as dishonest and evil. Even the prestigious and lay-controlled voice of French Canada, *Le Devoir*, lent its support to the *Achat chez nous* campaign urging French Canadians not to buy from Jewish merchants. Together, Quebec Church leaders, nationalist politicians, and the social elite united not only in support of a boycott of Jewish owned businesses but also in efforts to keep Jews out of the public square and, above all, to bar Canada's door to the further admission of Jews.

But anti-Jewish sentiment was not restricted to French Canada. Far from it. In English-speaking Canada, where a belief in Canada as a Christian dominion ran deep, the increasing number of Jewish immigrants entering Canada after the turn of the last century was a matter of public concern. And there is no denying that the early-twentieth-century growth of the Canadian Jewish population was both rapid and dramatic. The 1891 Canadian census counted only 6,503 Jews. Ten years later Canada's Jewish population had almost tripled to 16,717. Moreover between 1901 and 1911 the number of Jews in Canada increased another fourfold to 75,838. And by 1930 that number had more than doubled.

While this growth was striking, it was not just the increasing number of Jews in Canada that impressed itself on the public mind. Far more important was the unsettling realization that these Jews, most of them Yiddish-speaking eastern European immigrants, were more likely than any other immigrant group to subvert a Canadian immigration policy that prioritized the streaming of non-English-speaking immigrants onto farms on Canada's vast prairie agricultural frontier or into jobs in Canada's burgeoning interior mining, lumbering, and railway sectors. But Jews were conspicuously absent from rural and frontier Canada. In 1911 less than 6 per cent of Jews lived in rural Canada. Ten years later, fewer than 4 per cent lived in rural Canada; by way of comparison, more than 80 per cent of

Ukrainians, 75 per cent of Scandinavians and 70 per cent of Dutch and German immigrants to Canada were classed as rural. Indeed, no census group had a lower rural residency rate than Jews. Whether immigrant Jews originally came to Canada from big cities, small towns, or tiny villages, the now legendary eastern European *shtetl*, once in Canada they gravitated almost exclusively into larger urban centres. At the end of the First World War fully 80 per cent of all Jews in Canada lived in Montreal, Toronto, or Winnipeg.

Antipathy to Jews in English Canada found concrete expression in the construction of barriers to Jewish participation in community life. Even though Canadian law allowed Jewish immigrants to become citizens, until after the Second World War, discrimination on account of origin, race, and religion was widely and legally tolerated. Canadian Jews, immigrant and Canadian born alike, confronted widespread discrimination in employment and housing. On the eve of war in 1939, a "Report on Anti-Semitic Activities" compiled by the Canadian Jewish Congress noted that employment opportunities for Jews in English-speaking Canada were severely attenuated. Few of the country's teachers and none of its school principals were Jews. Both federal and provincial public services frowned on hiring Jews. Banks, insurance companies, and large industrial and commercial interests openly discriminated against Jews. Major department stores avoided hiring Jews as sales personnel. Jewish doctors, even Canadian trained, rarely received hospital appointments and universities and professional schools limited the access of Jewish students and did not hire Jewish faculty. The report also noted that Jewish nurses, architects, and engineers were often forced to assume non-Jewish surnames to get jobs.

Even as the organized Jewish community looked for ways to somehow counter discrimination, by the mid-1920s the battle against anti-Semitism had already been lost in one important area – immigration. Between 1919 and 1923 a series of regulatory reforms were approved by Cabinet that would reduce the intake of immigrants and especially Jews. Among these reforms was one that moved immigration inspection, including medical inspection, from the port of entry in Canada to the port of exit in Europe. By rejecting a would-be immigrant before he or she could set foot on Canadian soil, immigration authorities undercut the ability of lawyers, the organized Jewish community, or family members to intercede on behalf of the rejected. In many cases those rejected did not even know the reason for their rejection.

Without changing the Immigration Act, Cabinet approved several additional regulatory refinements designed to block remaining avenues open to Jewish entry into Canada. For example, the government narrowed the categories of family members eligible to be sponsored as immigrants by those already in Canada. This closed the door on immigration to all but the closest of family members and, in the case of siblings, only those who were unmarried. To assure that European Jews did not find an immigration loophole, in 1923 the government also approved new and draconian regulatory changes as transparent in their intent as they were absolute in their application. In a move said to forestall the entry of those described as belonging "to races that cannot be assimilated without social or economic loss to Canada," the government ruled that immigration preference should be given to those judged similar in "racial characteristics" to the Anglo-Canadian majority. It also closed Canada's door to all independent immigrants from central and eastern Europe except those who could prove they were bona fide agriculturalists. Accordingly, all new European immigrant applicants were slotted into one of three groups: the Preferred Class, the Non-Preferred Class, and the Special Permit class. The Preferred Class, made up of those from northern and western European countries including Germany, were exempted from nearly all restrictive immigration provisions except certain visa formalities. The Non-Preferred Class included those from Austria, Hungary, Czechoslovakia, Russia, Yugoslavia, Poland, Rumania, and the Baltic States. Immigrants from these countries were permitted into Canada within the provisions of the regulations, including especially guarantees that the immigration candidate expressed intent and had sufficient means to take up farming. The Canadian government also worked out a complementary arrangement with Canadian railway officials, who had a vested interest in selling both steamship tickets and western land, that essentially authorized them to act as Canadian immigration agents in Europe for the purpose of soliciting agriculturalists from non-preferred countries.

But Canadian immigration officials were not about to let Jews slip into Canada, not even experienced Jewish farmers with independent capital, no matter their country of origin, except those with the now more narrowly defined first-degree relatives already in Canada. Henceforth, all Jews, irrespective of citizenship or place of birth – including those from Germany (but excluding British-born subjects) – were to be lumped into a Special Permit Class with those from Italy, Bulgaria, Syria, and Turkey. Since the Fascist government of Italy had already moved to restrict emigration out of Italy, and the number of immigrants from other special permit countries was never great, it can be surmised that the Special Permit Class was devised and implemented in the main to restrict further immigration of Jews.

In effect, immigration officials and their Cabinet allies deliberately revised immigration regulations, without debate in Parliament, so as to make immigration more difficult for Jews than for others holding the same citizenship.

It worked. The 1923 changes in immigration regulations turned the Immigration Act on its head. Rather than permit the immigration of all except specifically prohibited classes, the regulations now prohibited all except specifically permitted classes. Except for those few who might still squeeze into Canada under the narrower family reunification category, only one route remained open for Jews hoping to immigrate to Canada. Cabinet had to approve a special permit that specifically granted a designated Jew or Jewish family permission to enter Canada in exception to prohibitive immigration regulations. By shifting the onus of granting Canadian entry from public servants to Cabinet, the immigration of Jews into Canada slid from the administrative process into the political arena. With no provision in immigration regulations for the routine admission of Jewish immigrants, the process of securing an immigration entry permit became a function of political influence and patronage. It was a process in which Jews would have few victories. "Between the upper and nether millstone," commented one Toronto rabbi, "the Jew as usual would be crushed."

Through the next two decades the Jew was indeed crushed. As *None Is Too Many* documents, once Canada's door was shut to Jews, it stayed shut. Even while the Nazis slaughter of European Jewry was taking place, the determination of immigration officials to withhold entry to those few Jews who might yet be rescued never wavered. Entreaties from Canadian Jews and the few non-Jews who lent their voice in support of refugee admissions had no impact. But while immigration officials continued to bar Canada's gate to the admission of Jewish refugees from Nazi persecution, it is important to acknowledge the sacrifice in lives and material that Canada suffered in the Allied struggle against Hitler and the Nazis. It is equally important to acknowledge that the Nazi genocide of European Jews, horrific though it might be, was regarded by most Canadians of the day as something separate and distinct from the Allied crusade. Simultaneous but disconnected, and certainly disconnected from Canada's war effort.

With victory, Canada, together with much of the western world, was gradually swept up in a human rights revolution. In the Canadian case, an informal human rights advocacy coalition involving the labour movement, liberal media and progressive political groups, and liberal churches and the organized Jewish community, began to lobby the government for remedial action to end racism and anti-Semitism in Canadian society. This struggle was not new to the organized Jewish community. In the interwar years, the Jewish community had vainly hoped to convince the larger Canadian public that their fellow Jewish citizens were, like themselves, upstanding and contributing members of Canadian society and, as such, should not be subject to discrimination. Results were meagre. At the same time the organized Jewish community also lobbied government to enact legislation prohibiting discrimination. Again, the results were meagre. Anti-Semitism remained as entrenched in interwar Canadian society as it was in immigration regulations.

Peace ushered in an era of change. And in Canada nothing so exemplified that change as the energy with which the Jewish community cranked up its campaign against anti-Semitism and, together with others in the human rights coalition, against racism of any stripe. Anything less than the eradication of state-sanctioned discrimination was now unacceptable. Canadian Jews, increasingly Canadian born, middle class, and educated, had sacrificed for the national war effort; they had given their sons and daughters to fight, some to die, alongside their fellow citizens. As partners in battle they were no longer prepared to tolerate the injustice of peacetime anti-Semitism.

As a resolute voice in the anti-racism cause, the Canadian Jewish community set as its minimum goal the end of anti-Semitism and the guarantee of equality of opportunity for all in employment, housing, and education. While other human rights advocates argued the need to educate Canadians to the injustice of discrimination as a necessary prerequisite to ending the problem, leaders in the postwar Jewish community increasingly took the position that convincing Canadians that racism was wrong was a fine goal but not to the point. Jewish leaders argued there would likely always be those in Canadian society who harboured racist and anti-Semitic views. If ending racism was made dependent on racists forsaking racism, racism would never be overcome. While not turning its back on efforts to promote religious and racial tolerance, the organized Jewish community put most of its energy into lobbying government for legislation that would make racism and anti-Semitism, whether individual or corporate and systemic, illegal in areas of employment, housing, and education. The softening of public attitudes, Jewish leaders contended, would only follow changes in the law and not the other way around.

The campaign for human rights legislation was gradually and increasingly crowned with success. Beginning in the late 1940s and continuing though the 1950s and 1960s, a patchwork quilt of provincially legislated human rights protections covered areas of accommodation and employment. Federal and provincial governments also began to consolidate these advances into more comprehensive human rights codes which, in turn, began to expand beyond race and religion to make other forms of discrimination illegal as well and also afforded human rights protection in areas beside employment, housing, and education. A singular achievement was the March 1982 royal assent granted to a far-reaching Charter of Rights and Freedoms as part of the Canadian Constitution. The Charter has allowed Canadians and the courts a new tool in advancing the struggle human rights in Canada.

Looking back, one is struck by how different Canada is today from the Canada that went to war against the Nazis in 1939. The parade of years has also brought us to a moment where the vast majority of Canadians have no lived memory of a Canada in which anti-Semitism was widely and legally tolerated. In as much as historians serve to link the here and now with the there and then, we researched and wrote *None Is Too Many* with full regard for the scholarly conventions of the historical profession. Through the four years it took us to write this book, our concern remained with historical accuracy – neither misrepresenting the past nor judging historical characters by the values of the present. While often troubled if not shocked by what our research revealed of the Canada of an earlier day, as historians we intended no larger statement than that which grows naturally from a diligent reconstruction of past events.

We believe that we have succeeded. But in our concern to be true to history, we did not foresee that from the day *None Is Too Many* was first published, it would speak to Canadians of more than just their country's past. To our continuing surprise, the events we document in this book have become an ethical yardstick against which events of our own day are measured. The book is repeatedly cited in discussions of present immigration and refugee policy, of bureaucratic callousness in the face of human suffering, and of the imperative that Canadians honestly and forthrightly address the dark moments in their nation's past. As a result, *None Is Too Many* has taken on a life of its own well beyond anything we, as its authors, ever intended or imagined.

If we never imagined the impact our book would have, we do take special satisfaction in knowing that in a small way it helped give thousands of refugees a new life in Canada. In 1979 the Vietnamese refugee crisis exploded. Canadians watched with horror as thousands of persecuted Vietnamese cast off into the South China Sea in small, barely seaworthy boats in search of a haven. Many died in the effort. As Canadians of good will pressed their government to act, one also heard the shrill warnings of the ominous racial consequences that awaited Canada should it participate in any refugee rescue program. For us, then still very much immersed in research on the Canadian response to the victims of Nazi brutality, these warnings had an uncomfortably familiar ring. More out of empathy with the hapless refugees than out of any expectation that we could influence those in power, we made a copy of a manuscript based on our preliminary research findings that we had just submitted to the *Canadian Historical Review*, put it in an envelope and mailed it to Ron Atkey, Minister of Immigration in the short-lived Clark government. Enclosed was a note reading: "We hope Canada will not be found wanting in this refugee crisis the way it was in the last." We expected no answer. We received none.

Only later did we learn that our article had been read by Canada's ranking immigration official, Jack Manion. A far cry from his counterpart during the crisis of European Jewry, Manion strongly advocated for a positive Canadian initiative on behalf of the Vietnamese refugees. After reading how a past Canadian government led the western world in rejecting refugees from brutality, Manion passed the article along to his minister, Ron Atkey.

Atkey later recalled reading the article at his retreat in Ontario's cottage country. Atkey was shocked and dismayed at the seeming historical parallels between the Vietnamese crisis and that of Jewish refugees from Nazis. Already decided on a path of activism on behalf of Vietnamese refugees, he later explained "The article stiffened my resolve to be bold." True to his word, he convinced the Cabinet that Canada must not turn its back on Vietnamese refugees as it previously had done to Jews. As a result of Atkey's efforts Canada's refugee resettlement program, enriched by unparalleled citizen participation, was second to none among nations of the world.

To the degree that our research added to the popular momentum leading Canada to open its door to those in desperate need of a haven, no impact of our work could be more gratifying or more unexpected. It remains our hope that *None Is Too Many* will continue to contradict those who argue that the only thing people learn from history is that people never learn anything from history. But, even as we write this new introduction, that hope is being tested. Those who measure the public mood tell us that increasing numbers of Canadians today suffer from refugee fatigue and that the magnanimous outpouring of humanitarian concern that moved Canada and Canadians to act with generosity during the Vietnamese crisis is no more. If this is so, it diminishes Canada and Canadians. Readers of *None*

Is Too Many have repeatedly told us they have been left moved and saddened by this tale of a dark moment in Canada's past. While it was not our intent when we wrote this book, we do hope that this tale also convinces readers that never again should "None is too many" be Canada's answer to those desperate for sanctuary.

PREFACE

To the condemned Jews of Auschwitz, Canada had a special meaning. It was the name given to the camp barracks where the food, clothes, gold, diamonds, jewellery and other goods taken from prisoners were stored. It represented life, luxury and salvation; it was a Garden of Eden in Hell; it was also unreachable.

In effect, the barracks at Auschwitz symbolized what Canada was to all the Jews of Europe throughout the 1930s and 1940s—a paradise, enormous, wealthy, overflowing and full of life; but out of bounds, a haven totally inaccessible. Why Canada was closed to the Jews of Europe is the subject of this book. It is a story summed up best in the words of an anonymous senior Canadian official who, in the midst of a rambling, off-the-record discussion with journalists in early 1945, was asked how many Jews would be allowed into Canada after the war. His response seems to reflect the prevailing view of a substantial number of his fellow citizens: "None," he said, "is too many."

Canada did not stand alone. Arguments still rage over whether more Jews might have been saved, or for how long rescue was possible. But such debates are futile. Had the democratic world tried to rescue the innocent—and failed—we might today find solace in the nobility of a lost cause, of a gallant crusade; but there were no rescue attempts. The nations of the world were put to the test and were found wanting; their failure was not a failure of tactics, but of will, of the human spirit.

One fact transcends all others. The Jews of Europe were not so much trapped in a whirlwind of systematic mass murder as they were abandoned to it. The Nazis planned and executed the Holocaust, but it was made possible by an indifference to the suffering of the victims which sometimes bordered on contempt. Not one nation showed generosity of heart to those who were doomed, not one made the Jewish plight a national priority and not one willingly opened its doors after the war to the surviving remnant of the once thriving Jewish community. Rescue required sanctuary, and there was none.

There can be no sadder irony in these events than that the democracies proved no more generous, and perhaps even more niggardly, in providing asylum than autocratic states. In countries where the voters could exact revenge on governments which initiated unpopular programs, political leaders carefully monitored the public mood. Nowhere was public sentiment in favour of the wholesale admission of Jews no matter how horrible the Nazi persecution, and nowhere did politicians display much courage in the face of popular antipathy to Jews. The Nazis read rejection of the Jews, especially by the democracies, as tacit approval of their policies. If no one wanted them, then the Nazis felt free to offer their own solution. The Holocaust followed.

Some Jews did find refuge, but measured against the millions who were murdered and the irreparable damage their deaths caused to the spirit of humanity, the number saved was pitifully small. During the twelve years of Nazi terror, from 1933 to 1945, the United Kingdom opened its doors to 70,000, and allowed another 125,000 into British-administered Palestine. Other states, with long histories of immigration, did even less. Argentina took 50,000, Brazil 27,000, and Australia 15,000. Some Latin American states, where life-granting visas were bought and sold like any other commodity, admitted but the trickle of Jews who could pay for their salvation.

The two North American democracies, the United States and Canada, share more than a common border and common values. Both are lands of vast empty space and great natural resources, lands underdeveloped and underpopulated, lands that pride themselves on being in the forefront of accepting the dispossessed and oppressed. They also share responsibility for the fate of the Jews of Europe. During the years of Nazi brutality, the United States, which eventually led the military crusade against Nazism, took only 200,000 Jews, including the select of European intellectual, cultural and scientific life. As for Canada: between 1933 and 1945 Canada found room within her borders for fewer than 5,000 Jews; after the war, until the founding of Israel in 1948, she admitted but 8,000 more. That record is arguably the worst of all possible refugee-receiving states.

Like the United States, Canada is today recognized as a nation of immigrants, a latter-day haven for refugees. From its very beginnings, as Canada edged away from Britain towards independent self-government, no area of public policy was more jealously guarded by Canadian leaders than control over immigration. Yet despite its pervasive immigration mythology, by the early 1920s Canada, once terminus of the Underground Railway, had effectively barricaded itself against "foreigners." If Canada, unlike the United States, never legislated quotas against particular groups, Canada's government still enforced a restrictive immigration policy with unabashed ethnic and racial priorities. With public support, it knew what ethnic and racial groups it wanted and how to keep out those it did not. British and American immigrants, especially agricultural immigrants, were always welcome, encouraged to come, recruited, made great promises, their journey often subsidized. When, out of economic necessity, Canada required immigrants from countries other than Britain and the United States, it gave preference to northern and central Europeans. Only in periods of great economic prosperity did it reach well down its ladder of ethnic preference to admit southern and eastern Europeans. These "foreigners" laboured in the mines, forests and marginal farms of Canada's vast interior plains or supplied the pool of cheap labour needed by the country's burgeoning cities and nascent industries. As Canada proceeded through the first half of the twentieth century, those groups that did not fit the national vision—especially Jews, Asians and blacks—were ever more often relegated by Canadian officials to the bottom of the list of those preferred. "Between the upper and the nether millstone," commented a Toronto rabbi in 1922, "the Jew as usual will be crushed." By the onset of the Great Depression, when Canada's doors slammed shut on almost all immigrants, Jews had already been locked out.

While in the 1930s and 1940s restrictions on immigration to both Canada and the United States had never been so severe, never before had the need for Jews to find a new home been so great. With the establishment of the Nazi government in Germany, both countries' immigration offices, as well as various Jewish agencies, were swamped by vast numbers of Jews looking for a haven. As Nazi control over central Europe increased, as their murderous intent towards Jews became more apparent, the number seeking refuge swelled. But immigration quotas barred admission to the United States to all but a few, and for those who turned to Canada, where anyone without a special permit was barred, there were few such permits. Thus, to almost every Jewish plea for admission, the response was the same: "Unfortunately, though we greatly sympathize with your circumstance, at present you cannot be admitted. Please try some other country." Most often there was no other country.

It is seductively easy to blame the democracies' dismal record on the Great Depression—easy, but wrong. Obviously, in the midst of such a debilitating economic crisis the governments of both the United States and Canada saw little reason to allow in any job-hungry immigrants. But the economic situation cannot account for the obdurate rigidity that led authorities to reject plans to offer succour to Jews even after the outbreak of war locked the democracies and world Jewry together in the same anti-Nazi crusade. Nor does it begin to explain the calculated and remarkably effective efforts after the war to insure that the admission of Holocaust survivors would be kept in check even as plans were laid to welcome many thousands of other displaced persons.

The destruction of European Jewry is a tragedy which extends beyond the inhumanity of concentration camps, the gassing of children and the annihilation of a culture. Horrible as these facts are, the Holocaust is a tragedy which also envelops and implicates the bystander. It claws away at democracy's pretensions to expose the anaesthetizing power of national self-interest. It cries out to warn all who will listen that there is no atrocity, no obscenity against life that mankind is not capable of committing. It demands that never again should none be too many.

ACKNOWLEDGEMENTS

This book took almost four years to research and write. It could never have been completed without the help and encouragement of many people. Robert F. Harney first suggested the collaborative effort out of which this study grew. He encouraged us at every step of the way, was always there when we needed to talk and generously made the resources of the Multicultural History Society of Ontario available to us. Our special thanks to Paula Draper, who shared both her research findings and good sense with us, and also to David Rome (Canadian Jewish Archives, Montreal) and Lawrence Tapper (Public Archives of Canada, Ottawa), both of whom gave of their time and energy to assure our access to those manuscript collections that now prove the backbone of this study.

Other custodians of the historical record offered us welcome and, when called for, bent rules sometimes beyond the breaking point to accommodate our research. We are particularly grateful to Jack Belwood (United Nations Archives, New York), Alf Erlandsson (United Nations Archives, New York), Jo Freeman (Department of Manpower and Immigration, Ottawa), Joseph Kage (Jewish Immigrant Aid Service, Montreal), Rose Klepfitz (Joint Distribution Committee, New York), Rabbi Moshe Kolodny (Agudath Israel Archives, New York), Sybil Milton (Leo Baeck Institute, New York), N. Nissen Ner (International Labor Organization Archives, Geneva), Louis Poch (Jewish Immigrant Aid Service, Toronto), and Sven Welander (League of Nations Archives, Geneva). We are especially grateful to Eileen Ready who allowed us access to her father's personal papers. We hope we have done justice to their trust.

Our work load was made lighter by the research aid of Rivka Augenfeld, Mrs. M. Gwynn, Bruce Lawrie, Danny Moore and Sonia Swartz and advice or help received from Barry Arbus, Yehuda Bauer, Leonard Dinnerstein, Susan Falb, Henry Feingold, Jack Granatstein, Andre Grushman, Benedykt Heydenkorn, Joy Houston, Ben Kayfetz, David Levine, Howard Palmer, Michael Slan, Bernard Wasserstein, Adele Wiseman and Larry Zolf. We are grateful for the hospitality freely offered by Raymond Breton, Barbara Hug and the World University Service (Geneva), Michael Marrus, Danny Mettarlin, William Moll, and Ralph Troper. Making sense of our hand-written notes, patching up our spelling and typing our manuscript was no easy task. We were fortunate for the efforts of Sharon Arbus, Margaret Brennen, Daisy Borden, Peggy Bristow, Susan Hall, Julie Parna, Gary Pyper, Toni Silberman and Beulah Worrell.

Our research was facilitated through the generous financial assistance of the John Simon Guggenheim Memorial Foundation, the Memorial Foundation for Jewish Culture and the Social Sciences and Humanities Research Council of Canada. We also gratefully acknowledge the encouragement of our colleagues in the Department of History, Glendon College, and the Department of History and Philosophy of Education, Ontario Institute for Studies in Education.

We are indebted to Lester & Orpen Dennys for easing the final stages of our project and, most of all, for having the wisdom to select so talented an editor to work with us. Janet Hamilton demonstrated abundant good humour, good sense and good will with respect to this project and its two authors. The American edition would not have been possible without the efforts of Susan Urstadt and, most especially, Corona Machemer of Random House.

We are also grateful to University of Toronto Press for ensuring that thirty years after *None Is Too Many* was first published, it will remain available to readers in print and now digital format. Special thanks to Len Husband for shepherding this edition through to publication and to Frances Mundy for her careful copy editing.

These acknowledgements would not be complete without a special note of appreciation to our families, Rosie, Jacob and Zachary Abella and Eydie, Carla and Sarah Troper. In large measure theirs were the countless small sacrifices that made this study possible and our collaboration a success.

I.A.
H.T.

NONE IS TOO MANY

1

WHERE THEY COULD NOT ENTER

It was May of 1938, and time was running out for the Kohn family of Bratislava, in Czechoslovakia. The Nazis had marched into Austria and were now making noises about pushing on. For some years the Kohns, a wealthy Jewish farming family, had been selling their land and other assets, while gradually transferring what money they could to a cousin who had left for Holland in 1935. It was now urgent that the Kohns make a decision, and a family conference of all the relatives—sons, daughters-in-law, brothers and sisters—was called by the patriarch of the family, seventy-year-old Julius Kohn. Like his father and grandfather, he had lived and farmed all his life in Czechoslovakia. But now it was time to go. The family must sell everything that remained, said the elder Kohn, and emigrate. As Jews the Kohns sensed what awaited them should the Nazis make good on their threat of annexing Czechoslovakia. As a family of successful farmers with a large amount of capital, they would surely be welcome anywhere, and they were already on the waiting list for visas to the United States; but Julius feared that the Germans would move in before the family could move out.

On October 1, 1938, the very day Nazi troops marched into the Sudeten region of Czechoslovakia, the Kohns boarded a train to join their cousin in Amsterdam. Once there, they planned their next step. Holland was already swarming with Jews who had fled Germany and Austria, and though some were content to remain in Holland, most were looking for a safer haven. Among the latter were the Wilner and Landau families of Vienna, both of whom had made fortunes in banking and farming and had left behind large estates; along with the Kohns, whom they knew through business dealings, they began the search for a country that would accept them. Fortuitously, Mr. Landau's sister had earlier moved to Canada and was urging her brother to join her. Though most European Jews knew that Canada was closed to Jews, the Landaus and their friends did not despair. With their determination, their wealth, their skills and their family connections in Canada, they felt they would have no difficulty.

On October 18 the group travelled to the nearest Canadian immigration office at Antwerp to apply for entry permits. The officer in charge, a Mr. Potvin, was candid and forthcoming. Here was a substantial group of potential immigrants, all of whom could legitimately qualify as farmers with hundreds, even thousands, of dollars to invest in their new country. Unfortunately, Potvin informed them, he must reject their application: they were all Jews and Canada was no longer admitting Jews. Shaken and horrified, Landau returned to Amsterdam, where he wrote to his sister in Canada for further instructions. He would pay whatever was required to get his family and his friends into Canada. His sister frantically contacted government officials in Toronto and Ottawa only to confirm Potvin's ruling. She wired back to her brother: "Kosher not welcome in Canada."

There was still hope however. One of the immigration officers Landau's sister had contacted inferred that with a judicious distribution of some money, including the transfer of all their funds to Canadian banks, the group might be allowed into Canada. One more bit of advice: they should also reapply as Christians. This they did at once, and within two months the entry visas arrived. Landau, Kohn, Wilner and their families, along with those of several other wealthy Jews masquerading as Christians, managed to join the group and were soon on their way to their new home.

Once in Canada all seven families kept up their charade. They bought farms, settled down to work the land and joined local churches. Some would never see the inside of a synagogue again; others would only feel confident enough to re-embrace their Judaism publicly after the war; and still others would convert—and remain to the present day active members of Protestant congregations. True, they had survived while so many perished—but only because they abandoned their faith.[1]

For most European Jews even this option was not available. Especially for those in Germany and Austria, life had become impossible.

On January 30, 1933, Adolf Hitler took the oath of office as newly elected chancellor of Germany. In his hunger for power, he soon gave short shrift to what remained of German democracy and civil liberties, and yet for Hitler political power was not an end in itself; it was but a tool in the service of his twin goals: resurrection of the Greater Germany and accession of the German people to their rightful place in the world order. Hitler's obsession with German living space—*lebensraum*—and racial purity—purity of blood—precluded any notion of co-existence with Jews. Nazis remained convinced that as long as Jews, or what Nazis defined as Jewish influences, remained abroad in the land, then Jews would remain a constant threat, undermining the Greater German state and sapping the life blood of renewed German peoplehood. For the Nazis, anti-Semitism was far more than a tactical rallying cry to be muted when power was achieved and the practical problems of governing the state confronted. On the contrary: power did not soften anti-Semitism, it legitimized it; power shifted anti-Semitism from speeches to policy, then from policy to law.

When Hitler took office as chancellor, Jews constituted approximately one per cent of the German population. To reduce, if not eliminate, alleged influence of these Jews on the state became a chief concern of the fledgling government. The wave of anti-Jewish boycotts and assaults on Jews and Jewish property that followed on the heels of Hitler's election to office was quickly legitimized by law. On April 7, 1933, the first of more than four hundred anti-Jewish laws and decrees was issued. In short order Jews were eliminated from all civil service positions, no matter how menial, Jewish lawyers were disbarred, teachers, including university faculty, dismissed, quotas placed on the numbers of Jewish children allowed in the schools and the practice of Jewish doctors restricted. Lest there be any confusion, a decree on April 11, 1933, asserted that for the purposes of German law anyone with so much as one Jewish grandparent was now legally defined as a Jew. Immediately, thousands of individuals who had had no previous contact with the Jewish community, who had never thought of themselves as Jews, were forced to cast their lot in with Germany's now terrorized Jewish minority.

The first wave of anti-Jewish legislation was followed by an eighteen-month period of legal retrenchment as the regulations took effect. Some individuals, including many Jews, may have been lulled into believing that the worst was over; but this was not so. After another year, in March 1935, a new wave of anti-Jewish demonstrations, acts of violence and terror broke out. The government, allowing if not encouraging anti-Jewish acts, seemed ill at ease with the chaos they effected. On September 15, 1935, the Nuremberg Laws were passed, laws that surpassed even the wildest hopes of the anti-Semitic demonstrators. Racial purity was decreed; marriage between Germans and Jews was outlawed; Jews were disenfranchised, their citizenship revoked. Stateless, with no access to the courts, no protection from the law, Jews were openly terrorized, Jewish businesses destroyed, children barred from schools, the sick from hospitals, the hungry from state assistance. But once again, the worst was yet to come.

As German frontiers expanded, with German annexation first of the Rhineland and, by 1938, Austria and Czechoslovakia, so did the number of Jews under German rule. The thousands of Jews who could were leaving for Poland, France, Britain, Holland, Belgium and Switzerland; hundreds of thousands more would have left had these countries allowed them in. None of these countries was, however, pleased with the influx of these unexpected—and unwanted—guests. They provided only a temporary haven and insisted that these refugees look for a permanent home somewhere else, anywhere else. Indeed, some countries—especially in Eastern Europe, where anti-Semitism was a way of life—began making noises about following the German precedent and forcing out unwanted Jews.[2] An acute refugee problem was fast becoming explosive.

International refugee organizations could not begin to cope with the problem. The League of Nations created the Commission for German Refugees but its accomplishments were pathetic, and most member states chose to ignore or belittle the plight of refugees, perhaps hoping that the problem would solve itself. Most nations argued wistfully that, if there was a solution, it must be on the basis of an accommodation between Germany and her non-Aryan population. No countries came forward to accept either those refugees left in Germany or those living temporarily in the countries surrounding her. Chaim Weizmann, then a leading Zionist and later first president of the state of Israel, neatly delineated the dilemma facing Jewish refugees. "The world," he said, "seemed to be divided into two parts —those places where the Jew could not live, and those where they could not enter."[3] Canada was in the latter camp.

That Jews were not welcome in Canada during the early

1930s is not surprising; neither was anyone else. With one-third of its people out of work, the country was understandably reluctant to accept job-hungry immigrants; in other words, that the economic consequences of the depression throttled immigration cannot be denied. But what should be stressed is that the depression also afforded Canadian government officials a dramatic opportunity to complete a process of restriction begun in the boom years of the 1920s.

Canadian immigration policy had always been as ethnically selective as it was economically self-serving. When economic necessity dictated the admission of non-British and non-American immigrants, it was always in descending order of ethnic preference. Following British and American immigrants, preference was given northern and then central Europeans. At the bottom were Jews, Orientals and blacks.[4] These "non-preferred immigrants" were acceptable as long as they were out of sight, risking life and limb in the mines and smelters of the west and north, holed up in lumber camps deep in the forest or farming the more marginal areas of the western wheat frontier. Those who escaped this life for perhaps the even worse one in Canada's urban centres, where they competed for jobs with native- or British-born artisans, were less acceptable. And to Immigration officials, the worst culprits, those most likely to settle in the cities, were Jews. Jews, according to the director of immigration, were "city people." To almost every request to admit Jewish farmers or agricultural workers, he had the same attitude: it was impossible to keep them on the farm or in the bush; every attempt to do so had failed.[5]

With the inclination on the part of less desirable immigrants to drift into the cities and a gradual decline in the demand for unskilled labourers, the Canadian government had begun, by the mid twenties, to restrict the immigration of those on the bottom rungs of the ethnic preference ladder. When in 1928 the deputy minister of immigration, W. J. Egan, ordered that the admission of eastern European immigrants be cut back by two-thirds, he explained that, although the economy was doing well, these "non-preferred country immigrants had drifted into non-agricultural work almost immediately upon arrival . . . and [were] filling positions that might have been filled by immigrants from the Mother Country."[6]

The onset of the depression then gave the government the opportunity to complete drawing the restrictionist ring around Canada. In 1930 an Order-in-Council was introduced, allowing into the country only those with enough capital to establish and maintain themselves on farms. In the following year another Order-in-Council effectively banned all non-agricultural immigrants unless either British or American. To all intents and purposes, Canada had shut itself off from the rest of the world just at the time when it was most needed. And for the remainder of the decade—and indeed beyond it—a determined federal government fought every attempt by the wretched European refugees to break through this protective wall of legislation.

The League of Nations' high commissioner for German refugees, James G. McDonald, repeatedly approached member states, including Canada, to loosen immigration restrictions. In the early spring of 1934 he wrote directly to the Canadian prime minister, R. B. Bennett, asking that Canada accept a share of the newly displaced. McDonald followed up his letter with a visit to Ottawa, where he held lengthy discussions with the prime minister and Immigration Branch authorities. Progress seemed to be made, and he was asked by the Canadian government to assemble a number of applications from German refugees detailing their full histories. There was one ominous rider on any deal made: government officials must be persuaded that all those put forward would "not become a factor in the labour market and [would] not become public charges." But as the high commissioner explained in confidence to Canadian Jewish officials, he was also assured some action would "be taken with a view to admitting a small number to Canada."[7]

The commissioner's office prepared the list requested; it was delivered to the prime minister on his visit later that year to the League of Nations headquarters in Geneva. In conversation with the high commissioner at the time, the prime minister was encouraging. Once he was back in Ottawa, however, everything changed. Immigration authorities persuaded Bennett that any breach in immigration restrictions, no matter how small, would only lead to more requests, more concessions; in the end the immigration tap would be turned on again—all this for the sake of a few Jews. Soon after, a contrite prime minister was writing the high commissioner that, although his cabinet's sympathy rested with the work of the refugee committee, the government would offer no help. "We cannot, in fairness to our population," Bennett explained, "authorize the admission into Canada of a number of people who must either remain idle or take the places now filled by Canadians, or for which Canadians are waiting an opportunity."[8] The matter was closed.

After the Liberal party came to power in Canada in 1935, the person entrusted with the task of insuring that restrictions on immigration were upheld was the director of the Immigration Branch of the Department of Mines and Resources, Frederick Charles Blair. Blair's small empire, the Immigration Branch, had been shunted from ministry to ministry as immigration had ground to a virtual halt. The decision finally to place it within the Department of Mines and Resources was likely made as much for administrative convenience as from any functional logic; as immigration receded further into the shadows of government priorities, it mattered little which ministry housed its operations.

Ostensibly, Thomas Crerar, minister of mines and resources, was responsible for immigration; in fact, Blair himself made policy and implemented it. Crerar, now well past his prime as a power on the Liberal party benches, knew little of the workings of the Immigration Branch and cared even less. He relied almost totally on its director for advice.[9] Thus, Blair made almost all decisions about who got into Canada; and nothing that touched his department escaped his personal scrutiny, whether it was authorizing the purchase of stationery or approving a routine application for admission to Canada. And from the point of view of European Jewry this was most unfortunate. Just when they most needed a friend at the gate, they had an enemy; instead of the philo-Semite they required, they had an anti-Semite; instead of a humanitarian, they got a narrow-minded bureaucrat.

Born in Carlisle, Ontario, in 1874, of Scottish parents, Blair joined the Department of Agriculture in 1903 and two years later became an immigration officer. In 1924 he was appointed assistant deputy minister of immigration and in 1936 he became director of the Immigration Branch with full deputy-minister status. He was a religious man, an elder in his church, a dedicated civil servant. Indeed, so devoted was he to his job that, when he officially retired in 1943, four years beyond normal retirement age, he had accumulated about two years of sick leave.[10]

As the man responsible for enforcing Canadian immigration policy, Blair mirrored the increasingly anti-immigration spirit of his times. He believed, said one observer, "that people should be kept out of Canada instead of being let in"; and he was, according to those who knew him, a tough administrator who "stuck to the rules," not so surprising as he had drafted most of them himself. Of course, Blair's ideas were entirely compatible with those of the Canadian government, which kept him in his sensitive position as long as it could. As James Gibson, a Department of External Affairs official, recalled, "He was the single most difficult individual I have had to deal with the whole time I was a public servant. He was a holy terror!"[11] And perhaps this is why he stayed for so long in his job: he was precisely the man the ruling Liberal government wanted; his inflexibility, his fetish for regulations, his wish to control unchallenged all matters of immigration—these traits suited an administration that had no intention of allowing in Jewish refugees but wished to avoid the reproach that might follow from not doing so.

For Blair the term "refugee" was a code word for Jew. Unless "safeguards" were adopted, he warned Thomas Crerar, Canada was in danger of being "flooded with Jewish people," and his task, as he saw it, was to make sure that the safeguards did not fail. Indeed, he was inordinately proud of his success in keeping out Jews. "Pressure on the part of Jewish people to get into Canada," he wrote, "has never been greater than it is now, and I am glad to be able to add, after 35 years experience here, that it was never so well controlled." Blair expressed a strong personal distaste for Jews, especially for "certain of their habits." He saw them as unassimilable, as people apart, as threatening people "who can organize their affairs better than other people" and so accomplish more. He complained bitterly that Jews were "utterly selfish in their attempts to force through a permit for the admission of relatives or friends." "They do not believe that 'No' means more than 'Perhaps'." And Jews, he lamented, "make any kind of promise to get the door open but . . . never cease their agitation until they get in the whole lot." Blair saw a conspiracy behind all Jewish attempts to get their co-religionists into the country, "to bring immigration regulations into disrepute and create an atmosphere favourable to those who cannot comply with the law." Self-righteous and justifying, he commiserated with the traffic manager of the Canadian Pacific Railway: "If there is any surer way to close the door in their own face, I do not know of it."[12]

But did Blair see himself as an anti-Semite? No, for he was, in his own view, just being realistic—realistic about Canada's immigration needs and about the unsuitability of the Jew to those needs. To keep Jews out of Canada, he would often argue, did Jews a favour, even if they could not see it. The arrival of Jews would create anti-Semitism in Canada, undermining the security of the existing Canadian Jewish community and little benefitting the new arrival. Those who saw anti-Jewish sentiment in Blair's position did so, Blair claimed, from self-serving motives. "I am sure," he declared, "the treatment received in Canada by Jewish people in no way warrants the charge of anti-Semitism. I suggest that those who hold such a view are putting it forward not on the ground of our past history but probably as an argument in favour of an open door policy, which under present economic conditions is impossible to adopt."[13]

Blair was of course an anti-Semite. His contempt for the Jews was boundless. In a revealing letter to a strong opponent of Jewish imigration, Blair elaborated on the reasons for his prejudice:

> I suggested recently to three Jewish gentlemen with whom I am well acquainted, that it might be a very good thing if they would call a conference and have a day of humiliation and prayer, which might profitably be extended for a week or more, where they would honestly try to answer the question of why they are so unpopular almost everywhere. . . . I often think that instead of persecution it would be far better if we more often told them frankly why many of them are unpopular. If they would divest themselves of certain of their habits I am sure they could be just as popular in Canada as our Scandinavians. . . . Just because Jewish people would not understand the frank kind of statements I have made in this letter to you, I have marked it confidential.[14]

But, though it was Blair who finally interpreted government regulations and who acted as the de facto judge and jury on individual requests for admission, to blame him alone for Canada's response to Jewish immigration would be both overly simplistic and incorrect; after all, he was, although powerful, only a civil servant whose actions reflected the wishes and values of his superiors. Not to accept refugees was a political decision, not a bureaucratic one. It was Mackenzie King, Liberal prime minister throughout most of the 1920s and again after 1935, and his cabinet ministers who, in the final analysis, were responsible for keeping Jews out of Canada.

Among the few voices raised in opposition to immigration restrictions were those from the Canadian Jewish community. But the community was small, politically weak and its protest barely heard. In 1931 Canadian Jewry constituted only 1.51 per cent of Canada's population, and although the Jewish population grew slightly over the next ten years, to 170,000, its percentage of the total population fell to 1.48 per cent.[15] The vast majority of Canadian Jews were central and eastern European immigrants or their children. As Blair was always ready to point out, they were urban people, most living in Montreal, Toronto and Winnipeg, Canada's largest cities. Each of the three Jews in Parliament at this time represented one centre of urban Jewish concentration—Samuel Jacobs was a Montreal Liberal, Sam Factor, a Liberal from Toronto and A. A. Heaps, a CCFer from Winnipeg—and together they constituted an ad hoc Jewish lobby in the nation's capital. However, despite the community's geographic concentration, Canadian Jewry was anything but monolithic. It was a community divided by its members' many countries of origin and by politics. Perpetual, often bitter conflicts existed between Zionist and non-Zionist, the observant and the secular, native-born and immigrant, and between an ostensibly well-integrated and generally monied Anglo-Jewish élite and the much larger, unassimilated and primarily Yiddish-speaking working class. In fact, Jews reflected almost every shade of political thinking on issues both domestic and foreign. No faction of the community seemed too small to form its own organization, yet few were the common causes strong enough to weld the factions together.

Efforts to establish a single national Jewish organization, built on a coalition of existing Jewish organizations, had begun in March of 1919 when the Canadian Jewish Congress (CJC) was established. At its founding convention, the Congress spawned the Jewish Immigrant Aid Society, then promptly foundered on the rocks of internal disharmony. It lay moribund, little more than a name on stationery letterhead, until the rise of Hitler in Germany and the growth of Fascist organizations in Canada. In response, then, to the threat of anti-Semitism at home and abroad, meetings were held in Toronto in 1933 and 1934, and the Canadian Jewish Congress was resurrected. It was reconstituted as a union of three semi-autonomous regions—East, Central and West—whose headquarters were in Montreal, Toronto and Winnipeg. A national executive, housed in Montreal, was elected with member of Parliament Samuel Jacobs as president.

Local differences persisted however. In Montreal efforts to unite the disparate Jewish elements under the CJC's umbrella failed. The far left remained outside of the Congress's fold, and, perhaps more importantly—at least for the success of the Congress—so did the "uptown" Montreal Jewish establishment, which saw the local Congress as a vehicle of the working-class, Zionist and Yiddish-speaking immigrant segment of Jewish life. Samuel Jacobs, even though president, was too preoccupied in Ottawa to concern himself with the day-to-day operations of the Montreal Congress. As a result, a well-intentioned but organizationally ineffectual Labour Zionist who had stood by the Congress through its long night of inactivity, H. M. Caiserman, took on administrative responsibility for the Congress in Montreal. If Caiserman was periodically able to tap individual uptown Jews, including members of the wealthy Bronfman family, for emergency transfusions of funds or token committee memberships, he was incapable of building either a secure financial base or a wide level of participation in Montreal. Thus, even after its resurrection in 1934 the Congress remained peripheral to Jewish life in Montreal.[16]

The role of the renewed Congress proved very different in the smaller Toronto Jewish community. As in Montreal, the extreme left remained outside the organization, but not the local Jewish élite. The Congress in Toronto was begun as a cooperative effort of Yiddishists, Zionists and *landsmannschaften* (mutual benefit societies often organized by men from the same region in Europe), working together with the affluent Anglo-Jewish leadership, the latter most often associated with Holy Blossom Temple, the home of Canadian Reform Jewry. Illustrative of the differences between Montreal and Toronto, the Toronto Congress did not delegate administrative responsibility to a senior member of the Yiddishist old guard, but made a young Canadian-born journalism graduate of the University of Toronto, Oscar Cohen, who had worked on the English-language *Canadian Jewish Standard*, executive director. Although under-financed, the Toronto Congress was never as chronically short of funds as was the case in Montreal, and it emerged as the centre of CJC planning and programming.[17] Winnipeg, as the headquarters of the western region of the Congress, therefore took its cue from Toronto, although it was more broadly representative of its constituents than either of the other two regions, largely because of the active role played by the left and by members of other small but energetic Jewish centres across western Canada.

The fractiousness that even a revitalized Canadian Jewish Congress could not paper over was set aside to some degree on the issue of immigration. Nevertheless, arguments over strategy and personal jealousies undermined unity. Only on paper did a neat and complementary chain of national and international organizations, in which the Congress was a link, exist to facilitate Jewish immigration to and settlement in Canada. First organized in Montreal in the late nineteenth century, the Jewish Colonization Association (JCA) was the Canadian branch of the New World Jewish colonization schemes inspired and originally funded by philanthropist Baron de Hirsch. Whatever its early dreams, by the late 1930s the association was sorely pressed to maintain a few Jewish agricultural colonies scattered across drought-ridden western Canada. In spite of its problems, the Jewish Colonization Association continued to press for organized Jewish agricultural group settlement and carefully maintained its links with HICEM, a union of world Jewish emigration and immigration organizations with headquarters in Paris.

The Jewish Colonization Association was joined in 1920 by the Congress's offspring, the Jewish Immigrant Aid Society of Canada (JIAS), which, unlike the association, engaged in personal intercession with government on behalf of individual immigration cases. As well, JIAS lobbied immigration officials to be more liberal and forthcoming in their application of the rules, assisted urban settlers and was largely funded through individual memberships and contributions from those who came to it for assistance—especially from those interested in bringing their relatives to Canada. Money, however, was always in short supply; A. J. Paull, the society's executive director, did not in 1935 put too fine a point on the problem. "Our own financial situation in Montreal is at present," he said, "quite precarious. We have absolutely no cash in the bank whatsoever and no other financial assets."[18] Indeed, at times it seemed that the struggle to insure the survival of the immigrant aid society threatened to supplant, as the organization's main activity, the struggle to assist immigrant Jews.

Jewish Immigrant Aid Society officials gradually developed a working relationship with Immigration authorities in Ottawa—not as partners in the immigration process but as supplicants requesting favours. As immigration restrictions grew more harsh with the depression, the society was unable to mitigate their effects. Rather than vociferously—and, as it knew, vainly—opposing the direction of government immigration policy, JIAS could only beg for indulgence on individual cases and hope, meanwhile, for better times. Every change, even in Immigration Branch personnel, was analysed, sometimes incorrectly, for its possible impact on policy. A 1936 reorganization of the Immigration Branch and even the promotion of Frederick Blair to deputy-minister status seemed to promise positive change; as the secretary of the society in Toronto wrote, "The opinions of the local immigration officials have it almost unanimously that with the reorganization of the Department and with Mr. Blair at the helm, the gradual introduction and human immigration policy [*sic*] may be reasonably counted upon. On the whole," he added, "Mr. Blair is regarded here very highly. Here is hoping and praying that with his appointment a ray of light will pierce the stark darkness of the heart-rending tragedy to our people."[19]

While the society's office in Toronto, opened in 1935, relied extensively on the Montreal office for assistance and advice, two dedicated Toronto businessmen, Sam Kronick and William Agranove, acted as an independent JCA field team, aiding agricultural settlers in southern Ontario. For the few farm settlers in this region these two men were a constant source of financial and moral support. With money in short supply the two spent almost as much time raising funds to support the farmers as they did actually dispensing them. They understood only too well that with farm failures endemic it was crucial that Jewish farmers succeed and, more importantly, be seen to stay on the land, if JCA's Jewish farm settlement schemes were to have any chance of approval in Ottawa. To Kronick and Agranove every agricultural success was a small victory in the struggle to gain approval for additional farm entries into Canada.[20]

In the west the division of responsibilities for immigration among the Jewish Immigrant Aid Society, the Jewish Colonization Association and the Canadian Jewish Congress was artificial. In reality, all responsibilities were combined in the hands of a few local Jewish functionaries, who reached for whichever letterhead was appropriate to the hat they were wearing at the moment. Nevertheless, to a small degree in the west and to a greater degree in Toronto and Montreal, the neat division of immigration jurisdictions set out on paper did not hold up in practice. Differences in rural and urban settlement needs, philosophy, money-raising techniques, attitudes toward urban drift, policy formulation and tactics for dealing with government officials repeatedly drew individuals and agencies into conflict.

Yet another problem complicated the Jewish immigrant aid picture in the 1930s. The immigrant aid societies, weak as they were, found themselves in competition with various private immigration entrepreneurs: lawyers, travel agents and political figures—the so-called "fixers"—who would intercede in Ottawa for a price to facilitate the entry of prospective immigrants. Although they had some success, angry JIAS officials claimed that these entrepreneurs undermined Canadian Jewry's collective effort to force the Canadian government to accept more immigrants, specifically refugees. Instead, the society charged, "fixers" encouraged tokenism and patronage. "It is our belief," the national director of JIAS explained to his new Toronto director, "that all immigration aid work should be done by our Society and that the steamship agents and the 'go-betweens' should be eliminated as far as possible from active contact with those of our people who need assistance in immigration, naturalization and visa matters. . . . It will therefore be our task to eliminate as far as possible the profit motive from Jewish immigration and immigrant aid work, and bring by all means at our disposal our people to our Society so that we may minister to their needs in our particular field."[21]

Thus, any notion of a Jewish community that was well-financed, well-organized and united in a common cause during the crucial years immediately preceding the war is a fiction. Divisions and fractiousness festered, and whatever national organization there was, was weak. It is therefore understandable that Canadian Jews—most of whom were immigrants, defensive and insecure, unsure of their political place and uneasy in the world of domestic power brokerage—would defer to the wisdom of the Jewish members of Parliament in their efforts to moderate government policy on immigration in general and refugees in particular. The Canadian Jewish Congress, often acting as the mouthpiece of these politicians, felt itself fortunate to have what the Jewish community termed *shtadlonim*, men of influence in the corridors of power who could speak on the Jews' behalf.[22] Ironically, in relying on *shtadlonim*, Canadian Jewry was in unwitting agreement with their anti-Semitic foes—both groups believed that Jewish politicians had far more influence in government than they actually had.

The three Jewish MP's, Jacobs, Factor and Heaps, won seats in the Liberal sweep of 1935. They, like the rest of the Jewish community, saw the 1935 Liberal victory as a harbinger of better things; after all, it was the Conservative Bennett government that had introduced the restrictive Orders-in-Council and had snubbed various Jewish delegations attempting to have these orders moderated. These predictions, however, were belied almost immediately following the election. In a meeting with Thomas Crerar, newly appointed minister of mines and resources and so responsible for immigration, Samuel Jacobs, MP, and Benjamin Robinson, the president of JIAS, were told that there would be no exception made for German Jews. Unless refugees met the requirements necessary for immigration—that is, unless they had sufficient capital to establish a successful farm—they would not be allowed in under any circumstance.[23] And Crerar kept his word. For the next two years almost no Jewish refugees arrived in Canada, and those few who did manage to come entered under specific Orders-in-Council, exempting them from the usual immigration requirements. Most of these immigrants were relatives of Canadian Jews, although some were admitted as favours to prominent government supporters, including Samuel Jacobs.[24] The latter was a cynical activity, but it worked; saving a few lives was better than saving none, and for the most part Canadian Jews, though restive, remained loyal to the Liberal government. They had little choice: Canadian Jews did not have the power to change government policy and, until they did, would accept what crumbs were thrown their way.

As for the Liberal government of Mackenzie King, it preferred to keep as removed from the refugee problem as possible. This was not always easy. When the League of Nations' high commissioner for refugees resigned his office, blaming the indifference of member states for his commission's failure, a suggestion was made that a Canadian might be appointed to the vacant post. Canada's response was predictable; in a memorandum to the prime minister, O. D. Skelton, under-secretary of state for External Affairs, tried to take the sting out of the commissioner's letter of resignation. "His criticisms were well warranted," Skelton admitted, "and the cause is a fine one. Unless, however, Canada is itself prepared to take steps to admit a large number of Jewish immigrants, it would seem anomalous to have a Canadian accept the thorny task of High Commissioner." King read the memorandum carefully and jotted in the margin: "I wholly agree." Nothing came of the suggestion. Canada had kept its distance from refugees and refugee support agencies.[25]

The Canadian Jewish Congress, for its part, established a refugee committee in 1937, but the committee's main function was to work with railway colonization officials, helping in the settlement of the handful of Jewish farmers able to break through into Canada. However, even this activity was short-lived. In April 1938, at the behest of Blair, who did not believe that Jews could be farmers, railway colonization agents in Europe were told to allow in as few Jewish agriculturists as possible. Indeed, when, for example, a German Jew, Hans Heinemann, applied to enter Canada as a farmer, he was told by an overly enthusiastic agent of the Canadian Pacific Railway in Hamburg that no Jews were being allowed into Canada.[26]

Previously, Jews, like other would-be European agricultural settlers, were routinely allowed to enter Canada if they met the stringent terms of the railway settlement schemes. By 1938 Blair, with the cooperation of Canadian railway colonization officials, changed all that. He removed the responsibility for processing Jewish applicants from railway personnel offices to his own, where he personally scrutinized each application, deciding on its eligibility. From among the thousands of Jews beseeching Canada for admission, Blair declared a few hundred eligible. From among those eligible, both national railways were permitted to select fifty farm families yearly.[27] It seemed, therefore, that by 1938 the Canadian government was carefully plugging the few loopholes through which some Jews were still entering Canada. As H. M. Caiserman, now the general secretary of the Canadian Jewish Congress, grimly informed Rabbi Stephen Wise of the American Jewish Congress, "The possibilities of an increased Jewish immigration to Canada at present are nil."[28]

In March 1938, just when Canada was further restricting Jewish immigration, Hitler marched into Austria and several hundred thousand more Jews became refugees—some, those who had escaped to Austria from Germany, were now refugees for a second time. As a response to this, and to quiet the storm of protest raised by more liberal elements in the United States, President Franklin Roosevelt took the bold step of issuing an invitation to more than thirty nations to meet together to discuss possible solutions to the refugee problem; what no one at the time knew but some suspected, the real purpose of the conference was, according to the author of the plan, American Secretary of State Cordell Hull, to give the United States the initiative "to get out in front and attempt to guide the pressure, primarily with a view toward forestalling attempts to have immigration laws liberalized."[29]

Had Canadian officials been aware of the Americans' real motives, they would have been relieved; but they were not. Thus, when the formal invitation to attend this conference arrived in late March 1938, they were decidedly uncomfortable. Even though the Americans had assured Canada that no country would be expected to "receive a greater number of emigrants than is permitted by its existing legislation" and that private organizations would be expected to fund this emigration, the Canadians felt Roosevelt was baiting a trap. Once committed to attending the conference, the Canadians would be expected to do something to alleviate the refugee problem. And this, King dreaded, meant "admitting numbers of Jews." His fears were reinforced by Under-Secretary of State Skelton, who warned that the publicity generated by the conference would likely result in strong "domestic pressure" in Canada to do something for the Jews.[30]

Blair too warned the cabinet against being stampeded by "a general Jewish drive for admission to other countries." He suspected that any concession offered the Jews in good faith would be abused. For instance, rather than Jews from Austria and Germany coming to Canada, distasteful as this might be, efforts might be made to foist Russian, Polish or other even less desirable Jews onto an unsuspecting Canadian public. This, Blair cautioned, Jews had tried before and this, he insisted, must be stopped.[31] The warnings of Skelton and Blair did not fall on deaf ears. The prime minister of Canada was obsessed with the notion that the admission of Jewish refugees might destroy his country. "We must . . . seek," King recorded in his diary, "to keep this part of the Continent free from unrest and from too great an intermixture of foreign strains of blood." Nothing was to be gained, he believed, "by creating an internal problem in an effort to meet an international one." Allowing Jewish refugees into Canada, he told his cabinet, might cause riots and would surely exacerbate relations between the federal government and the provinces. In effect, any action permitting an appreciable number of Jews to settle in Canada would, in King's mind, undermine the unity of the nation. This was no time for Canada to act on "humanitarian grounds." Rather, said the prime minister, Canada must be guided by "realities" and political considerations.[32]

The realities King had in mind were the attitudes toward refugees in general and Jews in particular within Quebec. He was absolutely convinced that Quebec would react violently to the admission of Jewish refugees; and with reason. Almost every French-language newspaper had warned the government against opening Canada's doors to European Jews. As *Le Devoir* asked, "Why allow in Jewish refugees? . . . The Jewish shopkeeper on St. Lawrence Boulevard does nothing to increase our natural resources."[33] And this was mild compared with vicious anti-Semitic utterances appearing regularly in such papers as *La Nation, L'Action Catholique* and *L'Action Nationale*. As well, many French-Canadian politicians spoke out—both within and without the confines of Parliament—against Jewish immigration. These Liberal members, in particular, Wilfrid Lacroix, C. H. Leclerc and H. E. Brunelle, led the anti-refugee onslaught. Indeed, in a speech in the House of Commons several months after Roosevelt's proposal was made, Brunelle denounced Jews as having caused "great difficulties" wherever they had lived.[34] In addition, both the prime minister and the Immigration Branch received many letters from such Quebec organizations as the St. Jean Baptiste Society, the councils of various counties, several *caisses populaires* and the provincial Knights of Columbus, all protesting any possible government backsliding on the refugee issue.[35] In fact, not long after Brunelle's attack on Jews, Lacroix delivered to the Commons a petition signed by nearly 128,000 members of the St. Jean Baptiste Society, opposing "all immigration and especially Jewish immigration."[36]

The prime minister and, more especially, his Quebec lieutenant and minister of justice, Ernest Lapointe, were also aware of the grievous situation in which the province's Liberal party found itself. Thrown out of office in 1936 by the right-wing Union Nationale led by Maurice Duplessis, the Quebec Liberal party was badly split and in a state of disarray. Anything that might further weaken it, King and Lapointe felt, would have to be avoided, no matter the cost. Thus, on Lapointe's recommendation, the federal cabinet swallowed hard and refused to revoke the heinous Padlock Act, giving Quebec's Attorney-General power to padlock the premises of any organization he declared subversive. To do otherwise would, according to Lapointe, have been disastrous for the Quebec Liberal party.[37] Allowing in Jewish refugees would also, at least in Lapointe's mind, play into the hands of Duplessis's nationalist forces and further weaken the Liberal party in Quebec. Whatever Lapointe's personal feelings on this matter—and there is no evidence that he otherwise favoured Jewish immigration—he felt justified for political reasons alone in taking a hard line with respect to refugees. And King believed that "if the Liberal party was to remain a national party," he had no alternative but to accept the views of Lapointe and his French-Canadian colleagues in the House.[38] The prime minister sincerely believed that illiberal policies were acceptable as long as the basic Liberal objective—national unity—was maintained.[39]

Mackenzie King was, therefore, reluctant even to attend the proposed conference on refugees, and the Americans, awaiting an official Canadian response to their invitation, were not unaware of the prime minister's preoccupations. The American chargé d'affaires in Ottawa, John Farr Simmons, met with officials of the Department of External Affairs to sound them out on the refugee question. He reported to Secretary of State Hull that the Canadians seemed "sympathetic"; but sympathy, he was advised, was not the trumpet call to action. Any possible Canadian policy shift in favour of admitting refugees would be measured against "the possible opposition to increased influx into Canada of Jews on the part of the Province of Quebec."[40]

For the better part of April 1938, while almost all other nations were replying positively to Roosevelt's invitation, and despite the anxious inquiries of the Americans, Canada did not respond. And while King and his cabinet dallied, the director of immigration was increasingly active. At the behest of Skelton, Blair drew up a draft response rejecting the invitation. Attending this conference, Blair said, might involve "the admission to Canada of many who by training and manner of life are not fitted for the development of any of our primary industries, but would add to the congestion and competition of our cities." More to the point, it was not "feasible . . . to encourage the influx of immigrants of one race and not of others." Blair privately told Skelton that it was unfair "to let down the immigration barriers for the benefit of any particular race or class." Personally, Blair did not feel that the refugee problem was all that serious. "No problem exists except for the Jewish people," and the refugee situation, he added, had been much worse immediately following the Great War. The government's first priority, Blair warned, must now be to decide "whether Canada can afford to open the door to more Jewish people than we are now receiving." "There is going to be," he predicted, "a general Jewish drive for admissions to other countries." The director thought little good to Canada would come from attending the conference; Canadian policy should be to maintain restrictive immigration practice, and if forced to attend the conference, simply to announce that the government would "show sympathetic consideration where possible to prospective refugee immigrants."[41]

What apparently most disturbed Blair was the possibility of a successful conference. "If the nations now asked to cooperate to save the Jews of Germany and Austria, manage by sacrifice to accomplish this purpose, it will please the Germans who want to get rid of this group . . . and it will encourage other nations to do likewise and this is probably the greatest danger. Can immigration countries afford to encourage such an eventuality? It is akin in a sense to the paying of ransom to Chinese bandits."[42] Clearly a real threat in Blair's view was that eastern European countries such as Poland, Hungary and Rumania would follow the German precedent and attempt to deport their unwanted Jews.

In addition, Blair had just been advised that the German government had officially announced that it would no longer allow Jewish emigrants from Germany back into the country. Blair at once informed Skelton that Canada had no alternative but "to refuse the admission of German nationals without presentation of passports endorsed as valid for return to Germany." His argument was as ingenious as it was cold-blooded: "If we accept people from Germany on one-way travel documents, we have no excuse for refusing a like class from other countries, and we will soon reach the place where the only persons we can deport will be British subjects and U.S. citizens. . . . I wish the immigration countries would take united action in refusing to admit nationals of countries who will not allow return by deportation."[43]

To the Jewish members of Parliament, on the other hand, the proposed conference on refugees seemed a godsend; they were convinced that the Americans would surely not have called a conference unless they had a dramatic gesture in mind. Canada, they reasoned, would be forced to follow suit with its own scheme to help alleviate the refugee crisis. At first, the MP's felt that they need only gently and quietly assist the government, especially the minister responsible for immigration, Crerar, choose the appropriate Canadian plan. With guidance, the cabinet would agree in advance to a secret but firm commitment to admit a specific number of refugees, which the government would then declare at the conference. It all seemed so simple. The Jewish members of Parliament allowed for delicate, even secret, negotiations with Crerar; but in their enthusiasm over the upcoming conference, some Canadian Jews saw the admission of refugees as a foregone conclusion. In Toronto, the local Congress executive met to consider calling their own conference on the anticipated refugees' settlement needs. The last thing the MP's needed, however, was a public Jewish conference on refugee settlement, which would attract wide media coverage. Quiet diplomacy had to be just that—quiet; no precipitous publicity should be undertaken without the members' consent. Caiserman warned Oscar Cohen, the Toronto Congress's executive director, that anything that could be construed as Jewish pressure on government might deter it from making concessions; the goverment could not be seen giving in to Jews. Caiserman explained, somewhat guardedly, that Samuel Jacobs had "contacted someone who is persona grata with the government" and that everything was "well in hand." He promised that good news would soon be forthcoming and counselled patience in the meantime.[44]

What Congress officials feared most of all was that meetings or demonstrations might both alienate the government and create an anti-Semitic backlash throughout the country. As Caiserman explained, "Experience concerning the refugee situation has convinced us that too much publicity has always proven detrimental to any request for the widening of the doors for the entry of our co-religionists to Canada. . . . In Quebec any public agitation for the entry of Jews would bring with it . . . a flood of counter agitation."[45] The Canadian Jewish Congress's role, therefore, was not to mobilize Jewish opinion but to monitor it—to guard against any Jewish outburst, spontaneous or otherwise, that might rebound against the community at large. And to win quiescence, Jewish members of Parliament repeatedly promised community leaders that a great victory was at hand. Caiserman, acting as spokesman for the MP's, assured Congress leaders that the quiet diplomacy was working. For example, he hinted to a restive Congress executive in Winnipeg that a breakthrough might soon be made on the vital issue of a Canadian pre-conference commitment to a broad refugee admission scheme, and once again he pleaded for Jewish restraint. It was crucial to "refrain from mass meetings, publicity and noise, because such methods would only nullify what we have in mind". "I am now in a position to inform you confidentially," said Caiserman, "that the Minister who has been seen is favourably impressed with the requests made on condition that no delegations and no publicity of any sort be made, and since this matter has to do with important financial obligation, we must all have the necessary patience until we are in a position to disclose what can be done."[46]

In fact, Jacobs, Factor and Heaps did hold informal conversations with Crerar, and they may have interpreted these conversations as negotiations but Crerar did not. He encouraged discussion partly to pacify Jewish voters and partly to keep himself informed on policy options; but there is no evidence that he took the suggested refugee scheme proposed by the Jewish MP's very seriously. There is, on the other hand, evidence to suggest that, if he had tried to carry these proposals to the cabinet for approval (which he did not), or to his ranking civil servants for preliminary discussion (which he also did not), he would have encountered insurmountable hostility. Indeed, while the MP's talked to Crerar about refugee schemes, the cabinet still talked of ways to avoid attending the conference. Thus, in spite of a self-deluded or inflated sense of their influence on the refugee issue, the three Jewish MP's achieved nothing—nor did their lobbying of a reluctant cabinet to attend the conference have any impact. Though they accepted the decision to attend as a great personal victory, it was not Jewish pressure that finally forced the government to go to the conference.[47]

It was in the latter part of April that King finally made his decision to attend the conference—probably because he had no choice. Under-Secretary of State Skelton warned the prime minister that "it would not look too well to be the only country, except Fascist Italy, declining even to sit on a Committee," and King carried this unpleasant message to his cabinet.[48] On April 26, 1938, the Canadian government officially announced that it would attend the conference, to be held in the small French resort town of Evian on the Swiss border. (Switzerland had already rejected the honour of holding the meeting on her territory.) At the same time King informed the Americans that he thought it wrong to encourage countries such as Germany, which were trying "to throw upon other countries the task of solving their internal difficulties." In the wake of this announcement Jacobs, Heaps and Factor determined to press their case. On May 16 Heaps wrote to Prime Minister King requesting a formal audience for seven pro-refugee members of Parliament, including the three Jews.[49] Rather than confront the seven directly, King asked them to meet a special cabinet committee, which he would appoint, to look into the refugee issue in advance of Evian. Then, to make sure their appeals got nowhere, King nominated to the committee the two Quebec ministers, led by Lapointe, who were the most adamant in their opposition to the admission of refugees.

Taken in by King's ploy, the Jewish MP's again assured the Jewish community that they were on the verge of a government commitment. Again Jews were cautioned to do nothing. The meeting with the cabinet committee was to be the final step to triumph for the *shtadlonim*. As a precautionary measure, however, the three decided to meet privately with the Quebec cabinet committee members, "with a view of winning them over," in advance of the formal meeting. Sensing that the long-awaited victory was finally within sight, the president of the Jewish Immigrant Aid Society confidently wrote to Oscar Cohen that, in the MP's upcoming meeting with the cabinet committee, "a policy of the government will be evolved, which I hope will be satisfactory."[50]

That Cohen was reassured by this news is unlikely. The quiet diplomacy had been too quiet for too long, and many in Toronto had serious doubts. Even the repeated assurances from Factor, Toronto's Jewish MP, were becoming more and more difficult to believe. And, as the local Jewish establishment again endorsed its politicians' call for restraint, Labour Zionists, Yiddishists and local *landsmannschaften* within the Canadian Jewish Congress were becoming increasingly impatient with the pace of negotiations.[51]

For them, the newer immigrant sections of the Jewish community, the refugees in question were not distant Jews, but family and friends. For those who had themselves so recently emigrated, it was impossible to deny the appeals from terrified kin in Austria or from those in Eastern Europe who, reading the handwriting on the wall, begged for escape. The oppressed had names and faces; each was a father, a sister, a cousin or a friend. A man in Montreal received a letter from his aunt, imploring him to save his cousin in Vienna—"Hitler came and took away all citizenship rights from everybody. They won't let him out of one country and won't let him into another country and he must, therefore, remain in prison until he gets an affidavit from somebody in some country where there is no quota."[52] There was nothing that could be done. A Jewish farmer in Hirsch, Saskatchewan, turned to the Jewish Colonization Association in Montreal to intercede on behalf of his wife's parents. Like many, he refused to believe that somewhere, somehow, there was no crack to be found in the wall of Canadian restrictionism. He asserted, "There is no rule which has no exception," but as far as his wife's parents were concerned, he would be proven wrong—dead wrong.[53]

To quell the growing unrest and, perhaps, to direct it along a more controlled and less noisy path, Cohen called an emergency meeting of the Congress council in Toronto to assess refugee strategy. "The many organizations in this community," he explained, "are holding the Congress responsible for the refugee situation and are not taking any independent or public action because the Congress has promised to do everything possible in this connection. It is essential, therefore, that we at least confer on this situation."[54] Heaps was furious. By its very nature a conference, he argued, would again generate press coverage, and publicity at this particularly sensitive moment might jeopardize the crucial meeting planned with the cabinet committee. Any organized Jewish demand for refugee admissions might create a backlash among non-Jews, especially in Quebec. Heaps demanded that the conference be cancelled or, failing that, that the first item on the agenda—the refugee question—be dropped. The director of the western region of Congress, speaking for Heaps, wired this message to the Toronto headquarters and added that at the very least the meeting be postponed for one week, until after the MP's met with the cabinet committee.[55]

Heaps and his fellow members were only partially successful in dealing with their increasingly impatient Jewish constituency. Although the Congress meetings were held with the refugee item still on the agenda, the discussions were, much to the MP's relief, kept private. Heated arguments reflected the anger of many who suspected the government was ignoring its Jewish members of Parliament, but it was decided that no public action would be taken in advance of the meeting with the cabinet committee. The single exception made was the establishment of a CJC national refugee committee; yet even this simple administrative step was symptomatic of the creeping crisis of faith in the power of the *shtadlonim*. The move to establish a Congress refugee committee was in itself an admission—the first—that the MP's might fail. Caiserman explained to the Winnipeg executive members, "While approving the activities of our three members of Parliament, a committee of seven . . . was selected and instructed to take the required measures in case the present negotiations for our MP's with the government do not bring desired results. The committee is also to make sure that if the concession is obtained it should be used in the best interests of Canadian Jewry."[56]

The meeting on which so many hopes rested took place on June 2, 1938. Jacobs, Heaps and Factor were joined by J. S. Woodsworth, leader of the CCF. They brought to the cabinet committee what they believed was a modest, workable refugee scheme; they were convinced it would be acceptable to the cabinet, to Quebec and to the Jewish community and that it would also give Canada its positive card to play at Evian. They proposed that Canada agree to admit five thousand Jewish refugees over a period of four years. All costs would be assumed by Canadian Jewry, who would also insure that these desperate people would never become public charges. In addition, as a palliative for Quebec, it was guaranteed that all refugees would be settled outside that province.[57]

Whatever hopes the delegation may have had of a positive hearing by the cabinet committee were dashed. Ernest Lapointe, the strong man on the committee, did not even bother to attend the meeting, and the rest of the committee listened but was non-committal, even uninterested. Halfheartedly, Crerar promised to take the MP's proposal back to the cabinet, but the public statement by the prime minister on the refugee question that the MP's expected to follow the meeting was never made.[58]

The *shtadlonim* had been crushed, quiet diplomacy had failed, and the fragile coalition of silence holding the divergent elements of the Jewish community together behind their members of Parliament crumbled. Heaps again promised to approach Crerar on the slim hope that something could still be done in the cabinet, yet he privately conceded to a confidant in Winnipeg that it would now be only "a waste of time." Nor would Heaps accept any personal responsibility for the failure, declaring that the Canadian Jewish Congress was at least partly to blame. He damned both the Congress's poor organization and the lack of full support from all elements in the community who, he claimed, played "peanut politics . . . with the refugee question."[59]

In spite of Heaps's accusations, the organizations represented within Congress had maintained a surprisingly united front in support of their members of Parliament. Even when many of the immigrant-oriented groups had privately expressed doubts about the wisdom of total reliance on the MP's, the fear of somehow upsetting delicate negotiations had kept protest in check. Unfortunately for the Jewish politicians, however, not every Jewish organization had allied itself with Congress. As if to underscore the impatience of many Jews with the seeming timidity of Congress to take action on its own, one group of Jews arrived in Ottawa on June 15, after the meeting with the cabinet committee, and did the unthinkable: it protested. A delegation from the People's Committee against Anti-Semitism (a front for the left-wing United Jewish People's Order, which had remained outside the CJC's umbrella) descended on Crerar's office claiming to represent ten thousand Jewish voters. In a hurriedly called meeting with the cabinet committee on immigration, the delegation angrily denounced the government's refugee policy.

If the minister responsible for immigration was shocked by the depth of feeling generated among Jews by the refugee crisis, he was also furious at the public nature of this protest. Crerar commented indignantly to Heaps on "the type of Jewish representatives who might be typical of the Jews in Canada." In turn, the embarrassed Jewish MP's felt betrayed by Crerar; the minister had consented to meet with an "outside" Jewish group when the MP's had assumed that they alone represented Jewish interests in Ottawa. Attempting to discredit the protesters, Heaps told Blair that the People's Committee members "not only represent the Communist element among the Jewish people, but are themselves distinctly Communist sympathizers."[60]

Perhaps sensing trail's end for *shtadlonim*, Heaps lashed out against the Jewish protesters and, perhaps more significantly, for the first time hinted that Crerar may have been two-faced in negotiations. Commenting on the adverse press coverage of the People's Committee meeting, Heaps wrote that "the delegation has done enormous damage. They double-crossed Crerar, and Mr. Crerar was not either frank or honest with us, I don't know which."[61]

But it was all too late; if there had ever been any real hope of the Jewish members winning concessions from the government, it had finally died. In a discouraging letter to HICEM in Paris, M. A. Solkin, executive director of JIAS, reported on both the failure of the members of Parliament and the sudden and symbolic death of Samuel Jacobs: "The remaining two Members of Parliament were finally compelled to give up their efforts after they concluded that the question had reached a state where they find themselves unable to be of any material assistance."[62] Canada's policy at Evian, whatever it might be, would owe nothing to Canadian Jewish interests.

Canada's long-awaited decision to participate at Evian had meanwhile stirred some international interest. The British, no more pleased with the prospect of Evian than the Canadians, welcomed Canadian participation. Unlike the Canadians, who feared admitting Jews domestically, the British were concerned that the Americans might be using the conference to pry open the door to Palestine, their League of Nations mandate territory administered much like a British colony since the First World War. Any country, such as Canada, that might agree to admit Jews would, the British hoped, deflect attention and pressure from the Palestine question. "The Canadian reply," one British Foreign Office official noted optimistically, "is more helpful than we expected."[63] But British pleasure was short-lived, for they soon discovered that Canadian willingness to participate in the conference, like that of its sister Dominions, was not attended by a changed attitude to refugees. Indeed, the British would soon find no more positive word than "discouraging" to describe the general position of the Dominions, and for Foreign Office officials a new fear was introduced. If the Evian Conference failed, as appeared likely, the Americans could conveniently blame the British Commonwealth of Nations unless they showed that they were "genuinely prepared to make an effort."[64]

The Americans, like the British, were already aware of Canadian discomfort at the prospect of attending the conference; the long delay in replying to the American invitation had carried its own message. But, if the Americans needed further proof, they soon received it directly from the Canadian under-secretary of state for External Affairs. In a conversation with the American chargé d'affaires, Skelton emphasized that Canada's attendance at Evian should not be interpreted by anyone to mean that a Canadian initiative was forthcoming; furthermore, he argued, any positive commitment from Canada, or anybody else for that matter, to accept refugees might prove counter-productive to those with the most to lose—Jews. He directed the chargé d'affaires to that section of the letter written by King to the American diplomat, suggesting that offers of freer immigration from Germany might give "rise to a renewed wave of persecution against German Jewish citizens." Who knows where positive action on refugees could lead? "Other governments with unwanted minorities must equally not be encouraged to think that harsh treatment at home is the key that will open the doors to immigration abroad. It is axiomatic that no state should be allowed to throw upon other countries the responsibility of solving its internal difficulties."[65]

Meanwhile, without much enthusiasm, the Canadian government was preparing for the conference. King appointed the Canadian delegate to the League of Nations, Hume Wrong, and the chief immigration officer in Europe, William R. Little, as Canada's representatives. Wrong's instructions were succinct: listen, make notes, say as little as possible and under no circumstance make any promises or commitments.[66] Canada was participating in the conference, the prime minister added, only to get information. King reminded Wrong that, because the League of Nations was shortly to discuss the universal problem of refugees, "it would be neither practical nor just to discriminate in favour of refugees from Austria or Germany." The director of immigration was at the same time instructing Little to take the offensive, to point out to other delegates that Canada had already done much more than required to solve the Jewish refugee problem, with fully twenty-five per cent of all special Orders-in-Council having gone to Jews. Rather than accept more Jews, Blair felt delegates might more fruitfully apply themselves to ways and means of stopping Germany from exporting its Jewish problem. He suggested that Little feel out other delegates on the prospects for a united front against accepting any refugees. If Jews had no place to go after Evian, Blair again argued, the Nazis would be forced to find a domestic solution to their Jewish problem. Canada and other states would be relieved of the need to continue rejecting those "without either capital or recognized citizenship." Of course, as Blair pointed out to Little in confidence, any general boycott of refugees would also be welcomed by Canada, because there was "not much enthusiasm in many quarters for any increase in . . . Jewish immigration."[67]

To make certain that whatever concessions forced on Canada at Evian were kept at a minimum, the creative director of immigration found a method both simple and clever: he delayed the admission of the handful of Jewish refugees whose applications had already been approved by his department, but whose names had not yet been forwarded to the cabinet for the necessary order-in-council. If Canada were forced to make a gesture, these names would then be sent forward; but these helpless Jews would meanwhile have to wait.[68]

Thus, as Evian drew near, Jewish Immigrant Aid Society officials began to notice that promised orders-in-council were being delayed, that Jews who would probably have won admission earlier were being rejected, and that these new terms were being applied to wealthy refugees, "coming with as much as $50,000."[69] Solkin, the society's executive director, reported on the unexpected tightening of regulations to his Toronto officers: "The situation in Ottawa has changed abruptly since a few weeks ago. It may interest you to know that at the present moment applications are no longer considered for the admission of people, no matter what amount of money they can bring with them. It is to be hoped that this newest restriction will be only of a temporary nature. Meanwhile, however, we have to be patient and bide our time."[70]

Jews in Europe, applying for admission through Canadian missions abroad, could not bide their time, yet found their applications rejected as soon as Canadian officials reached the line on the application indicating the applicant's religion. Zita Plaut, a Polish Jew raised in Berlin, had become a naturalized German citizen; the Nazis had then made her stateless and, in 1936, had confiscated the family business. Rather than await deportation, the family, except for Zita, had moved to Poland where they would eventually perish in various concentration camps.

Zita, newly married, moved to Vienna with her husband in 1937. Luck and the assistance of her husband's business contacts secured the young couple's escape from the Nazi incorporation of Austria. In spite of official inhospitality, they made their way across Switzerland and France and, finally, in July 1938, into Holland. From there, with the cooperation of family still in Germany, they hoped to ride into Canada on the coat-tails of this family's application. Zita later recalled the episode with some bitterness:

> They [her family in Germany] wrote to me that they had money in Holland, and would I please go to the Canadian consulate there and try to get a visa for them. That same day I went and told the official I had family in Germany who would like to emigrate to Canada; they have money—I think $50,000 in foreign currency was required. He said wonderful, and he let me fill out the whole form, and I signed it and returned it to him. Then he goes, Oh—their name is Rappaport? They are Jewish? I'm sorry, he said, we have no visas, and he tore the form up in front of me. Can you imagine—they say Germany alone was at fault. There were eight million people living in Canada. They were so under populated.

Zita Plaut and her husband would, nevertheless, be among the lucky few. The determined efforts on their behalf by an American cousin and the willingness of the American consul to bend the rules just enough won the couple lifesaving American visas, which came through on the very eve of their scheduled deportation from Holland back to Germany. In short order Zita and her husband were on a boat headed for New York. Zita did not get out of bed on the week-long journey: she was eight months pregnant.[71]

Back in Canada, Solkin at first publicly blamed the People's Committee against Anti-Semitism for the sudden rash of rejections coming from the Immigration Branch, but he was soon disabused of that notion. Although unsure of the exact reasons, he reported that "the Department apparently received instructions from above not to entertain any more application[s] of Jewish capitalists, regardless of the amount of money they may be able to bring"; and he was now aware that somehow everything hung on the events at Evian.[72]

As delegates to the conference began arriving, Wrong, the chief Canadian delegate, smelled a rat. The meeting, he predicted, was "going to be a most unpleasant affair" and his participation in it "an unwelcome duty." He described the proceedings as looking "very amateurish" and the entire concept "not the product of any well thought-out scheme," but simply "one of Mr. Roosevelt's sudden generous impulses." If the Americans were seriously concerned with helping refugees, he wondered, why would they send as their delegates Myron Taylor, "a steel tycoon," and two minor foreign service officers, one of whom was "a capable authority on the administration of the quota law." Though he realized that there was not much support for the admission of refugees into Canada, he nevertheless begged the prime minister not to make his instructions "entirely negative."

King ignored Wrong's plea; in a strongly worded letter, he reminded the Canadian delegate that Canada was at Evian only to "exchange information." Furthermore, Wrong was put on notice that, if the Americans made concrete proposals to solve the refugee problem, he should oppose them while trying neither to "lead in this opposition" nor to be "obstructionist."[73] Wrong, now depressed, wrote to his sister that it all seemed so painfully futile. "I have to go . . . to this wretched Evian conference on refugees," he complained. "The trouble is that the more that is done for them the more of them there will be. Help abroad will result in greater German militancy at home. So nothing will be done by Canada."[74]

The prime minister had already been informed by Blair that, from the point of view of the Immigration Branch, accepting German Jews would exacerbate the situation in Canada too. And Blair told Skelton that "the Jews of Canada will not be satisfied unless the door is kept open in some way to all the Jews from other countries"; Canadian Jews, he added, were largely from Eastern Europe and would apply unremitting pressure to admit fellow Jews from this area. Tireless, he also reminded Crerar that in 1923 Jews had "tricked" Immigration authorities into allowing into Canada more Rumanian Jews than had been agreed on. "We will not," he warned, "satisfy Canadian Jewry by a special effort limited to the Jews of Germany and Austria," and he forecast the day when Jews would use every loophole to bring in their co-religionists from Poland, Rumania, Russia and Hungary.[75]

Wrong realized as soon as the conference began that Canadian worries had been groundless. The chief American delegate, Myron Taylor, was the first speaker. Instead of the magnanimous gesture many of the representatives expected—and feared—the contribution of the United States government to solving the refugee crisis would be to fill its entire German-Austrian quota of 27,730, rather than let part of it remain unfilled as might have been done in years past. The delegates sat stunned: the nations of the world had been mobilized for this? A collective sigh of relief from the assembly was almost audible as Taylor sat down. For the Jews of Europe, Taylor's speech was a cruel letdown; for everyone at Evian, it was a reprieve. It was clear that the Americans saw Evian as an exercise in public relations; they had no concrete proposals to solve—or even to alleviate—the crisis. And, if the Americans were going to do nothing significant, it was hardly likely that anything would be expected of the other countries assembled.

Of course, for the next ten days delegate after delegate rose to announce that his nation was doing all it could to solve the crisis and that stringent immigration laws prohibited it from doing more. In a short speech Wrong echoed these sentiments, announcing that Canada had much sympathy for the impossible situation in which the refugees found themselves, but that it could do no more than it was already doing—which was a great deal. "Certain classes of agriculturalists" were welcome in

Canada; everyone else was out of luck.[76] Only one state, the Dominican Republic, committed itself to accepting more than a mere handful of refugees, and so the conference concluded with a unanimous resolution that the nations of the world were "not willing to undertake any obligations toward financing involuntary immigration." Almost as an afterthought the delegates also approved the creation of an Intergovernmental Committee on Refugees to study the problem.[77]

The formal meetings had proven a disagreeable duty to most delegates, but at least the town of Evian offered them some diversion. Forty years after the meetings the aging concierge at the Royal Hotel in Evian remembered the delegates who had come to discuss refugees:

> Very important people were here and all the delegates had a nice time. They took pleasure cruises on the lake. They gambled at night at the casino. They took mineral baths and massages at the *Etablissement Thermal*. Some of them took the excursion to Chamonix to go summer skiing. Some went riding; we have, you know, one of the finest stables in France. Some played golf. We have a beautiful course overlooking the lake. Meetings. Yes, some attended the meetings. But, of course, it is difficult to sit indoors hearing speeches when all the pleasures that Evian offers are waiting right outside.[78]

Evian had clearly shown that no one wanted Jews. The Jews were now solely Germany's problem, and having turned their backs, the nations of the world could hardly in conscience object to Germany's solution. In the eyes of the Nazis the world had given them carte blanche to solve their Jewish problem their way. As one Nazi newspaper concluded, "The Evian Conference serves to justify Germany's policy against Jewry."[79] Indeed, as the Jew had suspected but never really believed until Evian, he was on his own.

The tragic failure at Evian exposed the impotence of world Jewry in general and Canadian Jewry in particular. Not only did the latter have no influence on its own government's policy, it could not even discover what that policy was. Only days before the conference began, a Jewish Immigrant Aid Society official in Montreal complained to his colleagues in Paris that "it is quite possible that more will be found about the intentions of our Government in France than we learn on this side." Canadian

Jews, after the failure of the Jewish members of Parliament, had not expected much from their government, but were, even so, disappointed in how little they got. "It is quite obvious," the president of JIAS lamented, "that the most that can be expected of Canada is to be more lenient in its application of the present regulations." And when, a week later, after discussions with officials in the Immigration Branch, even this faint hope was dashed, he sadly confided to a colleague his worst fears. "I am more than ever confirmed," he said, "that Canada holds very little, if anything, for the refugees. For the sake of these unfortunate people I hope and pray that I should be wrong."[80] He was not.

For the Jewish Immigrant Aid Society and the Jewish Colonization Association, as for individual Jewish families across Canada, it was impossible to offer refuge to European Jews but heartbreaking to deny them hope. From Austria, Mayer Selzer, either failing to understand or unwilling to believe that the JCA could not deliver visas at will, beseeched Canadian Jewry for the rescue only a visa to Canada could bring. As he explained,

> We were very well situated up to the present because we all have very good positions. We have lost all that. You are no doubt well informed on our situation so that I do not have to go into details. We must under all circumstances leave this country as we have no means of existence. Our condition is getting worse from day to day. We are even afraid to lose our home and to remain homeless.
>
> It is well understood and I do not have to emphasize it, that when we will have the good luck to emigrate into Canada we shall accept gladly any work, as we do not want to become a public charge on anyone and as we are strong and capable of working. I plead with you to save us from our desperate situation and to obtain for us the necessary permits.[81]

Bertha Fugend-Witzer, from Vienna, pleaded on behalf of her husband and three sons. "I have nothing," she wrote, "and in no country have I relatives to whom I can address myself and if the only and last opportunity would be taken away to save my children, then I do not know what to do." The JCA replied, as it would again and again, that there was little chance of anyone entering Canada at the time. Writing a second time, Mrs. Fugend-Witzer pleaded with the association's director "once more not to spoil this my only hope and to help me, if that anyhow be possible for you to do so"; or, if it was not possible for her and her husband to come, then, she begged him, "to manage that my children get the permit of immigration at least."[82] Nothing could be done was once again the answer.

Leib Goldenstein was truly shaken by the sympathic but discouraging letter he received from the JCA office in Regina. For Goldenstein there was no room for "No" as an answer. "No" was a death sentence. He had a sister in Winnipeg who would guarantee that he would not become a public charge; Canada would not "undertake any financial risk." How, he protested, could there not be a way. "If you possess the sincere will to help me," he said, "you will surely find the right ways and relations and the right means to attain your aims."[83] But there were no ways, relations nor means, not for Mr. Goldenstein.

A few were luckier. H. Carl Goldenberg, a young Montreal lawyer, working in 1938 with the federal Royal Commission on Municipal Finances, approached Crerar directly in late June 1938; he had an elderly aunt, uncle and married cousins stranded in Vienna. Although, pending the outcome of Evian, Blair had just hermetically sealed Canada off from refugees, an Order-in-Council was soon drawn up for Goldenberg's relatives; the family's departure awaited only final cabinet approval and routine immigration processing.[84]

In late August the whole process hit a snag. Suddenly, Goldenberg's family had to be out of Vienna by August 30, or face arrest and imprisonment. Speed was called for and the concerned Goldenberg was at his wits' end. He wrote Crerar, Heaps and, in desperation, Mackenzie King; he was not disappointed. In a flurry of activity cables were soon sent his family in Vienna indicating Canadian approval of their visas. Such telegrams were reportedly enough to delay the Nazis from imprisoning Jews, at least for a while, so arrest was forestalled, and in early September, still in advance of official cabinet approval of the appropriate Order-in-Council, Goldenberg's family left Vienna for Hamburg and Canada.[85] A grateful Goldenberg wrote the prime minister: "You do not know how much I appreciate your kindness in attending to my request so promptly. I cannot adequately express the feelings of my Mother and myself for what you have done. I can only thank you for this renewed expression of your friendship."[86]

A month after Evian, the day after Goldenberg wrote Mackenzie King, Crerar met with Blair and other ranking Immigration Branch authorities to review the government's position on refugees. The previously uninterested Crerar had been moved by the tales of horror emanating from Germany and was prepared to do something to aid the refugees. As the minister told his officials, "Although great care should be taken, we probably should admit more of these unfortunate people on humanitarian grounds."[87] But the well-meaning and naive Crerar was no match for Blair and his "experts." By the time the meeting was over, Crerar, thoroughly confused, had in fact agreed to tighten restrictions even further. Apparently unaware of his own department's formal regulations, he agreed to raise the necessary capital required of prospective Jewish applicants from $10,000 to $15,000. There were not now many refugees with $15,000; Canada's official response to Evian was, in other words, to make it almost impossible for any Jews even to apply to Canada for admission. Perhaps most appalling about Blair's machinations was his admission not long afterwards that for some time he had been convinced that the destruction of European Jewry was at hand. In an all-too-prophetic letter to a pro-refugee Anglican clergyman, Canon W. W. Judd of Toronto, Blair stated that he feared that Jews were facing virtual "extinction" in Europe. But to allow more of them into Canada, he informed Judd, would not solve the problem.[88]

For A. A. Heaps, who had for so long counselled Canadian Jewry to remain silent and to trust its leaders, the government's response to Evian was the last straw. Screwing up his courage, he wrote a passionate, bitter and accusing letter to his friend Mackenzie King, stating that he had been betrayed by a duplicitous government whose "oft-repeated promise" of allowing a reasonable number of refugees to come to Canada had proved to be a cruel hoax. Though Evian had been traumatic for Heaps, he felt this one last desperate appeal to King, pointing out the iniquitous behaviour of his government, might shame the prime minister into some action. As Heaps wrote,

> The existing regulations are probably the most stringent to be found anywhere in the whole world. If refugees have no money they are barred because they are poor, and if they have fairly substantial sums, they are often refused admittance on the most flimsy pretext. All I say of existing regulations is that they are inhuman and anti-Christian. . . . Practically every nation in the world is allowing a limited number to enter their countries. . . . The lack of action by the Canadian government is leaving an unfortunate impression. . . . I regret to state that the sentiment is gaining ground that anti-

> Semitic influences are responsible for the government's refusal to allow refugees to come to Canada.

King shunted the letter off to Crerar and Blair for their consideration; Heaps did not get a reply.[89]

Options were now few, a change in strategy urgently required. Seriously weakened by the death of Samuel Jacobs in late September, the contingent of Jewish MP's was no longer a factor in the battle for the admission of refugees, and Heaps's letter was the last serious attempt by a Jewish MP to influence the government. Benjamin Robinson, the national president of JIAS, summed up the failure in a statement to his Toronto office. "I presume you feel as most of us do," he said, "that the old method of backdoor diplomacy has been of little avail even to the attitude of the Government toward political and religious refugees."[90]

The government, for its part, had successfully survived Evian and wished not to be bothered with the refugee issue again—not at the behest of Jewish members of Parliament or Jewish leaders. Indeed, if the MP's had not succeeded in moderating government policy, they had unfortunately succeeded in convincing the government that distant refugees were a Jewish problem, not a national one. And Mackenzie King himself was beyond reach. As far as he was concerned, the admission of refugees perhaps posed a greater menace to Canada in 1938 than did Hitler. If accepting Jewish refugees could threaten Canada's national cohesion, could there not be merit in Hitler's fears about Jews in Germany? "The truth is," King wrote, "Hitler and Mussolini, while dictators, have really sought to give the masses of the people, some opportunity for enjoyment, taste of art and the like and, in this way, have won them to their side"; and perhaps in a veiled reference to the Jews of Germany, King went on to say that "the dictatorship method may have been necessary to wrest this opportunity from the privileged interests that have previously monopolized it."[91]

A week after the Evian fiasco, the prime minister gave an informal party at his summer residence, Kingsmere. Sitting on the porch after dinner, he chatted for over an hour with his guests, who included the secretary of the American legation in Ottawa. Among other things, King fondly recalled his meeting with Hitler in Germany a year earlier. As the American diplomat reported back to Washington, "He described Hitler as being, in his opinion, a very sincere man. He even described him as being 'sweet.' He said that he [Hitler] had the face, as he studied it, of a good man, although he was clearly a dreamer and gave the impression of having an artistic temperament. During the conversation Hitler had sat with his hands folded and his only gesture was to raise and lower his hands from time to time without unfolding them. He [King] intimated that he had asked Hitler some very frank questions and that he had been satisfied with Hitler's answers."[92]

In September 1938, less than a year before Canada declared war on Germany, King was still mixed in his attitude to Hitler—sorrowful over Hitler's methods but understanding of his motives. "He might come to be thought of as one of the saviours of the world," King wrote. "He had the chance at Nuremberg, but was looking to Force, to Might, and to Violence as means to achieving his ends, which were, I believe, at heart, the well-being of his fellow-man; not all fellow-men, but those of his own race."[93]

2

THE LINE MUST BE DRAWN SOMEWHERE

In January 1939 a young man joined the Department of External Affairs. Escott Reid, a Rhodes Scholar, was then thirty-five years old and had been, for several years, the national general secretary of the Canadian Institute of International Affairs. His first posting with the department was as second secretary of the Canadian legation in Washington, where he arrived on January 27 to begin work a day later.

Reid's first day at the embassy was, he recalled, "most distressing."[1] What made it so was that he was given responsibility for dealing with Jewish refugees. As he wrote to his wife mid-way through that day, "My immediate file is concerned with unfortunate German Jews in the States who want to get their relatives out of Germany immediately and offer to support them in Canada until they can enter the U.S. Unfortunately I am afraid there is nothing we can do except turn them down. If I could find a loop-hole I'd feel I'd justified my existence before I become a machine-like cold-blooded bureaucrat."[2]

Two days later Reid told his wife that he had again spent several hours in the office on the German refugee files. "Some of the cases," he said, "reduce me to the edge of tears." Wealthy American Jews, he added, "cannot get starving relations" out of Germany because of American immigration quotas, while Canada "won't take people who are *en route* to the U.S.A." Even Cuba, he told his wife, "is much more humane" than Canada, and he advised these applicants "to inquire at the Cuban Embassy."[3]

Some weeks later Reid was asked by the chief Canadian representative in Washington, Loring Christie, to call on Mr. Justice Felix Frankfurter of the United States Supreme Court, who was attempting to have two elderly aunts in Vienna admitted to Canada. Reid was moved by the plight of these two old ladies and wrote, in his own estimation, "as persuasive a dispatch as possible" to Ottawa, requesting that they be admitted with the understanding that their nephew had promised to "finance them for the rest of their lives."[4] His request was rejected. Just over a month later an obviously troubled Reid described another painful experience to his wife:

> A terribly sad, good-looking and charming Jew came in to see me this morning about getting his parents out of Vienna. They are too frightened even to go to the U.S. consulate. His father has already been attacked on the street by some young hooligans. Every time one of them comes in it leaves me shaken and ashamed of Canada. I can't see any reason why we can't let these old people in when they are not going to work and their children in the States are willing and able to support them. It's like being a bystander at an especially cruel and long-drawn-out murder.[5]

The murdering had started in earnest four months before, on the evening of November 9, 1938, when, on the orders of the German government, the worst pogrom to that time was carried out. *Kristallnacht*—called crystal night because of the broken glass from Jewish homes and businesses littering the streets in every city, town and village in Germany and Austria —was organized by the Nazis to terrorize the Jews. Countless synagogues, Jewish stores and homes were plundered and razed; men, women and children were wrenched from their homes, beaten, and shot or dragged off to concentration camps; in all, scores were killed, hundreds injured, thousands arrested.

The tragic events of *Kristallnacht* finally moved the Canadian prime minister. "The sorrows which the Jews have to bear at this time," he wrote in his diary, "are almost beyond comprehension." "Something," he added, "will have to be done by our country." Coincidentally, on the following day King personally shared in Jewish grief as he attended the funeral of Mrs. Heaps, wife of the Jewish member of Parliament, and he was again overwhelmed by the breadth of the tragedy about to envelop the Jews in Europe. Writing in his diary that night, he noted that it would be "difficult politically" and his cabinet might oppose him, but he was going to fight for the admission of some Jewish refugees because it was "right and just, and Christian."[6]

The next week, when King was in Washington for talks with President Roosevelt concerning the upcoming visit of the Royal

Family, the conversation turned to the ghastly lot of Jewish refugees. While the president, Myron Taylor and the American secretary of state, Cordell Hull, discussed what could be done, King remained silent; in his own words, he "just listened," but during the conversation "felt more than ever" that, because countries with "more crowded areas," such as Great Britain and the United States, were accepting refugees, Canada must open her door. On his return to Ottawa he told Governor General Tweedsmuir that on humanitarian grounds alone Canada should allow in some refugees. "If we tried to keep our country to ourselves," he warned enigmatically "we would lose it altogether some day." It seemed at long last that Canada was prepared to do something for the desperate Jews of Europe.[7]

It was precisely at this time that the Jews of Canada mobilized for the last dramatic effort to help save Jewish refugees before the outbreak of war. Amid worldwide cries of repulsion and disbelief, Canadian Jews were for once united and unrestrained in their outpouring of grief and indignation. With a speed born of anger and frustration, mass protests were organized from coast to coast, though perhaps "organized" is the wrong way to describe a movement so spontaneous and ineluctable. The grass roots demanded action; for once Jews could not and would not be deterred from protesting, and the Canadian Jewish Congress organizers merely channelled the wave of protest into hastily planned demonstrations. Non-Jews swamped protest organizers with declarations of support and prominent Gentiles volunteered to stand side by side on platforms with Jewish leaders in a call for immediate action.[8]

On November 14, 1938, at a special emergency meeting, the executive council of the Congress decided to proclaim Sunday, November 20, a day of mourning, during which memorial meetings would be held across the country. It instructed its local organizations to insure that these meetings be non-sectarian, that non-Jewish community leaders play a prominent role and that most of the speakers be Gentile. These meetings were to "capitalize on the sympathy" felt toward the helpless victims of Nazi brutality and to impress the government with the fact that public opinion was in favour of admitting some of them to Canada. In addition, each community was sent a draft of a protest resolution to be adopted at these meetings and forwarded to Ottawa.[9]

Surprisingly, with only five days to prepare, the Congress achieved dramatic results. Across Canada, from Glace Bay,

Nova Scotia, to Victoria, British Columbia, mass meetings were held and resolutions passed, pleading with the government to open its heart and, more especially, its gate. And at almost every one of these meetings the featured speaker was a non-Jew. Mayors, judges, members of Parliament and businessmen took their place on the platform in support of the refugees. In Toronto people lined up in front of Maple Leaf Gardens in the morning for a rally that would not begin until that evening, by which time a crowd of more than twenty thousand packed the arena and spilled out onto the street. Eventually the large University Avenue synagogue, Goel Tzedec, was pressed into service to take some of the overflow, and speakers from the Gardens rushed to the synagogue to meet those denied a seat at the main meeting. Prominent non-Jews joined the speakers' platform; they included J. E. Atkinson of the *Toronto Daily Star*, Toronto's mayor Ralph Day, Agnes Macphail, Canada's first woman member of Parliament, B. K. Sandwell, editor of *Saturday Night*, George Watson, president of the Trades and Labor Congress of Toronto, Malcolm W. Wallace, principal of University College and ranking representatives of Catholic, Anglican and United churches. The meeting unanimously passed a resolution calling upon Canadians to "show their moral courage by taking action together with other liberal and democratic countries to provide havens of refuge for the victims of Nazi brutality."[10]

Similar demonstrations were mounted across the nation. In Winnipeg, 4,000 people turned out to protest; there were 600 demonstrators in Quebec City, 200 in Vegreville, Alberta, 800 in Niagara Falls, 1,200 in Kingston, and 300 in Humboldt, Saskatchewan. Telegrams, resolutions, petitions and letters poured into the offices of the prime minister and various members of Parliament. The demonstrations were, as reported in the Toronto *Globe and Mail*, an example of the "brotherhood of man asserting itself." Scores of newspapers across the nation —with the singular exception of the French-language press in Quebec—called for a more generous policy toward refugees.[11]

To capitalize on this outpouring of public support, a high-powered delegation of Canadian Jews arrived in Ottawa on November 22 to meet with the prime minister and plead the case for Jewish refugees. Unfortunately, it seemed they had come too late, for, on the day before they arrived, the cabinet took up the refugee question. Despite King's urging to make some "provision" for refugees, the Quebec ministers, still led by Ernest Lapointe, the minister of justice, were solidly opposed. Rather than force the issue and risk alienating Quebec, King announced to the press that the whole question needed further study.[12] This decision prompted a serious split within the Jewish community, and the *Hebrew Journal* of Toronto, castigating the Congress leadership for being too timid for too long, called for more militant action against a government that had humiliated the Jewish community by "shamelessly" making decisions concerning refugees the day before a delegation of Jewish leaders was to meet with the prime minister.

> Obviously it is easier to influence a decision before it is made than to change it after it has been announced. . . . It appears that our leaders have been too cautious—if not timid. . . . This exaggerated humility will be costly to the Jews.
>
> It is not our intention to be harsh on the Congress. We merely point out a fault with the hope that the costly experience of the past may serve as a lesson for the future. This is especially deplorable to the *Hebrew Journal* since it must bear part of the blame. We have continually exhorted the Jews of Toronto not to undertake any action on behalf of the German Jews unless it was directed by the Congress. We did so because we have been assured . . . that at the proper time everything would be done. It looks as if someone fell asleep.[13]

It was, then, a desperate group of Jews ushered into King's office on November 23. It included both Jewish MP's and the leaders of all the important community organizations, including the Congress, the Jewish Immigrant Aid Society and the Zionist Organization of Canada. They pleaded with King and his immigration minister, Thomas Crerar, to open up Canada's doors a crack and admit ten thousand refugees whom the community would guarantee would not become public charges. But they were politely rebuffed; King pointed out that unemployment in Canada was still high and that his first duty was "the avoidance of strife, . . . maintaining the unity of the country," and fighting "the forces of separatism." He said that he sympathized with the refugees, but had "to consider the constituencies and the views of those supporting the Government." Making virtue out of vice, King explained to an aghast Jewish delegation that *Kristallnacht* might turn out to be a blessing, that, rather than aggravating the Jewish situation in Europe, it might improve it: these tragic events had generated such revulsion worldwide that "the solution of the problem of immigration may have been facilitated." Germany, King explained, would be cowed by the international reaction to *Kristallnacht* and desist from further actions against the Jews.

How hard it must have been for the Jewish delegates to ignore the irony in King's claim that Hitler and his cabinet would be moved by the outcry over *Kristallnacht* when King and *his* cabinet had not been. Oscar Cohen, representing the Congress at the meeting, recalled that "it was a sweet minuet which was being danced, at the end of which everyone bowed to everyone else and left the room empty."[14] But the Jewish delegation took their leave shaken—shaken by the magnitude of the refugees' plight, by the weight of their failure to win any concessions in Ottawa despite the sympathy expressed in English Canada and by the bitterness of the grass-roots Jewish discontent that had now surfaced.

On the following day, November 24, King again met with his cabinet and, as he recorded in his diary, he once more asked them to adopt a "liberal attitude," to act as the "conscience of the nation," even though it might not be "politically most expedient, and to offer some aid. But again there was no response to his appeal; the cabinet, according to the prime minister, feared "the political consequences of any help to the Jews." What it was prepared to do, after some discussion, was to help find a home for these Jews "in some [other] land." King then dropped the issue as he "did not wish to press the matter any further."[15]

For Canadian Jews the cabinet's decision was a shock; for their leaders it was devastating. The prime minister had rejected every proposal and had told the Jews that they should go out and arouse public opinion if they wanted a change in government policy. This the Congress set out to do at once, but now with its options severely limited.[16] It was one thing to have unanimous agreement among Jews that action was called for; it was quite another to know what that action should be.

Canadian Jewry seemed poised, like a force armed for battle but without a plan of attack. The leadership of the Congress in western Canada declared its resolve: "Never before in the history of Jewry are we so united and ready to work and follow the instructions of the Congress."[17] Sadly, the Canadian Jewish Congress had all too few instructions to deliver. The influence of the Jewish MP's had been found wanting, direct appeals to King and Crerar had gone unanswered, mass demonstrations had gone unheard, delegations sent to Ottawa had come away empty-handed, and even the growing support in the English-Canadian press for a humanitarian gesture in the aftermath of *Kristallnacht* had left the government unmoved. That Jews ever had collective power to influence policy in Ottawa is doubtful; that they did not have it in the immediate prewar years is certain.

Nevertheless, defeat was unthinkable while newspaper headlines and letters from relatives and friends were an everyday reminder of the mounting horrors in Europe. Jewish leaders still preached communal restraint; no purpose would, they believed, be served by loud protest, at least not by Jews. And so, with no alternatives, they turned to organizational restructuring, first seeking influential allies—allies to whom the government might listen and for whom the refugee cause was not a private Jewish agony but a broad humanitarian cause.

Embittered and frustrated, Jewish community leaders began to consider seriously organizing a non-denominational, anti-Nazi lobby, which might more effectively act on behalf of the refugees. At its annual convention in October, even before the meeting with King and Crerar, the Congress had endorsed the creation of a non-sectarian body that could "approach the Government and appeal to them directly for favourable consideration on purely humanitarian ground."[18] Fortuitously, at exactly this moment a respected non-sectarian organization had decided, on its own, to undertake just this course of action.

For some time the Canadian League of Nations Society, an organization devoted to world peace and cooperation, had been without purpose and for the most part inactive, as irrelevant to a world that seemed hell-bent on another war as was the League of Nations itself. Most of its members were, however, deeply disturbed by the apparent inhumanity of the Canadian government's refugee policy, and, in a sense, the Jewish refugee issue proved to be a boon to the organization, giving it new life and new sources of membership and funds. It seemed to be the last great moral crusade of a dismal decade. In early October the society had announced that it would "place the strength of [its] entire organization behind a move to aid the Jewish refugees . . . by requesting the Canadian government to take immediate action." The society's president, the indefatigable Senator Cairine Wilson, a close friend and political ally of the prime minister, had stated that the organization was already beginning to mobilize its resources in an effort to change immigration policy. As part of that effort the Canadian Jewish Congress had promised covertly to finance the campaign, but fearful that the society might be tarred as a "Jewish front," had agreed that "Jewish representation should be small."[19]

Following the events of *Kristallnacht* the momentum toward establishing a non-sectarian, pro-refugee pressure group moved ahead unabated. On December 6, 1938, the Canadian League of Nations Society sponsored a national refugee conference at the Château Laurier Hotel in Ottawa. A deliberately small deputation from the Canadian Jewish Congress joined delegates from twenty-five national, or, rather, English-Canadian, organizations. Some of those representing non-Jewish organizations, such as Rev. Claris Silcox of the United Church and the Anglican Canon, W. W. Judd, had already worked closely with the Congress on refugee matters. No French-Canadian organization was represented.[20]

The meeting quickly constituted itself as the Canadian National Committee on Refugees and Victims of Political Persecution (CNCR). Senator Cairine Wilson took on the duties of president and an energetic and effective spokeswoman for the refugee cause just returned from studies in London, Constance Hayward, was made executive secretary. In cooperation with the Canadian Jewish Congress refugee committee, Wilson and Hayward immediately set about organizing local chapters of the CNCR across Canada. In many places the local Congress leadership was instrumental in suggesting sympathetic and prominent non-Jews who might actively support the new non-denominational group. The Congress also covered the direct and indirect costs of several CNCR projects, making cash contributions to the committee's operating budget and putting at the disposal of its permanent Toronto office printing and mailing facilities, address lists and other institutional services.

As one of its first efforts, a small CNCR delegation was granted an interview with the prime minister and several members of his cabinet at Senator Wilson's personal request; no Jews attended. Some of those attending the meeting, including Wilson, Silcox and Judd, spoke to King of the need for a humanitarian gesture by government on behalf of refugees, who included "Christians of the Jewish race in Germany, who had no organized body to speak for them."

King listened patiently; he had heard it all before, although not from this particular group of people. Thus, speaking as though to old friends, he applauded the committee's dedication and indicated his personal sympathy for its cause. He would, nevertheless, soon guide them, ever so gently, into the quicksand that was political reality. King advised the delegation not to approach the government with the specific number of refugees it wished to see admitted; that, he said, would serve no purpose. The prime minister's secretary recorded the conversation: "He then alluded to the constitutional problem presented by all immigration questions in which the Provinces, as well as the Dominion, had a measure of competence. He said it might be helpful to have the views of the provincial governments on the matter. He also pointed out the necessity of the government avoiding any action which would serve to increase the problem of unemployment in Canada, and indicated that the problem must be met without enhancing our troubles at home, and, above all, without creating dissension between one part of Canada and another."[21] With this, the CNCR delegation was excused. King had, once again, promised nothing.

The events of November 1938 both at home and abroad put the Canadian government on the defensive. The demonstrations by the Jewish community, the activities of non-Jewish, pro-refugee organizations and the critical tone of most editorials brought home to Canadian officials that something would have to be done. Even the British cabinet noticed how small had been Canada's contribution. Lord Winterton, the chancellor of the Duchy of Lancaster and chairman of the Intergovernmental Committee on Refugees, told his colleagues that, while "Australia was taking a substantial number [of refugees]," Canada, which had a great deal of "suitable land," had not as yet contributed anything to help solve the problem.[22]

The Canadian dilemma was best articulated by O. D. Skelton's talented assistant, the politically shrewd Norman Robertson. "We don't want to take too many Jews," Robertson said, "but, in the present circumstances particularly, we don't want to say so."[23] Although Canada's "capacity to absorb immigrants," Robertson believed, "is grossly exaggerated by Mercator's map, it undoubtedly can take in, in normal times, a good many more immigrants than it has in the last five or six years." He was, however, concerned that Canada would find it difficult to get "her share of the best type of Jewish refugee"—those from Germany and Austria—because most Canadian Jews were of Russian and Polish origin. German and Austrian Jews were, he argued, more likely to "adapt . . . to Canadian conditions than the Jew who is only one step removed from the ghettos of Poland and Czarist Russia."

On December 1, 1938, it seemed as though the Jewish community had won over its most important convert. On that day, during a cabinet meeting, Thomas Crerar, obviously troubled by his government's behaviour, announced to his stunned colleagues that he was prepared to recommend the admission of ten thousand refugees. But neither the prime minister nor his cabinet would budge. Disassociating himself from the hapless immigration minister, whose proposal he thought was made "without consideration" of the problems involved, King found a convenient solution. He suggested to his colleagues that they make use of the British North America Act to justify their inaction; King himself would publicly announce that nothing could be done for German Jews until the provinces were consulted, as, according to the constitution, immigration legislation was concurrent. At the same time he chided Crerar, telling him to do his homework and prepare a statement which the cabinet would discuss.[24]

Crerar's defection clearly troubled King. Even more bothersome, however, was the announcement on the same day by the Australian government that it was now prepared to admit fifteen thousand refugees over the next three years. Crerar at once warned the prime minister that Canada would be put under "a great deal of pressure" to follow suit. As well, King received a trenchant letter from A. A. Heaps, saying that the Australian's decision had made him "ashamed" as a Canadian and that the government's policy was "inhumane" and "lacking principle."[25]

On December 13 the cabinet took up the refugee issue once again. Aware that he had support neither from his cabinet colleagues nor his department officials, Crerar read a statement—drafted by Blair and Robertson—that said nothing about the admission of ten thousand refugees but simply recommended the easing—ever so slightly—of the present immigration regulations.[26] After wavering somewhat, Crerar had again been brought into line, and a relieved cabinet accepted the new position, not to change the regulations but to interpret them "as liberally as possible." According to the prime minister, what this meant in practice was that Jews already landed in Canada as tourists would be allowed to remain, while no more Jewish refugees would be admitted to Canada "lest it might foment an anti-Semitic problem . . . and [create] a new problem." Thus, after months of wrestling with the question of Jewish refugees, the cabinet had at long last found an answer: keep them out.

For Jewish refugees eager to come to Canada it was unfortunate that the Canadian high commissioner in London was, to say the least, no partisan of Jewish immigration. Vincent Massey, the prominent scion of the wealthy Massey family, had in fact become a fringe member of the aristocratic, largely pro-German and anti-Semitic Cliveden set, centred around Lord and Lady Astor. Though he was much too "Anglophilic" to have the confidence or even the trust of Mackenzie King—indeed, the prime minister had once told Massey that he was "quite wrong on his views on most things"—Massey's recommendations still carried weight with the government, especially when they were in line with policies already endorsed by the cabinet.[27] And, on the question of Jewish refugees, their positions coincided.

Massey was enthusiastic about the anti-Nazi Sudetens displaced by the Munich agreement, most of whom were Social Democrats or Catholics. Many of these refugees, he told the prime minister, were skilled craftsmen, professionals and farmers—exactly the kind of settlers Canada wanted; and perhaps even better, only a small number were Jews. Massey immediately saw an opportunity to score some public relations points for Canada at minimal cost. The British government was applying heavy pressure on the Dominions to admit Sudeten refugees; indeed, immediately following the Munich agreement, Malcolm MacDonald, the Dominions and colonial secretary, called together all the high commissioners to inform them that "all those concerned with the recent settlement in Czechoslovakia had a greater responsibility in the matter than fell upon them, for example, in respect of the Jewish refugees in Germany and Austria."[28] Would it not be a wonderful tactic, Massey suggested to King, to accept "as many as possible Aryan Sudeten Germans"; these, he stated, were surely "more desirable" than other refugees, but, more to the point, he said, "if we could take a substantial number of them it would put us in a much stronger position in relation to later appeals from and on behalf of non-Aryans." The government, Massey also pleaded, should consider Sudeten Germans "quite separately from other refugees, . . . as they include . . . many persons who would be much more desirable as Canadian settlers and much more likely to succeed in our country than certain other types of refugees." Privately, Massey wrote the prime minister that admission of Jewish refugees would "naturally swell the already substantial Jewish population of [Canada's] larger cities" and help create an "anti-Semitic feeling." It would be much "easier," he told King, "to refuse to make a substantial increase in . . . admissions of Jewish immigrants" if Canada allowed in a substantial number of "political refugees from the Sudeten area." And in case the prime minister missed the point, Massey drove it home: "These refugees are of a superior type to certain other categories of refugees who are engaging our attention."[29]

Such cynicism was clearly not unappreciated in Ottawa, and Under-Secretary of State Skelton was quick to assure Massey that his suggestions were "in line" with proposals already before the cabinet. In fact Skelton's assistant, Norman Robertson, had recommended sometime earlier that an offer of admission be made to these Sudetens rather than to other refugees—"Men of their type and history should be a really valuable asset and acquisition to this country." As well, the chairman of the Intergovernmental Committee on Refugees, Lord Winterton, had assured the Canadian prime minister that, although many of the Sudetens were called "non-Aryan Christians, . . . in fact [they had] very little Jewish blood . . . and . . . would make excellent settlers."[30]

Within days of receiving the high commissioner's recommendation, the government decided again to keep out the Jews but let in the Sudeten Germans. Massey was delighted; he congratulated King, informing him that there were indeed a large number of central Europeans "of means and education" who would enrich Canada "in both the material sense and otherwise," but for Canadian immigration laws, which were "too wooden." Canada was missing a golden opportunity, he said, if it did not accept these people. Naturally, Massey did not have in mind Jews but "the numerous non-Jewish people who [found] life quite intolerable under the Nazi regime." He urged the prime minister to announce publicly that Canada was prepared to admit an unspecified number of non-Jewish German political refugees from the Sudeten.[31]

The lesson of the Sudeten refugee experience was not lost on at least one American observer. John Goodyear, the vice-consul in Vancouver, noted that, although the Jewish refugee problem had existed for years, "it [was] the babes of the refugee contingent," the Catholic and non-Jewish Sudetens, who were offered haven. "A solicitous attitude towards the Sudeten minority," he concluded, "has prompted more practical action on its behalf since it became a problem in September, 1938, than has any comparable feeling towards the Jews over a period of several years. The inference is indisputable that the Jew is unpopular in Canada."[32]

By 1939 an unofficial, unholy triumvirate had been forged, with the Immigration Branch, the cabinet and, to a lesser degree, the Department of External Affairs opposing the admission to Canada of refugees in general and Jewish refugees in particular. The intransigent and morally obtuse Blair, as director of the Immigration Branch, gave vent to his anti-Semitism by placing every possible bureaucratic obstacle in the path of the refugees; meanwhile, Ernest Lapointe corrected any cabinet backsliding, including that by the prime minister; and Vincent Massey worked through External Affairs as best he could to keep Jews out of Canada. Individually, each man had significant power, his own sphere of influence; but on the refugee issue their spheres overlapped and, collectively, they seemed beyond challenge. There is no evidence that they consulted on the refugee issue—and they likely did not—but what united them was the conviction that Canada did not need more Jews.

The prime minister was not a prisoner of this anti-Jewish coterie, yet he could not help but be influenced by it. When the foremost immigration authority, the leading French-Canadian politician and the nation's senior foreign diplomat spoke, King listened (especially because they were all saying the same thing). King himself vacillated; at times his humanitarian and religious instincts overcame his advisors' arguments. His sympathy for the refugees was genuine, and he sincerely wanted to find them a home—anywhere but in Canada. Only a vast public outcry, he told a delegation from the Canadian National Committee on Refugees, could overturn the barriers to immigration, and he urged the delegates to go to the nation, to provide it with a "proper education on this question."[33] Just how much public support would have to be generated before the government would change its policy, King did not say. He did not have to. The combined forces of Jews and the CNCR could, he knew, never overcome the government.

Above all else King was committed to keeping Canada united. He feared that allowing in Jews would disrupt that unity —and not only within Quebec.[34] Anti-Semitism, perhaps most overt in that province, was prevalent throughout English-speaking Canada as well. In a meeting earlier that year with the premier of British Columbia, T. D. Pattullo, the prime minister had been put on notice that, although that province was prepared to take refugees, it did not want many Jews.[35] Jewish quotas existed in various professions, universities, medical schools and industries. Jews were restricted from buying property in some areas, from holidaying at some resorts, from joining many private clubs or using their recreational facilities and even from sitting on the boards of various charitable, educational, financial and business organizations.[36] Anti-Jewish sentiments were being voiced regularly—and with impunity—by many respectable newspapers, politicians, businessmen and clergymen, and by leading officers of such groups as the Canadian Corps Association, the Orange Order, the Knights of Columbus and farm and business organizations.[37] There was even some violence as Jew and anti-Semite confronted one another on the streets of Toronto, Winnipeg and other Canadian cities. So extensive was Canadian anti-Semitism that the American chargé d'affaires remarked on "the rapidity of its spread." He informed his superiors in Washington that Canadians had "no desire to have . . . Jews emigrate to [their] country" and that the entry of Jewish refugees "would be regarded privately as a calamity by most people here." Anti-Semitism, he added, was increasingly "finding expression in private conversations."[38] Indeed, so grave did this problem appear that at its founding convention the CNCR resolved as one of its major priorities to combat the anti-Semitism that seemed so rife in Canada.

If it is possible to overemphasize the extent of anti-Semitism in Canada at this time, it is not possible to ignore it. It existed and King was well aware of it. Any move to admit Jewish refugees, he feared, might cost him political support. Although some organizations and high-placed members of religious groups, such as the Anglican and United churches, actively campaigned on behalf of Jewish refugees, most Canadians seemed indifferent to the suffering of German Jews and hostile to their admission to Canada. Indeed, in March 1939 Reverend Silcox, now general secretary of the Social Service Council of Canada as well as a leading pro-refugee advocate, delivered what he called a "post-mortem" on Canada's refugee policy to a large audience at the University of Toronto. He listed a series of reasons for Canada's failure to respond to the crisis, ranging from timid leadership and a bad economic situation to the success of Nazi propagandists and xenophobia in Quebec; but, most important, he claimed, was "the existence throughout Canada . . . of a latent anti-Semitism."[39]

Despite all obstacles to success Jewish leaders persevered; they had no choice, for after *Kristallnacht* the requests from European Jews trapped in Germany and Austria multiplied dramatically. They arrived daily at the offices of the Congress, JIAS and various other Jewish organizations. Each bore its own story of suffering and helplessness; each told of the horrors of Nazi oppression; each begged for mercy and above all for hope. They were, in the memory of Oscar Cohen, the most painful letters he had ever read, and the one thing they all asked for was the one thing Canadian Jews could not provide—entrance to Canada.[40]

For Jewish officials, responding to the letters was a difficult task, and for some, an impossible one. What could be said, for example, to the Stein family of Vienna who reported that their business had been shut down for eight months, that they had been "left without means of assistance and with no possibility of earning a living." They were homeless, stateless and penniless. Particularly affected were the two children—a nine-year-old boy and a seven-year-old girl. As their father Jacob explained, "Our distress . . . increases daily and there is nothing left for us but suicide. . . . Our only hope for survival is admission to Canada."[41]

The Steins, like almost everyone who wrote at this time, had been relatively well-off until the Nazis came to power. Indeed, petitions were flowing in from scientists, doctors, bankers, judges, merchants, musicians, professors, skilled craftsmen, lawyers, entrepreneurs, as well as hundreds of farmers; all were Jewish and all wrote asking for help. From the Hebrew Immigrant Aid Society (HIAS) in Paris came an urgent wire to Jewish authorities in Montreal, informing them that thousands of Jewish professionals who were highly qualified and would be "extremely useful for Canadian industry" were now stranded in France, "penniless and distraught"; their only hope was emigration. The Jewish Immigrant Aid Society office in Toronto alone dealt with so many of these "heartbreaking letters" during the latter half of 1938 that much of the ordinary work of the staff had to be put aside in order to deal with the correspondence.[42]

Pleas for help came from individuals, families and entire communities. A successful middle-aged Austrian engineer wrote on behalf of his sixteen-year-old son. "You are parents too," he said. "You will understand our distressful and desperate care concerning our child's future. Thus you will understand also that I apply to your Jewish kindred heart for your care in my son's interest. For our children give contents and meaning to our life now so full of trials. They are our only hope. . . . I should like if my son's talent would not be wasted. . . . You would save the future of the grandchild of a rabbi."[43] A seventeen-year-old boy, the son of "respectable parents of the Jewish middle class," wrote from Berlin on behalf of himself. As a Jew, he said, he could neither work nor survive in Germany. He had to leave, and was therefore begging for admission to Canada.[44] From Czechoslovakia a group of two hundred farm families, "with a total of one million dollars in capital," begged for entry visas. They were aware that "the Canadian government dislikes . . . to get any Jews into the country," yet had no other choice but to leave their homeland before the Nazis arrived.[45]

For the twelve members of the Zuckermann family of Austria, the situation was almost hopeless. As Samuel Zuckermann wrote to the Jewish Colonization Association, "In great distress and desperation a whole family directs itself to you with an appeal for help. . . . We have here no possibility whatsoever to maintain ourselves. If no assistance will come to us forthwith, we shall all go under. Please help us and save us. You are our last hope." Even more poignant was the position of Leopold Kluger and his family. A wealthy Jewish merchant, Kluger had been imprisoned in Vienna on *Kristallnacht* and was released only on condition that he leave Austria by April 1939. Canada was his last hope; he was, he said, in a "state of despondency beyond description" and would soon be dead if he could not find refuge. Similarly, Professor Maximilian Low, a renowned linguist, asked Jewish officials in Canada if they could find a way to admit him and his family. "We have lost," he wrote, "all rights of existence and life as human beings."[46]

To each of these letters the response of Jewish organizations was the same: "Though we sympathize . . . with your plight, . . . the Canadian government is not yet admitting Jewish refugees. . . . Try some other country."[47] But for the Steins, Zuckermanns, Klugers and Lows, for the thousands of Jews trying to get into Canada, there were no other countries.

Of course the cries of these Jews were also heard by the Canadian government, through letters or Jewish Immigrant Aid Society and Congress intermediaries. "We are almost inundated," Blair complained to Conservative opposition leader Robert Manion, "with applications for the admission of Jewish people from the whole Continent of Europe. In all the years I have been connected with Immigration, I have never seen anything to compare with the appeals that are now being made." And he told the consul general of the American embassy that he was under extreme pressure from Jewish groups. The 165,000 Jewish residents in Canada, he said, "most of whom seem to have relatives or friends in Central Europe, . . . are naturally anxious to get these relatives or friends . . . to Canada."[48]

The Immigration Branch was, however, wholly unmoved by these heart-rending appeals. Its task, as Blair kept reminding anyone with whom he talked, was to see that the regulations were not subverted.[49] The scientists, physicians, surgeons, craftsmen and other professionals applying to his office were all rejected as part of the "inadmissible classes." Rejecting the application of Leo Recht, a Jewish doctor from Vienna, Blair explained: "We have now reached the place where I think every person around the Department is delighted when he comes on a case that can be granted." But there were few such cases.[50] Dr. Recht was, Blair said, "merely one of the tens of thousands of people who are in the same position."

The Immigration Branch made it clear that it would accept only bona fide agriculturalists with "sufficient capital" to establish a farm; yet, for the Jewish refugee who could qualify, there was still a hitch: Blair and his officials believed that Jews could not farm. The "fundamental difficulty" with Jewish immigrants, he told his chief officer in Europe, was that "the Jewish people do not . . . take to farming." Ironically, the last thing Canada needed in the 1930s—a decade of disappearing export markets, low agricultural prices, dreadful harvests and cruel weather—were more farmers. In reply to a senator who had commented on Canada's "wide-open spaces" and its "meagre if not stingy policy . . . towards refugees," Blair retorted that "so far as most of the refugees are concerned, Canada need not be any greater than Montreal or Toronto as they exhibit little or no interest outside of these cities." The Immigration Branch had tried "various ways" for twenty years, he told Robert Manion, "to tie these people to the land but with little success." Jews invariably promised to be farmers "merely as a means of getting into the country," but rarely remained on the land. "It is quite common," he later told the leader of the opposition, "for Jewish traders to represent themselves as farmers only for the purpose of getting into Canada and when they have succeeded in entering they pay no further attention to farming." He also took it upon himself to tell Under-Secretary of State Skelton that it was impossible "to keep these people on the land," and if the government harboured any schemes for settling refugees on farms, it should be aware that all such schemes involving Jewish settlers had failed.[51]

Blair was not alone in fearing that regulations were being subverted by Jews anxious to be admitted to Canada. Little, Canada's chief immigration officer in Europe, confided to the director of immigration that he had concluded that "the term 'agricultural background' in the minds of many of these people meant a small plot at the back of the house or flower pot at the front." It was "becoming increasingly apparent," an immigration inspector reported to Blair, "that a great many refugees are turning to the supposed loop-hole of farming in order to get into Canada."[52]

For Jewish officials the government policy of admitting only farmers with capital was a cruel joke. "It was only conceded by the Government in principle," said the director of JIAS, "and, in the light of our experience, with the tongue in their cheek."[53] Almost no Jewish farmers, Solkin ruefully conceded to his staff, were being admitted, no matter how legitimate their qualifications or substantial their assets. The general secretary of the Congress's western region exaggerated only slightly when he claimed that, "while the farmer family settlement scheme has been in operation, there were no Jewish families allowed on the grounds that there were no Jewish agriculturalists." The head of the Jewish Colonization Association in Europe, still the clearing-house for much of the Jewish agricultural immigration to Canada, complained bitterly that Canada seemed to have put an end to the immigration of Jewish farmers; all those applying, he added, were being rejected. Further, he reported to his counterpart in the United States that the Canadian railway and shipping companies in Europe had been ordered "not to consider requests from Jewish agriculturalists, even if they comply fully with the law." Meanwhile, because ostensibly only farmers were allowed into Canada, Jewish officials impressed on the many doctors, engineers, scientists and other professionals who were applying that they must emphasize only their "ability to engage in farming and their suitability for a farming life."[54]

As the flood of refugee applications began to overwhelm the Immigration Branch, government authorities decided to keep raising the admission standards for prospective refugees. Between January and November 1938 alone, the capital required for a Jewish family to enter Canada had risen from $5,000 to $15,000. And even this amount was often not enough to guarantee admission. Solkin told Jewish authorities in Poland that admission also depended "on the size of the family and the occupation of the proposed immigrant." By December 1938 the Immigration Branch was rejecting Jews able to bring $20,000 or more with them, and by 1939 even that amount was insufficient. A distraught Solkin told incredulous HIAS officers in New York that despite herculean efforts he had been unable to gain an entry permit "for dress manufacturers with capital as high as eighty-five thousand dollars." Even worse, just days before the outbreak of war the JIAS director reported to his counterparts in Europe that they should discourage Jews with any amount of capital from applying to Canada as the government had already rejected "people with as much as $170,000 . . . on the grounds that their industry might compete with others."[55]

A major obstacle for Jews with assets was the Immigration Branch's assumption that their capital was spurious. Blair and others in the department were convinced that once again the Jews were attempting to hoodwink Canadian authorities. The funds these refugees claimed to possess were, in Blair's mind, only "show money," money deposited in a Canadian bank by an American Jew "to the credit of some person in Europe," who then applied for admission. It was, he warned, "a crooked business," an attempt to evade Canadian laws.[56] Similarly, Little cautioned his superiors that he had learned from "an authority, which cannot be questioned, that many of these wealthy refugees who transfer their money to Canada immediately file Powers of Attorney assigning various sums to different people."[57]

The task of Jewish authorities in Canada seemed hopeless. The Jewish Immigrant Aid Society was already reporting that more refugees were arriving in Canada on their way to Australia than were staying; much of its time and effort, a society spokesman said, was spent shepherding these people from Halifax to Vancouver.[58] Indeed, so many refugees were passing through Canada in transit that a French-Canadian member of Parliament worried aloud that some were remaining behind. He asked Crerar in the House of Commons if more people were arriving in Halifax than were sailing from Vancouver, but did not get a reply.[59] Nor did Solkin when he pointedly asked whether the government kept "changing the regulations . . . and creating obstacles . . . just to keep out prospective Jewish immigrants."[60] But the society's director did promise that Canadian Jews would not give up; they would continue to "apply pressure" on the government and to "hope for an improvement of conditions."

The attempt to improve conditions for refugees' admission to Canada began in January 1939, when, bowing to pressures from the Jewish community, Samuel Bronfman agreed to become the president of the Canadian Jewish Congress. An aggressive, strong-minded entrepreneur and one of Canada's wealthiest men, Samuel Bronfman had long kept his distance from the Congress. The Congress, he believed, was a "useless organization . . . which was doing Canadian Jewry more harm than good."[61] But he was deeply touched by the plight of Jewish refugees and was determined to do something on their behalf. With him, he brought to the largely working-class, immigrant organization the wealthier, more integrated Jews of Montreal. As far as Bronfman was concerned, the days of well-meaning but ineffectual amateurs, constrained by limited budgets and, perhaps, even more by limited expectations, must end; the Congress, would now become a power with which the government would have to contend.[62]

Bronfman at once called a meeting of Jewish organizations outside the umbrella of the Congress, such as B'nai B'rith and the Zionists. He impressed upon them the need for unity, and they, in turn, agreed to create a new refugee committee to take charge of all Congress activities in the area of immigration. After a series of regional meetings, the Congress's refugee organization was renamed the Canadian Jewish Committee for Refugees (CJCR), with Bronfman as chairman. At the same time a young, dynamic, articulate Montreal lawyer, Saul Hayes, was hired as the refugee committee's full-time executive director, and would shortly go on to become executive director of the Congress itself. Hayes was promised and given both the staff and financial resources necessary to initiate what all hoped would be a massive propaganda campaign designed to change government policy. It at last appeared that—even in Montreal—all Jewish factions were under one organizational roof, ready to lobby on behalf of Jewish refugees.[63]

One of the first tasks of the new refugee committee was to underwrite "educational tours" by various pro-refugee speakers. In January, for instance, Claris Silcox was sent on a speaking tour of western Canada. Officially, he was travelling under the banner of the non-denominational CNCR to address community groups and service clubs; actually, his tour was "originated, arranged and financed" by the Canadian Jewish

Committee for Refugees.[64] A gifted public speaker, Silcox attracted both wide media coverage and editorial support. He also made himself available to local Jewish groups and helped organize refugee committees throughout the west; the local committees then worked with the national refugee committee to publicize the successful business ventures begun by refugee industrialists in Britain and the United States, pointing out the opportunities that Canada was missing by keeping refugees out.* Similar arguments were made respecting the potential wealth of scholarly and scientific manpower that could be Canada's for the asking.[65]

Unfortunately, these activities had no impact on government thinking. Also in January, in a speech to his Montreal constituents, the secretary of state, Fernand Rinfret, would sum up the government's position. "Despite all sentiments of humanity," said Rinfret, "so long as Canada has an unemployment problem there will be no 'open door' for political refugees here." Government restrictions, he said, would remain, especially against "that element who is assimilated with difficulty among the English and French of our country."[66]

A week later Rinfret's speech was the subject of a "lengthy and sometimes heated" debate in the House of Commons.[67] A. A. Heaps launched a vigorous attack on the secretary of state who was, fortuitously, absent from the House. Should government policy, Heaps asked, be announced at a constituency meeting before it was announced in Parliament? He accused both the minister and his cabinet colleagues of using "harsh and brutal language" and of being "devoid of sentiment and humanity." The government, he charged, had made promises to the Jewish community that were never kept; it had reneged on every single commitment to allow in refugees. In support of Rinfret, the prime minister answered that, although he was probably misquoted, the secretary of state was clearly

* An intimate relationship soon developed between the CJCR and the CNCR. Programs organized by the Congress were sometimes publicized under the banner of the national refugee committee in order to downplay the Jewish connection; indeed, the two organizations' function, programs and funding sometimes overlapped. Although the CNCR's mandate was to work in non-Jewish circles and the CJCR was delegated tasks in the Jewish community, the interests of the Jewish group were in fact all served by the independent and non-sectarian committee. If there was a problem in the relationship, it was that it might be seen as too close by outsiders, who might then dismiss the CNCR as a handmaiden of the Jews. Consequently, on the surface, relations were fraternal but distinct.

enunciating government policy. There would, King said, be no door opened for refugees by his administration.[68]

The activities of the pro-refugee committees, combined with a general unease among some Canadians over their government's policy, brought forth from Canadian newspapers an almost unanimous denunciation of the "pusillanimous" behaviour of the King administration. Since *Kristallnacht* most of the press—including even the odd paper in Quebec—had urged the government to be more generous toward Jewish refugees. The *Financial Post*, for example, encouraged the government to make a more concerted effort to bring in refugees: "If Canada really wants desirable immigrants from Europe, now is the time to get them. The present opportunity is not likely to be repeated."[69] The *Windsor Star* condemned the government's attitude toward Jewish farmers. "There is in some quarters a belief," its editor wrote, "that Jewish settlers would not be suitable agricultural pioneers. We have become used to the Jew in business in Canada, but not on the farm. Yet a glance at what has taken place in Palestine shows that Jewish farmers can succeed since the Jewish colonists in Palestine have made that country a garden and the products of Jewish farms are being exported widely throughout the world."[70] To *Saturday Night* the government's behaviour was "un-Christian"; to the *Vancouver Province*, "inhumane"; to the *Toronto Daily Star*, "stupid." The *Globe and Mail* wondered whether Canada was really a nation: "Does it stand for anything?"[71] After a survey of the press's attitudes to the refugee problem, the *Canadian Press* concluded: "Across Canada from coast to coast, editorial opinion, of all political shades, is urging that Canada should play her part . . . in meeting the vast international problem of the refugee."[72] Less sanguine was the American vice-consul, who noted that, although most newspapers were pro-refugee, some were "unfavourable or lukewarm according to their particular reactions to the problem."[73] Most hostile, he said, was the French-Canadian press, particularly the publications of the Catholic Church, which took the position that Canada had already received "too many immigrants of the Jewish race . . . who do not assimilate with either of the two elements which have built Canada."

Support for this anti-Jewish view came from a surprising source. Speaking to a Quebec audience, Conservative leader Robert Manion stated that he was opposed to any immigration, "so long as any Canadian remained unemployed."[74] His speech immediately caused a storm. Jewish leaders were apoplectic. Manion's speech, said Caiserman, was "a great blow."[75] *Saturday Night* decried it as not doing "justice to the humanitarian feelings of the people of this country," and other English-language newspapers then joined in denouncing the leader of the opposition.[76] Yet Manion's argument was well received by most Liberals and by the French-Canadian press.[77] And a young history professor at Mount Allison University, later one of the nation's leading academics and Lieutenant-Governor of New Brunswick, applauded Manion and his speech: George Stanley pointedly condemned "those who shed tears over the fate of the Jews in Europe and who raise funds for the assistance of foreign refugees, . . . [while they] ignore the poverty and distress on their own doorstep." "Charity," he said, "begins at home."[78]

At about this time, the somewhat more charitable students at Mount Allison University overwhelmingly supported a resolution, forwarded to the prime minister, that asked for "a relaxation in immigration laws to permit controlled entry to Canada of . . . refugees from Germany." The students even voted to raise funds to support several refugee students at the university.[79] And a view considerably different from Stanley's was held by another historian, Professor George Wrong of the University of Toronto, who poured out his heart in a letter to Manion:

> I am quite sure that the more thoughtful of our people are growing uneasy in consequence of our doing so little in regard to refugees from Europe. We have a land half empty, and refined people, victims of brutal injustice are homeless, tortured in mind and body, dying in grim desolation for lack of a place of refuge. Barely half of them are Jews. I fear Nemesis on our country if we close our ears to their cries of distress. We can not only ease our consciences but benefit ourselves by opening our doors to those among them whom we might select. . . . We must act and act quickly. Our own fibre will be improved if we face and overcome the difficulties.[80]

Manion later said privately that he had been "badly misquoted" and that he opposed only "large-scale immigration," not the admission of "carefully-selected refugees."[81] If "Mr. King," he told A. A. Heaps in confidence, "will agree to bringing in a reasonable number of refugees for humanitarian reasons, I will certainly support him."[82] Publicly, Manion said nothing.

Buoyed by numerous supporting editorials and convinced

that there was now a groundswell of popular support in English Canada, Jewish leaders were again in Ottawa in late February 1939 to meet with the prime minister. They fully expected "a definite and favourable decision," and would later share their optimism with their community. "It was felt that by now," a delegate reported, "opinion has been crystallized and the government is in a position to tell the Jews of Canada what it intends to do." Indeed, the government was. Crerar and Blair congratulated the Jewish delegates on their success in coalescing so much national support in so short a time; they were polite and sympathetic; they offered them nothing. Indeed, a disingenuous Blair told the delegates that, with respect to the Sudeten refugees, there would be no discrimination against Jews, "a number of whom would be included in the allotment." Two weeks later, after a careful study of every family, Crerar announced in the House that he could assure the members that "probably 95 percent of these people are Roman Catholics."[83]

The meeting with Crerar and Blair finally disabused Jewish community leaders of any notion they still cherished that the government would change its policy. The director of the Jewish Immigrant Aid Society declared that nothing could be expected from any meetings with the Canadian government: "From my frequent conversations with the high Department of Immigration officials, I know only too well that the government is as far from admitting refugees as they ever were and that any attempt to obtain a general relaxation in immigration is doomed to certain failure."[84] Although Solkin could not deny the chance of there being some moderation of specific regulations, his overall prognosis proved all too correct. Thus, while the Canadian Jewish Committee for Refugees at last promised activity to a Jewish community accustomed to inaction, it could not hope for any meaningful concessions from the government—only, as Solkin confessed, for an early federal election. Perhaps, he mused, "the new government would no longer have to placate the whims of anti-Semitic Quebec or retain the good graces of other reactionary elements in this country," and so might adopt "a more reasonable immigration policy."[85] The subsequent actions of the Immigration Branch could hardly be called "reasonable." As late as March 1939, it was attempting to expel Jews who had only tourist visas back to Germany. When a Liberal member of Parliament told Blair that this would be like "passing a death sentence" on these Jews, the director was unmoved—"not at all frightened" by the fate awaiting deported Jews, the

MP told a constituent.[86] Indeed, neither Blair nor Crerar admitted that any Jew deported from Canada to Germany would be "going to his death." They were concerned solely that the regulations be upheld.[87]

Just how negative government officials still were to the prospect of Jewish immigrants came as a surprise to the American diplomat, John Farr Simmons, who had been alerted to Canadian immigration policies at the time of the Evian Conference. After meetings with Norman Robertson, from External Affairs, and Blair, Simmons reported that there was little chance of Canada doing very much for the refugee cause. Robertson, he said, although "a humanitarian," categorically stated that Canada might accept more Sudeten Germans "as a group," but would accept Jews "on individual applications only." Setting quotas for refugees, the assistant under-secretary of state said, would "set the country on fire." According to Simmons, Blair had "adopted a much more rigid attitude." "Even a limited number of refugees once admitted," the director had told him, "would form an entering wedge for progressive and continual increases in this type of migration."[88]

It was now almost too much for Canadian Jews to bear. There was no longer any hope of convincing the King administration to change its mind, yet with newspapers full of horror stories of German Jews being whipped through the streets, thrown off roofs and dehumanized in every possible way, Canadian Jewry could not possibly admit defeat. Failure was unthinkable, even as the unthinkable was beginning to happen in Europe. And once again large numbers of individuals and organizations within the Canadian Jewish community were voicing bitter criticism of the Congress. Particularly in Toronto, the abject failure of the Congress's tactics was the subject of attack by trade unions, *landsmannschaften* and other Yiddish-speaking groups. Meetings were held, door-to-door collections begun, fund-raising campaigns launched—all to help form yet another pro-refugee coalition. The Zionist Organization of Canada made it clear that it would campaign for funds on its own because its purpose was not simply to assist refugees, but to insure "the establishment of a homeland for Jews in Palestine." S. M. Shapiro, publisher of the *Hebrew Journal*, led the campaign.

> There is no point in being reticent any longer about the fact that . . . the matter of refugees has been neglected by the

> leaders of the Congress . . . and that the policy of secret diplomacy pursued until now has not brought results. The public was duly impressed by the arguments advanced that any undue publicity was likely to do harm to the cause. . . . For two years the leaders of the Congress sought to assuage any misgivings on the part of the Jewish public by assuring it that they were negotiating with the authorities in Ottawa. The impression was conveyed that they were given some secret commitment by the government. Yet . . . it is becoming apparent that the secret negotiations accomplished nothing and that our leaders had no more promises from the Ottawa government than if they had done nothing at all in the matter.[89]

Shapiro further condemned Jewish leaders for their failure to "launch a mass movement," while "thousands of Jews perished and were rendered homeless." "The masses," he warned, were now "restive," convinced that only action on their part would force the government to move on the refugee question. "If we play the game of secret diplomacy," he warned, "we only play into our enemies' hands."

Just how prophetic were Shapiro's words was brought home to Canadian Jewry by the infamous "Voyage of the Damned." On May 15, 1939, nine hundred and seven desperate German Jews set sail from Hamburg on a luxury liner, the *St. Louis*. They had been stripped of their possessions, hounded first out of their homes and businesses and now their country. Like many who had sailed on this ship before, these passengers had once contributed much to their native land; they were distinguished, educated, cultured; many had been well-off but all were now penniless. Their most prized possession was the entrance visa to Cuba each carried on board.

The Jews on the *St. Louis* considered themselves lucky—they were leaving. When they reached Havana on May 30, however, their luck ran out, for the Cuban government refused to recognize their entrance visas. None of these wretched men, women and children were allowed to disembark, even after they threatened mass suicide.[90] The search for a haven now began in earnest. Argentina, Uruguay, Paraguay and Panama were approached, in vain, by various Jewish organizations. Within two days all the countries of Latin America had rejected entreaties to allow these Jews to land, and on June 2 the *St. Louis* was forced to leave Havana harbour. The last hope was Canada or the

United States, and the latter, not even bothering to reply to an appeal, sent a gunboat to shadow the ship as it made its way north. The American Coast Guard had been ordered to make certain that the *St. Louis* stayed far enough off shore so that it could not be run aground nor any of its frantic passengers attempt to swim ashore.[91]

The plight of the *St. Louis* had by now touched some influential Canadians; on June 7 several of these, led by George Wrong and including B. K. Sandwell of *Saturday Night*, Robert Falconer, past-president of the University of Toronto, and Ellsworth Flavelle, a wealthy businessman, sent a telegram to Prime Minister Mackenzie King begging that he show "true Christian charity" and offer the homeless exiles sanctuary in Canada. But Jewish refugees were far from the prime minister's mind. King was in Washington, accompanying the Royal Family on the final leg of its triumphant North American tour. The *St. Louis*, King felt, was not a Canadian problem, but he would, nevertheless, ask Skelton to consult on the matter with Lapointe and Blair. Lapointe quickly stated that he was "emphatically opposed" to the admission of the *St. Louis* passengers, while Blair claimed, characteristically, that these refugees did not qualify under immigration laws and that in any case Canada had already done too much for the Jews. No country, Blair added, could "open its doors wide enough to take in the hundreds of thousands of Jewish people who want to leave Europe: the line must be drawn somewhere."[92]

And the line drawn, the voyagers' last flickering hope extinguished, the Jews of the *St. Louis* headed back to Europe, where many would die in the gas chambers and crematoria of the Third Reich.

As the clouds of war gathered over Europe, as refugees knocked ever more often and loudly on Canada's locked door, the Canadian National Committee on Refugees worked tirelessly to promote a pro-refugee movement that would force a change in government policy. To the delight of the Jewish refugee committee, the refugee cause—at least in English Canada —was now frequently interpreted as a humanitarian one. Through the spring and summer of 1939 the *Globe and Mail*, the *Toronto Daily Star* and the *Winnipeg Free Press* continued their editorial assault on what they termed "a cowardly" government policy. "Canada is missing the boat on the refugee question," wrote the *Winnipeg Free Press*, just six weeks before the onset of war.

> This country still has the bars up and the refugee who gets into Canada has to pass some mighty stiff obstacles before he finally reaches his destination, . . . obstacles deliberately placed there by government. . . . A new type of immigrant is available if we want to take advantage of it. . . . Immigration bars . . . are undesirable now. Resources of capital and manpower, forced from the countries of their origin by political and racial persecution, now seek new outlets. Many countries are opening the door to them. . . . We are deliberately keeping out of this country men and money who would greatly add to our productive revenues. We are cutting off our nose to spite our face.[93]

As well, voices for so long silent were remonstrating the government from pulpits across the land and in church publications. Led by Claris Silcox, Canon W. W. Judd and Raymond Booth of the Quakers, ministers were preaching on the refugee problems (although the Catholic Church—despite the pleas of some of its prominent lay and clerical leaders—was still largely silent);[94] and American and British church leaders, invited by local CNCR committees, spoke to Christian audiences on the necessity of saving German Jewry. William Birks, president of Henry Birks and Sons, angrily told Robert Manion that he felt that the "Canadian approach . . . had been narrow, bigoted and very shortsighted," and he wrote to Thomas Crerar that he did not "wish to hang [his] head in shame as a Canadian at Canada's lack of interest and initiative in facing the problem in a big and decent way." He defiantly told the immigration minister that "Canada should have sent trade missionaries to beg such people to come and not wait for them to seek and beg us."[95] CCF leader J. S. Woodsworth admitted that he felt "helpless" and "ashamed at . . . Canadian smugness and selfishness."[96]

But support in English Canada, gratifying though it may have been, was not enough, and the combined efforts of the national and Jewish refugee committees proved too little too late. Neither group had successfully breached the well-defended wall of government hostility, which deemed refugees, especially Jewish refugees, a divisive force in Canada and a potential tool in the arsenal of Quebec nationalists, and which doubted that a capricious English-Canadian public would long support the arrival of large numbers of refugees. And, in the final analysis, Canadian Jewry, weak and divided, had neither the influence to effect any positive change in government policy nor any idea of the low esteem in which they and their cause were held by cabinet members and civil servants. Their sense of being outsiders in their own home, of being *in* Canada but not *of* it, left them uneasy in dealings with government, deferring to *shtadlonim* in the form of their members of Parliament, who themselves turned out to be powerless. Thus, the general timidity of Jewish leaders, even under pressure from their own rank-and-file, and their obsequiousness in the face of government authority led in the end only to friction within the Jewish community.

Would other tactics have succeeded? Would loud public protests, what might today be called the politics of the street and advocated at the time by leftist Zionists, Yiddishists and *landsmannschaften*, have succeeded where more moderate approaches did not? Probably not, for the pro-refugee forces, particularly Canadian Jewry, were too disorganized, too fractious and, most importantly, too distant from the seat of real power to effect any change. If resolution of the refugee crisis ranked high among the priorities of Canadian Jewry, the government only wished the issue would go away. Delay and obfuscation were the order of the day.

The Canadian government's success in withstanding pressure from pro-refugee groups, both Jewish and non-Jewish, was virtually complete. To the very end Blair was even proud of his achievements. Only days after the *St. Louis* was turned away from Canadian shores, he told Little that, although he had noticed "a disposition" on the part of Jews to claim that Canada was "not doing anything for refugees," it had in fact done much. He had no intention, he said, of "advertising what had been done," though what had been done gave him "a good deal of satisfaction."[97] Thus, the unyielding opposition of certain key officials, the depression, the general apathy in English Canada, the outright hostility of French Canada, the prime minister's concern for votes and the overlay of anti-Semitism that dominated official Ottawa combined to insure that no more than a mere handful of Jewish refugees would find a home in Canada.[98]

The government had adamantly refused to admit refugees, to see the refugee problem as its own. On September 1, 1939, the Germans invaded Poland, soon offering their solution as the final one.

3

DER FETER YIUV IST BEI UNS

Three months after the invasion of Poland began, an envelope arrived at the home of the Goldstein family in Toronto. It was from the Red Cross in Geneva and contained a letter one of its officials had smuggled out of Poland—the first word anyone in Canada had received about what was happening to that country's Jewish community. The Goldsteins knew the writer well; he was a rabbi and a nephew of Mrs. Goldstein. And they realized that he was writing in code, fearful that the letter might fall into the wrong hands. But they could make no sense of it, nor could any of their relatives and friends.

The note was brief: "Der Feter Yiuv ist bei uns." Literally translated from the Yiddish, it meant that Uncle Yiuv was with them; but the Goldsteins knew no one called Yiuv. Frantic, the family took the letter to the Jewish Immigrant Aid Society. Everyone at the Society was mystified too, yet certain that the simple sentence contained important information. After pouring over the message for hours, one of the staff suggested they consult a rabbi, and a call for help immediately went out to two of the leading sages of the community, Rabbi Weinrib and Rabbi Silverstein. Within minutes—both lived near the society's office —the two white-bearded scholarly men had arrived and gone behind closed doors to study the letter, while the society's entire operation had come to a halt, the staff waiting outside the room for the rabbis to announce their verdict.

The two venerable men pondered over the letter, debating its possible meanings. It was clear to them that "Yiuv" referred to the Book of Job; they asked for a Bible. But which verse did the young rabbi have in mind? They knew too that the only word underlined, "bei," was significant, that this word was clearly the key to unravelling the code. Minutes later Rabbis Weinrib and

Silverstein had the solution; by giving the three letters of "bei" their numerical equivalent in the alphabet and then adding them together, they got the number 16. They did not even have to look in the Bible, so well known was Job, chapter 1, verse 16: "A fire of God has fallen from heaven and hath burned the sheep and the servants and consumed them, and I only have escaped alone to tell thee."

This was an answer Canadian Jews had expected but did not want to hear. It was the first indication of the fate of Polish Jewry.[1] Other messages, brought to the society's office by anxious relatives, soon confirmed the worst. One aged woman brought a letter from her daughter smuggled out of Warsaw, a letter that needed no interpretation: "Since the Germans have come Uncle Lechem [bread] has not been home. We eat as if it were Yom Kippur and dress as if it were Purim."[2] And aware that this latest disaster rendered them helpless, society officials quickly discarded plans to set up a tracing system to help Canadian Jews find their relatives in Poland.[3] They realized that they would, all too soon, know their fate regardless.

The Canadian government was at this time most assuredly not concerned about refugees in general or Polish Jews in particular. On September 10, 1939, following Britain by one week, Canada declared war on Germany. For the second time in twenty-five years, armies had to be created, new industries built, men outfitted. Little time could be spent worrying about the millions of people clamoring to get out of Europe before engulfed by the Nazi tide.

The German government itself was scurrying about trying to find a way to dispose of the millions of Jews it had ingested with Poland's surrender in September 1939. At the time its policy was one of extrusion rather than extermination; any Jew who had a place to go, could leave. Nazi officials contacted both the British and American government through the Intergovernmental Committee on Refugees, offering up as many Jews as any country would have.[4] Predictably, there were no takers; most of the world's nations had other things on their minds.

Indeed, only the United States seemed to have the time to think of the refugees. Unencumbered by the problems of war—of mobilization or rearmament—the American government invited Britain, Canada and several other countries to a conference in Washington to discuss the new refugee problem created by the onset of war. Hoping that the Americans would relieve the continuing pressure on Palestine, the British quickly agreed to attend, while Anthony Eden, British Dominions secretary, privately warned Roosevelt that his government "could no longer help solve the refugee problem," because no country at war with Germany "could assist in any way the exodus of enemy nationals from territories under enemy control." Nor could the British agree even to talk about those stateless after the collapse of Poland.[5]

Enthusiasm for refugees was even more muted in Canada. Jewish refugees in Britain and France were besieging Canadian consular offices with requests for visas. The director of immigration's instruction to his immigration officers was to the point:

> I see no reason why Canada as one of the partners of the fight should encourage these people to leave France and Britain where they have been given a haven of refuge, until it is known that they have at least offered their services where they might be valuable to the country in which they are living. . . . Someone has facetiously said that numbers of our Jewish refugees lustily sing "Onward Christian Soldiers" but are very content to stay here and grab up all the opportunities. . . . When the Empire is fighting the battles for the liberty of these people they at least ought to have enough red blood in their veins to find out, before running away from the areas of the conflict, whether their services will be of any value to the country which has given them shelter.[6]

And when informed by the under-secretary of state for External Affairs that the British were refusing visas to "enemy aliens," Blair smugly told the prime minister that this simply underscored his policy of refusing entry to refugees, "who are nominally enemy aliens." Under no circumstance, he told his officials, would nationals of Germany or "of any country occupied by Germany" be admitted to Canada, whether they were refugees or not.[7]

Unaware of the government's ever-hardening attitude, the Jewish community again lurched into action. To protect itself against charges of disloyalty, Congress officials undertook an energetic campaign to persuade Jews to enlist in the armed forces. "The Jewish community," H. M. Caiserman explained, "is being watched carefully and we must give a good accounting of ourselves. Failure to do so may create a tragic weapon against us."[8] At the same time the Congress increased its funding of the

Canadian National Committee on Refugees, making it possible for the committee to hire a public relations expert and to issue over fifty thousand pieces of literature to various newspapers, radio stations, religious organizations and trade unions.[9]

And once again Jewish delegations tramped off to Ottawa to plead for a more lenient immigration policy. To a Jewish Immigrant Aid Society group requesting the admission of Jewish farmers from England and neutral countries, Blair appeared quite receptive.[10] In fact, however, the director was adamant—at least in private—in his opposition. As he informed Robert Manion, he had, over the past decade, turned down "thousands" of applications from young Jews who wished to enter as farmers; "the likelihood that a Jewish young man will be content to stay on the farm is very remote," he stated. "I have seen it tried many times. What usually happens is that the Jewish worker finds that he cannot eat Jewish food, and so he takes an early opportunity of leaving the farm and going to the city, which is about the only place he can find his fellow countrymen."[11]

Nor did Blair put any more faith in young Jewish women and children. He sternly rejected a JIAS appeal for permission to bring to Canada Jewish domestics, because, as he explained, "it is almost notorious that Jewish domestics or supposed domestics do not remain in housework for any length of time." And he turned away the society's request to bring children: Canada could "render a greater service by undertaking to look after groups of those children in the countries where they are now resident rather than incur the expense . . . in moving numbers of them across the ocean."[12] So resistant was the Immigration Branch to allowing in refugees that a JIAS officer reported with disbelief that an application by three Polish Jews in France, "with a combined capital of $120,000" and access to $100,000, had been rejected because they wished to establish a tannery and the Canadian government felt the country did not "need another tannery."[13] In another instance, the British war cabinet's refugee committee, aware of the Canadian attitude, had to decide to "encourage Latin American countries to accept" the fifty thousand refugees then in Great Britain. There was no point in pressing Canada.[14]

Yet what could Canadian Jewry do? By January 1940 thousands of letters had flooded the offices of the Jewish Immigrant Aid Society and the Canadian Jewish Congress from European Jews begging for help. Thousands of letters had been received by individual Canadian Jews from relatives and friends overseas. The requests were all the same: "Save us before it is too late"; "We have been fleeing the Nazis for two years. Is there no country which will rescue us? Please, we pray, force your government to let us in! We have nowhere else to go." By the spring of 1940 the director of the Jewish Immigrant Aid Society was complaining bitterly that the activities of his organization were still reduced to meeting the hundreds of refugees arriving in Canada on their way to the United States or Australia. "We meet them," Solkin said acidly, "care for them, feed them and then take them to the American border."[15] And by the summer even this was becoming impossible as the Canadian government had peremptorily cancelled transitory rights for most European refugees. Immigration authorities feared that their visas might be found unacceptable by the receiving country and that they would then be stuck in Canada. Ottawa even discontinued pre-examination procedures, whereby refugees destined for the United States could enter Canada in order to secure a non-quota visa. As the American National Refugee Service complained, "The termination of this procedure is a deterent to aliens who have come in [to America] as temporary visitors . . . but who have in the past been granted the privilege of Canadian pre-examination."[16]

Clearly, Canada was determined to barricade herself against all refugees. When Blair was alerted that two Lithuanian Jews had arrived in Vancouver with expired visas from the Canadian embassy in Tokyo, the director rushed to warn Under-Secretary of State Skelton that the government should act at once to prevent these refugees from coming to Canada. "Unless we take prompt action," he warned, "word will go back to Europe that the route [through Russia to Japan and China] is open and there will be many of these people clamoring for entry." The embassy in Tokyo, he insisted, must be told not to grant visas to European refugees; should any of the latter still manage to arrive in Canada "without the required forms," Blair would have them deported.[17] Accepting the director's advice, the Department of External Affairs ordered the legation in Tokyo "to refuse to grant visas to European aliens wishing to come to Canada . . . even if they hold provisional letters of entry."[18] The embassy agreed, but asked to be allowed to issue transit visas to Jews on their way to Latin America. Blair once again advised rejection. No aliens, he told Skelton, should be allowed into Canada—period.[19] Thus, by the end of 1940 all the holes had been plugged; almost no refugees were gaining entry into the Dominion even if on their way elsewhere.*

There were some Canadians who passionately disagreed with their government's behaviour, and one of these was a Danish immigrant who had settled in western Canada following the First World War and had gone to work for the Canadian Pacific Railway. By the 1930s Mark Sorensen had worked his way up to become the railway company's agent in Copenhagen, responsible for all passenger traffic from the Scandinavian and Baltic states. It was while in this position that Sorensen learned first-hand of Canada's restrictive immigration policies.

Time after time Sorensen had attempted to acquire visas for able, young and well-off Jews, but his every effort to bring a Jew to Canada had ended in failure, each application rejected in turn by Ottawa. Sorensen could scarcely believe—and could not accept—the myopia of the Immigration Branch. How, he wondered, could it turn away immigrants with skills the country badly needed and with huge amounts of capital to invest? So distraught did he become that by 1939 he began keeping duplicate records of the decisions handed down by the government. "One day those responsible for this inhumane policy will be brought to the bar of justice," and the attitude of the Canadian government, he wrote, will be seen as "a shameful chapter in the history of Canada in this period. . . . It will record regretable opportunities lost for the expansion of the country and for the exercise of the nobler and gentler qualities of the nation."[20]

Sorensen's personal files (which he brought back to Canada after the onset of war) would, he was sure, provide a scathing indictment of the immigration policies of the Government of Canada in these years. And indeed they do. Sorensen interviewed many of the thousands of Jewish refugees who had made their way from Germany, Austria, Czechoslovakia and Poland to Scandinavia and the Baltic States between 1933 and 1940, as well as the Jews already living in Lithuania, Latvia and Estonia and anxious to leave. Sorensen was impressed with these men

* There was in fact one group of refugees that arrived in Canada in 1940. These were the so-called "accidental immigrants," the interned aliens shipped over to Canada from Britain. Two thousand of these men and boys—mainly German Jews—were plunked into prisoner-of-war camps from which most would not emerge for the next two years. Their story has been well told by Paula Draper, "The Accidental Immigrants: Canada and Interned Refugees," *Canadian Jewish Historical Society Journal*, 2, no. 1, 2 (1978), and by Eric Koch, *Deemed Suspect*: *Canada's Wartime Blunder* (Toronto, 1980).

and women, telling his superiors in the CPR that they were "good . . . potential settlers of a type Canada pretends to welcome if the Grandmother is in order."[21] They were people, he added, "who have never been a burden on any community [and] when they land in Canada they will dig in and make good." Sorensen duly arranged passage to Canada for many of those he had interviewed, but they were time and again rejected by the Immigration Branch. Sorensen was horrified. He had assured Ottawa that a large number of these Jews were experienced and successful farmers, "amongst the most progressive" in Europe, and had thousands of dollars with which to buy land in Canada. But even those with liquid capital of several hundred thousand dollars could not break through Blair's blockade. Virtually none of the hundreds of Jewish farmers interviewed by Sorensen in the Baltic countries was allowed into Canada; almost all—with their families—were soon afterwards murdered by the Nazis.[22]

Equally unsuccessful were the large number of Jewish industrialists and professionals who asked Sorensen for help. Most of these were men with considerable assets who had left behind thriving businesses and well-paying jobs. All were denied admission to Canada on what Sorensen called "the flimsiest of excuses." The Immigration Branch, he charged, "functions as a policeman." It was, he said, "the most soulless Canadian institution" he had ever encountered, consisting of "a gang of old men using a negative policy to hide their incompetence." And, perhaps worse, the department was "entirely out of tune with the needs of the times and the desires of the Canadian people." Sorensen's contempt for Immigration was shared by the CPR's European colonization manager, H. C. P. Cresswell, who complained that "Ottawa [was] determined to reject all applications irrespective of merit." How else could one explain the rejection of Gustav Barth, who had managed to flee Czechoslovakia and had transferred to a London bank the $100,000 that he wished to take with him to invest in Canada. He was turned away, Blair said, because "this money could be used to [better] advantage in Great Britain during the present emergency than in Canada."[23]

Barth's case was not unique. Paul Eisner, another Czech Jew, wished to move his metal-refining plant to Canada. Despite Cresswell's assurances that Eisner would bring with him over $100,000 in cash and materials, as well as significant metallurgical processes, and would employ upwards of twenty Canadians in his factory, he was refused admission on the grounds that he was "a national of a territory now occupied by an enemy country." Joseph Mahler, an Austrian Jew who had fled to London and had intended with his considerable capital to set up a paper plant in Canada, was told by Blair that Canada would not accept him because "all available transportation facilities should be reserved for British subjects or others whose evacuation from the British Isles is considered advisable." In July 1939 Mr. and Mrs. Leo Bauer applied from London for a temporary permit to Canada to visit Mrs. Bauer's ailing father. Not only were the Bauers extremely wealthy German Jews—they promised to transfer to Canadian banks some $200,000 if admitted—but they were also the beneficiaries of $160,000 from the estate of a recently deceased American banker. It would be "better," Blair told railway officials, "not only for us but for themselves" if they applied to the United States. And if they were successful he would "gladly allow them visiting privileges in Canada."[24]

Most illustrative of the commitment of the Immigration Branch to keeping refugees out of Canada was the case of Otto Sygal, a Hungarian Jew, an experienced airplane mechanic and an expert in the manufacture of Diesel engines. His rejection by Ottawa in June 1940 infuriated Sorensen, who noted on the file: "At a time when the services of a skilled aeroplane fitter is at a premium, when stirring appeals are sent out over the Empire for more and still more aeroplanes because it is a matter of life and death, [how] is Ottawa capable of turning such applications down? Capital not working for us is working against us and so with aircraft mechanics and fitters. Those who are not making British planes are making them for Germany and Italy."[25]

But it seemed that no amount of pressure could budge the unyielding Immigration Branch. Influential scientists throughout the world pleaded with the Canadian government to admit Dr. Maximilian Wiernick, a German Jewish pharmaceutical manufacturer. Before being removed by the Nazis he had headed a company that had over two hundred employees and annual sales of two million dollars. Even the chief commissioner of the CPR in Canada wrote Blair in early 1939 to assure him that Wiernick had sufficient capital to build a plant in Canada that would supply his export market and employ a considerable number of Canadians. For over a year the department sat on the application, until in March 1940 Blair told the railway's head office that "there [was] no particular advantage to Canada in our [admitting him]."[26]

Canadian Pacific Railway immigration officials were thoroughly aghast. They could scarcely believe what was happening. Almost every single refugee they had tried to bring to Canada had been rejected. These were people, said Cresswell, who at another time—and had they not been Jewish—"would have been welcomed with open arms." As he lamented to his superiors in Canada, "It is becoming increasingly clearer to me that for the sake of decency the time will come when it will not be possible for Canada to keep people out, the way they have been doing it. . . . Other countries less adapted to it have had to take the burden of hospitality to those in need. . . . Will Canada allow it to be recorded that she kept her doors closed for those seeking shelter in the storm?"[27] And for Sorensen, who was even more bitter, the negativism of the Canadian government finally became too much.[28] When Ottawa turned down a refugee family with nearly a million dollars to invest in Canada and refused to admit a world-famous academic with $150,000 and a private income of some $10,000 a year, Sorensen threw up his hands in disbelief: "Has Ottawa gone stark staring mad?"[29]

In the late spring of 1940 Sorensen was ordered to close his Copenhagen office. On his arrival in London he poured out his heart to the railway official Cresswell. "Cut off from the Continent," he wrote,

> we have come to the end of a chapter in our Canadian immigration. It is now too late to amend our ways to recover opportunities lost—and rare opportunities we had these last six years—but we may well give thought to it, consider where we ourselves have failed, and the forces working against the movement to Canada of qualified people who were in so urgent need of the refuge we so well could have offered them.
>
> The mean and the damnable aspect about the whole affair is that if these people had not been in need of a refuge, they would have qualified. . . .
>
> I cannot consider myself a Free Lance, but if I were I should make this the biggest wartime scandal in Canadian Public Life short only of treason. You have been in an even better position than I to survey Ottawa's attitude to refugees, and I do not wonder what you will write on the margin of this question: Could the Fifth Column have done it any better? . . .
>
> What is wrong with the money we could have introduced to Canada and what would have been wrong with the production of the farms and the factories of our clients? Is it

realized that the money that could not be put to production in the Empire is working against us now. If not, might such a measure of foresight and intelligence not have been expected from those who administrate the Immigration Law?

And can you wonder that thoughts stray to the Fifth Column?

Of all the Government Services the one the least heard of in Canada, the one known the least and hiding, as it were, the best from public attention, is the Department of Immigration. This, of course, is in perfect harmony with their negative policy. . . .

If we had experts and men with a rudimentary appreciation of Political Economy in the Department of Immigration they would have corrected public opinion in Canada instead of resorting to the mob for endorsement of their negative and self-sufficient attitude. . . .

You may say that it is of little avail to ease myself of my feelings about the Department at Ottawa, but I reply that these men must go, and we must find ways and means for their removal. We must have men we can work with, men of vision and with a horizon, men of wisdom. . . .

That the cause of this war is partly owing to maldistribution of population you will not dispute, but Mr. Blair and our Mr. Little would not understand, nor would they see Canada's responsibility or the cards they for years were putting into the hands of Hitler and Mussolini. It has been given Canadians to be trustee of a large estate but they are simple-minded who think that possession of it means that it need not be accounted for. . . .

Lest anyone should question my justification for using the term sabotage, I invite them to find a more apt expression, but let them consider the cases I have handled, presented and had rejected.[30]

There were other Canadians who shared Sorensen's concern. One of these was Georges Vanier, the Canadian ambassador to France, who was deeply affected by the plight of the thousands of refugees in that country. Canada had a "wonderful opportunity," he wrote King, to be generous and yet profit by accepting some of these people.[31] On May 24, 1940, the Canadian war cabinet met to discuss the refugee situation in general and Vanier's suggestion in particular. Moved by the ambassador's report, the minister responsible for immigration drafted a cable offering to accept a substantial number of refugees from both France and Britain. He found little support in the cabinet. King felt the cable was "very muddled in thought and expression, . . . far too wide open and [undertook] too much in the way of government obligation," while the minister of finance, J. L. Ralston, expressed fears that too much money might be spent on the project.[32] It was decided that Canada should simply join with Britain in asking the Americans to help solve the problem.

Not long after the cabinet had rejected the Vanier proposal, it was confronted by another. The Polish ambassador to Canada, Victor Podoski, requested the admission to Canada, "for the duration of the war," of some two thousand Polish exiles—many, the wives and children of Polish civil servants—as well as one hundred Jewish children.[33] After wrestling with this petition for some time, the cabinet agreed only to consider allowing in these exiles if there were guarantees of "adequate financial support during their stay in Canada"; but it made no mention of the Jewish children. Of course from the moment Podoski had made his request, Blair had been on his guard. He pleaded with the cabinet to reject the proposition. "A certain group will dominate amongst these refugees," Blair warned, "and will want to settle permanently in Canada"; he insisted above all that Canada not admit any Jewish child who was not an orphan, as this would mean, he advised, admission of other family members at a later date, who would then not likely return to Europe. His department, he told Skelton, had "definitely turned down this movement."[34]

At the request of the World Jewish Congress (WJC), a Jewish representative of the Polish government-in-exile, Ignace Schwartzbard, called on Canada House in London to lobby for the admission of these Polish Jewish children. His reception was, to say the least, unexpected. He was told by the senior immigration officer that Canada might accept "Roman Catholic Jewish children," but no others. When Schwartzbard answered Little that there were no such things as "Roman Catholic Jews," Little simply said that "Jews cannot be treated as a nation or a religious group but [only] as a race" and that "the interest of Canada is to prevent Jewish people from coming to Canada." Schwartzbard was flabbergasted and angry. He countered that Canada's policy—if accurately represented by Little—was that of "Hitler and company." "We were supposed to be fighting for democracy," he added, "where there is no distinction between Jews and non-Jews." According to the Polish diplomat, Little then arose and, ordering him out of his office, shouted out: "Never mind what you think. I am telling you what I think and what we want."[35]

Schwartzbard, of course horrified, then approached a British refugee official, Major MacNeil-Moss of the Children's Overseas Reception Board, who interceded on behalf of the World Jewish Congress with Canada House. Bypassing the unpleasant Mr. Little, MacNeil-Moss spoke with a Massey aide, Major Simpson, who promised that Canada would accept twelve Polish Jewish orphans. Canada in the end agreed to accept only four orphans, two of whom were Jewish.

Schwartzbard's report of his meeting with Little caused a sensation among North American Jewish leaders. Rabbi Stephen Wise of the American Jewish Congress angrily wrote his friend Gladstone Murray, general manager of the Canadian Broadcasting Corporation, asking him to apprise the Canadian cabinet of Little's behaviour: "Something should be said to Little which will make him feel that it is not wise or just to say these things and to act in this way." Wise also asked Congress president Samuel Bronfman to "make the strongest possible representations." It was "inconceivable," Wise thought, that Little spoke with the authority of his government—apparently, however, it was not. When Gladstone Murray forwarded Wise's complaint to Skelton, he was told it was an "internal matter" and the government would take no action. Similarly, Canadian Jewish Congress petitions went unanswered. Not only was Little never reprimanded, officials did not even bother issuing an explanation of his behaviour. It was finally clear that Little had indeed articulated Canadian policy.

While European Jewish leaders were shocked by "the unexpected, unfriendly attitude" of Canada, Canadian Jews, beyond being surprised by their government's attitude, simply and doggedly opposed it. Heaps urged the CNCR to pass a resolution at its next conference condemning the Immigration Branch for its "scandalous" behaviour in depriving Canada "of the possibility of a rich increment of immigrants culturally, artisically and scientifically," because of the "bias" of Blair and Little. The Canadian Chamber of Commerce joined in supporting the resolution, and William Birks, a member of the Chamber of Commerce, personally sent "a strongly worded protest" to his friend Vincent Massey.[36]

By the end of 1940 the director of the Jewish Immigrant Aid Society had sadly to report to his board that immigration to

Canada was at a "standstill," though some Jews were still arriving in Canadian ports on their way to the United States or Latin America. Jews, Solkin explained, were escaping to other countries; only Canada had shut itself off. Emigration from Germany "was unrestricted," and the society, its director claimed, was prepared to bring out German Jews to Lisbon or to Japan; it had, however, been unable to convince the Canadian government to issue the necessary entrance permits, and, even worse, the government was regularly rejecting refugees with large amounts of money. "Those who had sterling assets were not acceptable," said a JIAS official, "since, according to Ottawa transfers of sterling tend to upset the financial equilibrium of Britain by depressing the value of the pound." Those with American funds were somewhat more acceptable, but, as Blair told society officials, "Ninety per cent of refugees admitted to establish businesses never do . . . and live unproductively on the interest of their capital."[37]

Occasionally the attitude of the Immigration Branch rankled officials in other departments. Under pressure from the British, External Affairs had asked the Immigration Branch to allow two German Jews, Judge Oskar Shenker and his physician brother Alfred, who had escaped to Japan, to land in Vancouver on their way to safety in Chile. When the request was rejected in early 1941, Skelton begged Blair to change his mind: although the decision, he assured the director, was "reasonable and probably unavoidable," it left "these wretched people . . . in a rather desperate predicament." He left unsaid that it also embarrassed the government. Skelton, like King, feared that at any time Canada would confront the same "panic exodus of European refugees from the Far East" that Germany had "thrust on her neighbours after 1933." Would it not be advisable, he suggested to Blair, to "stretch regulations . . . to dispose of individual cases . . . rather than wait until we are asked to take them en bloc and without any financial means whatever?" The director was firm, warning Skelton that refugees who landed in Vancouver could refuse to leave. "I wish we could save some of the Finns, Norwegians, Danes, Dutch, Belgians and French," Blair offered, "but any opening of the dam will result in absolutely nothing but a movement of Jewish refugees." He told Skelton that, if the government changed its policy and decided to "open the door wider" to Jews, he would follow orders; but he reminded the under-secretary of state that the Jewish refugees already in Canada were guilty of "misrepresentation" and were using Canada simply as "a convenience to get to the United States."[38]

Meanwhile, the refugee situation in both Britain and Japan was growing more intolerable, with thousands of refugees pouring into these countries. Feeling "overwhelmed," the British government pleaded with the Canadians to take some three to four thousand Allied nationals—many of them Polish and Czech officials and their families still in continental Europe—for the duration of the war. "Their fate," the high commissioner in London, Vincent Massey, told King, "if they fall into German hands, does not bear thinking of."[39] Among those Massey felt most strongly about were 150 Polish Boy Scouts stranded in Rumania, of whom only ten per cent were Jewish; the rest were children of the Polish intellectual class.

Ever watchful, Blair warned that Britain's estimate of three to four thousand was far "too low," because he himself knew that there were thousands of refugees in Spain and Portugal. He also noted that Massey had not supplied a breakdown of the refugees, who, Blair suspected, were "80% Jewish . . . and who would all settle in our cities and engage in the same occupations as are followed by Jewish residents in Canada." Jews, he warned, were not in Canada simply for the duration of the war: "There [is] little likelihood of their return to Europe." He suggested that the Canadian government attempt to persuade these refugees to go to the Belgian Congo.[40]

The Canadian war cabinet agreed to accept only one thousand of these refugees, "as long as their governments agreed to bear all the costs of transporting and maintaining them," but, aware of Blair's reservations, left it to the Immigration Branch "to decide the preference." The cabinet made it clear to Blair that it would accept some Dutch, Czech and Polish immigrants, but "would prefer not to have too many Jews." As well, word went out to the Polish ambassador in London that Canada would take one thousand of the two thousand refugees Podoski had inquired about, if the Polish government guaranteed their costs, "their repatriation after the war" and, above all, "limited the possibility of Jewish refugees."[41]

Within a week after the cabinet decision, the Canadian ambassador in Japan urgently wired home that Canada should join with other parts of the Empire to accept Polish nationals. Ambassador Podoski informed Norman Robertson in External Affairs that these Poles, "chiefly of the Jewish race," must leave Japan to make room "for other Polish refugees from Eastern

Poland [to] save them from deportation under the most tragic circumstances to Siberia." He pleaded that seventy-nine of the 450 refugees be admitted to Canada. Along with his request, he sent the acting under-secretary of state some "sample letters" from those exiled to Siberia, graphically depicting the bestial conditions in which they lived, as well as the hunger, fear and death that were their constant companions. The letters, affecting even Blair, were, he said, "enough to make one's heart run." "The brutality which treats these poor people worse than civilized people would treat animals is a shocking disclosure of how close we are to complete savagery."[42]

The director of immigration was not sufficiently moved, however, to allow any of these "poor people" into Canada. Some thirty Polish nationals who had come to Vancouver from Japan to join the Polish army in Great Britain were sent back. Blair took a smug view of the affair: "All were Jews . . . who had no interest in war service . . . [and because] this was merely a scheme to effect entry to this country we closed the door." Blair told his minister, Crerar, to inform the cabinet that there would be no more "loopholes," in other words, no more transit visas issued; most of the Polish refugees in Japan, he explained, "will be Jewish and will not come here for the duration of the war but to remain." Nonetheless, the cabinet agreed to Podoski's request to allow in seventy-nine Poles from Japan with the understanding that this number would be part of the contingent of one thousand agreed to earlier.[43]

As Blair had feared, this was only the first act in a many-act drama. As Nazi horrors escalated in occupied Europe, so did the number of Jews attempting to escape them and so did the pressure on Canada to accept refugees. Both Portugal and Japan felt they had a surfeit of refugees; they would allow in no more until those already there had left, and they threatened to deport those without exit visas. Podoski told Blair that deportation was most dangerous for refugees in Portugal, who would then be placed in camps—"where the Gestapo will have free access to them."[44] There were, the Polish diplomat added, several hundred Jews in Portugal and two thousand in Japan who had to leave at once. Because Brazil had accepted two thousand refugees from Portugal "without any financial restrictions," could Canada not do the same? In particular, there were seventy-five refugees, he claimed, who had job offers in Canada, but could not make their way across the Atlantic because Britain had frozen the Polish government's sterling accounts.

Blair was not taken in. He did not believe that these seventy-five had legitimate employment opportunities; in any case, Canada, he stated, was not going to relax its immigration restrictions no matter what the situation. He was particularly unnerved by Podoski's attempt to get more refugees in from Japan. Petulantly, he reminded Crerar that the Canadian ambassador in Tokyo had reassured his government that the Russians "had shut down the movement [of Jews] to Japan." The Soviets, he charged, were not living up to their commitment.[45]

On April 23, 1941, the Canadian cabinet met to discuss Podoski's request to allow in 450 Poles from Japan and 300 from Portugal. After some discussion it was decided that only the group in Portugal be accepted, "as part of the one thousand." That evening, Dr. Tadeusz Brzezinski, the learned Polish consul in Montreal, phoned his acquaintance, Simon Petruszka, of the Federation of Polish Jewry (FPJ), to tell him that the Polish government had received permission from Canada to admit a "large number of refugees without distinction of race or nationality." The news electrified the Montreal Jewish leadership. For eight years there had been no good news concerning refugees forthcoming from the government. Finally, it seemed, a breakthrough had been made.[46]

On the following day a delegation of federation officials expectantly gathered in the Polish consul's office. Brzezinski immediately asked if the Jewish community could guarantee the maintenance of all the Jewish immigrants who might arrive. With a show of bravado, the FPJ leaders not only promised to take care of all the Jewish refugees, but to assist Polish Christian immigrants as well.[47] Though they had few funds of their own, they were certain that the treasury of the Congress, of which the federation was an affiliate, would be at their disposal. After all, when might there be another chance to save some of Europe's Jews.

Rumours had now begun to circulate throughout an excited Jewish community that the Canadian government was prepared to accept thousands of Jewish refugees. Both the Congress and JIAS offices were flooded with offers of assistance and money. The president of the Federation of Polish Jewry, Lazarus Phillips, phoned the Immigration Branch to arrange an interview, but was told by Blair's deputy that he had no knowledge of what arrangement had been made. Nonetheless, Phillips informed the Immigration office that the Jewish community was prepared to support fully any refugee admitted.[48]

When informed of the activities of the federation, Blair was enraged. Jewish guarantees for non-Jewish refugees, he told Ambassador Podoski, were "unacceptable." He charged that the Polish consul, Brzezinski, had "stirred up expectations" in the Jewish community; he warned that he would meet no Jewish delegations and told the Polish ambassador to deal with the matter "in such a way . . . as to avoid creating [false] impressions." He then phoned Phillips and made clear to him that, because the agreement was "between governments and not between individual organizations," neither he nor his government was "prepared to deal with Jewish or any other organizations on these matters." Finally, the Polish consul, he complained, had no business speaking to a Jewish organization about refugee policy. If Jews were prepared to offer guarantees, he stated, they should offer them to the Polish government. Blair was determined that there would be no repetition of what he called the "Roumanian affair" of 1921, when, he believed, the Jewish community had tricked the government into allowing into Canada five thousand Rumanian Jews, though permission had only been granted for a much smaller number. He warned Norman Robertson, who had replaced Skelton as External Affairs' under-secretary of state, that small numbers of Jews, "clutching visas," were still arriving at British Columbia ports and again asked the under-secretary to order his officials in Tokyo to desist from issuing these visas. "We fear that a desperate effort is now being made in Japan to get the door open for at least 1,500 Jewish refugees," he cautioned, reminding Robertson that the Canadian ambassador in Tokyo had been told in August 1940 to stop granting entry permits and should now be reprimanded for persisting. Jews in transit from Japan, he added, "are unlikely to complete their journey and would undoubtedly remain in Canada."[49]

By May 5, after consultations with Podoski, the Polish consul had changed his tune. Brzezinski told a delegation from the Federation of Polish Jewry that there had been a "slight misunderstanding," but he now understood that it was the Polish government that would guarantee the refugees' maintenance. The Jewish community, he said, should offer aid, but he could not tell them what form that aid should take. On the next day, a joint conference of Congress and federation officials—including Saul Hayes—was held, with Podoski and Brzezinski present. The Polish ambassador confided that the motivating factor behind his government's request to Canada was the "unfortunate situation" in Portugal, although conditions for refugees in Japan were also deteriorating rapidly. He also said that Blair would not accept guarantees from societies and institutions because, in the director's experience, "these did not fulfill their obligations 100%." The Polish prime minister, General Sikorski, had promised that his government would subsidize each refugee with $25.00 per month, and Podoski asked the Jewish community to come forward with generous cash grants—$60,000 was the figure he had in mind—to the Polish government. Pointedly, he told the assembled Jewish officials that, though Blair had insisted that "Polish Jewish refugees should be admitted in the proportion of Jews to Christians in Poland [about 12 per cent]," the director would commit himself to offering one hundred visas to Jewish refugees.[50]

Naturally the Jewish leaders were disappointed. Their vision of thousands of refugees arriving in Canada had been reduced to a hope for a paltry one hundred. Hayes was particularly distraught. That it was up to the Polish government to see that a "fair proportion" of Jews was included among the refugees, he found disturbing. Yet he believed that Podoski would try to bring in more Jews than the Canadian government wished. "The reason is not wholly philanthropic," he said. "It lies in the fact that it is up to [him] to see that a sufficiently large number of Poles get out of Portugal and Japan in order to allow room for other Polish refugees and, inasmuch as the vast majority of those in Japan and Portugal are Jews, I imagine he can't help himself." Nevertheless the executive of the Congress's refugee committee, now reconstituted as the United Jewish Refugee Agency (UJRA), decided to guarantee the Polish government the funds it required. At the same time it condemned the Canadian government for refusing to deal with Jewish organizations, charging that Blair was "unfair and not . . . reliable."[51]

Jewish leaders now undertook their most heart-rending task. The Federation of Polish Jewry had been asked to choose the seventy-nine Jews who would be admitted from Japan under the Immigration Branch's allowance. Though the Congress attempted to keep the information secret, within a community starved for news of any sort it proved impossible. The Congress was soon besieged by a desperate throng of people hoping to save their relatives. Pressures—and tempers—mounted daily. The Jewish Labor Committee was anxious to bring over a group of Bundists who had made it out of Russia; Zionists were lobbying for their compatriots; the Federation of Polish Jewry was intent on bringing over intellectuals and writers.

However, one group proved persuasive, so persuasive that its demand for all the entry permits could not be denied. Out of the inferno that was Poland three hundred students and staff of two leading seminaries had escaped to Russia. These Yeshiva boys and their teachers had been promised entrance into the United States by the American consul in Moscow, and on the basis of this commitment, the Japanese government had allowed them entry. Once they were in Japan, however, the American government had second thoughts. Fearing that some of these rabbis and their students were Communists or had relatives in Russia who "might force them to work for the Communists in the United States," the American government declined to honour its consul's promise, and the Japanese were now threatening to ship the group back to Russia. As Rabbi Oscar Fasman of Ottawa, their most important Canadian supporter, reminded the director of Congress, "In atheistic and proletarian Russia, a tailor who is sent back might be given a chance to work, but a religious leader is doomed." These scholars, he went on, "embody the wealth of Jewish sacred learning the like of which can no longer be duplicated [because of the Nazi atrocities]. . . . We are saving not merely a people but a holy culture which cannot otherwise be preserved. . . . It is certainly horrible to save only a few, but when one is faced with a problem so ghastly in nature, he must find the courage to rescue what is most irreplaceable."[52]

Supporting Fasman were many rabbis, religious organizations and seminaries in the United States. Rabbi Kalmanowitz, an influential New York rabbi, led American Orthodox organizations in a massive campaign on behalf of the unfortunate Yeshiva boys. They contacted Canadian political leaders, members of various Jewish organizations and representatives of the diplomatic community; they wrote letters, raised large amounts of money and lobbied unceasingly. Indeed, they were so aggressive that Hayes complained privately that, with "Blair up in arms," they had done the refugee cause in Canada "a lot of damage."[53]

On May 14 Kalmanowitz arrived in Ottawa with a list of those rabbis in Japan who should be given priority, but Ambassador Podoski refused to pass the list on to the director of immigration because it included far more than the seventy-nine

Canada would admit. At the same time the Polish ambassador received from the FPJ a list with 133 names, which he sent back to the federation with a patient reminder of the quota set.[54] Caught amid conflicting pressures, the Congress itself threw up its hands, resolving that it would not take the "responsibility of selecting the names" because it could not know "who [was] most deserving and urgent." It was decided to ask the Polish embassy in Tokyo to consult with the Jewish community in Kobe, Japan, in making the choice. This would "not only save [the Congress] from a great deal of heartache and worry," Saul Hayes remarked with some relief, "but is the most humane manner of dealing with it; . . . otherwise the names would simply be the people we happen to know in Japan."[55]

Predictably, the Congress's decision infuriated the North American religious leadership. To allow the Polish embassy to make the decision, charged Fasman, would "pave the way for a great deal of graft and bribery in Tokyo, for it stands to reason that those who have reached Japan with money will use every dollar they have to persuade the Polish embassy to help them."[56] He pleaded with Hayes to reverse the Congress's decision and to allow the North American Jewish community to select the refugees it wanted. His plea was echoed by the Federation of Polish Jewry, which desperately wanted both to maintain its high profile on refugee matters and have some input into the selection of refugees.

The activities of the federation had long been a sore point for Hayes. Refugee matters, he insisted on reminding its members, were the responsibility of the Congress, not of its affiliates. The Congress's director was particularly angered by the attempts of the federation to insinuate itself with the government as spokesman for the Jewish community and, above all, by what he saw as its ineptitude in this task. The federation, he told a colleague, had decided "to seek a place in the sun"; the Congress would have to "clip its wings." Hayes's major complaint was that he spent only "one quarter of [his] time on . . . constructive work and the balance repairing the damage done by others."[57] And so in order to limit this "damage," Hayes informed Podoski that in future he was to deal only with the Congress on refugee matters. Hayes insisted that, because the Congress was being asked to fund the refugee program, it expected to have some influence in its formulation. "On the theory that there should be no 'taxation without representation'," he said, "[the Congress] would like to be apprised of what is going on . . . so that we will know what we are guaranteeing."[58] Podoski, not used to being scolded, was not amused. He angrily told Hayes that the Jewish community should start working together; "the Polish Government has not taxed you in any way," he added. A chastened Hayes quickly apologized, but insisted that, though the federation acted on "excellent motives," it was now the United Jewish Refugee Agency that represented the Jewish community of Canada on all refugee matters.[59]

When the Federation of Polish Jewry executive got wind of Hayes's activities, they were apoplectic, complaining bitterly to Bronfman about Hayes's letter to Podoski: "Imagine a responsible Jewish organization writing to non-Jewish officials with reference to another Jewish organization . . . against its basic interest! This is an irresponsible act." Unless Hayes withdrew his letter and apologized, the organization would, it threatened, sever its relationship with the Congress.[60] At the same time the federation went on the offensive. A leading member, Hershel Wolofsky, told a Congress leader that, not only was the federation "not to be criticized, . . . but it [was] worthy of deep gratitude": it alone was responsible for the seventy-nine visas for refugees in Japan. "One must know how to deal with the Poles," said Wolofsky. "They are very sensitive with reference to honour and approach. The Federation of Polish Jews . . . knows what to do."[61] He pleaded that the federation be delegated to deal with the Polish government on all matters affecting refugees.* After a series of bitter, recriminatory meetings between the Congress and federation, an agreement was finally reached: a special committee of the Congress's United Jewish Refugee Agency that included representatives of the federation

* As well, in a meeting with both Congress and FPJ officials, Wolofsky told Hayes that his own organization's members were "in a much better position to handle this work." "They appreciate the various nuances of expression of the Polish consul," he said, "speak the same language . . . and are in close contact because of their common heritage." Hayes could barely contain himself. He charged that the federation had caused the refugee cause much damage, that it had "no following outside Montreal and no funds," and that it was responsible for limiting the seventy-nine visas to Yeshiva students, which was, Hayes charged, a "major mistake." In dealing with Blair, he said, they had been irresponsible, especially when they promised that the rabbis and students from Japan would shortly after their arrival go to the United States. This, said Hayes, "shows their absolute ignorance on refugee matters." "Anyone with a knowledge of immigration matters knows that the best way to prevent refugees coming to Canada," he chided, "is to advise the Immigration Branch that the prospective immigrant is here preparatory to going somewhere else." Canadian Jewish Congress, Montreal, United Jewish Refugee Agency Papers, Hayes memorandum, June 11, 1941; ibid., Hayes to Zion, May 28, 1941; ibid., Hayes to Bronfman, June 7, 1941.

would deal with Podoski on this specific refugee scheme, with "all correspondence being forwarded to either or both organizations."[62]

Meanwhile, the entire Japanese arrangement seemed to be collapsing. Blair was committed to insuring that not one more refugee than already agreed on would arrive in Canada. He told Podoski that, as some Jews had already arrived from Japan, he was reducing the number eligible for admission from seventy-nine to sixty-eight; and of these Canada would accept neither anyone who had previously applied for an American visa nor anything but complete family units. "We will not take a mother and daughter," he warned Podoski, "if there is a father or brother somewhere in the background."[63] Indeed, the embattled director of immigration saw the entire project as the work of "Americans." Only through American Jews, he believed, had Jews who had just arrived in Japan managed "to get their names and occupations so quickly to the Jewish community in Canada."[64] The desperate attempts of Jews to leave Japan for Canada disgusted Blair; he said he was reminded "of what I have seen on a farm at hog feeding time when they are all trying to get their feet into the trough." Informing External Affairs that it "was perfectly evident" that American Jews were trying to get rabbinical students, refused admission into the United States, into Canada, he stated that no Jews on the American quota list should be admitted. As he told an External Affairs official, "One would have thought that the ordinary rank and file of the Jewish people in Canada would have been able to include their relatives and friends if they had any in Japan. . . . [The activities of Kalmanowitz] are about the most barefaced attempt at bringing people into Canada who have no connection with this country. . . . It would not surprise me at all if we find that Jewish people in the United States have paid very considerable sums to Jews in Canada [for the refugees] to be included on the list."[65]

Much to Blair's horror a sheepish External Affairs official then informed him that through some error the Canadian chargé d'affaires in Tokyo had issued 120, not 79 or 68, visas to Jewish refugees. At once the director pleaded with both the department and Ambassador Podoski not to tell Canadian Jewish leaders. "This would be regarded," he said, "as evidence that the door can be shoved open if they press hard enough." As well, in an attempt to undermine the plan's legitimacy, Blair persisted in informing everyone involved—from the Office of the Prime Minister to the Polish ambassador—that it was the American Jewish community that was behind the scheme, "making a determined effort to fill the quota . . . with refugees who desire to go to United States but have been refused entry."[66]

Finally, an opportunity to torpedo the whole project presented itself. After a chance meeting with Avra Warren, chief of the United States Visa Division, a Canadian official posted in Washington reported that the Americans believed all of the two thousand Jewish refugees in Japan were "working in full collaboration with the Japanese against the Russians." In addition, of the 22,000 European refugees in Shanghai, he advised, "8,000 are known to be Japanese agents . . . and of the remaining 14,000, one in four obtained transit visas through Russia upon a written undertaking that he would become a Russian agent in the Americas should he succeed in reaching this hemisphere." Warren reportedly claimed that from Japan the United States would admit only forty "celibate rabbis," if a way could be found of doing so "without at the same time granting admission to others," while from Shanghai it would accept only complete family units to avoid remaining family members becoming "hostages," their relatives in America "subjected to great pressure."[67] Made aware of Warren's decision, Blair proudly pointed out to Norman Robertson that Canada's "caution" in accepting these refugees was clearly "not ill-advised."

Meanwhile, the lot of Polish Jews in Portugal was rapidly deteriorating. The representative of the World Jewish Congress in Lisbon, although pessimistic about Canada's response, wired in desperation that "every minute counts" and pleaded with the Canadian Jewish Congress to lobby for more entrance visas, as the Portuguese government was threatening to deport Jews who did not possess them. In addition, the Polish government-in-exile in London was attempting to limit the number of Jews included in its quota. According to the World Jewish Congress, the Jewish quota as stipulated by Polish officials was to be between two and ten per cent. When Saul Hayes asked Podoski that one-half of the three hundred visas allocated to Portugal by the Canadian government be used for Jews, the ambassador responded that Canadian officials were insisting that the ratio of Jews to non-Jews be based on the proportion of Jews to non-Jews in Poland; again, about twelve per cent. The Canadian government would not allow in the 150 Jews from Portugal, he added, and he himself might be "vulnerable to attack . . . on the grounds that [he was] not saving Polish Christian citizens but

[was] concentrating on Jewish refugees."* The World Jewish Congress publicly condemned Canada's policy of "racial percentage" in granting visas to Poles: "[Jews] are allied to the whole civilized world in the great struggle and are also allied to the people of Canada." As a WJC spokesman put it, "Canada is a country so spacious and so rich and yet so sparsely populated. Two thousand visas could make so many people happy. . . . Does the conscience of the world never respond to a call from the Jewish nation."[68]

By July 1941 small numbers of Jews had begun to arrive in Canada from Japan and Portugal, the first ship of some twenty-one Jews from Japan landing in Vancouver on June 18. According to a district immigration officer, every single Jew on board had submitted lists of relatives in Canada who were "fictitious." Thus, when Podoski complained to Blair that none of the rabbis and their students still in Japan had yet been issued a visa, Blair answered that Jews could not be trusted. "The interest in Canada of these rabbinical students arises," he said, "only because they have failed to get into the United States"; the "Jewish population of this country," he added, "is not sufficient to absorb a group of eighty rabbis." Podoski then approached Hugh Keenleyside, a first secretary in the Department of External Affairs, who promised to speak to Blair. The Polish ambassador also advised Congress officials of his problems with Blair, and suggested that they indicate to government authorities that they were prepared to create "a special centre" in Montreal for the rabbinical students coming from Japan.[69]

It was now clear that in order for the rabbis to come to Canada an end run would have to be made around the Immigra-

* At about this time, Jewish leaders debated meeting again with Immigration Branch and cabinet officials to discuss Canadian policy. The Congress executive had feared that it would be "a waste of ammunition to go to Ottawa to discuss generalities on the fate of Jewry"; but the specific agreement with the Polish government might, Hayes said, provide an "opening wedge . . . and a splendid opportunity to traverse the whole question of offering asylum to Jewish refugees for the duration of the war." The Congress felt it was of utmost importance that it meet with government officials—this would be the first meeting between the two since the onset of war—but Thomas Crerar did not feel the same way. In rebuffing the Congress, he insisted on knowing precisely what the Jewish representatives had in mind. At the same time, ironically, Crerar reassured the Congress that he was fully aware of the "trials and tribulations" of the Jewish people and that his department was "dealing with Jewish refugees as favourably as possible." Public Archives of Canada, Department of Immigration Records, Hayes memorandum, June 15, 1941; ibid., Crerar to Bronfman, June 18, 1941.

tion Branch. The point man for this new strategy was Keenleyside, a veteran External Affairs official and a man who seemed sympathetic to the plight of the refugees. At a hastily arranged meeting, Keenleyside discussed the fate of the rabbis and students with a delegation from the Federation of Polish Jewry and for the first time, he was told of the horrific situation facing them, of the importance of the *yeshivot* to Jewish religious life, and of the scarcity of these scholars, who would greatly "strengthen the religious feelings of the Jewish people in Canada."[70] Impressed with the urgency of the case, Keenleyside asked Saul Hayes if he could meet "a specimen" of this culture; fortunately, an Hassidic rabbi, Eli Chazan, had just arrived in Canada from Japan, on his way to the United States, and was hurriedly brought to the first secretary. From the Jewish point of view the encounter was a success; after meeting the rabbi and discussing the situation with Hayes and Podoski, Keenleyside declared that neither he nor Under-Secretary of State Robertson "shared the views of Mr. Blair," but were "in full accord . . . with the views . . . that these people should be admitted to Canada." He promised to use his influence to get the Immigration Branch to issue the visas for all eighty rabbis—forthwith.[71]

Clearly time was running out for the Jews in Japan. Immediately after Keenleyside's meeting, External Affairs asked its embassy in Japan what would happen to the refugees should they not be given entrance visas, and were told that they would be deported to Shanghai when their current entrance visas expired. An urgent cable from the most senior of the rabbis in Japan to New York warned the Jews of North America: "Act instantly, Torah's sons, before it is too late." Requests went out at once from leading American Jewish leaders to their Canadian counterparts to intensify their lobbying. The Congress wrote Crerar pleading for a meeting, Samuel Bronfman stating emphatically that "the lives of the Rabbis and seminary students are in jeopardy and unless asylum is offered to them at once, their fate will beggar description." And even the Department of External Affairs seemed to be alarmed. In a strongly worded letter Norman Robertson asked Blair to meet with him to discuss the rabbis. "I am very much afraid that this matter is going to be taken directly to the Prime Minister," Robertson warned Blair, "unless we can dispose of it before that occurs."[72]

But the director of immigration was a man not easily browbeaten. On August 5, meeting with Robertson and Keenleyside, he demanded to know how they had learned about the putative visas. When told the information had been conveyed by both Jewish leaders and the Polish ambassador, Blair warned that the Jews were "merely getting the door open." "It was a well-known fact," he added, that Jews "make any kind of promise to get the door open, but . . . never cease their agitation until they get in the whole lot." When Keenleyside suggested to Blair that the Jewish community send a letter to the government assuring it that the community would be satisfied with the eighty visas, Blair simply insisted that the only thing to do was send the Jews in Japan "back to Vladivostock which was nearby."[73]

Finally, on August 6, 1941, the minister responsible for immigration agreed to meet a Jewish delegation. Blair was itching for just such a confrontation; he later admitted that he was in a belligerent mood and that it took him, in his own words, "only thirty seconds to turn the tables and put the delegation on the defensive." Emboldened by his deputy, Crerar told the assembled Jews that Canada could do no more for them; it could not "create precedents [that] would . . . tie its hands for the future." He also warned them against going outside his department with their demands, and that, should appeals come before the cabinet, "no relief" would be forthcoming because immigration matters were of "such a contentious nature . . . [that] the Cabinet would never consider them." And, as though to win the Jewish community's trust, he promised to allow in a total of two hundred refugees from Japan (naturally, these would come out of the one thousand promised to the Polish government), but threatened to cancel the arrangement should the Jewish community petition the cabinet anyway. When a member of the delegation asked Crerar if he was prepared to leave "the balance of the 450 Jewish rabbis and students to the mercy of the Japanese," the minister did not respond. Nor did he say anything when the representatives pleaded that more Jews be allowed in from Portugal and Shanghai. At this point Blair ended the discussion, cautioning the Jews to act with "care . . . [as] there was a danger that the movement might stop altogether."[74]

It seemed as though Blair was determined that it should. Immediately after the delegation departed, he quietly informed his minister that some Jewish refugees in Japan were actually Nazi agents; when Saul Hayes later submitted a list of refugees in Japan with relatives in Canada, the director of immigration responded that his department was in no hurry: that anyone "who tries the rush act is going to find out that it does not work." Furthermore, he even claimed that Crerar had made no definitive promise to let anyone in. The "whole movement," Blair finally said, "should be turned down without any further work on our part." Nor was the director prepared to live up to other commitments to bring refugees to Canada. As part of an agreement with the Allied countries, Canada was supposed to accept Czech officials and their families in Spain or Portugal. Unfortunately, the immigration officer in London, Little, reported that, though he knew how important it was to "maintain a reasonable racial balance," this would be impossible as forty-two of the forty-five Czechs applying for visas were Jewish. Blair was clearly not gratified that his warnings had come true. He complained bitterly to Crerar that "we have now reached the place where practically all refugees . . . are Jewish." He insisted that the "racial balance" be preserved, if only to insure that fewer Jews were granted admission.[75]

As the lot of European Jewry worsened, their desperation to escape increased. Some thirteen Polish refugees managed to flee occupied France and make their way, after harrowing experiences, to Argentina. From there they applied to enter Canada as part of the complement of one thousand. The Canadian trade commissioner in Buenos Aires informed the Immigration Branch that these men and women were "preferred immigrants, . . . including professors, nurses, translators, artists, furriers, and lawyers"; all were healthy, spoke French fluently and were Jews. Blair informed Podoski that these people did "not come within the classes whose services would be valuable to Canada."[76]

Even more poignant was the case of fifty Czechs who, having escaped as the Nazis were rounding up the Jews in their area, began a ten-month tragic odyssey to Argentina. Only twelve arrived—without entry visas or funds. The Czech consul general in Canada, Otto Pavlasek, pleaded with Canadian Immigration Branch authorities to admit these people, as part of the Czech allotment, who would otherwise be deported to Czechoslovakia and the Nazis. "They will be sent," he stated, "to one of the Jewish colonies newly established in devastated Poland and will perish there." Pavlasek said he knew them, could vouch for their character and would guarantee their maintenance. They are "in danger of their lives," he added unnecessarily.[77] But the director of the Immigration Branch was mostly curious about how these refugees had got out of Europe without visas. When one of these wretched individuals personally wrote to Prime Minister King, volunteering to enlist in an Allied army once in

Canada, Blair asked why, if he wished to fight, had he left Europe?[78] Neither the twelve Czechs nor thirteen Poles were admitted to Canada, and Blair explained to Norman Robertson why it was necessary to refuse permission to those wishing to enter Canada on their way to some other country: "If we were not careful we would soon find ourselves with a large number of cases . . . [and] we would be faced with allowing practically everybody to remain in Canada who enters in transit. We have already had so many cases of this sort especially amongst refugees of a certain type that we had to refuse transit privileges to numbers of these people at both Eastern and Western ports."[79]

By the beginning of September 1941 the Canadian government had finally issued instructions to its embassy in Tokyo to grant permits to the Yeshiva boys. At once the embassy contacted the Polish ambassador. After long discussions with leaders of the Jewish community in Kobe, Podoski prepared a final list of those who were to go to Canada, and within days eighty young men left Japan on their way to Shanghai where they would board a ship taking them to safety in North America.

Unfortunately, a problem that had plagued the Orthodox refugees since their arrival in Japan threatened their journey before it had even begun. Because of the International Date Line, Orthodox Jews were uncertain when to celebrate the Sabbath and their holidays. Should the Sabbath be on Sunday to coincide with the day Jews elsewhere were observing their holy day? Or should it be on the Japanese Saturday, which coincided with Friday throughout the rest of the Jewish world. Various rabbis among the refugees gave their opinions: some said Sunday; others said Saturday; a few suggested that observant Jews should celebrate on both days—just in case. An opinion was even sought from the chief rabbi of Palestine. It was, however, an issue never resolved and it profoundly affected and divided the group.

Those bound for Canada felt certain they had left the dispute behind, but, ironically, they were now to begin a debate just as divisive—and for some much more tragic. On their arrival in Shanghai they learned that their ship, the *General Pierce*, would be on the high seas for Yom Kippur, the holiest day of the Jewish calendar. Various opinions were offered about the correct date on which Jews were obligated to fast and pray. The most senior rabbi in the group stipulated that it would be necessary to fast and pray for two days—in effect, to observe Yom Kippur twice—but fifty-one dissenting members of the group announced that they would not sail on the *General Pierce*, but take the next ship. Thus, on November 2, 1941, only twenty-nine refugees arrived in Vancouver.

The ship scheduled to pick up the remaining refugees never arrived. A month later the Japanese bombed Pearl Harbor, and only five years later, four of which were spent in a Shanghai internment camp, did these hapless youths make it to Canada.

By November, after the twenty-nine Yeshiva boys had arrived in Canada, Saul Hayes reminded Crerar of his promise to admit two hundred more, and when Blair rejected the idea, the Federation of Polish Jewry took matters into its own hands.[80] At the request of the Congress they wrote a representative of the Polish government in London, asking it to intervene with Canada "as an ally for the humanitarian act" of rescuing the thousands of Polish Jews in the Orient.[81] Five days later Podoski contacted Blair to express the dismay of his government concerning the Polish refugees in Shanghai. The director of immigration flatly informed him that it was not in Canada's interest to take any Jews from the Orient while it was trying "to help the refugees who are still in Europe—[and] not those who have left to proceed to other countries"; publicly, he added that Canada had "helped a great many more Jewish people than Gentile"[82] and, privately, that he "would not be surprised if some person connected with [the UJRA] . . . is in the immigration business for money." Canadian Jews, he charged, were acting in bad faith: "It is the old plan which I have seen tried scores of times, to represent that the problem is less than actually exists and on the basis of the smaller problem get some promise which is then immediately stretched to cover the larger number. Taking one thousand additional Polish citizens out of the Far East still leaves 22,000 untroubled. . . . Evidently the only way we are going to control this is to close all doors because nothing short of an open door will satisfy these people."[83]

Even entreaties from abroad had little effect. When the chief rabbi of the British Empire pleaded with Canada to admit 370 rabbinical students in Shanghai, Blair told Robertson that the rabbi should mind his own business; he told him that Canada was under severe pressure from world Jewry to help solve the refugee crisis. "It is an ill wind that blows nobody good," he said. "We have already got far more than our share of Rabbinical students." The director of immigration also rejected an appeal from Rabbi Kalmanovitz. The rabbi's pleas, he told Podoski, "weigh with us nothing at all."[84]

To overcome the anti-refugee sentiment that seemed to permeate Ottawa, the Federation of Polish Jewry began a campaign on its own to trumpet the role played by recent Jewish arrivals. In letters to the editors of several newspapers the federation pointed out that many of these refugees had joined Allied armies or were involved in various war industries. According to Podoski, Blair took umbrage with these accounts. It "was a different group of Polish citizens," he said, "who supply heroes to the armed forces from the group which claims credit for it and seeks benefit in the shape of visas for Canada." And Blair was not alone. The Polish ambassador himself was taken aback, and told Saul Hayes that the FPJ campaign was both "not wise" and "misleading"; neither was it welcomed by Immigration authorities, who felt it was merely an attempt to play public opinion against government departments. It was difficult enough, Podoski said, to get Jews into the country. He had "struck an impasse" with government officials, who felt that too many Jews had already arrived in the Polish contingent; and few of these, he said, "ever enlist in the army." Podoski intimated that he agreed with the government's complaints and that he found it intolerable to be attacked by the Jewish community for not having done enough. He felt as if he were being "placed between Scylla and Charybdis" and that all he got, he added, mixing his metaphors, were "shots in the aft of my ship." Though embittered by the continuing government hostility, Hayes told Lazarus Phillips, the president of the federation, that he wondered what federation officials now thought about their claim that, "because they were Polish Jews, they knew how to deal with the Consul" and that Hayes himself "would only gum up the works."[85]

It was not only Polish Jews who were considered non-desirables by the Immigration Branch. When the Czech consul appealed to Canada to allow some of his countrymen in North Africa to use Canada as a transit base on their way to join Czech forces in Britain, Blair refused. Some people, he told the Czech representative, "use these movements as a means of access to Canada without any intention of training or proceeding to any theatre of war." These, he told an official in his department, were invariably Jews, and because there were so many Jews on the Czech list, "we had to take the stand that these people not be included"; they usually "contrived to get out of volunteering and would instead remain in Canada."[86]

By the end of 1941 it seemed that Canada would, for all intents and purposes, accept no more refugees for the duration of the war. The attack on Pearl Harbor had closed the door to the Orient. The Immigration Branch itself had closed the door to Europe. Of course to European Jewry the sound of doors slamming was not a new one; they had been hearing it for the past decade. It was a sound, however, that Canadian Jewry could not get used to—especially by the beginning of 1942 when the stories of Nazi barbarity were slowly leaking out from Poland and Eastern Europe. The Polish underground and government-in-exile were beginning to reveal to the world the unimaginable enormity of the Nazi campaign of horror. Almost every week reports were smuggled out of Poland about another Jewish community destroyed, about Jews being deported in vast numbers from cities and towns, then disappearing.

As early as March 1942 Ignace Schwartzbard, on behalf of the World Jewish Congress, was asking Jewish communities throughout the free world to set aside a special day—the eve of Passover—to commemorate the destruction of Polish Jewry and to inform their governments of the Nazi atrocities.[87] A horrified Canadian Jewry did as it was asked. Jewish newspapers carried graphic accounts of the destruction and Jewish organizations held meetings and petitioned local politicians. The Canadian Jewish Congress sent out press releases and pleaded with the federal government to denounce the Nazi campaign of terror.[88] There was little response from either Canadian politicians or the press, and two months later, the Polish National Council sent out a detailed account to the governments and press of the Allied countries of the slaughter of Polish Jewry. The report listed the villages, towns and cities in which Jews had been massacred and estimated the number of Jews killed at over one million. It also gave gruesome details of the bestial murder methods employed by the Nazis.[89] But again there was little reaction. Those papers that did report the story expressed some scepticism; there was no comment of any kind from the Canadian government.

Overwhelmed by the catastrophe in Poland, Canadian Jewry could not understand the lack of response of their fellow Canadians. The spotty newspaper coverage and the silence of the politicians left them demoralized and angry. A leading Congress official in Winnipeg, Samuel Sheps, complained bitterly to Bronfman that "the impression is all too prevalent that the Jewish population of Europe suffers to the same extent, but no more, than the general population of enemy-occupied countries." It was essential, Sheps added, "that the mass slaughter of Jews in occupied Europe . . . be brought to the attention of the Canadian population, so that the sympathy and protest of all Canadians may be mobilized." Along with other Jewish leaders in the west, he urged the Congress to organize demonstrations before "Communist-dominated groups . . . took advantage of the situation and endeavoured to capture Jewish sympathy by organizing a series of Dominion-wide protest meetings."[90]

In central Canada, however, Jewish leaders were much less militant. They saw little advantage in demonstrations. Archie Bennett, president of the Congress's central region, even viewed them cynically: "It seems that every time Jewish leaders feel a little bored they decide to call a mass meeting and everybody has to get excited with them. . . . It seems that no matter how much we try to train our community to act with dignity according to long range policy, we must always be subject to the eruption of hysteria-mongers in our midst."[91]

Bennett nevertheless agreed to a protest meeting—"If the Congress didn't [organize it] other bodies perhaps less responsible would undertake the project and make a mess of things"—and on July 20 a group of disgruntled Congress officers met in Samuel Bronfman's office to discuss strategy. They were aware that Canadian Jews were demanding action. Already the American Jewish Congress had announced plans for a huge rally in Madison Square Garden in New York. Most of the Congress executive opposed the idea of a meeting, but all knew that "they must bow to the general pressure."[92] Bronfman himself feared that any demonstration would be "a disservice to the British Commonwealth" and warned that the subversive organizations had "whipped up a spurious demand" to serve their own political purposes. Although all the executive agreed that "logically there [were] more reasons not to have the meeting than to have it," they felt they had no alternative but to sponsor a demonstration. Despite the apparent urgency of the crisis, they chose a date almost three months away, October 11, 1942, as a "general day of prayer for the success of the Allied cause and for mourning the fate of European Jewish life."[93]

As October 11 approached, new tales of murder and torture emerged from Poland. On September 15 the World Jewish Congress confirmed that an organized massacre of Jews was taking place in Poland, and that hundreds of thousands were being deported from the Warsaw ghetto to camps somewhere in Poland. The Allied governments said nothing. Rabbi Stephen Wise reported that the American State Department was sceptical of the story's origin, while both Podoski and Brzezinski said they had received no official authentication of the report.[94]

The Congress devoted much effort to insure that the October 11 demonstrations, planned in all of the country's major cities, were "dignified and effective," and the day of protest did go as the Congress had hoped. Thousands turned out across the nation; various government officials attended, including Norman McLarty, the secretary of state, and the American ambassador, J. Pierrepont Moffat; the Canadian Broadcasting Corporation carried some of the speeches on a nation-wide hook-up; and resolutions were passed praising the Canadian government for its war efforts and condemning Germany for its brutality. On the following day editorials across the country praised the Jewish community for its "loyalty" and "moderation."[95] Yet in the end nothing was achieved. The Canadian government did not adopt a new policy toward refugees; the newspapers did not spend any more time detailing the barbarities perpetrated against the Jews; and, obviously, the Nazis did not stop their massacres. All the protest did was all it could do—allow the Jewish community a needed catharsis and the Canadian Jewish Congress a chance to show that it still spoke for Canadian Jewry.

By the end of 1942 the nature of the Nazi's final solution had been gradually disclosed to the Allied governments. Although they had had several unimpeachable sources of information about the holocaust engulfing the Jews of Europe, Allied officials were reluctant to accept what these accounts depicted. But the weight of evidence—the enormity of the crime—could no longer be ignored. The Allies were now coming under even more severe pressure from Jewish organizations, from the Polish government and from prominent citizens to denounce the genocide.

On December 8, 1942, the British government informed Canada that Jewish organizations had created "considerable publicity regarding the existence of a detailed German plan for the extermination of Jews" and had asked the Allies for a joint statement "condemning the German policy and threatening retribution." The British now had "little doubt" that the Germans had indeed adopted "a policy of gradual extermination" of the Jews and had turned Poland into a "slaughterhouse" for Jews from all over occupied Europe. They asked Canada to join the other Allied governments in condemning "this bestial policy of cold-blooded extermination" and in warning that "those responsible for these crimes should not escape retribution."[96]

Because the proposed declaration would not involve any subsequent action, the King government agreed to sign it, especially after Hume Wrong, deputy under-secretary of state for External Affairs, warned that failure to do so would cause "agitation" among Canadian Jews.[97] At a press conference on December 17, the day the declaration was issued, Wrong stated that the Allies knew definitely that two million Jews had already been massacred and that the remainder were being used for slave labour. When Wrong was asked, however, whether Canada was now prepared to rescue some of these Jews by admitting them to Canada, he demurred. He told the press that the solution was not to admit refugees to Canada, "but to defeat Germany and thus liberate the Jews of Europe."[98]

As though to underscore Wrong's reasoning, on the day of the Allied Declaration the Immigration Branch dealt with the application of Rudolph Pick. For some years Pick, a wealthy German Jew, had tried to gain entrance to Canada, even transferring $42,000 to a Canadian bank to forward his case. Yet the government had twice rejected his application. Finally, he had managed to flee, always one step ahead of the Nazis, through France and Portugal to Cuba. Now, in December 1942, Pick was pleading again for admission—on December 18 his application was again rejected. A Jewish Immigrant Aid Society official noted the government's rationale—it did not want "to initiate a movement of refugees from [Latin] American countries to Canada." The government would not, by the way, allow Pick to transfer his funds to Cuba. The JIAS report was caustic: "With thousands of dollars in Canada, the man is penniless in Havana."[99] It was indeed evident that it would take much more than a detailed knowledge of what was happening to the Jews of Europe to force Canada to open her doors.

CANADIAN JEWISH CONGRESS ARCHIVES

(Left) Saul Hayes
(Below) Seated (left to right): Georges Vanier, Vincent Massey. Standing (left to right): Lester Pearson, Ross McLean, an aide.

PUBLIC ARCHIVES OF CANADA

PUBLIC ARCHIVES OF CANADA

PUBLIC ARCHIVES OF CANADA

(Top) Norman Robertson (left) and Georges Vanier, August 1941. (Bottom) F. C. Blair (left) after investiture with highest award for meritorious service to the country at Government House, November 1943.

J. L. GRANATSTEIN

PUBLIC ARCHIVES OF CANADA

(Top) Anthony Eden talks to Mackenzie King with Norman Robertson in background at the U.N. in 1945. (Bottom) A. L. Jolliffe, January 1947.

CANADIAN JEWISH CONGRESS ARCHIVES

(Above) Samuel Bronfman receiving a *torah* from one of the orphans brought to Canada in 1947. (Right) Royal Hotel, site of the Evian Conference, July 1938.

NATIONAL ARCHIVES, WASHINGTON

JOINT DISTRIBUTION COMMITTEE

(Left) Some of the children who never came. Children interned in Vichy France, 1942. (Below) A refugee family from Portugal in Montreal in 1944.

CANADIAN JEWISH CONGRESS ARCHIVES

CANADIAN JEWISH CONGRESS ARCHIVES

NATIONAL ARCHIVES, WASHINGTON

(Top) The first *seder* in freedom. Jewish refugees from Portugal in Montreal in 1944. (Bottom) Vanier and U.S. Congressional Committee visit crematoria at Buchenwald immediately following liberation of the camp in 1945.

JEWISH IMMIGRANT AID SOCIETY

CANADIAN PACIFIC

(Top) Jewish refugees en route to Israel in 1948. (Bottom) Displaced persons disembarking from the S.S. *Beaverbrae* on arrival in Canada in 1948.

"Inasmuch as ye have done it unto one of these... ye have done it unto Me"

Something Every Warm-Hearted Canadian Should Know About the REFUGEE PETITION

WHY IS CANADA AT WAR?

Is it not simply to preserve a place in the world for human decency? Is it not because we believe no man or race has the right to enslave or destroy another man or race? Is our unaccountable expenditure of lives, labor and wealth justifiable for any lower reason?

If the cause of humanity is worth such an effort, it is also worth the consideration of the plight of a few thousand refugees at present stranded mainly in Portugal. Putting it another way, the whole Canadian war effort is weakened unless the principles which motivate it are applied in the specific, immediate and practical issues. Fighting Hitlerism means fighting Hitler's most bestial acts. It means rescuing those whom he would kill, giving sanctuary to those lucky enough to escape from him. It means admitting some of those refugees to Canada.

All this should be obvious. But it is not. Canada, one of the richest and most sincere of the United Nations, should be first in giving refugees the right and room to live, which they were robbed of by Hitler. But she is among the last.

THE CANADIAN GOVERNMENT is presently being petitioned to offer haven to these derelicts. Because many readers of this newspaper might not otherwise have an opportunity to join in the petition, it is printed herewith. It should be clipped, signed and mailed immediately by all Canadians who believe in what they are fighting for. To refrain from signing it is to endorse the present attitude toward the refugees, an attitude little better than Hitler's.

Meanwhile it might be pointed out that at the very outside there are probably no more than 15,000 or 20,000 victims of Nazi tyranny who are in a position to come to this or any other sheltered land, and of these Canada might be expected to take in only a thousand or so. And, although the Government recently announced that a representative would be sent to Lisbon to facilitate the entry of refugees into Canada, how much Canada will actually do will undoubtedly be greatly influenced by the number of signatures secured for this petition.

Let Canada remove this moat from her eye so that she can better see the beam in Germany's. Thousands of Canadians have already written in their own blood their responsibilities to Hitler's victims. We back home can, at least, put our responsibility in ink.

WE CAN SIGN THE PETITION.

This Appeal Is Made to You!

READ HOW YOU CAN HELP – BUT PLEASE ACT NOW

This space is contributed by the Saskatoon Branch of the CANADIAN NATIONAL COMMITTEE on Refugees and Victims of political persecution.

DR. J. S. THOMSON, *President*

PROF. G. W. SIMPSON, *Secretary*

Canadian National Committee on Refugees

220 QUEEN ST. WEST — TORONTO 2-B, CANADA

THIS petition is to be signed by Canadian citizens of 18 years and over.
People are requested not to sign in more than one group.
Return the sheets promptly to the Committee's national headquarters or to the distributing organization

Name of Group, Church, Club., etc., and Address ....

Petition

WE, the undersigned citizens of Canada, do respectfully petition His Majesty's Government and the Parliament of Canada as follows:

Realizing our responsibility in common humanity to relieve the suffering and distress of victims of Nazi terror:

We urgently entreat the Government of Canada:—

1. To offer the sanctuary of Canada to refugees from political or religious persecution without regard to race, creed or financial condition.
2. To take immediate steps to facilitate the entry into Canada of refugees (especially those stranded in Portugal) whom it is still possible to rescue.
3. To make any changes in the Immigration Act, Regulations or administration thereof necessary to admit such refugees into Canada.

Signatures

NAME	ADDRESS	NAME	ADDRESS

Signature and Address of Group Officer ....

Pro-refugee petition from the *Saskatoon Star-Phoenix*, December 7, 1943.

4

THE CHILDREN WHO NEVER CAME

For no one was the onset of war more terrifying than for the children of Europe, and for no one did the people of Canada show more concern. Even before the start of the war the Canadian National Committee on Refugees had managed to force out of a reluctant government an agreement to admit one hundred refugee children who had made their way to England. There were approximately nine thousand of these children in Britain, some of them orphans, many of them separated from their parents, all of them frightened. All of those to be admitted to Canada, the cabinet stipulated, must be orphans and between the ages of three and twelve.[1]

Once war began, however, the Canadian interest in the refugee children waned as the threat to British children became more real and as pressure began to build on the Canadian government to evacuate endangered British mothers and children.[2] Committees of Canadian women formed to help organize the movement, led by Charlotte Whitton, one of the nation's most prominent social workers, a key member of the CNCR, secretary of the Canadian Welfare Council and an influential voice in Ottawa. Whitton seemed little interested in Jewish children; indeed, the Canadian Jewish Congress saw her as an enemy of Jewish immigration. According to Oscar Cohen, she "almost broke up the inaugural meeting of the CNCR by her insistent opposition and very apparent anti-Semitism." Cohen charged that she had since then carried on "guerrilla warfare" against the Canadian Jewish Congress and had "tried to block the refugee children project." On her own Whitton had sent a memorandum to welfare councils throughout the nation, warning of the problems inherent in Canada's admitting large numbers of non-British refugee children, eighty per cent of whom, she had added, were Jewish. She had followed this with a cross-country tour in which, according to Congress officials, "she interviewed all child welfare provincial authorities and indicated the difficulties involved in the immigration of refugee children." And Cairine Wilson, the national refugee committee chairman, suspected that Whitton had even discussed her opposition to the project with Blair. It was, finally, largely because of the Whitton campaign that the Congress decided not to apply for the admission of any Jewish children "until at least a few non-Jewish applications had been submitted."[3]

Whitton was not alone in her preference of British over Jewish children. The immigration director privately voiced strong opposition to the scheme, arguing that most of the continental children in Britain were not orphans and that the program would be very costly.[4] In a curious dispatch the Canadian embassy in Washington informed Mackenzie King that the American government opposed the admission of Jewish children, fearing that, admitted to Canada, they might then enter the United States. "If they [Jewish children] were given comparative liberty of movement," the embassy wrote, "Congress and the competent United States authorities would be constrained to believe that efforts would be made by friends and relatives in the United States to try to get them across the border into the United States. . . . No such feeling . . . would be aroused by the admission to Canada for temporary or permanent residence of British-born children, or the children born in France, the Netherlands, Belgium and in the Scandinavian countries."[5]

Meanwhile, the situation in Britain was worsening, with thousands of refugees still pouring into the country. The head of the British Movement for the Care of Children, Sir Charles Stead, anxiously cabled the CNCR in January 1940 that Canada must move swiftly to help alleviate the children's refugee crisis. At once the committee wired the prime minister, urging the government to act promptly and to admit nine thousand refugee children. King agreed to meet a delegation from the committee, but his cabinet rejected out of hand the CNCR's request. To accept nine thousand children, "ninety percent of whom were of the Jewish race and mostly of German citizenship," was totally unacceptable to government officials.

But to accept ten thousand British children was not. Thus, on May 25, 1940, the government agreed to accept this number of children as long as they were of British, French, Belgian or Dutch origin. Within days of this decision Vincent Massey informed Ottawa that British officials did not expect that there would be many British children among the ten thousand. Rather, the British were anxious that Canada help relieve it of the "more immediate and pressing" problem of continental refugees. At the same time the Canadian government made it clear to its ambassador in France, Georges Vanier, that, if necessary, "it would be possible to take a certain number of children of French descent," because "some thousands" of French children could be placed in Quebec homes for the duration of the war; their way would be paid for by the Canadian government.[6]

On June 14 Immigration Minister Crerar announced at a cabinet meeting that Canada could now receive five thousand children immediately. The prime minister expressed some concern at this number, fearing preparations to accommodate so many, so soon were inadequate. More worried was Ernest Lapointe, who warned about the "difficulties involved in receiving such a large number."[7] Nonetheless, Crerar's scheme was given the green light—as long as it was restricted to British children.

It was clear that in the rush to accept British evacuees, the prewar plan to admit some one hundred children from continental Europe had fallen by the wayside. As Geoffrey Shakespeare, the Dominions Office's under-secretary, told the British House of Commons, the Canadian scheme "applied only to Allied boys and girls, not to German-Jewish refugees." This restriction, he said, was "in harmony with the wishes of the Dominion Government."[8] Charlotte Whitton was more blunt: "It is not refugees whom we want to receive, . . . it is part of Britain's immortality, part of her past, part of all the hope of her ultimate future that we take into our keeping."[9]

For the Jewish community, the shift in emphasis from European to British children was a major disappointment. The Congress and the Jewish Immigrant Aid Society had spent months arranging homes for the expected influx of children. Funds had been raised, negotiations with schools had been completed. Now it was all for naught. Unless the British included Jews among their evacuees, there would be no Jewish children arriving at all. As Saul Hayes bitterly asked, "If it is a bad thing for Jewish children to be admitted into Canada, well and good, even if unfortunate, but if it was a good thing for six or eight months, why is it a bad thing today?"[10]

Aware of the Canadian government position, an official of the Council of Austrians in Great Britain pleaded with Jewish leaders in Canada to force a change in policy. He was particularly concerned about the thousands of Jewish refugees and their children still in France, who would "face death" if extradited to the Germans. As Great Britain had taken "many tens of thousands" of refugee children from French ports, could not Canada open her door to some? The JIAS response was all too familiar: "We regret to say that for the time being admission of these refugees is impossible."[11]

On July 9, 1940, an Order-in-Council was passed that specified that the government would undertake to evacuate to Canada British children and their mothers. There was no mention of refugee children from the continent already in Britain, even though Vincent Massey had assured his superiors that there was shipping available for at least five thousand children.[12]

Through the offices of Victor Podoski, Polish ambassador to Canada, the Jewish community made one last effort to get some Jewish refugee children included in the complement. Podoski officially petitioned King to admit one hundred Polish Jewish children who were in England. At the request of the prime minister, Blair personally informed the Polish ambassador that Canada might admit some orphans, but would refuse admission to children whose parents were still in Poland, "as that would mean the admission of entire families sooner or later." The Jewish community, Blair again explained, "could not do through his office by the back door what we had refused to do at the front door on other applications"; and he added that the minister responsible for immigration had accepted this position in the belief that Jews were "not coming [to Canada] for the duration of the war but to remain permanently."[13]

Jewish leaders complained bitterly about the restriction. Many Jewish children, a CNCR official argued, did not *know* whether they were orphans or not; their parents "were last heard of in Prague—or Vienna," and could be presumed neither alive nor dead. The *Toronto Daily Star* also condemned the government. "It is not altogether clear", the editorial stated, why Jewish refugee children "now in England . . . have been excluded from this mass rescue movement. . . . They have suffered as much—and probably much more—than British children. . . . They have been torn from their parents, some of whom were sent to concentration camps, to prison or to slave labour fields"; for Canadians to open their hearts and homes to these children would be "a humane Christian act." The government would not be moved. Though in the end it received about forty-five hundred British children—including some British-born Jews—it took none of those who had managed to escape from the Continent.[14]

Two years later, in 1942, the Canadian government was again put to the test. After the fall of France in 1940 the pro-Nazi Vichy government in the unoccupied part of the country began interning refugee women and children in camps, where they lived under the most trying of conditions; and as war progressed, conditions deteriorated even further. Thousands of children separated from their parents were imprisoned in camps in southern France, in filthy, pestiferous barracks, with little food. As one observer described it, "Famine, parasites, cold and disease—this is the fate of these unfortunate children."[15] Worse awaited them.

In the summer of 1942 the French government began rounding up Jews and deporting them to the East. Thousands of children were now abandoned and left behind in the internment camps. Though few Jews had any doubt about their own fate, some still hoped for their children's escape. One desperate parent slated for deportation managed to smuggle a letter to his relatives in Toronto, begging them to save the life of his son. He and the boy had attempted to escape from unoccupied France, but had been captured and interned. Now he had been told that he would be transported to an "unknown destination"; his son would be left behind. "My Erich," he told his relatives, "has grown up very nicely, speaks French perfectly and until recently was a pupil of the Second Grade and Public School. . . . I beg you implicitly, dear family, . . . keep Erich with you. God will repay you for what you have and what you will do for him." The letter's end was plaintive: "I now take my farewell with my son and can write no more. . . . I can only beg you repeatedly to have him with you. He and I will never forget you. It is indeed sad that a child as Erich should perish. I thank you once more and for the last time. . . ."[16]

There did seem to be some hope that the thousands of Erichs in Europe just might be saved. Since the fall of France the American Friends Service Committee had acted as the representative in France of various North American refugee-assistance organizations. It had managed to smuggle numbers of families out of France to Spain and Portugal, and to inform the Allied governments about the details of the deportations and the conditions of the internment camps.[17] Above all, the service committee was actively involved in attempting to convince Vichy officials to allow the emigration of these abandoned and helpless children.

Pressure was also building on the Vichy government not to deport the children to Poland. The French Catholic Church issued a strong statement, supported by the Pope, denouncing the deportations;[18] and newspapers throughout the free world were savage in their denunciation of Vichy's behaviour. But the government paid no heed. According to a recent study, the children "were not seen [by the Vichy government] as victims, but as a problem."[19] When the American chargé d'affaires arrived to deliver to Pierre Laval, the Vichy prime minister, his government's protest, he was astounded when Laval offered him all the children he wanted. At once the American asked his government to take up the offer.[20] At the same time the surviving Jewish welfare organizations in France appealed to the Allied countries to permit the immigration of those children whose parents had been transported.[21]

It was now the turn of the Allied governments to bear the brunt of the pressure. North American Jewish groups immediately besieged their governments with requests to admit the children. The leading American Jewish groups sent a joint protest to Washington pleading for assistance. As the leading American Yiddish newspaper, *Der Tag*, put it, "Is it too much to hope and expect that these countries will open their door just long enough to admit the Jewish exiles at France. . . . It's now or never. Either these Jewish victims hounded and persecuted beyond belief and imagination are now given a home in the countries beyond the seas . . . or the free world, when it rises on the ruins of the war, will see only graves where living Jews with ability to create and a desire to contribute to human happiness had roamed. . . . Is it too much to ask that these children be given a new lease on life."[22] Within days the American government intimated that it would accept at least a thousand of these waifs, and by the end of September, American Secretary of State Cordell Hull officially told Vichy that the United States would admit up to five thousand.[23]

The Jewish community in Canada was also off the mark quickly. The Joint Distribution Committee (JDC), an organization devoted to rescuing Jews in Europe, phoned Saul Hayes from New York, and the Congress director, alerted to the possibility of saving some children, was quickly on the phone to the Immigration Branch. Neither Blair nor Crerar took his call, so he left word that he would soon be presenting the government with a proposal regarding these children. Hayes also cabled HICEM, which coordinated refugee efforts, that Canadian Jewry would "leave no stone unturned" in attempting a rescue. The *Kanader Adler*, the largest Yiddish-language newspaper in Canada, joined the chorus of voices on behalf of the children. In an eloquent editorial it pleaded with Canadian Jews to submit petitions to their government and, especially, to make common cause with the leaders and people of Quebec. It urged the Canadian Jewish Congress to point out to the Government of Quebec that church leaders in France had condemned the deportations —perhaps the people of the province would perform more satisfactorily if they were being asked to help refugees from France rather than from other parts of Europe. "Let us at least quiet our conscience that we have done all we could, but at least not less than our brethren from the United States."[24]

On September 8 the Congress received a cable from the HICEM representatives in Lisbon informing them that the deportation of the French children was about to begin. Immediately Hayes wired the Immigration Branch asking the government to follow the American lead and admit several hundred of these orphans for the duration of the war. The Congress would provide "full maintenance and support." The director also requested a meeting with Crerar and his officials to discuss "this emergency matter." Crerar's response was noncommittal. There was "no object" in a delegation meeting with him at this point; rather, the Congress should send "full particulars . . . in writing," and then the government would be able to respond.[25]

There was clearly no time to waste. At the same time as Crerar's response came to the Congress office, so did an urgent letter from the Joint Distribution Committee: "There are [in France] approximately 5,000 children, aged two to fifteen, whose parents have been deported eastward and who are themselves in danger of being deported." "Arrests," the letter added, "are being made daily in the street, and as a result of the terror and panic there are many suicides. . . . Unless speedy action is taken in the next few days, the hope of saving even a part of these children may be gone." The JDC pleaded with Hayes to persuade the Canadian government to act to save "these innocent young children."[26]

Within hours Hayes and Congress president Samuel Bronfman composed a letter to the prime minister, detailing the agony of French Jewry. King was asked to protest to the Vichy government against "these heinous crimes" and to warn the French that "the Free Governments in the world [would] bring the perpetrators of these crimes to boot." The Congress again appealed to Crerar to allow several hundred of the refugee children into Canada. It was pointed out that countries such as the United States and the Dominican Republic had already agreed to accept some, and that the Congress would be responsible for all the expenses incurred in bringing these orphans to Canada and would provide total maintenance once they had arrived.[27]

For once the usually backward—at least about Jewish causes—Canadian bureaucracy responded quickly. The Department of External Affairs had been receiving intelligence reports for several weeks that the Vichy government was beginning to deport Jews in a "barbarous fashion" to "an unknown destination across the Rhine." On September 12 Hume Wrong informed the prime minister that these deportations were "equivalent to a sentence of death." The deputy under-secretary suggested that the Vichy minister in Canada be called in to hear "a strong verbal protest" against the behaviour of his government. This was, Wrong said, something he had wanted to do even "before the arrival of Mr. Bronfman's letter."[28]

The Immigration Branch reacted as promptly though less positively. Blair told Norman Robertson in External Affairs that his department would not waive any of the "technical details," such as mental and physical examinations, required for admission to Canada, when considering the refugee children; he granted only that it was "alleged" that the children were in "immediate danger." Blair did promise to cooperate with American authorities, and he asked External Affairs to get from the United States details of its proposal. As well, Crerar informed Bronfman that his department would act in concert with the United States, and that, though the government could do nothing at the moment, he himself was "personally most sympathetic."[29]

On September 15 Wrong met a member of the Vichy delegation and conveyed "the grave concern" of the Canadian government over Vichy policy. He stated that Canada wanted the deportations stopped and all those in the internment camps released. The French representative—"off the record"—agreed with the Canadian protests, though denied that either Marshal Pétain, president of Vichy, or Laval was anti-Semitic. After dismissing the Vichy diplomat, Wrong informed King that Canada could not emulate the Americans by accepting as many refugees from France because this was "a large order" and even if Canada "were willing, . . . there [was] next to no transportation available."[30]

Replying to a Canadian request for information regarding its policy toward the children in France, the American government admitted privately that it had been subject to much pressure and had agreed to accept approximately one thousand children; it had not, unfortunately, worked out "the details of the plan" and so could provide no information to Canadian authorities. What the Americans did do, however, was summon the Vichy ambassador in Washington to a meeting at which Secretary of State Hull gave him a severe dressing down. Hull described the Vichy policy of deportation as "so revolting and so fiendish that it defied adequate description." At a press conference on the same day Hull categorically denied reports that Laval had offered to "send the Jews to America if she would have them."[31]

The Canadian government was in a quandary. The Americans, whose policies and procedures it hoped to emulate, had yet to announce any. And the pressure to act quickly was growing daily. On September 21, on behalf of his government, Victor Podoski asked the Canadian government to grant Canadian visas to a number of Polish Jews in France. These visas, the Polish ambassador said, "may make it possible for them to obtain exit permits . . . and to seek temporary asylum in Switzerland or Portugal, and thus save themselves from the hands of the Gestapo." Several days later the head of the Intergovernmental Committee on Refugees, Herbert Emerson, cabled King urging Canada to give temporary asylum to refugee children in France "as the only means of saving them." On behalf of Canadian Jewry, Samuel Bronfman "unconditionally guaranteed" that any refugee accepted as a result of the Polish government's entreaty would be fully subsidized and maintained by the Canadian Jewish Congress. It was clear to the Department of External Affairs that events were coming to a head, that Canada would have to act soon.[32]

The British government was also considering its response to the developments in France. Though it joined in the denunciation of Vichy, it would do little for the French children. When Emerson met with the British home secretary, Herbert Morrison, he was told that Britain could do nothing for these Jewish children because of the "anti-Semitic feeling which [was] quite certainly latent in this country." The Foreign Office agreed that Britain should hold out for non-Jewish children. "I feel very strongly," a ministry official explained, "that we must stick out for equal—or better—facilities for Allied nationals. . . . Humanitarian considerations alone are not regarded as good enough for the Allies to get their nationals into the United Kingdom and I see no reason why Jews as such should receive preferential treatment."[33]

Canadian Jews, increasingly impatient with their government's dilatory attitude, now formed a committee, made up mostly of Federation of Polish Jewry members, to go to Ottawa and complain personally to Prime Minister King. If King would not see them, they threatened "to camp on his doorstep until he [did]." A panic-stricken Hayes phoned Wrong asking when the government would make its decision. He warned that the Congress was under great pressure to send a delegation to the capital. Wrong cautioned that a visitation by Jewish officials would be a mistake and promised a decision shortly.[34]

Meanwhile, Blair was attempting to find out from Jewish officials more about the children and arrangements for their stay in Canada. How many were refugees? How old were they? Would they be adopted or put in foster homes? Were they to remain only for the duration of the war or were their parents to join them in Canada once hostilities had ceased? How many could the Jewish community absorb and who would take responsibility for their placement, maintenance and care? Personally, he did not know what could be done by Ottawa, but he was "quite sure that [Crerar was] sympathetic." However, he warned Hayes not to give his letter "any publicity" until it was decided whether the government would approve the movement.[35]

On receipt of Blair's letter, Hayes felt that the director was baiting a trap. Any suggestion to the Immigration Branch that these children were not refugees, or too old to be considered as minors, or that they intended to stay in the country permanently, or that their parents might join them, would be sufficient grounds for the scheme's rejection. Hayes very carefully drafted his response. These children, he said, were all refugees and under eighteen years of age. Canadian Jewry had asked the government to grant asylum to these children, not to their parents, almost all of whom had been deported to Eastern Europe. There were no plans to ask for the admission of the parents at present or after the war. In cooperation with various welfare agencies, the children would be placed in foster homes until they could be repatriated. Finally, he reminded Blair that this was "a matter of life and death for a number of innocent children."[36]

Hayes was also concerned that the government might lump Podoski's plea for Polish refugees in France together with the Congress's request on behalf of the refugee children. He said that the two applications were separate, should not be confused and did not "concern the same people." Sure enough, on the following day Wrong wrote Bronfman asking if the two arrangements were identical. The Congress president hurriedly assured him that they were not, and that the Jewish community would support all refugee children who arrived in Canada, not merely those of Polish origin.[37]

Hayes's precautions were wasted, for Blair assumed he was lying. In a briefing paper for his minister, the crafty director of immigration stated that it was "evident" that what was "being pressed upon" the government by Canadian Jews was "not a movement of children only, but also of adults"; and as far as he was concerned, the number involved far exceeded five thousand. The situation, he said, reminded him of the Evian Conference, which had failed because the task of finding a home for the tens of thousands of Jews Germany wished to get rid of was too difficult; Germany was, Blair said, now desperately trying "to get rid of whatever thousands of Jewish children or adults there are, whose labour they cannot utilize." Blair told Crerar that the Jewish community would find it very difficult to look after even one thousand children satisfactorily: "Regular welfare organizations have expressed criticism a number of times of the Jewish method of handling earlier movements." It was Blair's opinion that Canada might accept five hundred at first, and "if the Jewish peoples can take care of that many," maybe a thousand later. Of course no adults would be admitted.[38]

On October 2 Blair met with Crerar to discuss the project. The minister overruled his director's suggestion that the matter be discussed by the cabinet; he would, on his own, authorize the admission of five hundred children, with another five hundred to follow—"only when we are satisfied that the Jewish community will be able to properly absorb them." These children would be admitted as "non-immigrants" for the duration of the war, would not be able to bring in their "parents or other relatives at a later date," and were not to be adopted but placed in foster homes.[39]

On the same day the British government decided to admit all

those refugee children in France under sixteen years of age who had a near relation in Britain; this action would not be limited to Jews. When told that the Canadian scheme involved only Jewish children, a Foreign Office official noted that his department, with the support of the Home Office, had "held out against . . . this suggestion." Though by the end of September the Americans had agreed to accept up to five thousand children, the Canadian government was not officially informed and learned of the proposal through the press. This was most disconcerting to External Affairs officials because the Americans had been told that they would be responsible for examining and transporting the children accepted by Canada.[40]

For political reasons Ottawa had asked the United Jewish Refugee Agency to give its decision no publicity. Hayes therefore warned Jewish community leaders that "publicity might kill any plan," and that all public discussion of the children's movement must cease. The JIAS director informed his officers that it was necessary to keep the decision quiet lest Quebec, learning of it, attempt to have it reversed, as it had succeeded in doing with previous schemes to bring refugees. But word of the plan was rapidly spreading in the Jewish community, and the government's and Congress's attempts to forestall public reaction failed. Those with relatives in France descended on Congress offices or sent letters, giving the last known address of their sons, daughters, nieces and nephews. Requests even came from the United States. From New York City, for example, a letter arrived at Congress offices from a woman begging that her two young cousins, both under fifteen years of age, be included in any rescue attempt. Their parents had been deported "to the East," and the children were now alone. "We are clutching at the ray of hope of some help," she wrote, "as a drowning man clutches at a straw." A man in Ottawa wrote about his seventeen-year-old sister, a refugee from Germany now in a camp in unoccupied France. He had no idea where her parents were, but thought they had been sent to Poland. Her life for the past five years had been "wretched," and this was her last chance for survival.[41]

For everyone concerned, this seemed like the last moment in which to wrench a loved one from the murderous hands of the Nazis, and the Congress was fully aware of its weighty responsibility. Hayes still tried to get the Canadian government to be more forthcoming. He phoned Wrong and asked if the government was going to grant the Polish ambassador's request to allow in a number of Polish refugees from France. The deputy under-secretary of state warned him that it "would be unwise to pursue this matter in view of [the government's] consent to admit refugee children."[42] Hayes did not pursue the matter.

Perhaps because of the awesome nature of the task, or perhaps because of the prestige that would accrue to the organization succeeding in it, Hayes was determined that the Congress's United Jewish Refugee Agency must take sole charge—and sole credit—for the refugee children project. Even though he had reassured Blair that the "entire facilities" of the Jewish Immigrant Aid Society—all their field workers and expertise—would be made available, he was in fact determined to minimize its role. On the other hand, after several years of playing second fiddle on immigration matters to the UJRA, the immigrant aid society was determined by 1942 to regain what Solkin, its national director, called its "place in the sun." In a meeting on October 2 between representatives of the two organizations, it was agreed that JIAS play a key role in placing and maintaining the children. Immediately following this conference, Solkin informed his officials that, if the society wished to "retain the position of leadership, . . . [it would] have to show initiative and produce results." He cautioned that there was to be "no competition" however, but "friendly teamwork" with the refugee agency; both had "a goal of common concern and interest."[43]

Hayes saw the matter differently. To him it was a Canadian Jewish Congress project from beginning to end, and the immigrant aid society would be allowed to participate only as a good will gesture; it would do only those things which the UJRA told it to do: "I would like to make it very clear that the Minister [responsible for Immigration] has turned over the entire project for reception, placement and after care to the UJRA."[44]

The Congress's attitude and behaviour rankled society officials. Nonetheless, both groups tried to paper over the divisions. The society's national president, Hyman Barsky, sent a long conciliatory letter to Bronfman stressing that the "unprecedented extent of the Jewish catastrophe" required that all Jewish organizations work together, and he offered the Congress the "full co-operation" of JIAS. The Congress's "arrogance," however, proved too much for the society's leaders. When informed that the UJRA had planned a meeting in Toronto to discuss the children's project but had failed to invite a society representative, the president of the Toronto JIAS, Dr. John

Atkins, exploded: Toronto members, he said, go to Congress meetings and "sit back and listen" to Hayes "praise himself" and the UJRA without even mentioning JIAS; no one had spoken to him of the French children's project; Solkin was not "battling for JIAS policy and rights"; his "shoulders [were] not big enough to carry the burden of fighting for and defending JIAS" against Hayes. If the Montreal JIAS wished to be "grand fellows" and give in to the Congress, that was fine, but Atkins resolutely promised that the Toronto JIAS was not going to be the "scapegoat."[45]

Both Solkin and Barsky tried to soothe the nettled Toronto doctor. The former praised him for his "personal devotion," but assured him that he was "unduly alarmed," that there were no "schemes to ignore" his society. He repeated that Hayes had confirmed "his determination to abide by the agreement" and that Atkins's anger would "create undesirable reverberation and antagonism" with the Congress. What was required was "judicious calm." Similarly, Barsky commended the Toronto JIAS for "the way . . . it had persistently and zealously stood up for the prestige of JIAS," but suspected the effect of its "total loyalty." "You are sometimes so sensitive that JIAS should not be ignored," he said, "that you see a storm ahead . . . when it is merely a passing cloud." He assured Atkins that Hayes had promised the society a complementary role in the French children's project.[46]

The Congress was of course perturbed by the developments in the immigrant aid society. Hayes chided Solkin for the disorder in his ranks and denied the charge that he was leading "a diabolical plot" to eliminate the society's participation in the children's movement. Solkin himself told Atkins that his charges against him were "wrong and undeserved."[47] He had again spoken to Hayes to reaffirm the arrangements and was fully confident that the United Jewish Refugee Agency would live up to its commitment.

Solkin was wrong. At a UJRA meeting in Toronto on October 15, Congress officials stated that they had "secured the permits [and] would take charge of the entire project." When Atkins, who was present, complained, he was told by Congress leaders that they had "no knowledge of the arrangements . . . between JIAS and UJRA." Now the Toronto society president could crow that his Montreal colleagues had been hoodwinked and that he himself had "no confidence in the promises and assurances of Saul Hayes." As Atkins and other society activists saw it, their organization no longer had any credibility nor a "justification for existence." They worried that, because of the Congress's high profile, it, not JIAS, would handle the expected postwar immigration boom. There would be nothing left for the society but "to pick up the crumbs from their table." At an emergency meeting of the Toronto executive of JIAS on October 18, it was decided that the organization take its case to the public and ask the Congress to apologize in the Jewish press. Hayes in particular was attacked—for failing to notify UJRA officials of his agreement with Solkin and for publicly slighting JIAS. It was now clear to the ever-patient Solkin that Hayes could not be trusted. He agreed with Atkins that the society was "up against it." Yet he still felt it necessary to take a "mild tone" with the Congress as "challenging attitudes [might] aggravate things beyond repair."[48]

The national executive of the Jewish Immigrant Aid Society decided to ask Hayes for an explanation of his behaviour and to find out whether his agreement with Solkin was binding. In response a fiery Hayes stated that he could only make recommendations to his board; there was no binding agreement until it had approved the arrangement. "Every second piece of publicity issuing from this office is the subject of complaint on the part of the JIAS," he complained. Would the society not support the children's project unless it received proper publicity? Hayes said he wished the animosity to end and to focus on the success of the project.[49]

On the same day Hayes issued a press statement announcing the children's project. In the ten-paragraph release not only was there no mention of JIAS, but the UJRA's "direct and complete" control of all phases of the program was stressed. It was by now evident to even the most die-hard supporter of the society that the United Jewish Refugee Agency would reign supreme on immigration matters at least for the war's duration. The society reluctantly agreed to take a back seat to the Congress on the children's project, and as consolation, the UJRA executive formally invited the society "to co-operate in a capacity compatible with its status." Solkin agreed, adding that he would do "everything in [his] power to secure a prominent place for JIAS in the project." When informed that Congress officers in the west were "anxious . . . not to have any co-operation or assistance from any other organization" and would under no circumstances give any credit to JIAS, Solkin merely shrugged. His only hope was that Hayes, with "experience," would soon come to "view things in proper perspective"; until then JIAS would lie low.[50]

Both the United Jewish Refugee Agency and the Canadian government seemed to realize the urgency of the situation in France and were desperate to conclude preparations. On October 8, 1942, Hayes met with officials of the American Friends Service Committee, the Joint Distribution Committee and the United States Refugee Service. It was agreed to choose first those children "in the greatest danger," with infants given priority. The American Friends Service Committee would make all selections. The children would be brought to Lisbon by French nationals and met by American doctors and nurses and consular officials. They would then be transported to the United States where those on their way to Canada would be met by Canadian officials. The External Affairs Department had already asked its Washington embassy to discuss the question of transit visas, while the Immigration Branch had requested its American counterpart conduct the necessary medical examinations. Blair generously promised that the mental and physical standards used by the United States would be acceptable to Canada. Indeed, the director seemed to be going out of his way to expedite the project, urging Hayes to have his "agents move very quickly in Unoccupied France . . . since the situation . . . might change so rapidly . . . that [it] might become Occupied France and everything would be in the hands of the German government." Indeed, so forthcoming was Blair that the Congress executive officially offered him their "deep and lasting thanks" for his "sympathetic" approach to the project and paid tribute to his "kind consideration and human instincts."[51]

These instincts, however, did not apply to other refugees from France. Since the fall of France, Jewish groups had been frantically lobbying the Immigration Branch to issue visas to relatives of Canadian residents stranded there. The Orthodox community pleaded with the government to allow in 250 "outstanding rabbis and religious laymen who faced immediate deportation." The Jewish Labor Committee sent a list to Crerar of labour leaders, intellectuals and scientists—"men of outstanding merit"—who were likely to be killed by the Gestapo for the "sole crime . . . that they have resolutely propagated the ideals of democracy and freedom."[52] With the support of Ambassador Podoski, the Federation of Polish Jewry was constantly sending petitions to the Immigration Branch asking for the admission of Polish Jews in France. To all of these the government's response was the same: it sympathized with the unfortunate lot of these people, but could do nothing for them.[53]

Increasingly, government bureaucrats resented the pressure. Hume Wrong warned a colleague about to take on responsibilities in the area of immigration that he would be subject to "a good deal of pressure from Jewish agencies." Knowing the sensitivities of important bureaucrats, Hayes made it a point to try and dissuade delegations from going to Ottawa unless he himself had cleared it with the appropriate Ottawa authorities. Thus, when word came to him that the Federation of Polish Jewry was planning to meet with the prime minister about Podoski's most recent petition, he hurriedly phoned Wrong. Wrong told him that "public injection of new immigration issues . . . would be unwise and potentially prejudicial" to the children's project, so Hayes had Bronfman tell the federation to stay at home. When informed by Hayes that the Jewish Immigrant Aid Society was intending "to approach Ottawa to formulate a clearer and more lenient policy regarding . . . refugees," the deputy under-secretary advised the Congress to stop the delegation, as their going to Ottawa might force a hardening of the government's attitude. The delegation did not go. Indeed, so determined was Hayes not to upset influential civil servants that almost every attempt by a Jewish group to make representation in Ottawa was rejected by the Congress—and few organizations were heady enough to take on Hayes and his associates.[54]

Naturally, this attitude did not go down well with some. The Zionists, the *landsmannschaften*, the trade unions and the Federation of Polish Jewry were always nagging the Congress to be more aggressive. Their brethren were being slaughtered in Europe, and they were being asked to remain silent. These organizations were coming under increasing attack from their own rank-and-file to do something—anything. "It is needless to stress the danger in which our people find themselves in France," the federation executive complained to Bronfman. "Their deportation to 'unknown destinations' we know means extermination. Negligence in such cases on our part to do our utmost is unpardonable." The federation demanded that the Congress send a delegation to Ottawa to insist on the entry of refugees in France with relatives in Canada.[55] In order not to jeopardize the children's project, the Congress resisted all such urgings.

It seemed, in any case, that all the energies of the Canadian

Jewish Congress were devoted to the children's project. Plans were underway to find homes, schools and other services for the one thousand children, with approximately thirty-three thousand Jewish households in Canada being solicited for contributions of every kind. Two boats chartered by the Joint Distribution Committee would leave Lisbon in early December with the precious cargo. Doctors and nurses had been chosen, and social workers were being given "crash courses" in the problems they might encounter among the children. American and Canadian Jewish organizations pledged over three million dollars to the cause. Committees were set up in every centre with a substantial Jewish population. Hayes himself went on a cross-Canada tour to discuss potential problems with provincial cabinet ministers and agencies, as well as with local Jewish leaders. The enthusiasm and energy of Canadian Jewry, so long pent up while waiting on something to do, now burst forth. Everyone, it seemed, was ready to act, if only a handful of Jewish children could be saved.[56]

What the Vichy government intended was not so clear. From the start, it had not committed itself irrevocably. Indeed, Prime Minister Laval was all along being warned by the Germans that he should not allow the children to be used by the Allies as anti-French or anti-Nazi propaganda. Negotiations with the Americans moved at a snail's pace as neither Laval nor his ministers—nor his German overlords—could decide how to proceed.[57] Toward the end of October 1942 the Americans became convinced that the French would not issue any exit visas at all, and word was soon filtering down from United States authorities to a disbelieving Jewish community that it best not expect any children. Jewish leaders promptly denounced these warnings as "guesses" and "rumour-mongering," but were careful not to give the project any publicity. They thought news of the scheme would encourage "anti-French" propaganda, in turn placing the project in "jeopardy."[58]

The fate of the French children's project was sealed in the early days of November 1942 when the Allies began their invasion of North Africa. Within a week both Canada and the United States had broken off diplomatic relations with the Vichy government, and on November 11 the Germans moved into unoccupied France. There would be no rescue of, no haven for, the refugee children of Vichy. They would soon be transported not to North America but to Auschwitz, not to new homes, families and lives but to gas chambers, crematoria and their death.

Canadian Jewry was staggered by the shock. All the preparations, the hopes, the expectations had been for naught. They found solace only in the realization that the invasion might hasten the end of war. As Hayes said, "Although we naturally feel very discouraged about the fate of these 6,500 or more children, . . .we cannot but feel glad that the ultimate happiness of millions of people will be quicker assured by the events in North Africa. It is certainly a step towards victory and the fate of children all over the world will be the more easily guaranteed by these events." The Congress director was, however, determined meanwhile to keep pressing the government. Hayes told the director of immigration that the news from North Africa was "glorious," then pursued his end. Although "the children's rescue scheme [was] infinitesimal beside the rescue of all the world from the enthralldom of the axis," the Congress had no intentions of giving it up. Until a "clearer picture" emerged from Vichy, Jewish organizations were only "marking time," said Saul Hayes.[59]

Canadian and American immigration officials thought the project "dead," or "in complete abeyance," but they were soon surprised and the Jewish community delighted when in December rumours began circulating that some children had escaped France and were now in Spain and Portugal. The Joint Distribution Committee confidentially informed Hayes that there were several hundred children now being cared for by Jewish relief agencies in Portugal and that the Americans were prepared to accept all those under sixteen. There remained twenty between the ages of sixteen and eighteen, and on December 29 the Congress officially asked the Canadian government to admit the twenty as part of the French children's movement, their request arriving with an identical one from the American government. The Department of External Affairs told the American State Department that these teenagers would be readily admitted, and reassured Hayes that the government had "no objection" to the movement. Laurent Beaudry, an External Affairs officer, who had taken over the program from Hume Wrong, did not see any difficulties in meeting the Congress's request, but waited on the Immigration Branch's opinion.[60]

The department's opinion was, when it came, unexpected. Since Hayes's original letter to admit the children had arrived,

Blair had been wondering if the Jewish community was not attempting another one of its "questionable ploys." He had been told by his officals in London that 250 Jewish children and their parents had gone to Spain and Portugal from France, and his deputy, A. L. Jolliffe, had immediately suggested that the twenty children might be part of this group and therefore inadmissible because they had parents. To Blair it seemed as if Hayes was being duplicitous. "An attempt is being made to bring Jewish children under what we call the thousand children refugee movement, who do not belong to that group at all," he told External Affairs. Canada had agreed to accept only orphans or those children whose parents had been deported; "children who were with their parents," Blair told Beaudry, "cannot be included in this movement."[61]

The External Affairs Department was shocked and embarrassed by Blair's response. Wrong agreed that the government "never undertook to receive Jewish refugee families," but felt that Canada should ask only that the children were "in fact separated from their parents and [had] no place of refuge." Even a phone call from Beaudry could not unbend the punctilious director of immigration. Beaudry found Blair "quite clear that this [was] an attempt to open the door to some action different from the agreement and . . . strongly opposed to any action being taken to open the door." As Blair cold-bloodedly put it, "There can be no manner of doubt that the children we were trying to rescue were not children living with their parents but children who had become orphans." Indeed, the director told Hayes that "someone had got their wires badly crossed" on this issue and that the United Jewish Refugee Agency was trying to bring into Canada children who did not belong in the children's project. Further, he implied that Hayes had been aware of this all along.[62]

Left no other option, External Affairs officials informed their American counterpart that Canada would not accept the teenagers. The Americans pointed out that they themselves admitted those whose parents did not accompany them as long as the parents signed an agreement not to apply later for entry into the United States using their children's presence as grounds. They asked Canada to consider adopting the same procedure.[63]

Blair would not budge. And he was being pushed not only by the Americans, but by a number of refugee relief organizations, including the Unitarian Service Committee and the Joint Distribution Committee, which warned that children in Spain and

Portugal were "in great danger," that unless they were removed no new refugees would be allowed into those countries. Even the Canadian embassy in Washington was alarmed; it was likely that some children had been granted entry visas in Lisbon and were already on their way to Canada—could not they be admitted though they did not qualify? The children, Blair answered, would not be admitted "unless they came within the agreed scheme."[64]

Hayes was still ready to take a new tack. On behalf of the United Jewish Refugee Agency he sent a telegram to the immigration director agreeing that children with parents did not qualify for admission. He was, therefore, applying to have seventy-five children admitted whose parents would "voluntarily surrender" them for the rest of the war. These were children in "great danger"; a "dire fate" awaited them if they could not leave immediately.[65] In a confidential note sent to the director the next day, Hayes claimed that it had been "a privilege" to work with him. He hoped that he would "sympathize with the UJRA request, [as] the ordinary peacetime view of separating children from parents [was] not now tenable": "By insisting on it one may find both go to their doom together." Hayes concluded: "At least the children would be saved."[66] The Immigration Branch could not be moved. Crerar himself now joined with Blair, and Blair simply rested on precedent. "For more than twenty years," he said, "we have refused hundreds of times to deal with families otherwise than as family units."[67]

So offended was he that the usually diplomatic Hayes promptly drafted a bitter reply accusing the government of basing its refusal on a "policy of 20 years standing in times of peace" when the world was now confronted with the "most dastardly crimes in history." He accused the government of having no feelings for the Jewish people "in their travail." "Surely the decimation of a people," he wrote, "has not so steeled us to tragedy as to deny an application for an infinitesimal movement on humanitarian grounds because of a peacetime principle." Unfortunately, the letter was never sent. Hayes argued in its favour against Bronfman and other Congress leaders who felt such a reply would only alienate the government; Hayes was so enraged, felt himself "even more disturbed than the letter would suggest" and so believed the letter "somewhat discreet"; he was, nevertheless, dissuaded from sending it. In a second letter Hayes simply expressed his "deep disappointment," and requested an interview between Congress leaders and Crerar. Bronfman meanwhile wrote the minister directly, pleading with him to admit just forty-five children; they "may well be caught," he wrote, "in a Nazi trap if sanctuary is not found for them in time." He asked for "a half hour at most" of Crerar's time. He did not get a minute. The minister of immigration said Canada would not "abandon one of the principal safeguards of immigration"—the integrity of family units—even for the children in Spain and Portugal.[68]

Pressure from other departments on the Immigration Branch to soften its resistance continued as well. On behalf of External Affairs, Norman Robertson asked Blair to allow in children for the duration of the war whose parents promised not to use the presence of their children in Canada "as a basis of admission for themselves or other relatives at a later date." This, said Robertson, was American policy. Would it not be wise, he asked, "to adopt the same policy as the United States while insisting on the same safeguards?" Canada was "being pressed by the United Kingdom," he added, to accept refugees from the neutral countries in Europe. Since the government was "reluctant to make any commitment," its position would be "stronger," he stated, "if we did all that we could to make a reality of the Government's specific offer of temporary admission to the Jewish child refugees in Western Europe."[69]

No amount of persuasion or pressure, however, could move the obdurate director and his like-minded minister. Blair told Robertson that his conclusions were "erroneous." And to Senator Cairine Wilson's complaint to the prime minister, Blair had an answer: "All the cases Senator Wilson has brought to my attention in the past four years have been Jewish." External Affairs officials threw up their hands. "The man resolutely sticks to his point," Wrong told Norman Robertson—the point being "not to separate children from their parents." Yet "we did exactly this, of course, in taking British children as 'war guests' in 1940." There was nothing more the department could do but take the matter to the cabinet, and Wrong knew that that was a "bad" idea. Robertson was thus forced to tell Lester Pearson, chief Canadian representative in Washington, that the Americans should not expect Canada to admit any Jewish children except bona fide orphans. Thus, when the first shipload of children landed in the United States and no passenger thought himself headed for Canada, this, said Pearson, saved the government much "embarrassment." Henceforth, Canada need not anticipate any "objectionable" children coming its way, he added, as the Americans had been informed of the country's "exact requirements."[70]

The children's project, seemingly laid to rest by 1943, would be resurrected once more, a year later. The initiative came this time from the British and the Intergovernmental Committee on Refugees (IGC), the committee born of the Evian Conference and responsible for coordination of refugee resettlement programs. On December 3, 1943, the British alerted the State Department that it might be possible to get as many as six thousand children from France to Switzerland. Shortly thereafter the British and Americans privately agreed to negotiate with Switzerland, while they referred the question of the children's numbers and whereabouts to the Intergovernmental Committee. According to French underground and Jewish sources, there were approximately three thousand Jewish refugee children with Christian families who might "escape detection"; the rest— about ten thousand—were doomed unless evacuated. A Jewish agency official in Lisbon reported that "the hunt of hidden Jewish children is going on by the Gestapo in the most horrifying way." He advised immediate Allied action if any children were to be saved.[71]

The IGC executive met on January 4, 1944, to discuss the situation. It was agreed that every attempt be made to get the children out of France. Both Switzerland and the Irish Republic would be asked to approach German and Vichy authorities to grant exit permits, and various nations would be asked if they would provide asylum. The Canadian government at once agreed to live up to its earlier commitment as long as the children were given "the necessary examinations." The Americans informed Canada that it would likely use the Red Cross to examine the children, but would "not be too severe on the question of physical standards [because] most of these children [would have suffered] from malnutrition." Of course the Immigration Branch reminded External Affairs to include in any communication with the Intergovernmental Committee: the children "must be orphans or . . . [children] whose parents' whereabouts are unknown."[72]

Canada was preparing to reply positively to the IGC, when A. L. Jolliffe anticipated in a memo "some awkward problems": if children were admitted to Switzerland because Canada agreed to admit them after the war, and if those same children were "found to be inadmissible . . . on medical grounds," what would happen? Because there was a "danger to the public health from refugees coming to Canada," Jolliffe, who had some months before replaced Blair as director of immigration, demanded that there be no "lowering of the standard of health requirements."[73]

On January 24, with the Immigration Branch's caveats in mind, External Affairs officially informed the Intergovernmental Committee that its original offer to accept Jewish refugee children in France who were "orphans" was still valid, but it would under no circumstances "give an absolute guarantee that children admitted . . . to Switzerland [or Portugal] for temporary domicile would later be admitted to Canada if transportation became possible."[74] In other words, in the twenty-eight months since Canada first committed itself to accept children from unoccupied France, during which time almost all external circumstances had been transformed, the government did not revise the conditions for entry in any appreciable way. Though no one could any longer doubt their fate, Canada was not prepared to liberalize its requirements to help even some of the Jewish children trapped in France.

By February 1944 there seemed little hope that any of these children would survive. An IGC official reported to Sir Herbert Emerson that all refugee children in France, "whatever their age," were being deported. A month later a Joint Distribution Committee representative in Geneva worried about the fate of the Jewish children with false identity cards who were being concealed by sympathetic Christian families. Would it be better, he asked IGC authorities, to try to get them out or leave them where they were? In either case they did not stand much chance of surviving. It was by now readily apparent that the Vichy government would not grant any exit visas to these children; all approaches by the Swiss government had been rebuffed. The last remaining hope was a desperate plan, which the World Jewish Congress broached to the British government, to send in "underground teams" to lead the children to safety over the Pyrennees into Spain. The Foreign Office rejected the plan out of hand on the grounds that the British and American government disliked "sideshows."[75]

The American State Department remained convinced that it was still possible for groups of children to be smuggled across the border to Switzerland. To reassure the Swiss, the Americans authorized entrance visas for four thousand refugee children in that country, "irrespective of nationality, religion, or citizenship status." According to the State Department, this was done "to assist in the escape of orphaned or abandoned children from enemy occupied . . . areas and to assure the Swiss Government that the children will not remain in that country after the war." It also suggested that Canada "adopt a similiar course of action, . . . [taking] 1,000 children."[76]

Canada was not impressed with the American offer. It "really involves no great danger," said Norman Robertson, "since by the time movement of the children out of Switzerland would be possible, it would be equally possible and much easier to resettle them . . . in their countries of origin." The whole purpose of the gesture, he told Immigration officials, was "to encourage the Swiss to admit an equivalent number of other refugees." Even less impressed—predictably—was the Immigration Branch. Canada should make no compromises and must adhere to all its conditions, said its director, as any change in the requirements "would raise a number of difficult questions . . . such as . . . the admission at a later date of one or both parents and other members of the family." Nor would he accept the proposition that Canada might share the cost of maintaining the children in Switzerland. Hume Wrong answered the Americans that before Canada would alter its policy, it would need a great deal of "additional information." And just as External Affairs officials had suspected, none was forthcoming.

There were no more schemes to help save the refugee children. None were needed. By the time of the Allied invasion of France in June 1944, most of these children had been deported and murdered. Not one of them had made it to Canada.[77]

5

OTTAWA OR BERMUDA? A REFUGEE CONFERENCE

By 1943 the Nazi death camps were working overtime. From all over Europe, Jews by the hundreds of thousands were being shipped in crowded cattle cars to Auschwitz, Sobibor, Treblinka and the other German murder factories. The Warsaw ghetto was being razed and well over a million Polish Jews had been murdered. Millions more, it was clear, would soon be.

One of these was Chaim Kahane, a Polish Jew who had moved to Berlin following the First World War and had become a successful banker. His brother, Simon, had meanwhile emigrated to Canada. Following *Kristallnacht*, Simon, now a wealthy merchant, began a concentrated campaign to get his brother and his family into Canada. Money was no obstacle. Unfortunately, the Immigration Branch was. Every request from Simon, his lawyer and his member of Parliament was turned aside. The Jewish banker from Berlin and his family, a department official said, "did not qualify for immigration to Canada." In 1939 Chaim, his wife and four small children were expelled by the Nazis to Poland. Again Simon pleaded for their admission. He guaranteed that he would support his brother and his family and was willing to put up a bond of $50,000, but Immigration Branch authorities would not hear of it. Again the reply came that the family was "inadmissible."

When the invasion of Poland began, Chaim was supplied with funds by his brother and fled to Lithuania. Shortly afterwards, he cabled Simon to "do everything possible" to send a visa that would allow him to buy tickets on the trans-Siberian railway to safety in Japan or Shanghai. Simon immediately travelled to Ottawa to plead his case personally with Blair. The director would not see him. Nor would the immigration minister, Thomas Crerar. For two days, Simon went from office to office with no success. Eventually he met a junior immigration officer who took down the details of his brother's situation and promised "to be in touch." He never was.

In January 1941 Simon Kahane lost contact with his brother. Suddenly, in the latter part of 1942 a cable arrived from Chaim. Somehow, probably making good use of the money his brother had sent, Chaim and his family were now in Vichy France. The message both heartened and horrified Simon: "Send permit for your family otherwise we soon join Mother." It was heartening to Simon because it meant his brother and his family were still alive; it was horrifying because their mother had been killed by the Germans at the beginning of the war. Again a frenzied Simon pleaded and cajoled. It was now, he knew, a race against time. He beset the Immigration Branch with letters; he wrote the prime minister; he met with Jewish Immigrant Aid Society and Canadian Jewish Congress officials; he hired lawyers—but it was all to no avail.

In Febrary 1943 Chaim Kahane, his wife and four children were rounded up by French police, transported to Auschwitz and gassed.[1]

The Allied governments were largely aware by 1943 of what was happening to the Jews of Europe. Not only did they get detailed information from the Polish government-in-exile about events in Eastern Europe, but their own intelligence sources confirmed the Polish government's stories. It was apparent to the Allies that something would have to be done. But what? Already they had issued a declaration denouncing the massacres, but this was hardly the appropriate response to the slaughter of millions, and both the British and American governments were coming under increasing pressure from many quarters to do more.

Reluctantly, the British created a cabinet-level committee on Jewish refugees, but the difficulties confronting the committee were made quite clear at its first meeting. Almost before the members were in their seats, the home secretary announced that Britain could not accept any more than a few thousand Jews as "there was considerable anti-Semitism" in Britain; if it accepted more, it would "be in for serious trouble." As well, because Palestine, according to Oliver Stanley, the colonial secretary, would not be permitted to take any more Jews, the only havens in the empire might be the Dominions and the colonies. At its next meeting, the Dominions secretary, Clement Attlee, dashed that hope: he reported that the only Dominion close enough to help was Canada, but that it had already accepted five hundred refugees and "would take no more." The committee then concluded that the only succour available to Jews might be the United States, and decided to approach the Americans to see if they would help in relieving the refugee problem in Spain and Portugal. As an afterthought, British officials also decided to ask Canada if it would accept more refugees. They did not expect a positive response, and they were not disappointed.[2]

On receiving the British request, Norman Robertson, under-secretary of state for External Affairs, asked Blair to specify what Canada had done on behalf of Jewish refugees, and warned King that Canada should make some contribution "towards the solution of this pressing problem." It "concerns at present," Robertson said, "non-Jewish refugees probably to as large an extent as Jews. . . . The problem obviously transcends the normal limits within which immigration questions are considered." The director of immigration, however, thought differently. Although he conceded that only "several hundred" Jews had entered Canada since 1939, he pointed out that Canada had shown "favourable treatment" to the Jews since 1919 and that most refugees in Canada were Jewish. This was so, he added, because "no other race" had exhibited such a fanatic "desire to get away from Europe prior to the outbreak of war" and because of the "well-known ability of Jewish people to organize and carry out movements." If Canada did assist the refugees, Blair cautioned Robertson, it must set "some ratio of Jews to non-Jews, otherwise the former will, as in the past, succeed in filling a large part of the quota set"; Blair pointed out the "considerable uneasiness" in Canada over the possibility of more Jewish refugees arriving.[3]

Concerned that the government might in fact submit to the British request, Blair told his minister that the "refugee problem . . . is almost wholly a Jewish problem," even though the cabinet might not think so. He pleaded with Crerar to inform his colleagues that it would be "impossible" to set "a reasonable racial balance" because Jews always found a way around these ratios. As if to underscore Blair's fear of unremitting British pressure, on the day before the cabinet met to discuss the issue, the British again officially asked Canada to accept more refugees.[4]

Blair need not have worried. In his report on the refugee crisis to the cabinet, Robertson wholly accepted the director of immigration's arguments. He told the cabinet that the refugee problem was largely a Jewish one and that Canada had done much for the Jews since the First World War. He warned that the admission of refugees would give the advantage to Jews over non-Jews, and recommended that Canada not give preference to the admission of "close relatives" in dealing with refugees. "In the case of Jews," he said, "this often means that the entry is allowed of Eastern European Jews of not a high standard of education and skill in preference to Jews from Central and Western Europe possessed of greater attainments . . . since the great bulk of Jewish immigration to Canada had come from Eastern Europe." The cabinet accepted Robertson's suggestion that it not accept any refugees until the United States had responded to the British request. Although it was not discussed at the meeting, the cabinet decision was made easier by a public-opinion poll released that same day by the Canadian Institute of Public Opinion. It reported that a vast majority of Canadians were opposed to the full-scale immigration of Europeans to Canada. Fully eighty per cent of those responding to the poll opposed any attempt to bring large numbers of immigrants to Canada. Copies of the poll were made available to the ministers at the meeting.[5]

While Canada dallied and searched for reasons not to admit refugees, the British were mounting an energetic campaign to involve the Americans in helping alleviate the refugee crisis. After careful consideration by the Foreign and Colonial offices and by the British cabinet, a memorandum was sent to Washington outlining the British position and pleading for American assistance. The British admitted that it was "impossible" for them to deal with situation without help. They pointed out that the problem was not "wholly Jewish," that others were suffering as well, and they warned that "Allied criticism would probably result if any marked preference were shown in removing Jews" from enemy territory. "There is also a distinct danger," the memorandum went on, "of stimulating anti-Semitism in areas where an excessive number of foreign Jews are introduced." The British feared most that the Nazis might "change over from a policy of extermination to one of extrusion, and aim as they did before the war at embarrassing other countries by flooding them with alien immigrants." Yet, the statement continued, it is "impossible to make merely a negative response [to pleas] to rescue people threatened by Germany's extermination policy." Patting its own back, Britain claimed that she and her colonies had already done everything they could for the refugees and that it was time for the United States to offer some assistance or, at the very least, to agree to "some kind of private conference . . . with the minimum of publicity."[6]

It was a significant memorandum, a document that the historian Bernard Wasserstein would describe as "one of the fullest and most considered British statements of policy on the refugee problem." And the Americans took their time responding to it. Indeed, they took so long that the British government despaired. It even contemplated "a major gesture"—admitting a large number of refugees to shock the United States and Canada into following suit. Cooler heads prevailed, however, and the British cabinet decided to wait to hear from its overseas allies. Meanwhile, it again approached the Canadians and Americans through their representatives in London and urged them to convey to their home governments "the precise urgency and scope of the question." In addition, the British suggested to the Americans that a conference of all the Allied countries be held in London to consider the refugee problem, and that, in the interim, both countries issue a number of special visas to refugees in neutral countries.[7]

On February 25, 1943, the Americans finally responded—much to the chagrin of the British, via a press release. It was an anodyne reply. The United States detailed its massive contribution to the refugee cause since 1933 and claimed it could do no more because it was "bound by legislation enacted by Congress."[8] The Americans were agreeable to a meeting with the British, as long as the refugee problem would not be considered "as being confined to persons of any particular race or faith." What was most shocking to the Canadians, however, was that the American government suggested that Ottawa be the site for this meeting.

Both the British and the Canadians were annoyed, the British, because the Americans had made its response public and so had made it appear, in the words of one disgruntled British official, that they "had taken the initiative"; the Canadians, because Ottawa had been suggested without even the pretense of a consultation. The State Department apologized "profusely" to the Canadian government for the oversight, but only after Lester Pearson, representing Canada in Washington, had chastised his American counterpart. He also informed Ottawa that the British embassy people were also "mystified" and "embarrassed" by the Americans' behaviour. Officially, the British government itself told the Canadians that they were "caught by surprise" by the American reply and were bewildered over the choice of Ottawa. They were curious, however, about whether or not the Canadian government had been consulted and whether it might allow the meeting to proceed in Ottawa. Robertson hurriedly assured them that Canada had not been approached by the Americans, nor was it anxious to host any meeting.[9]

Pearson also informed his superiors that the British had expressed their dismay to the Americans, who were nevertheless "unrepentant." According to American Under-Secretary of State Sumner Welles, "British propaganda had attempted to show that the United Kingdom had done far more than any other country to solve the refugee problem." The American response, he claimed "was designed to correct this impression." Pearson also warned Robertson that, if Canada wished to abort the selection of Ottawa, it should begin making representations "at once."[10] The British agreed to meet the Americans in Ottawa if Canada was agreeable, but it was quite apparent to London that Canada "was furious at the United States choosing Ottawa" and that it was likely that Canada would try to have the venue changed. In any case, the British Foreign Office saw the conference as simply an American "political ploy" to placate its restive Jewish population.[11]

Political ploy or not, Canada was now unexpectedly thrust front and centre into a refugee drama that it preferred to sit out. The British Foreign Office fully understood the Canadian dilemma. As it pointed out, "Apart from injured feelings [at not being consulted], holding a conference there might draw attention to their own refugee record." The Canadian cabinet even feared being invited to attend the conference. Canadian newspapers were already trumpeting loudly that Canada had agreed to host and participate in a conference to help alleviate the refugee problem. A harried Robertson quickly reassured the cabinet that Canada knew nothing about these arrangements. Privately, he confided to Malcolm MacDonald, the British high commissioner, that Ottawa would not be an "acceptable location" for such a meeting: an Ottawa conference, he explained, would "lead to misunderstandings and possible awkward questions in Parliament and publicity in the press." As there was "a regular guerrilla warfare" between External Affairs and Immigration over the refugee question, a meeting in Ottawa would "add to the embarrassment."[12]

The news of a possible Allied attempt to save some refugees once again electrified the North American Jewish community. A "monster rally" was quickly organized by various American Jewish organizations, to be held in Madison Square Garden in New York City. Approximately fifty thousand demonstrators milled inside and outside the Garden, listening to prominent speakers urging both their government and that of Palestine to open their doors to the ravaged Jews of Europe.[13] Among those present was a Canadian External Affairs official who reported back to his superiors on how moving the occasion was. Yet, what stuck in his mind, he added, was the gall of American Jews who "would dream of rescuing the dying Jews of Europe by asking them to seek refuge in Palestine."[14]

The Jewish response in Canada was, predictably, more restrained and hesitant. On hearing of the putative conference, Congress director Saul Hayes arranged an extraordinary off-the-record interview with Robertson. As soon as he was ushered into the under-secretary's office, Robertson treated him as a long-lost friend. He assured him that he personally supported the Jewish case for increased immigration; although he thought the Ottawa meeting would have "a good deal of trouble . . . in starting off . . . under favourable auspices" because of the "indiscreet statement" by the Americans, he believed there was some hope of success. Surprisingly, he told Hayes that "at no time has the Canadian government been so susceptible to pressure as it is at the present time." According to Hayes, he suggested to the Jewish community that it might obtain success if it "exerted . . . sufficient pressure." Robertson urged the Canadian Jewish Congress to send briefs to the government that were "specific." "The humanitarian side," Robertson said, "will not move the government . . . to the same degree as the factual story of numbers taken by the United States, the United Kingdom and other countries." "If Canada has not done its share," he assured Hayes, "then something might be done to rectify this." Above all the under-secretary stressed that Jewish requests, "to be effective, must cite chapter and verse of what other countries have done."[15]

To Hayes's astonishment, Robertson also shared the Jewish community's low opinion of the Immigration Branch. When Hayes informed him of that department's record of refusing Jewish children from France and, later, Spain, because of the family unit rule, Robertson seemed sympathetic. Such a policy meant, Hayes told him, "that if you cannot save two people then it is better that both perish than one be saved," and Robertson nodded and added clearly that "some missionary work" was necessary amongst Immigration officials. After the interview Hayes concluded that the under-secretary was "more than sympathetic to the plight of refugees and to the idea that Canada should agree to take a goodly number." Hayes also felt that Robertson was "a bit ashamed of Canada's not too generous policy of the past." "If left to Robertson," Hayes believed, Canada "would be giving refuge to many."

On March 9, 1943, the executive of the Canadian Jewish Congress held an emergency meeting in Montreal to plan strategy for the upcoming Ottawa conference. Representatives arrived from all over Canada. After several hours of heated discussion, a program was drafted that would govern the activities of Canadian Jewry. The purpose of the program would be to mobilize public opinion in Canada for the admission of Jewish refugees and to point out to Canadians why Jews were more in need of rescue than were any "other of the conquered peoples of Europe." The Congress's plan of attack was twofold: the Congress itself would undertake a petition campaign which every Jew in Canada would sign, would mobilize all pro-refugee groups in the country and would lobby the governments attending the conference to admit more Jews; as a complement to this, it would create an "inter-denominational and non-partisan" committee which would sponsor radio programs, issue press releases, coordinate a media advertising campaign, organize a day of prayer for both Christians and Jews and sponsor tours by pro-refugee speakers. As well, the latter group would deal with the religious bodies, particularly the Catholic Church, and would lobby various politicians and labour and other organizations. The entire cost of this campaign would be borne by the Jewish community.[16]

At the outset of the meeting there had been considerable opposition by those who had always opposed mass demonstrations as counter-productive. Even the most faint-hearted, however, were won over when messages were read from Nachum Goldmann, head of the World Jewish Congress, and Joseph Hyman, of the Joint Distribution Committee, stating that leaders of the Jewish community in the free world were planning to attend the conference and wished to coordinate all Jewish activity with the Congress. They called for a large-scale campaign in Canada which would "dove-tail" with the activities planned by the World Jewish Congress.[17]

Meanwhile, Jewish leaders in both the United States and Britain were informing Hayes that their "government sources" were clearly concerned that Canada would not allow the meetings to take place in Ottawa. Hayes himself wrote Robertson telling him of their concern. He pleaded with the under-secretary to put to rest these fears and to associate Canada "with the noble and practical objectives of the projected meeting." Robertson's reply was noncommittal.[18]

The pressure was indeed mounting in Canada to allow the meetings to be held in Ottawa. Throughout the country editorialists were delighted that Canada was to host such a significant conference. Some church leaders castigated Canada for delaying its response. Not since the debate over whether to attend the Evian Conference had the Canadian government faced such fierce pressure. In a curious letter to his superiors, an official of the British High Commission in Ottawa wrote that there was "considerable" pressure on the Canadian government, "especially from the English-language press." Significantly, the French-language press has, he added, "lined up solidly against the idea of finding a home for any large number of refugees." The letter then made a final gratuitous—and incorrect—claim: the Zionists "do not appear to have granted [their] support to the campaign [because] . . . in rescuing numbers of European Jews, Canadian Jews fear that they may risk becoming the victims of anti-Semitic campaigns in Canada."[19]

Aside from the Canadian government, there were others shocked by the choice of Ottawa. *Der Tag*, for instance, was outraged. "Why should such a conference involving Jewish refugees," it pointedly asked, "be held in a country like Canada whose record in admitting Jews is terrible?" Also outraged, and yet at the same time aware that he might score some easy public relations points, Hayes made a stinging response to the paper, sending a copy of his letter to both Robertson and Blair. He castigated *Der Tag* for its narrow-minded view and claimed that Canada's record, "though bad, was no worse than any other country's." Holding the meeting in Ottawa, the Congress director said, might force the Canadian government "to do something," and he chided the editors with their naivety: "Where would the ideal locale for a conference be? Perhaps the ideal place is on another planet. Let's have the conference and work for its success and not worry too much whether it is in Ottawa (whose record of immigration generosity is bleak) or anywhere else. . . . We don't know the views of the capitals of Saturn,

Venus or Jupiter, but presumably they will be tough also."[20]

The Canadian government, meanwhile, was keeping a low profile. Although it did not accept the choice of Ottawa, it could not, for political reasons, refuse. The less said about the selection, the better. Thus External Affairs totally ignored the projected conference. It neither asked the Americans why they chose Ottawa, nor did it ask the British to intervene. The hope of the Canadian government, of course, was that if it ignored the matter it might go away. Thus, when the British high commisioner asked Robertson whether either the Canadian or American governments had "followed up" on the Ottawa site, he was reassured that neither had. The British had previously assured Pearson that they would not force the Ottawa choice on an unwilling Canada. As well, the British government was itself getting cold feet about an Ottawa venue, especially after receiving a warning from Myron Taylor, a delegate at Evian and now a member of the Intergovernmental Committee on Refugees, that a conference in Canada might "result in unexpected developments and commitments." "Certain it is," Taylor predicted, "that it will bring out a great Jewish gathering in Ottawa."[21]

Domestic agitation for a conference was increasing in Britain. Already a parliamentary debate was being scheduled for March 23 to discuss the Commonwealth's refugee policy and the future of the Ottawa conference. The British were anxious to know Canada's refugee record since 1933 and, particularly, its views on the projected conference. Looking for help, Norman Robertson asked Blair to detail Canada's record and, above all, to recommend "the line which [he] would like the Government spokesmen to take in the [House of] Lords about the proposed Ottawa conference." Predictably, Blair saw no need for such a meeting and pointed out that since 1933 Canada had accepted at least forty-five hundred Jewish refugees. "Perhaps," Blair added, "we should do more, but looking over the record and comparing it with our population, I think our contribution to the refugee problem has already been worthwhile."[22]

It was now quite apparent that the Canadian ploy had worked. By refusing to be drawn into discussions on the conference, the government had made it obvious that Ottawa had no intention of hosting it—or even attending it. The British government, after getting no answer to even a direct question, had no choice but to inform the Americans that the Canadians "obviously did not want the conversations to be held in Ottawa." Slyly, the British then asked the Americans if Washington "would not be a convenient locale"? The American response was predictable. Choosing Washington, or London for that matter, would, in the words of Secretary of State Hull, "give rise to a good deal of embarrassing public agitation." It was now clear that the meeting would have to be held in a site far from the centres of Jewish population, where the participating countries would not be subject to "public pressure." The British suggested Bermuda. The Americans accepted at once.[23]

And no one was more relieved than the Canadians. Pearson exultantly wired Robertson that the pressure was off and that, "in the circumstances," Ottawa was no longer "a possibility." And, he added, of even greater importance, Canada would not even be asked to take part in the conference. Especially gratified was Mackenzie King, who, since the Americans had first broached the idea of an Ottawa conference, had been subjected to unsettling questions in the House concerning Canada's position. To each he had replied that the American document was only "a working paper," and that Canada was keeping all of its options open and would not actively seek participation in such a conference. He, for one, was glad Canada could again go back to the sidelines.[24]

It also seemed that the Americans were now having second thoughts about getting involved. In a personal letter to Roosevelt, Cordell Hull stated that, because of the Canadian attitude, the proposed meeting would be moved from Ottawa to Bermuda. He warned the president that the United States was, however, under "great pressure" from various groups throughout the country to be more forthcoming on the refugee issue and that there were "manifestations of a deep sentiment on the part of the Jewish elements of [the] population."[25] Four days later Roosevelt and Hull met with Anthony Eden to firm up arrangements for the Bermuda Conference. They asked the British foreign secretary what to do about those Jews in Hungary, Bulgaria and elsewhere in southeastern Europe who were "threatened with extermination." Eden warned that it would be impossible to offer any solace to the Jews of that area. "If we do that, then the Jews of the world will be wanting us to make similar offers in Poland and Germany," he explained. "Hitler might well take us up on any such offer, and there simply are not enough ships and means of transportation in the world to handle them."[26] They decided they could do nothing until the Bermuda Conference.

Meanwhile, the Canadian Jewish community was busy organizing its campaign to coincide with the Ottawa conference. Committees were organized, influential members of the community were contacted and plans were underway for the "biggest petition campaign" in Canadian history.[27] At last, the Jews of Canada were being given their chance. The eyes and ears of the world would be focused on Ottawa for the duration of the meeting; Canadian Jewry was determined not to fail. By sheer force of numbers, rather than by force of argument, they would bring the cause of European Jewry to the attention of the Allied leaders, to say nothing of their own government.

No one in government circles had bothered to tell the Canadian Jewish Congress, first, that the conference would not be held in Canada and, second, that Canada would not go to Bermuda. It was not until a distraught Cairine Wilson phoned Hayes that the Jewish community was made aware of the sudden turn of events. Hayes concluded that there was "no point" to any campaign if Canada was neither hosting nor attending the conference, while Ben Sadowski, a prominent Toronto Jewish leader, announced that he would oppose the "spending of a tremendous amount of money on a nebulous project." Only on March 30 did Robertson officially inform Hayes that Canada would not be going to Bermuda because the United States' and Britain's aim was so limited: they wished only to "survey the situation," Robertson explained, "[to] see if there is any purpose in calling on other governments to act." The conference would "not be [like] Evian," he added; it was only "exploratory" and "preparatory," and Canada was not even going as an "observer." Once again, Jewish hopes had been dashed.[28]

With Canada's refusal to play a role in the refugee conference, the Canadian Jewish Congress set about rethinking its strategy. In a long policy statement Hayes urged Congress leaders not to accept defeat lightly. He admitted that the Bermuda Conference was likely a "fruitless" exercise; but Canadian Jewry, he insisted, must work in concert with their brethren in America and Britain to make sure the conference would not be "detrimental . . . to the cause of European Jewry . . . by acting as a soporific and serving to lose valuable time in the course of which our fellow Jews in Europe are massacred by the thousands daily." Above all, he urged that Canada must be forced to "set an example for the whole world" by agreeing to allow in a large number of refugees. He pointed out, however, that the Canadian government was likely to use Bermuda as "an excuse" for doing nothing. Though he hoped that non-Jewish groups would be in the vanguard, he noted sadly: "Such representative and 'safe' leaders of Canadian public opinion have not evinced any interest in the entire question which is, itself, a sad commentary on the callousness of the citizenry and, consequently, the Government of our country."[29]

Having raised the hopes of Canadian Jewry, the Congress felt it had no choice but to carry on the campaign. But it also knew that Jews alone could not sway government policy. Only "influential members"—non-Jewish ones—of Canadian society could interest Canadian policy-makers in the Jewish refugee issue, Hayes glumly informed the Congress president. He also planned to continue the petition campaign which he felt was part of "a much larger scheme." "The petition has a specific role," Hayes said, "which is the maintenance of interest factor. Moreover it will be the 'mise en scene' but not the play."[30]

What was most encouraging to the Jewish community was the response of Canadian newspapers. The vast majority of the English-language press was condemning the pusillanimous behaviour of the Canadian government and decrying the extent of native anti-Semitism. "The sacrifice Canadians . . . are making," wrote the editor of *Saturday Night*, "will have no enduring value . . . unless we can get rid of the unreasonable and unChristian racial prejudices which have bedevilled us for more than a generation."[31] And even more forthright was the *Winnipeg Free Press*:

> It would be encouraging, indeed, to hear some day very soon that the Canadian Government was taking active steps to open our country's doors to the victims of murderous Nazi persecution who, by some miracle, escape from the clutches of tyranny that seeks to destroy them. . . . But what will it avail them if the gate being opened, the doors of the free countries remained bolted in their faces? . . . It would be the occasion of rejoicing if Canada led the way. It would be a permanent blot and shame upon us, if the chance, being offered, we rejected it. . . . The government can, by the stroke of a pen, legalize the entry into this country of whatever it chooses of those wretched, starved and penniless people. . . . The horrifying racial persecution that marks the spread of Nazi conquest has had its counterpart . . . in the restrictive rulings which . . . have completely destroyed the basic conception of sanctuary among western civilized people. . . .

> Anti-Semitism, shameful though it must be to admit it, has far too large a footing among Canadians. . . . Gross prejudice and gross exaggeration sadly mark every discussion of the historically fateful Jewish problem. . . . The percentage of persons of the Jewish race in Canada is 1.56. . . . We . . . have a duty which we can neglect at our peril.[32]

The Canadian government was, however, implacable. Pressure from Jewish groups and their sympathizers had been faced —and withstood—before. Editorials could be ignored. As long as the vast majority of Canadians and the provincial governments remained silent—and they did—the Canadian government did not have to move. And no one understood this better than did the leadership of the Jewish community. After the initial optimism and excitement over the putative Ottawa conference, Canadian Jewry was again depressed and cynical. Its leaders knew they had been, in the words of Louis Rosenberg, a Congress official, "had." As he confessed to Hayes, "Ostensibly the Canadian Government will not attend because it is not invited. Actually . . . the Government would have felt very much embarrassed if it were invited, and must feel quite relieved at this way out. No international conference concerning refugees and migration can be of any use unless countries like Canada which will eventually have to absorb some of the population are officially present and take part." Like most of his colleagues in the Congress, Rosenberg realized that the choice of Bermuda was "ominous" for the cause of the Jews: "As good a place to bury our hopes as any," he said. Nonetheless, he warned that Canadian Jews "must not throw up [their] hands." "We must do everything we can do," he declared, "to crystallize vague sympathy into action."[33]

American Jewish leaders had also lost hope. At a meeting with their under-secretary of state, Sumner Welles, and Anthony Eden, they were told by the British foreign secretary that their goals—of establishing sanctuaries in Allied and neutral countries for refugees and of opening up Palestine, the United States and the British Commonwealth to those who had managed to escape Hitler—were "fantastically impossible of achievement." According to one of the Jewish representatives at the meeting, when the suggestions were made Eden "froze into a state of almost complete immobility." Somewhat later Welles privately told the Jewish leaders that he did not share Eden's opinions. Embittered, the delegation felt Welles was merely playing "smart politics," in that the Americans knew that "the buck [could] now be passed quite confidently to the British." At the same time Roosevelt met another Jewish delegation and told it that "the shipping situation was not the bottleneck . . . since there were hundreds of ships proceeding to the continent which were returning empty for more cargo." Jews left convinced, however, that the American president would do nothing to fill those ships with refugees.[34]

After these meetings American Jewish leaders came away convinced more than ever that the Bermuda Conference would be "a farce and a fraud." At a meeting with Hayes, they said that it would accomplish nothing and that it was meant "simply to forestall great clamor and merely to capture and then channel the emotion of the present time." It was, they said, "a ploy to the public and meant nothing." Nonetheless, like their counterparts in Canada, these Jewish leaders were determined to mobilize public opinion at home "so that it would be impossible for the Conference to fail." They also urged Hayes to form a "distinguished committee" in Canada to support resolutions to "open Canada's doors," and to keep in close contact with the appropriate British and American lobbying groups.[35]

Immediately on his return to Montreal, Hayes began his task. As usual, all he could do was write letters. Everything else had already been tried—and had failed. Writing to Jewish leaders across the nation, he urged them to get behind the petition campaign. It was, he said, "one of the largest undertakings of Congress in its . . . history. Its objective is securing the signed support of *all* the Jews of this country. . . . This does not mean many or even a majority. . . . What is required is *all* the available signatures."[36]

Then, following the advice of his American colleagues, Hayes composed a letter to the Canadian National Committee on Refugees asking it to set up various subcommittees to lobby members of Parliament and church, labour and business groups; to sponsor media campaigns and speaking tours; to gather pro-refugee resolutions from "influential" organizations; and, in effect, to take over the lobbying activities of the Congress. Naturally, he finished, these activities would be subsidized by the Congress. What was most discouraging, he said, was how unresponsive the Canadian people had been. He noted that only the press had been active—"Over three score newspapers have devoted editorials to the plight of the Jews in Europe." "But more is necessary," he added, "if one of the great peoples of the world is not to be exterminated utterly. . . . Every day's delay in dealing directly with this problem sees the death by famine and by massacre of thousands of innocent Jews." If only Canada would admit some Jews, he pleaded, this "would encourage other U.N. and neutral countries to follow suit."[37]

Two days later the CNCR submitted a brief to the prime minister, pointing out that, while Canada was doing "remarkable" work for the war effort, it had failed to do its "share in actively rescuing those who by intervention on our part would have been saved." While other countries, it noted, had evinced their humanity "by saving the hunted and the ravaged, . . . Canada has done little." The committee pleaded with King to accept refugees from neutral countries "to save them from slaughter and torture."[38] There was no response; there was nothing to say.

On the following day—the day before the start of the Bermuda Conference—Hayes went to see the prime minister. He wished to discuss with King the refugee issue and to get from him a favourable declaration, which "would be publicized at the opening of the Bermuda Conference." Not surprisingly, on his arrival at the Prime Minister's Office, Hayes was told that the scheduled meeting had been cancelled and that King would be "unavailable" for the forseeable future. All the downcast Hayes could do was to leave with the prime minister's secretary a copy of a Congress memorandum calling for "an inspiring demonstration of sincerity and good will" on the part of the Canadian government, that is, admission of refugees into Canada.[39] Once again, there was no reply.

Yet, surprisingly, some Jews had not lost faith in King or his government. The Toronto philanthropist Ben Sadowski bitterly opposed any type of campaign that might embarrass the government. The strategy outlined by the Congress, he suggested, "would involve tremendous costs and when it was all done, I would see no purpose that it would serve." He denounced the petition as an "emotional programme." If the Jewish community, he added, "knew we were spending a fabulous sum of money to relieve their emotions, . . . they would recognize . . . that it was a most impractical useless expenditure." He called the Congress plans "impractical and ridiculous." King, he announced, had his full confidence. "I think it is our duty to find out what Mr. King thinks," Sadowski said. "I have maintained from the start that that would guide our efforts completely and absolutely because if Mackenzie King expressed a favourable attitude, and I cannot believe he would do otherwise, and that the only reason he has not come out of the wide open spaces and shouted it from the housetops is probably due to the political exigencies of the moment." Sadowski pleaded with Hayes not to be guided by Jews in Britain or America—because "their population and political situation is different." The Congress, he demanded, should be guided by the political exigencies at home.[40]

Stunned by Sadowski's bitter response, Hayes felt betrayed. Everything he had tried had failed; every suggested step he had cleared with Congress officers. As he admitted to himself, there were Jews who would remain loyal to the Liberal party "through hell and high water." Nonetheless, he had no alternative but to decipher somehow King's private views on the Congress's strategy. He phoned Cairine Wilson for advice. Within an hour she responded that she had been told unofficially by Norman Robertson "that a certain amount of publicity will do no harm." Gratified, Hayes then called a staff meeting to plan another publicity campaign. This time, he suggested, the campaign and resolutions should be "non-political," their appeal "humanitarian not legislative." It was recommended by David Rome, the Congress publicity director, that Jews should not carry out "any programme among the 'goyim' " and that a "pro-Jewish committee of 'Gentiles' " be set up to lobby for Jewish causes. As that had already been tried with little success, the meeting ended with no new ideas. It was clear to all those present, as well as to most Canadian Jews, that no campaign could succeed until the government wished it to.[41]

On April 19, 1943, on the eve of the Jewish Passover and on the day when the final struggle of the doomed Jews of the Warsaw ghetto began, the Bermuda Conference opened. Canada had not been invited, but had been put on warning by the British government that it would be expected to admit two thousand refugees. It had also been put on warning by French Canada. *Le Devoir* castigated King for not demanding "avec insistance et fermeté" that Canada attend the conference in that Canada would likely be asked to accept refugees. Other Quebec newspapers cautioned the prime minister that he had best keep his guard up lest the Allies attempt to "dump" a large number of Jews in Canada's lap. Would it not be in Canada's interest, they wondered, to attend the conference to insure that the "Jewish problem" was solved by other countries? In any case, King had long ago been informed by the British that the conference would not amount to much. The objectives of the meeting, the Dominions Office told King, were limited. All Britain was prepared to discuss was the setting up of some camps in North Africa to receive refugees from Iberia, the convocation of an international conference at a later date, and, finally, a joint declaration that refugees were a problem for the United Nations. With such restricted goals, had it been invited, Canada would likely have attended. There was no reason not to. It was clear that neither the Americans nor the British could—or, indeed, even wanted to—solve the refugee problem.[42]

For world Jewry the Bermuda Conference was a fatal betrayal. After months of frenetic lobbying and zealous activity, Jews had literally forced the Great Powers to acknowledge responsibility for solving the refugee crisis. Yet, in the crunch, all the British and Americans would do was send some delegates to meet on a semi-tropical island to talk in general terms about the problem without in any way coming to grips with it. From the outset both nations had ruled out any idea of attempting to rescue Jews from occupied Europe and both were determined not to accept any significant number of new refugees.[43] As a result, the head of the British delegation, Richard Law, warned Eden as soon as the conference began that the results would be so "meagre" that he had told the British representatives to keep "on as good terms as possible with the press"; otherwise, he cautioned, "they will murder us." Though he knew the conference would be "abortive," Law nonetheless saw some benefits emerging from it: "The Americans are here seeking our support to enable them to state unpalatable facts to their own public opinion. It shall be correspondingly helpful to us to be able to enlist their support against our own Archbishops. For this negative, but not unimportant point of view, I think some good may come out of Bermuda."[44] This, it seemed, would be the only good to come from the meeting.

After ten days of discussion a press release was issued stating that the two countries had both reached agreement on certain "concrete" proposals, but these would remain secret. In fact, the proposals—thirteen in number—dealt largely with technical matters, such as, revitalizing the rather ineffectual Intergovernmental Committee on Refugees and involving the United Nations. There were also some references to admitting small numbers of refugees to North Africa, Britain and the United States. It was, as Law foresaw, an "abortive" conference. Not one single refugee would be saved as a result of its deliberations. As the British delegation privately conceded, "So far as immediate relief to refugees is concerned, the conference was able to achieve very little." All that Canada was expected to do, according to the Dominions Office, would be to join in some amorphous declaration on the need to revive the committee created at Evian and to resettle "displaced nationals" who could not return to their native lands.[45]

Immediately following the conference, Robertson wrote the Congress. The prime minister hoped, he said, "that methods may be developed which will relieve the suffering of the Jews of Europe as rapidly as the circumstances of the war permit." There was no hint that Canada itself was prepared to help devise some of these "methods." Indeed, the attitude of the Canadian government had not escaped the attention of others. In a stinging editorial the *New York Times* attacked both the British and Canadian governments, which together, it argued, could still save a large number of Jews. "The truth is," it said, "the dead hand of yesterday's politics is still at the throat of the European Jews. The British Government can save these people but does not want to do so." European Jews could be saved not by "changing the immigration laws of the United States or by shipping them thousands of miles overseas to Australia or South America." Rather, they could be saved if both Britain and, especially, Canada were more receptive. It urged Canadians to "demand" that their government be more forthcoming.[46]

The director of the Immigration Branch was not impressed by the arguments in the *Times*. In a message to his minister and to officials in his department, Blair indicated that the newspaper should not be taken seriously because it was "controlled . . . and owned by Jewish interests." Their criticism, he added, "would be very much more effective if our Jewish friends were more popular where they live." He warned Crerar that the results of the Bermuda Conference would give "rise to a wave of protest and publicity directed by Jewish people" and that this "propaganda" should be ignored. Its aim, he stated, was to show that Canada and the Allies had done "nothing" for Jewish refugees but that "the solution could be readily found . . . if the Allied Governments wanted to do so." Above all, Blair feared that Canada would be flooded by Jews because of their innate "ability to move . . . once an open door [was] obtained." Jews should be saved where "possible," he added, but "semi-hysterical statements that ignore the real difficulties sow seeds of distrust and dissension and create the impression that the salvation of the Jews rather than the successful prosecution of the war, should be the Allies' main concern." Canada, he concluded, must continue to act as before.[47] But Blair was not entirely convinced that it would be possible to keep Jews out of Canada. As he told a member of Parliament, "Jewish people are usually first on the move, and, therefore, nearest the door when the door is open". "This characteristic," he added, had "its origin in the many migrations of the Hebrew people."[48]

The failure of the Bermuda Conference again tore apart the fragile coalition among Canadian Jews. Yiddish-language newspapers, *landsmannschaften*, rabbis, Zionists and other community leaders were raising questions about the effectiveness of the Congress. Even Congress officials themselves were voicing doubts. A pained Caiserman suggested to Hayes that it was time to take off the gloves and urge on the community "spontaneous action." Canadian Jews, he warned, are "instinctively pressing for action," and the Congress must take the lead before the community turns its "ears to other active groups." Fearful that Jewish leadership would fall into "irresponsible" hands and that their activities would be "counter-productive," Hayes warned against panic. No one had expected much from the conference, so that logically no one was overly shocked by its results. "The Canadian Jewish Congress must continue its policy and its program as if there had been no Bermuda Conference," he added. Especially the petition campaign, Hayes insisted, must proceed. "The Canadian Jewish public," he told a dubious Sadowski, must be allowed "to state its case." The petition was important both as "a matter of self-respect" and as "a matter of assuaging public opinion." "If only a few thousand lives can be saved by the dramatic pressure of our campaign," he claimed, "then this will justify the bustle, the noise and the activity."[49]

Sadowski was not assuaged. The petition campaign, he again charged, was "a lot of fuss by people who should be able to find more positive and constructive things to do," and, besides, it "will not save any lives." Though, he continued, it was "a lot of wasted time and effort and will do absolutely no good," he would "watch efforts with interest from the sidelines." By contrast, at the executive meeting of the eastern division of the Congress, Hayes came under attack from some delegates for not proceeding with greater haste on the petition campaign and for not having done "enough" on the refugee issue. Others felt that the petition was useless—"everyone knows that Jews are in favour of admitting refugees"—but after a bitter debate, it was agreed to go forward with the campaign.[50]

A despondent Hayes told Sadowski: "we are damned if we do and we are damned if we don't." Jewish organizations, he explained, "will not be satisfied until something is done." Since, he argued, the petition will do "no harm," and, in fact, is "an essential action for our self-respect," then it is a "worthwhile" project. He reminded Sadowski that the Congress, "as the instrument of Canadian Jewish activity, should not be allowed to become a bureaucracy." The petition should go forward, "even if it only does the Jewish groups in this country some good."[51]

Meanwhile, Hayes was also fighting a rear-guard action with his own immediate superiors in Montreal, Congress president Samuel Bronfman and FPJ president Lazarus Phillips. Hayes had wanted to send a strong response to Robertson's letter of May 7; it was, he said, "high time we looked at pious statements offering help and put them in their proper perspective." But both Bronfman and Phillips felt that Hayes's draft was "too argumentative." They pointed in particular to a section in the letter in which Hayes had told Robertson that Canada could act alone—without Allied cooperation—to admit Jews from Spain and Portugal because Portuguese steamers were available to ferry "eight hundred and one thousand" people. In addition, he had asked the government to loosen up "its rigorous standards of pre-war days" and allow in Jewish children from Iberia whose parents might still be alive. It was a hard-hitting letter—too hard-hitting, it seemed, for the leadership of the Canadian Jewish Congress.[52]

Hayes was ordered to redraft his response and, reluctantly, he did so. Swallowing hard, the Congress director sent out a letter over Bronfman's signature that referred to the "friendly attitude" toward refugees of the prime minister and which thanked Canada for approaching this issue "in a spirit of sincere sympathy." The letter did, however, take up King's hope that "methods might be developed" to assist refugees, and it set out some possible steps Canada might adopt including admitting refugees from Spain and Portugal. Robertson's reply was succinct. There was little he could add to what he had already said in his previous letter, but he was grateful for Bronfman's suggestions and for the "friendly" tone of his letter.[53] Perhaps the Congress letter would have been less friendly had Bronfman been aware of a meeting in another government office on the same day Robertson was sending his response. In a discussion with the Dutch chargé d'affaires, who was inquiring whether Dutch Jews in neutral countries could be granted asylum in Canada, Blair stated that "Jews and other undesirable elements" would never be admitted to Canada.[54]

Nor was President Roosevelt more forthcoming. In his private response to the Bermuda Conference he told Hull that the United States must "comply strictly" with its immigration regulations and that he thought it "extremely unwise" to send a large number of Jews to North Africa. As well, the British informed King that to avoid "pressure" it would issue no statement on the conference. The British saw the conference as a "success" as it would require of them "no magnificent gesture" and no change in their immigration policy.[55]

Like Evian, the Bermuda Conference in failure was a triumph for everyone concerned, save the person most affected, the hapless European Jew. For him there would be no salvation—no rescue attempts and no havens. His suffering might stir the free world, but not sufficiently. The Jew of Europe was in a world of his own where conventional moral standards did not apply. The Nazi massacres would continue unabated.

6

IN THE FREE AND CIVILIZED WORLD

The Bermuda Conference had successfully failed. Except for the few administrative changes cosmetically enlarging the scope of the Intergovernmental Committee's mandate to include refugees from all Nazi-controlled areas and the few expressions of sympathy, little was done. But the refugee crisis would worsen, all knew it, and Britain's delegates to the conference knew pro-refugee activists would not let up. One delegate warned London that "refugee enthusiasts, mainly Jewish-inspired," would settle for nothing less than mass rescue of the Jews in Hitler's hands. But this, he insisted, was impossible. Even if the complex diplomatic, military, financial and technical problems of any rescue could be ironed out, one undeniable fact remained: nothing could be done as long as "the present combination, in so many countries, of pity for Jews under German control and extreme reluctance to admit further Jews into their borders" persisted.[1]

This was no secret to Jewish leaders. The president of the Synagogue Council of America decried the fiasco at Bermuda as failure by design. "Victims are not being rescued," he charged, "because the democracies do not want them. . . . The job of the Bermuda conference, apparently, was not to rescue victims of the Nazi terror, but to rescue our State Department and the British Foreign Office from possible embarrassment."[2] Again the Jews of Europe seemed consigned to their fate. The liberation of Europe and the final revelation of the extent of the Jewish catastrophe still lay ahead; but this is not to say that information on what was happening in Europe was not available. Jewish officials in North America drew together the scattered threads of information to reveal a terrifying pattern of unchecked, systematic and unrelenting mass murder. In a seemingly indifferent and unbelieving world, it seemed impossible for Jewish leaders who knew the truth, who believed that truth, to make others heed it. Those Jews whom the Western world had denied admission now faced extinction, and there seemed no way of galvanizing governments, let alone the larger public, into any effort to rescue the few, largely in neutral Europe, who, Jewish leaders hoped, might still be saved. An escapee from Poland carried a bitter message to allied Jewry from those still trapped; his was the voice of those who would soon die: "Tell them [Jews outside Nazi-occupied countries] that there are moments when we hate them all; we hate them because they are safe 'there' and do not rescue us . . . because they do not do enough. We are only too well aware that in the free and civilized world outside, it is not possible to believe all that is happening to us. Let the Jewish people then do *something* that will force the world to believe us."[3]

If world Jewry proved ineffectual, it was not for lack of will. While American and British representatives met in secret session in Hamilton, Bermuda, Canadian Jewish leaders met in Montreal to assess their program and consider any options to encourage the removal of European Jewish refugees to Canada. As it became increasingly apparent that Bermuda would bring no relief, the mood at the Montreal meetings became pessimistic. Canadian Jewish Congress leaders knew only too well how unlikely it was that Canada would move any further or faster than its American or British allies. They also knew that, "in the final analysis, any plan of rescue must be based upon an offer of refuge for the victims of the Axis." There were no offers.

One slender hope persisted. If Canada could somehow be committed to some relief effort, no matter how small, perhaps, just perhaps, this might prove the thin edge of the refugee wedge. With more fanfare than enthusiasm a three-point proposal was drawn up by Saul Hayes and the Congress's United Jewish Refugee Agency and approved by the delegates in Montreal. The Canadian government should be approached, first to grant asylum to "a number of Jews, especially children, who may by this means find freedom from Axis slavery," second to initiate a scheme for sending food and medical supplies to the Jews of Europe (much as basic supplies were then entering and sustaining civilians in Nazi-occupied Greece) and, third, to make itself the standard bearer for international relief efforts on behalf of stricken European Jewry.[4] A letter outlining these approvals, signed by the national president of the Congress and the chairmen of the regional divisions, was sent to Prime

Minister King. A meeting in Ottawa attended by the Canadian National Committee on Refugees executive and several sympathetic members of Parliament dutifully endorsed the Jewish refugee agency's program; the members of Parliament pledged to raise the refugee problem in the House.[5] Nobody expected much from the exercise.

On the morning of June 4, 1943, almost two months after the Bermuda Conference, a Jewish delegation led by Samuel Bronfman and Saul Hayes was ushered into the office of Thomas Crerar to meet with the minister and his director of immigration. Blair, as always, kept his own notes of the discussion, which in this instance lasted just over an hour. Hayes, spokesman for the delegation, led off, expressing his disappointment at what he termed the "failure" of the Bermuda Conference. It was, however, this failure, Hayes argued, that now gave Canada the chance to "step out in the forefront and give a lead to the rest of the world."

The Congress director drew Crerar's attention to a case in point. In Portugal and Spain recent Jewish escapees from France, many of them children, remained in mortal danger. Although these Iberian countries were for the moment neutral in the European war, there was no guarantee they would remain so. If either or both were attacked by the Germans or coerced into war by the Axis powers, these escapees would surely fall into Nazi hands. If, on the other hand, these refugees could be transferred elsewhere and the Iberian Peninsula remain neutral, it was likely that Spain and Portugal would continue to shelter temporarily the trickle of refugees smuggled across the Pyrenees. By either scenario, any concrete Canadian pledge of haven for the refugees would mean far more than all the declarations of sympathy the free world might issue. Hayes pledged all the usual financial and other support for refugees, Jewish and non-Jewish.

Crerar listened patiently, even sympathetically. He was not uncaring, only powerless. When Hayes finished, the immigration minister promised to consider the suggestions.[6] Blair, however, reading between the lines, was livid. To Blair the program proposed as a means to put Canada out front in humanitarian action suggested only a dangerous and well-orchestrated plot to "make all the other Allies ashamed." Who could possibly benefit from shaming the Allies except those who wanted to undermine Allied unity and strain domestic tranquility? This was a heavy price to pay for a few Jews. "I regard this as a dangerous business," Blair later warned External Affairs, "and [it] requires very careful handling especially as practically all the refugees we are likely to get will be of the Jewish race"; if Canada was compelled to make any gesture on behalf of refugees, it should be only in the direction charted at Bermuda—a narrow course which Blair knew led nowhere.[7]

But Blair, for once, was outmanoeuvred. This time pro-refugee advocates, including the few sympathetic members of Parliament, successfully slipped the refugee issue out from under his control and into the Office of the Prime Minister's. Rather than addressing the issue as a facet of national immigration policy, the MP's exploited the Bermuda Conference (which Canada had so assiduously avoided) and characterized it as a problem for External Affairs. In this incarnation the refugee problem fell directly into the prime minister's lap, as King had remained his own secretary of state for External Affairs.[8]

As prearranged by the members, several questions were addressed to the prime minister in the House of Commons concerning Canada's official reaction to the Bermuda Conference. King, sensing that some public response was called for, used these questions as a pretext for readying a statement on refugees to be read in the House.[9] External Affairs, in consultation with Immigration authorities, was assigned the task of drawing up a draft for cabinet approval. Finally, some hoped, Canada would act.

In the meantime, King sent a noncommittal but appropriately sympathetic letter to Samuel Bronfman, a reply to Congress's proposed three-point program. Without promising specific action, King indicated his government's readiness "to do its part in cooperative efforts to deal with the tragic position of the victims of Nazi persecution." He did not indicate what that part would be, but expressed the hope "that methods may be developed which will relieve the suffering of the Jews of Europe as rapidly as the circumstances of the war will permit."[10]

The prime minister's statement to the House would match the tone of his letter—reassuring and noncommittal. For almost six weeks External Affairs drafted and redrafted it, a contentious word here or word there edited out, any phrase open to misinterpretation as a commitment to action scrapped. Every word was weighed, every phrase a bulwark against hope.

Blair, standing on the very threshold of retirement, was not too preoccupied to caution the cabinet one last time against relaxing the policy on Jews, especially with respect to quotas:

"In any movement of refugees that takes place there must be at least fifty per cent of non-Jewish refugees and . . . this percentage must be maintained during the entire movement so as to prevent the usual course of getting all Jews in first and run the risk of getting others later."[11] Blair's warnings were designed not so much to shape the prime minister's forthcoming statement as to limit the implementation of any promises it might make. And others who suggested revisions of a draft statement circulated by External Affairs were no more charitable in their thinking than the director of immigration. One civil servant submitted a redraft that, he offered, had four advantages over the original. It bespoke "Canadian cordiality toward refugees," it contained "less material likely to provoke further discussion," it did "not make so much reference to the Jews, which had obvious advantages," and of no small benefit to an otherwise busy cabinet and Commons, it was "one page shorter."[12]

External Affairs officials, for their part, were inclined toward a sympathetic statement, more for its symbolic value to other nations than for its actual usefulness to European Jews. What harm could there be in more concerned wording, the undersecretary of state for External Affairs asked, when "the frontiers are closed against [Jews'] departure"? Perhaps a few Jewish refugees might still flee to neutral Europe, but there would be no wholesale exodus. External Affairs had just been confidentially advised that a scheme to release forty-five thousand Bulgarian Jews had fallen through under Nazi opposition.[13] With Jews trapped, with little or no prospect for their rescue, a magnanimous offer was safe. It would have few, if any, takers.

On July 7, 1943, the Canadian cabinet met. Squeezed between discussions of federal subsidies of water supplies for Dawson Creek, British Columbia, and the thorny question of whether or not Canadian armed service personnel in Britain should be eligible for a British issue of war medals, the cabinet hurriedly reviewed and approved a statement on Canada's refugee policy.[14] Two days later King rose to address the House on several External Affairs issues, one of which was the refugee problem. King did begin by decrying the magnitude of the catastrophe befalling European Jewry, but he rejected any notion that the Allies had any power to ease their plight immediately. Beyond warnings to the Axis, "there is nothing that the allied governments can do to save these hapless people," King said, "except to win the war as quickly and as completely as possible. They cannot be removed from Axis territory. Efforts to aid them, even if aid was feasible, would prolong their agony if these efforts were to prolong the war."

The key to King's statement was, however, the Bermuda Conference. He explained that his government generally concurred with the limited recommendations following upon conference deliberations. He then hid behind the confidentiality of these same deliberations to forestall any meaningful debate.

On assistance to refugees in neutral territory King held out some hope. It was within the spirit of Bermuda "to aid those who [had] escaped but [had] not yet found a safe asylum." While those in Switzerland and Sweden did not need Canadian help, those in Spain, Portugal, the Middle East and Africa did, and without being specific, King offered that they might "be moved to places where they [could] remain until peace [was] restored." He was also even-handed enough to reassure both the anti-refugee forces: any refugees admitted to Canada would be on temporary visas; and the anti-Jewish lobby: refugees need not all be Jews.

Lest anyone still think the prime minister might open Canada to the wholesale importation of refugees, King also announced a series of prerequisites for admission. Anyone aware of conditions in Europe knew that they were so demanding as to cut off any flow before it could start. Anyone admitted would come "under international auspices, with consideration to the possibilities of transport, of repatriation at the end of the war and of useful employment in the war industries." In case these proved too encouraging, King promised restraint on the number of refugees allowed in, to avoid any "invitation to the German government to distribute . . . their spies and secret agents." And having introduced the bogey of Nazi espionage, King added flatly: "I cannot state how many additional refugees Canada will be prepared to receive." He allowed that the offer to take one thousand Jewish children from France was still open if all the conditions associated with this scheme could be met. Of course many of the children earmarked for Canada were already dead. Finally, King enumerated Canada's past achievements in refugee and relief work, strangely including the imprisonment of "the many thousand prisoners of war who [had] been transferred to Canada for safe custody" and modestly praising the country's record overall. "We have not, of course, done all we could have done and perhaps we have not done all we should have done," he offered. "Our record, however, is better than it is frequently made out to be and I think it will stand comparison with the records of other parts of the British commonwealth and of the United States."[15]

Pro-refugee members of Parliament, especially the small CCF caucus, were of course disappointed by King's statement. The CCF member for Winnipeg North Centre, Stanley Knowles, led off the debate, castigating the government for its lack of positive action on behalf of refugees. Pointing an accusing finger at the government benches, he berated them with doing too little too late. As far as he was concerned, the government continued to yield to anti-Jewish sentiment just as it had done in the past. "We know there are people who have a dislike for the Jewish people," he said. "I believe it [allowing Jewish refugees to enter Canada] would increase our sense of humanity, and increase our own consciousness of the fact that we are willing to get rid of racial hatred, prejudice and antagonism. Somehow we in this country should rise up and do the generous and humane thing for these people."

Fellow CCFers M. J. Coldwell and Clarie Gillis joined the attack. Coldwell lamented that so little was being done, while Gillis pointed out that King had neglected to mention one area in which Canada might have some influence in saving Jews. Picking up on King's own words, Gillis agreed that "Hitler [had] a policy of complete extermination of these people" and that admission to Canada, though offered halfheartedly, could save a lucky few. But haven in Palestine remained a realistic solution for many. It was Canada's humanitarian duty, Gillis insisted, to protest by word and deed the British rigidity over Palestine. To do otherwise would be a sad admission. "We have not," Gillis declared, "lifted a finger, to save thousands and thousands of lives."[16]

King knew an opening when he saw it. Correctly sensing that the largely CCF pro-refugee group would find few kindred spirits elsewhere in the House, he interrupted Gillis. The prime minister's patience had been tried on the refugee problem; he had made his statement and now would have done with it. Ridiculing Gillis, King said that if Canada had "not lifted a finger" to save refugees, it had boldly raised a fist. The prime minister played to the House: "Does Gillis attach no importance to all the Canadian army, navy and air force do in this war to alleviate the situation in Europe, and in particular, the terrible position of these very people." (In the desk thumping on both sides of the House that followed King's quip, few would sense the cutting edge of his words. In the heat of debate the prime minister was unconsciously coming close to parroting a Nazi propaganda line—the Allies and Canada were fighting a war, the Nazis repeatedly asserted, demanded by Jews to save the Jews.) Side-stepping the thrust of the CCF attack, King had the last word on refugees: "Where it is possible to have them brought over, Canada is prepared to receive them." He did not then feel it necessary to say when or how that might be done.[17]

The United Jewish Refugee Agency, although publicly silent on the government's statement, was deeply disappointed—not because Canada alone could have actually done much to alleviate the Jews' suffering, but because the government seemed still so reluctant to offer the pittance then possible, especially to those in Iberia. The moderateness of the community's purpose is perhaps best summed up in Saul Hayes's vision of the tragedy: "There simply are not any other refugees [except those in still neutral Europe] to be moved. The question of the migration of the balance is nothing that either Canada can do or the United Nations can do. It is almost solely with Germany or its satellite countries, France, Bulgaria, Roumania, Hungary. Until they agree without any quid pro quo which makes it impossible for us to accept the conditions, there will be no movement. It is a hard tragic fact but there is no use refusing to face it."[18]

Despite all the government's restrictions, King had still offered hope for Iberian refugees. Yet, Jewish community leaders sensed no commitment to action. A. Leon Kubowitzki of the World Jewish Congress related the obvious: "On the whole, the statements made by Mr. Mackenzie King are much less helpful than we have been led to expect on the basis of reports in the Jewish press."[19]

Weeks passed. Finally, and as though to prod the refugee issue back to life, Hayes wrote Crerar, reminding him of the standing Jewish community guarantee to underwrite the total cost of any refugee movement to Canada. He questioned the reasons for delaying further a program in Spain and Portugal; shipping from Iberia was no longer a problem, he pointed out, as neutral Portuguese vessels were "leaving Portugal half empty". In fact government officials had given thought a month before King's statement to the logistics of organizing some sort of refugee movement out of Spain or Portugal (which, Blair agreed with Hayes, was "probably the only area from which refugees [could] be moved immediately.") But a cursory review of the situation by Blair and his deputy generated a series of restrictive guidelines for any refugee movement that were draconian in their effect. The Immigration Branch's criteria, in a general way, had been incorporated into King's statement in the Commons as the basic rules under which refugees might prove eligible to apply under any subsequent refugee scheme. There was, of course, no guarantee that those judged eligible to apply would subsequently be judged suitable for admission. The specifics of Blair's and Jolliffe's guidelines would see to that.[20]

Almost symbolically, the restrictive criteria designed by Blair to cripple any proposed movement of Jewish refugees to Canada became his last major policy thrust before he retired in the summer of 1943. Blair, who would shortly be invested with the highest award given a public official for meritorious service to the country, was succeeded by his deputy, A. L. Jolliffe. It was no secret within the Immigration Branch that Blair and Jolliffe did not get along. Jolliffe, a thirty-year veteran of immigration work when appointed to replace Blair, was, by all accounts, a more flexible, accessible and agreeable individual with whom to deal. One observer was later to recall of Jolliffe that he consistently endeavoured "to interpret Canada's immigration regulations in a generous and liberal sense."[21] For all this, however, Jolliffe was no less a civil servant than Blair. If, unlike Blair, he was not personally an anti-Semite, he certainly knew the intent of government policy in the summer of 1943 and recognized the likelihood that any tinkering with that policy, even as the new director, would not be received well in the cabinet or by the civil service organization he now headed. Even with Blair gone, his policies would dominate thinking in the Immigration Branch for years to come.

In mid August 1943, six weeks after King held out hope of some Canadian refugee initiative in Spain and Portugal, the minister responsible for immigration summoned Jolliffe into his office for a discussion. Crerar was clearly concerned. Some External Affairs officials seemed intent on pushing some sort of Iberian refugee scheme through the cabinet in line with the prime minister's statement. Immigration authorities, with their experience and administrative apparatus, would undoubtedly be made responsible for administering any actual movement. Crerar did not want to be caught with others initiating programs for which his own ministry would do all the work.

An Immigration Branch proposal on Iberia, based in large part on the earlier Blair and Jolliffe memorandum, was hurriedly pulled together. Neither Crerar nor Jolliffe was inclined to dramatic or magnanimous gestures. The minister seemed satisfied that Canada's admission of one hundred families from the Iberian Peninsula was a "gesture toward relieving the situation." Crerar, inclined to be a little more generous than the newly retired Blair, would allow that seventy-five, not fifty, per cent be Jewish. Jolliffe, for his part, cautioned the minister to go slow, but Crerar was anxious to play a role in the cabinet. He instructed his new director to press the Branch's refugee scheme on External Affairs—before it was too late.[22]

It seemed that Crerar would have his way. Ten days after his meeting with Jolliffe, ranking External Affairs and Immigration officials met. They agreed to recommend to cabinet that the Immigration Branch open an office in Lisbon and screen an unspecified number of refugee families using the Blair–Jolliffe criteria. Refugees were and would remain refugees, never immigrants; project costs, including some of those incurred by government personnel abroad, would be recovered in part or full from the Jewish community or international refugee relief agencies.

The scheme went to cabinet in early September 1943, after Jolliffe, in a manner reminiscent of Blair's, had warned of possible pressure from Jewish groups should they learn of the project and had won agreement that both the seventy-five per cent quota and total number of admissions be kept secret. The cabinet, as a possible concession to External Affairs, then allowed that the maximum number of refugee families admitted be raised from one to two hundred, while sensing that "the number actually able to move [would] probably be very small." One sensed King's political artistry: the refugee scheme should have a high enough profile to still those voices demanding action, while, it was hoped, protests against the wholesale admission of Jews could easily be countered by pointing to the small numbers arriving.[23]

The cabinet discussion was brief and approving. Jolliffe was assigned to prepare a press release for King; he was instructed "not to mention the limit of 200 families to be placed on the movement," and was himself aware that "it would be inadvisable to place the emphasis on the reception of Jewish families." The Intergovernmental Committee on Refugees was notified, in confidence, and long-time immigration officer Odilon Cormier travelled secretly to Lisbon to open an immigration office.[24]

On November 2, 1943, King informed the press.[25] Any hope King had of finding and then riding a popular pro-refugee tide was to be sorely disappointed. Refugees, especially Jewish refugees, had remained a political hot potato. Even if Canadians were nearly unanimous in their sympathy for the victims of Nazi terror, this unanimity did not extend to a wish to relocate victims to Canada. The cabinet knew it. King knew it. If anything they underestimated it. Commenting in his diary on a conversation with a Jewish visitor about the storm that instantly broke with the announcement of the government's refugee scheme, King observed again that there were few, if any, votes in aiding Jewish refugees. What a statesman might do, a politician could only dream of. King was, above all, a politician. He explained to his visitor that for a government "to adopt any policy of open door would only cause the other partee [*sic*] to take an opposite stand and gain thereby in a general election." "I thought," King then reflected, "after I was out of politics altogether, I might sometime speak on the need of Canada following Britain's example and becoming a haven for peoples of all countries who were refugees from political persecution especially if there were careful selection of standards, etc."[26]

For once King's political artistry failed him, and the government's efforts to pacify pro-refugee groups with the promise of saving refugees in Iberia (without revealing just how small would be its contribution or how selective its application) backfired loudly. Anti-refugee interests read press reports and feared the worst—an unchecked deluge of refugees coming to Canada and a seeming collapse of the government under the pressure of the Jewish lobby. Pro-refugee groups, especially Jews, found their initial hopes giving way to frustration as the limits of the refugee scheme were confirmed. If the government was surprised by the sharp response, they also had proof for what they had always suspected: there was less public sympathy for refugees than the pro-refugee coalition had argued. If the government's limited relief scheme could cause an outcry, what, they must have wondered, would a real commitment provoke? One could almost hear Blair's 'I told you so.'

Anti-refugee arguments unquestionably cloaked widespread anti-Jewish sentiment. Many feared that any move to assist refugees by bringing them to Canada was but backdoor Jewish immigration. Even the Jewish community's staunchest allies on the refugee question, local CNCR chapters across Canada, were squeamish when it came to the immigration of Jews. Temporary refugees, including Jewish refugees, were one thing, Jewish immigrants another. A Jewish official in Winnipeg confided to a colleague in Toronto that committee sponsors in his city were, if not anti-Semitic, at least backward. "They fear the question of [Jewish] immigration as much as the Devil is said to fear holy water," he said. "They are all in favor of Canada offering 'sanctuary for the refugees' at the present time, but they do not wish this issue to be confused with the question of opening the doors of Canada to non Anglo-Saxon immigrants after the war. Many of them are in favor of 'refugees' but opposed to 'immigrants'."[27]

The CNCR's national office faced the problem head on. In cooperation with the United Jewish Refugee Agency, it launched a Canada-wide petition campaign to drum up support, not just for aid to refugees, but for their immigration. Constance Hayward, national secretary of the CNCR, dismissed local chapters' concern over the petition appearing too closely associated with Jewish immigration. "We have come to the place," she boldly asserted, "where anti-Semitism in Canada must be faced and if the Petition ignores this issue or is silent upon it, its effectiveness will be greatly reduced."[28] But the petition, designed to gather half a million signatures, soon ran into resistance,[29] with Professor Watson Thompson of Winnipeg among the first to sound the alarm. "There seemed to be a great racial prejudice, the chief argument being that the bulk of these refugees were Jews," he explained, "but this sort of thinking was only Fascist thinking."[30]

Fascist thinking or not, the petition received only limited support. King's July refugee policy statement in the Commons may have dampened the sense of urgency felt by its supporters, along with the mixed response from the press. While some in the English-Canadian press urged readers to sign the petition, others argued that sympathy for the Jewish plight did not necessitate bringing them to Canada. Which position accurately reflected the views of most English-Canadian readers? James H. Gray, editor of the *Winnipeg Free Press*, thought it was the latter and condemned it. "It is unfortunately but decidedly untrue to say that the people of Canada are unanimous in desiring to see justice done the Jews," he wrote. "It is unfortunately but decidedly untrue to say that they desire to see all measures taken to relieve the plight of the Jews. . . . As for the editorials, far too many of them weep crocodile tears but take no stand on the refugee problem."[31]

Some editorials did not even "weep crocodile tears." They

were openly hostile to the petition and to Jews. In Alberta, the *Hanna Herald*, "A Paper with a Conscience," warned its readers against signing a petition to loosen immigration regulations. It called for Canadians to reach beyond "ordinary humanitarian instincts" and ask why Jews were "the most universally disliked people in the whole world." The *Herald* allowed that "anti-Jewish feeling [could] not be explained or defended" and "was contrary to Christian teaching and to ordinary humanitarian ideas." But: "It persists and will be aggravated if the Jews universally persist in their attempts to bring thousands of European refugees of that race into Canada." In southwestern Ontario too, newspaper readers were cautioned against signing the refugee committee's petition. The *Sarnia Observer* decried its consequence: "If translated into law, the doors of Canada would be flung wide open." Canada, the *Observer* allowed, might need more people, but before one additional soul was allowed in, the government must check "which races and which sections of the globe and even countries yield the highest percentage of criminals, such as, bootleggers and gunmen." Published just north of Toronto, the *Simcoe Reformer* was more concerned with the pro-refugee lobby than with the refugees. If one began with the notion that refugees, especially Jews, were undesirable, what might one suspect of the motives of those who would bring Jews into Canada? "The suspicion aroused is that those who have set these petitions afoot are more concerned with increasing the foreign population of Canada, to serve their own ends, than they are with the welfare of the European refugees or the good of Canada."[32]

Thus, by November 1943 the government Iberian refugee scheme, hand-in-hand with the CNCR petition, had stirred up a hornet's nest of nativist passion. Among the first to go on record against the plan was the Manitoba Command of the Canadian Legion. Others followed. Again, confusing temporary refugees with immigrants, Legion chapters across Canada moved resolutions opposing the admission of "undesirable Europeans" and calling for a program of postwar British immigration. What of refugees? "The future of Canada depends on the preservation of British institutions." The *Canadian Veteran*, house organ of the Legion, lumped refugees together with the interned Japanese further to define its social vision: "There is no room in Canada for cut throat competition of Japs or refugees until every last man or woman who gave their service to their country in time of need has been properly and happily reabsorbed into the national structure."[33]*

This rising tide of anti-refugee and anti-Jewish sentiment was only too apparent to Canadian Jewish leaders. Lest any of the Congress leadership was still oblivious to the national mood, the Congress director would alert them. "By all reports based on examination of the press of Canada and even according to special reports prepared for government departments," Hayes said, "anti-Semitism in Canada is rising among all sections and classes of the population. This is no less true among English-language groups than it is among the people of French Canada."[34]

And the results of a Gallup Poll in January 1944 tended to confirm this view. The poll repeated a question asked one year earlier—should Canada open its doors to immigrants after the war or should it keep them out? With so much debate still confusing temporary refugees with immigrants, there is little doubt that immigrants or refugees were both understood to mean just one thing—Jews. The national percentage favouring an open-door policy fell slightly, from fourteen to thirteen per cent. Those who favoured even limited and selective immigration fell from fifty-nine to fifty per cent, while the number of bedrock restrictionists—those who would keep everyone out—rose from twenty-one to twenty-nine per cent. Most frightening to the Jewish community and the CNCR, now over five years into their campaign of public education, was that those favouring a closed door grew by about eighteen per cent in Quebec and by a shocking fifty per cent in English-speaking Canada.[35]

In a lengthy and confidential analysis of this poll, the government's War Information Board in Ottawa observed that the majority favouring some restrictions would select immigrants "first by their racial or national origin, secondly by their suitability

* The veterans' call was answered by at least one powerful voice. Ontario's premier, George Drew, unveiled his own scheme for selective postwar immigration also in November 1943. "We need young and vigorous people from Britain—that is what I mean by selective immigration." And Drew went even further, cautioning that Canadian policy must be more selective: it must be active. If Canada wanted better immigrants, it would need to go after them. In the coming era of postwar reconstruction, Australia, New Zealand, South Africa and others would all want these same settlers. Drew, for one, would be ready. He committed the full resources of his government to postwar planning in this direction. Anything else, he warned, would leave Canada with very poor pickings. *Sarnia Observer*, December 23, 1943; *London Free Press*, December 29, 1943; *London Ledger*, December 30, 1943.

for life in this country." Jewish refugees lost out on both counts. Many of those Canadians who listed "adaptability" as the single most important criterion for admission to Canada also argued that Jews did not adapt well. Among those who emphasized the need for strict racial selectivity, many, especially French-speaking respondents, specified "No Jews."[36]

With the force of nativism on the rise across Canada, it was still most concentrated and vocal in Quebec. Even before King's July policy statement, Quebec was rife with talk of Jews poised to flood Canadian ports of entry. The Immigration Branch had picked up a rumour sweeping Quebec and dutifully passed it along to the wartime "Rumour Clinic": the government was ready to admit one hundred thousand Jewish refugees "as an example to the rest of the world."[37] After the November 1943 press release from Crerar's office, refugees became a major electoral issue in Quebec. Maurice Duplessis, charismatic leader of the Union Nationale opposition and once premier of Quebec, fired up loose talk of a refugee invasion from Iberia into political dynamite. He chose a sleepy pastoral village of about one hundred and fifty persons, Ste. Claire in Dorchester County, from which to launch his attack. At a pre-election political meeting following Sunday mass, Duplessis treated the townsfolk and farmers from the parish to a rousing assault on the Liberals, federal and provincial. To cap his performance, he charged that they were in league with a so-called "International Zionist Brotherhood," an organization of his invention. In return for financing Liberal candidates, Duplessis charged, the non-existent organization would be allowed to settle one hundred thousand Jewish refugees in Quebec. To prove his charges, he waved about a copy of a letter that, he claimed, detailed the plot.[38]

Denials, accusations and cries of disgust echoed across the political landscape.[39] Yet, if Duplessis's allegation was a patently false, cruelly cynical and pernicious political manoeuvre, it nevertheless struck a responsive chord in the prevailing anti-refugee, or anti-Jewish, spirit in Quebec. In symbiotic fashion, charges and countercharges fed off one another, and denials only enlivened the issue. Shortly thereafter, Duplessis was again elected premier of the province.

The national and Jewish refugee organizations were kept busy exposing the Duplessis fraud, and worried too about Ottawa's reaction to the uproar. CNCR president Cairine Wilson publicly charged Duplessis with "trying to build up his own political position on racial prejudice," and hoped that the sympathetic understanding of Immigration Branch officials would not be undermined.[40] The executive director of the Jewish Immigrant Aid Society confided his fears to his Toronto president:

> On the one hand it is quite conceivable that Mr. Crerar and the rest of the Government anticipated some reaction from Quebec to his pronouncement on an Iberian refugee scheme and scarcely expected such reaction to be enthusiastically favourable. On the other hand, however, the repercussions of Mr. Duplessis' sensationalist "revelations" may have the same effect on the Spanish refugee project as the protest resolution circulated by the St. John [*sic*] Baptiste Society had upon the Jewish farmer movement which this Society [JIAS] brought about in 1938.[41]

Most alarming to Jewish leaders was not Duplessis's making political hay of this one scheme, but the degree to which his transparent fraud, this Quebec variation on the Reichstag fire, found a credulous public. Indeed, raw anti-Semitism, disguised by the anti-refugee movement, took on a new respectability. La Ligue Nationale circulated province-wide an anti-refugee petition that soon outstripped the faltering pro-refugee effort. In Montreal the Association des Jeunes Laurentiens held a public debate on the question "Visitor or Not in Wartime." An enthusiastic crowd of five hundred repeatedly cheered anti-refugee spokesmen, and warnings that tens of thousands of Jews stood poised to overrun Quebec and trample its institutions, religion and heritage rang through the hall.* What, one speaker demanded, had the existing Jewish community in Quebec done to earn its place in the community? Little, except elect Communist Fred Rose to Parliament. (Rose was referred to by the speaker as "Red Rosenberg" lest anyone miss the point.) The moderator closed the meeting by encouraging all those present to join the anti-refugee crusade: "Not to follow a minority of Jews," one observer recalled him saying, "who far from helping

* The day of the debate the president of the Lafontaine Branch of the Association des Jeunes Laurentiens in Montreal wrote to Crerar. He warned that Quebec would neither forgive nor forget those politicians who would abet Jews entering Canada. "The presence of Jews in cities," he said, "already constitutes a very serious problem for our leaders. Would not the admission to this country of thousands of Jews who are not Christians and who do not believe in our faiths aggravate the problem and make it unsolvable? These thousands of Jews know neither French nor English and what would their presence therefore bring to us if not difficulties for both races, the French and the English." Public Archives of Canada, Department of Immigration Records, File 673931, J. Z. Leon Patenaude to Crerar, November 18, 1943.

the conadians [*sic*] are grabbing everything their crooked fingers can get hold of."[42]

The French-language Quebec press did not wholeheartedly support Duplessis or the more shrill nationalists; it did, however, demand the rejection of Jewish refugees. Except for the Montreal weekly, *Le Jour*, dismissed by one anti-refugee activist as a "cabbage leaf," the French press spoke with one voice.[43]

While Jewish leaders assessed the announcement of the government's refugee scheme and the consequent anti-Jewish backlash, news from Europe stunned the community. Revelations, for example, of the mass murder of sixty thousand Jews outside Kiev two years earlier were confirmed. Eyewitness accounts published in *Liberty* magazine and picked up by the English-Canadian press detailed an orgy of death that might earlier have been dismissed as Allied propaganda. One eyewitness, begging to be believed, described the ravine of Babi Yar near Kiev that gradually filled with bodies as the killing continued, "the little children . . . hurled alive into the gully, there to lie broken and maimed until they died," and the sounds of gunfire and screams, heard as one during the three days of continuous slaughter. The article didn't stop there, for neither had the horrors of means and ways to murder. Many *Liberty* readers might now read for the first time of technologically advanced and scientifically efficient death camps. Names like Treblinka, Belzec and Sobibor entered the lexicon to become synonymous with previously unimagined brutality. "Speak of propaganda if you will," *Liberty* challenged its readers. "Close your eyes and ears and hearts against the horror and the cruelty of the *Judenrein*. Call the Jew an alien race. Wash your hands of responsibility as Pilate did. But a Gentile race that does not call for justice for the Jew will be forever accused."[44]

The Canadian government was pursuing its refugee scheme meanwhile. Its agent in Portugal, Odilon Cormier, had been at his post for several months, working with British embassy officials (out of sight of Jewish agencies) to determine the legal status and number of the refugees: "how many there are of each nationality with mention of percentage of those of Jewish race." Cormier invoked all the Immigration Branch's restrictions when making his calculations—health standards, racial quotas and family composition: only complete family units (father, mother and children under eighteen) would be admitted. At last, he reported secretly from Lisbon that, of an estimated thirteen hundred bona fide refugees in Portugal, most were Jews; but the government need not worry, for only a few complete families were present. "From this," Jolliffe dutifully explained to his minister, "we are going to get no movement from Portugal on the basis of the Government's decision to admit up to two hundred families."[45]

Cormier sent another message to confirm that he would not be approving many applications. He suggested that Allied war successes lessened the sense of urgency among some refugees for an immediate exit from Europe; others were far from enthusiastic about a temporary, rather than immigrant, visa to Canada. But if these factors contributed to some refugees' hesitance, it was Cormier's unyielding and overtly obstructionist interpretation of the family unit rule that deprived virtually everyone of consideration. He showed a fetish for detail that might well have made Blair gasp. Was it with pride or concern that, after three months in Lisbon, Cormier could write: "I have not had occasion to issue a single visa to anyone to date."[46]

Estimates as to the actual number of refugees in Iberia varied. Jewish sources claimed there were approximately thirty-five hundred; British sources, on which Cormier relied, claimed there were thirteen hundred Jewish and non-Jewish refugees in Portugal alone, of whom the vast majority were Jews.[47] One could attribute these statistical differences to problems of separating bona fide refugees from illegal refugees, to varying definitions of who was a Jew, or simply to guesswork on everyone's part. But Cormier was not so much concerned with the number of refugees as with the numbers of complete and acceptable family units.

Once the government's scheme was officially announced, the Joint Distribution Committee, acting for the United Jewish Refugee Agency in Lisbon, directed a steady stream of refugee families to Cormier; but it soon complained that fifteen families might be the total number eligible unless modification of the family unit rule could be arranged. In a hurried meeting with Jolliffe, Saul Hayes and the JDC's New York director pleaded for a more liberal interpretation of the rules. They requested, for example, that single-parent families, families with grandparents, families with children over eighteen and families who had earlier succeeded in getting children out of Europe (usually to the United States) be allowed to apply for Canadian visas. Even these changes might only increase the total eligible to ninety families or three hundred persons.[48]

As this concession would not violate the government's two hundred family quota, Jolliffe could afford to be generous; he instructed Cormier to include children over eighteen and grandparents as part of family units. But Cormier was in no mood to relent. He again applied regulations in such a way as to subvert their intent. If the age limit of eighteen years had created a problem, Cormier made its elimination an even bigger problem: he now ruled that all children in a family, including married children, must apply as a unit. And as grandparents were now eligible as part of the family unit, he ruled that they were family heads, and all children and grandchildren must also be included. This imposed a new, almost impossible, precondition. One refugee family of a wife, husband, several children and the wife's father, for example, was declared ineligible for consideration. The grandfather had another child, an adult son, in Palestine, and according to Cormier's reading of the more liberal rule, this son would be required to travel to Portugal before the family was "complete."

Again under pressure to relax family unit restrictions, Jolliffe allowed that a family with a "member missing or in a place unknown" would be eligible for consideration.[49] Again Cormier stood ready. He refused, in one case, to consider a Jewish family from Yugoslavia. They had a son fighting with the Yugoslav resistance, neither missing nor in a place unknown, but a partisan fighting with the underground. Because this son was unwilling or unable to travel to Canada as part of the family unit, the family was not eligible for consideration. Obviously, as the Joint Distribution Committee protested, Cormier, with authority from Ottawa, intended to keep the number of refugees moving to Canada low, whatever the regulations.[50]

The family unit rule was applied in tandem with the strict medical exam. Individual family members, often elderly grandparents, were disqualified by reason of health, undoing the entire family's eligibility. In addition, by imposing the tightest immigration regulations on country of origin and financial guarantees, it was easy to exclude family members. Initially, for instance, Cormier stipulated that refugees come only from conquered Allied countries. Applying existing immigration regulations rather than the spirit of a refugee rescue program, Jews from Germany, Italy and Hungary were inadmissible for entry into Canada. For those from Allied countries, he also demanded a $1,000 deposit per refugee family, as was the case with immigrants, in spite of the United Jewish Refugee Agency's financial guarantees. These particular stumbling blocks were eventually cleared away, but in the meantime nobody was processed.[51]

Equally troublesome was Cormier's demand for strict documentation, travel papers and identification, even from refugees who smuggled themselves across the Pyrenees with little but the clothes on their backs. Refugees who had escaped the Nazis only because they had false identification papers or phony visas and passports now confronted the no-nonsense Cormier. Cormier remained unmoved by any argument that discovery of the very documents he now demanded would have meant certain death for refugees trying to get out of Nazi territory. The regulations called for authentic documentation. Anything less was unacceptable.

And then not all documentation, even if genuine, was acceptable. Because the Polish government did not recognize ecclesiastical marriages, the *ketuvah*, the age-old rabbinical marriage contract, was not accepted as documentary proof of marriage in the case of Jews from Poland, although it might be for Jews from European countries that recognized it. While Saul Hayes tried to win an exemption to this rule from the director of immigration, the Joint Distribution Committee tried to organize civil marriages for Polish couples (a difficult process for foreigners in Spain and Portugal), some of whom had been married for as long as twenty-five years. In recognition of Cormier's obvious predisposition to rule against eligiblity where possible, Hayes also sought an additional guarantee. Where civil marriages could be arranged, Hayes wanted Jolliffe's assurance that Cormier would not then claim that, having "lived in sin" for so long, these Polish Jews were guilty of "moral turpitude." (Persons guilty of "moral turpitude" were, of course, ineligible for admission to Canada.)[52] As was so often the case, Hayes won his point, but it took precious time.

Cormier's antics kept the movement of Jewish refugees in check. They also cast doubt on the sincerity of Canada's commitment to refugee relief even within the international community. In January 1944 the Joint Distribution Committee representative in Lisbon complained bitterly about Canada to Emerson of the Intergovernmental Committee on Refugees. Emerson took up the gulf between Canadian words and deeds with Charles Ritchie of Canada House in London and was reassured that tough regulations should not be misread as restrictions; they were, rather, guiding principles which merely gave the immigration officer in Lisbon direction in these unusual circumstances. Diplomatic double-talk aside, Ritchie conceded to External Affairs in Ottawa that these regulations, especially the family unit rule, "continued to undermine the possible movement out of the Peninsula."[53]

He was right. After five months of work, assessing and reassing would-be applicant families, a group was ready to sail—not the 200 families cabinet secretly agreed upon, but 114 families, 235 adults and 58 children. Processing would continue for several more months with now-liberated North Africa incorporated into Cormier's mandate. But the final count—less than 450 refugees—would still fall short of 200 families.[54]

In March 1944 Jewish officials in Lisbon completed arranging transport for the few refugee families approved to that date. In spite of some reservations on the part of Canadian Jewish leaders about sending all those approved as a single group, "due to the reaction of that part of the Canadian public opinion which [was] hostile to any immigration during and after the war," all those with visas left together. It was decided, however, to divide the group evenly between Montreal and Toronto: if anti-refugee sentiment could not be denied, it might be pacified by lessening refugee visibility during the settlement process.[55]

On April 6, 1944, the eve of Passover, the S.S. *Serpa Pinto* slipped into the port of Philadelphia with 280 Canada-bound refugees, mostly Jews, aboard.[56] With press watching, refugees were hurried through American landing formalities. They were then divided into two groups, bussed to waiting railway cars and promptly locked inside. The refugees, who stood pressed at the windows looking out at America, saw "enough police to provide an armed guard for each refugee."[57] American authorities were taking no chances on any refugee attempting to overstay his short visit. Once the train began to move, Canadian authorities and Jewish refugee officials entered the cars. They processed the families as best they could, while the cars rolled northward. In Montreal or Toronto they were greeted with a welcoming Passover Seder.[58]

A second voyage of the *Serpa Pinto* carried only seventy-four Canada-bound passengers, again mostly refugees. Their journey proved far more hazardous. In mid-Atlantic the neutral Portuguese vessel was intercepted by a German U-Boat. At 2:00 A.M. on May 25 all passengers were awakened and assembled on deck. Terror gripped the group as word spread that the

U-Boat, its guns poised, was about to sink the unarmed vessel. The captain ordered everyone into life boats. A sixteen-month-old baby girl bound for Montreal with her parents was lost overboard. In faltering English a passenger later recalled the tragic events for JDC officials: "You . . . know of the death of little Betty Trapunski, who the mother had reached down into the life-boat before climbing down herself the rope ladder. In that moment the boat went to pieces and the sailor who had held the child had to struggle for his life and apparently during that struggle he lost the baby. You can imagine that the poor mother nearly went crazy—she is still in . . . hospital in Montreal."[59] While he interrogated several American passengers, the U-Boat commander radioed Berlin requesting instructions whether or not to torpedo the then empty vessel. Word arrived at 8:00 A.M. After six hours bobbing about in lifeboats, passengers and crew were allowed to reboard the *Serpa Pinto* and resume their journey.[60]

On Friday, October 1, 1944, a final group of forty-five Iberian refugees on the S.S. *Nyassa* landed at Philadelphia en route to Canada. If their crossing had been uneventful, their first few days in North America were not. The Jewish refugees, among them an Orthodox religious group, were processed by American officials, once again with armed guards at the ready, then taken to the nearby railway station to board special cars on a waiting Montreal-bound train.

Soon after the Jewish refugees gathered on the train platform, they learned that their train would only depart after sunset, after the Sabbath had begun. A rumble of protest ensued. While bewildered officials and armed police looked on, the Orthodox refugees conferred for a moment, then announced they would not violate the Sabbath by travelling. Following the lead of a man carrying his eighteen-month-old baby, the group picked up their hand luggage, turned and proceeded to walk out of the railway station in the direction of the port. The entire group walked back to the *Nyassa*; shocked officials and armed guards trailed behind. Sabbath was spent on board ship.

The group was rerouted to Montreal by way of New York on a train leaving the next evening—after sunset and therefore after the Sabbath had ended. The New York to Montreal leg of its journey was scheduled to leave on Sunday evening. Once again pandemonium broke out. Sunday sundown began the Jewish Festival of Tabernacles, Succoth, which precluded travel for another two days. It also required the faithful to eat all meals in a temporary wooden structure, a *succah*, through the roof of which one might see the stars. In deference to this group's determination to observe the ritual, arrangements were hastily made for the refugees to spend Succoth at the Hebrew Immigrant Aid Society shelter in New York. Here a *succah* was put at their disposal—all under the watchful eyes of armed American guards.

This last group tried the patience of officials and taxed the resources of the Jewish community—a small price to pay for a first taste of religious freedom. For their part, these refugees both understood and appreciated the deference shown their special needs. The mother of the eighteen-month-old baby expressed her gratitude in very personal terms. "I am jubilant," she wept, "to be back from the dead. I am happy to bring my child to a country where he can grow up to be anything he wants to be."[61]

This mother's jubilation might have been somewhat muted had she understood that she and her child might not be able to stay. Refugees were not immigrants. Officially, these refugees were only visitors for the duration of hostilities. In an article outlining the Iberian refugee scheme, the *Moncton Transcript* noted the limited nature of the Canadian sanctuary. "They are not being admitted as immigrants," the paper explained, "but are being given wartime refuge only. . . . Canada is not playing the role of the good Samaritan to these people. Its role rather is that of innkeeper who admitted the victim upon the payment of cash in advance with the promise of more if needed."[62]

Canadian officials were also uneasy lest at some point these victims might need to be evicted from the inn. The Bermuda Conference had only called upon the Allies and neutrals to offer temporary haven for refugees. Canada promised nothing more. With an end to hostilities, repatriation of these European nationals back to their countries of citizenship, along with those admitted earlier from Japan, could be ordered. Therefore, while Cormier inched his way through the procedures that brought refugees into Canada, RCMP and Immigration officials in Ottawa prepared to move with lightning dispatch in removing these same people from Canada. They mapped out contingency plans for a swift roundup of all temporary refugees for immediate deportation if and when the signal was given. Some officials may have suspected that all these temporary refugees might eventually be allowed to stay—nothing might prove so permanent as a temporary solution. But this was conjecture.

Ever-prudent Immigration Branch authorities joined the RCMP in completing a list of refugee addresses, at home and work, and for children at school, to insure a smooth, efficient, quiet and, above all, quick deportation of refugees from Canadian shores if necessary.[63]

Jewish leaders knew full well that the refugee visas were temporary. They felt assured, however, that, having granted haven to Jewish refugees, Canada "would be somewhat inconsistent pressing for the immediate departure of its guests before the emergency [was] over." But when might the emergency be over? The Iberian scheme had only been authorized because of a real and present danger to refugees in Spain and Portugal. Refugees who had made it to safer, albeit temporary, havens elsewhere in Europe or Latin America were not eligible for consideration. Jolliffe was unmoveable in this regard. As he explained to an External Affairs official, "Our chief concern has been with refugees in danger of their lives and those suffering hardship through persecution or want, and it has not been our policy to consider those who have escaped from war areas to safety in other countries as being entitled to special consideration."[64]

But, in truth, the whole Iberian rescue program had been a "special consideration." Positive news from the war fronts—the Germans were in retreat across Europe—removed any immediate threat to the remaining refugees in Spain, Portugal and newly liberated North Africa. In the late summer of 1944 External Affairs agreed there was no justification for continuing the Iberian program just to fill a secret, two-hundred-family quota. Immigration officials were only too pleased to terminate operations as soon as possible. No announcements were made, but Jewish Immigrant Aid Society officials were not long in picking up signals to that effect. In September 1944 Solkin explained to society workers in Toronto: "To all practical intents or purposes the refugee movement from Europe is definitely a closed chapter." Three days after the *Nyassa* landed in Philadelphia in October 1944 the Canadian immigration office in Lisbon closed. Cormier had done his job. Canada had taken in all the wartime refugees it was going to take.[65]

Most refugees who arrived from Spain and Portugal settled in well. They found work and soon realized a stability and security unknown since they first fled the Nazi terror. For a few, however, it was more difficult. The fears and memories they brought were not easily set aside, not even in Canada. For others their Iberian refugee experience, during which time they were not allowed to work and forced onto the dole of refugee agencies, made dependence seem normal. For those who had expected a warm public welcome in Canada, the existence of a deeply rooted anti-Semitism, even in English Canada, came as a disappointment. One refugee woman in Toronto wrote to a friend in Lisbon expressing both her gratitude for the warmth shown her by the local Jewish community and her shock at the virulence of anti-Jewish prejudice she found in the city. "Anti-Semitism here," she observed in a letter copied by Canadian military censors, "is developed to a degree unimaginable with us. Of course, we had no illusions in advance with regard to this, but it exceeds our boldest expectations."[66]

For those few who suffered a jolt at shifting from a dependence on charity forced on refugees while in Iberia to the fiscal self-reliance expected of them by Jewish agencies in Canada, problem followed problem. Some damned JIAS officials, responsible for settlement matters, with charges of penny pinching. Society officials, in turn, complained bitterly to international relief agencies about being unable to meet standards of aid refugees claimed to have received in Iberia. One disgruntled refugee wrote bitterly to a friend in Barcelona: "I will give you some advice, *do not* leave. As nice as you have it in Spain, you will never have it again." Another refugee in Montreal tacked onto her complaints of tight-fisted Jewish officials a none too flattering assessment of life in her new haven. To a friend in Caldas she complained of Montreal: "Life here is horribly monotonous as the people here are very primitive and the country is like a big village."[67]

Jewish Immigrant Aid Society officials, generally satisfied with the adjustment of most refugees, still expressed concern over some. "They appear," wrote one officer, "reluctant or even unwilling to cease being refugees. . . . The flesh pots of Egypt are a bit too full and fat." Relief officials in Iberia expressed surprise if not amusement at requests from society officers in Canada for their guidelines on support levels offered refugees in Spain and Portugal. One JDC agent in the field explained that Jewish relief groups did not match relief levels maintained by other agencies or governments-in-exile. Furthermore, he noted in passing, this was the first time he had ever confronted an inquiry suggesting support levels for refugees were too high instead of too low.[68]

The image of Jewish refugees in Spain and Portugal having given up lives of luxurious indolence to come to Canada persisted. Admittedly, these Iberian refugees, unable to work, depended on aid; with time heavy on their hands, milling about and anxious for every snippet of information from home or rumour that Spain or Portugal might enter the war, they were easy prey to anti-Semitic caricatures. After being read by Canadian military censors, copies of several unflattering letters home from Canadian airmen interned in Portugal were widely circulated among Ottawa civil servants. Typical was a letter from one airman, sitting out the duration in Caldas de Rainha, also the location of a Jewish refugee camp:

> My only hope, Doll, is that Canada doesn't take all these Jewish Refugees home from Portugal, like they are planning. Cause they are people who will never work and they say they won't work. They are no good too [*sic*] themselves. Just hunks of flesh that all sit around in cafes and talk and conspire and live off the money sent them by Charity organizations from England, Canada and the States. . . . I sure would hate to come home after the war is over and find Canada overrun with these Jewish Refugees. Doll, they receive the treatment they've been getting cause they ask for it. . . . I honestly hope that the Canadian Ministers smarten up and keep them out of Canada cause we've got enough Jews in Canada now. I wish I had a say in that matter, but I guess my job is to fight for a country that will probably be unfit to live in when its overrun by the conniving Jews.[69]

Canada was not to be "overrun" by Jews. Canada's active wartime refugee schemes, limited as they were, ended with good news from the war zones. Canadian authorities also avoided making or even hinting at future relief commitments. Of course, this did not rule out ritual expressions of concern for the fate of Nazi victims. If the government did not feel it was Canada's place to initiate international condemnation of the Nazi horrors, it was generally ready to endorse the initiatives of others.

Canada had supported a 1942 Allied Declaration against Nazi war crimes. In the spring of 1944 domestic American pressure forced the White House to prepare another statement, this time threatening retribution for war criminals. British officials were not pleased with the notion of another statement. As the British Dominions Office explained to Ottawa, the 1942 Declarlation "did not have the desired effect." It was, the British claimed, counter-productive. Following a line of reasoning that cautioned restraint in public declarations of this kind, the Dominions Office alleged that the Germans "may have felt that they could hit Allied nations by tormenting or killing large numbers of Allied Jewish nationals." This came close to arguing that the Nazis might not have murdered the Jews had they not been incited by outsiders. In any event, the Dominions Office was definite in arguing against any declaration because, it cautioned, "repeated warnings of this kind tend to debase the currency."[70]

External Affairs agreed with the British but little seemed at stake. They decided the best way to get along with the Americans was to go along. Lester Pearson, Canadian minister in Washington, was informed by Ottawa that, if the Americans persisted in their plans for a declaration, "it will probably be desirable for the Canadian government to associate itself with such a warning." Pearson reported that the Americans were, indeed, intent on some sort of statement, which they believed "could do no harm and might do some good." Pearson's sources also indicated that Roosevelt, who was behind a statement, had vetoed a proposed draft as too narrowly concerned with Jews. He wanted a "redrafted" statement that reduced the emphasis on victims in favour of one focusing on villains. This done, an American statement was issued on March 24, 1944, warning Germany, Japan and their allies of the consequences of war crimes. The British could not duck the issue and were forced to follow suit. Their parallel statement, directed at Nazi satellite governments, warned of a postwar reckoning and the "stern judgements" that would be meted out to all collaborators in war crimes. If, however, the Jewish angle had been deliberately downplayed in the American statement, it was eliminated in the British one.[71]

As was the case in 1942, the Canadians endorsed the Allied moves. Forewarned of the impending American declaration, a complementary Canadian statement was drafted for King to read in the Commons. The Commons statement reviewed the Canadian effort on behalf of refugees, deplored Nazi brutality but promised nothing, certainly no additional admission of refugees or moves toward a postwar relief policy. In any event, what more could Canada do in wartime? If the Allies might once have worried, as observed by Myron Taylor, that a door too widely open to refugees might carry a "danger of inviting the Germans to dump the Jews on the Allies," this no longer seemed likely. "The general refugee situation . . . is," a Canadian diplomat in London reported to Ottawa, "that Jewish refugees cannot succeed in getting out of the iron ring of German-occupied Europe and its satellite countries to places of refuge."[72]

Canadian Jewish leadership also understood that there were few Jews to be rescued outside of Iberia, but for those who might seek relocation out of difficult or inhospitable locations in the Caribbean or Africa, the answer from immigration authorities was almost always the same—no. The week of the American, British and Canadian statements, an exasperated Solkin complained to HICEM headquarters in New York. "I am sorry to say their [the government's] attitude to refugees from other than Spain or Portugal is as negative as ever before," he said. "This attitude clearly cannot be reasoned away. Relief may be expected only with a change in the sacrosanct regulations which, incidentally, remain the same as they were before the war regardless of all that happened and continues to happen in the world."[73]

The Canadian government felt no contradiction in time and again denying entry to refugees who had somehow successfully eluded the Nazis, while it publicly professed sympathy for those still victims of the Nazis—none of whom could escape. The government would find it more awkward, however, when called upon to grant haven to these victims, who could be snatched from the jaws of death if only they had a place to go. And despite earlier assurances from External Affairs that this could not happen, the cabinet faced exactly this dilemma in the summer of 1944. The issue was now Hungarian Jews.

In the late winter of 1944 the Nazi-allied government of Hungary, now convinced of an Allied victory, sought ways to open communication with the Allies. They hoped to negotiate a surrender, especially if it would forestall their being overrun by Soviet troops pushing in from the east. A pawn in the diplomatic game were 900,000 Hungarian Jews, the last major European Jewish community that had not yet suffered the "final solution." Perhaps because the Nazi death machine was fully occupied elsewhere, perhaps because the self-governing Nazi ally had hedged its bets, Hungarian Jewry remained, temporarily at least, intact. If they were subject to persecution and ghettoization, they were still alive. In January 1944 Ritchie reported to External Affairs from London on their status: "Although the Hungarian Jews suffer from disabilities they have not been subjected to ill-treatment."[74] One might question Ritchie's definition of "ill-treatment," but in any event the situation of Hungarian Jews deteriorated quickly after January 1944.

The Nazis, fearing a Hungarian capitulation to the Allies, moved quickly. They installed a new and more ardent Nazi supporter as prime minister, and in the early spring the new government was reinforced by German troops. With the troops came Adolf Eichmann and, with him, the deportations. By late summer over half of the Jews of Hungary had been transported to the camps of Auschwitz, Birkenau and Treblinka. In a report to the executive officers of the Canadian Jewish Congress, Saul Hayes outlined the immediate crisis in Hungary:

> Reports recently received would seem to indicate that the situation now in Hungary is desperate. The original hopes that Germans would be so busy at strategic military positions that they would not be able to ferret out the Jews in non-military areas has, unfortunately, not proven to be a fact. About 150,000 have been sent to Polish concentration camps, particularly the extermination centres as Oswiecim and Treblinka. Moreover, the situations of those who are not sent to concentration camps is desperately bad.[75]

In the midst of the Nazi roundup and deportation of Hungarian Jews came word of a strange, even bizzare, episode. Out of the shadowy world of international intrigue emerged a Nazi offer to trade Jews for commodities. In June 1944 External Affairs was informed that as many as one million Jews, largely from Hungary, might be released to Portugal or Spain in return for food, soap and other goods for civilian use: if, however, this "offer is rejected," the British told the Canadians, "they will proceed with their programme of whole-hearted liquidation." American and British governments, sensing that the offer might be authentic, agreed to keep discussions going. According to British sources, the Allied effort was "to gain time and induce Germans to hold their hand." At first it appeared the ploy had failed. In mid July 1944 the Dominions Office advised External Affairs that any hope that "the murder of the Jews" would "cease temporarily" had ended. The Hungarian question again seemed closed.[76]

Two weeks later it was open again. The British and Americans had now received signals that the Nazis in Hungary were again interested in a deal which could mean release of their remaining Jews. External Affairs was informed by the British that deportations of Jews had halted. The International Red Cross, acting as intermediary, anticipated Nazi approval for the release of children under ten years of age and adults with visas to

Palestine. Once this group was free, the International Red Cross hinted, any remaining Jews guaranteed admission to the United States or "British Commonwealth and Empire" might be allowed out. The British, fearing new pressure to take these Hungarian Jews into Palestine, began pressing the Americans to seek Latin American cooperation in admitting any released Hungarian Jews while they, for their part, would attempt to do the same with the Dominions and their self-governing colonies.[77]

The first pitch to Canada and the other Dominions was low key. The British outlined their Hungarian and Palestine problems and in a thinly veiled appeal for assistance, spoke to the urgency of the situation:

> We have already made considerable efforts to give asylum to Jewish refugees. A large number have recently entered Palestine and in conjunction with the United States Government and UNRRA, camps for the accommodation of 100,000 persons have been or are being established in the Mediterranean area. These camps will be almost entirely filled with Jews who have escaped from Yugoslavia via Italy. The problem of finding alternative destinations for any new influx of Jews from Hungary is acute but solution must be reached without delay, especially in view of the fact that we are meeting much ill-informed pressure due to ignorance of the restrictive capacity of Palestine.[78]

The pace of events moved quickly. Before External Affairs could weigh the consequences of any reply, it was advised by the British that a joint British and American declaration would be issued accepting the offer to release Jews. The proposed declaration would assure both Allies and neutrals that the British and Americans would arrange for the care of all Jews permitted to leave Hungary who reached neutral or United Nations territory, and would "find for such people temporary haven." In a separate communication to Ottawa, the British explained that their acceptance was not quite as open as it might seem at first. A close reading of the approved Allied Declaration still referred only to the initial offer of haven for children under ten years of age and those children and adults eligible for admission to Palestine. Nevertheless, the British had to consider the alarming prospect of a wholesale removal of Jews from Hungary, and they now dropped their soft sell. They explained to the Canadians that, if the terms in the joint declaration were accepted by the Nazis, it could soon lead to a flood of Jews out of

Hungary beyond anything the British could or would accommodate. In preparation, Canada and the other Dominions were requested to consider whether there were any steps that could be taken toward "furnishing temporary asylum for some of these Hungarian Jews."[79]

The British were not the only ones now applying pressure on Canada. The Americans, also not wishing to be saddled with all these Jews, looked for assistance wherever they could find it. They resurrected an old Canadian offer, and formally asked the Canadian government to "extend its acceptance in principle on this matter to [one thousand] children from Hungary as well as from France."[80] Also, at a plenary meeting of the Intergovernmental Committee on Refugees, the Hungarian crisis was added to the agenda, and it was expected that the British and Americans would apply pressure on Canada as a committee member to accept Hungarian Jews.

Canadian Jewish Congress leaders, briefed by American contacts on events unfolding in Hungary, also appealed to Canadian authorities. A telegram to External Affairs over the signature of Samuel Bronfman pleaded for a positive Canadian gesture at the upcoming IGC meetings. "Implore Canadian government," it said, "to instruct Canadian representative to offer some measure of participation in rescue scheme for our compatriots trapped in Nazi area and for rescue of children in those and contiguous countries. Indifference to the fate of these refugees will fully sign their death warrants. In this hour of approaching victory let us add luster to Canada's shield by a practical measure of full support."[81]

Vincent Massey, Canada's representative at the Intergovernmental Committee meetings, was so negative when it came to Jewish refugees that, barring direct instructions from Ottawa to the contrary, he could be counted on to reject any suggestion of a Canadian initiative to assist Hungarian Jews. He received no such instructions. Furthermore, Massey had already dismissed the whole Hungarian rescue scheme, or at least efforts to involve others besides the Americans in it, as naked political hucksterism by Roosevelt. At a meeting of Dominion high commissioners on August 10, 1944, Massey joked with the assembled diplomats about the American Democrats' current aims in this, an American election year. "They apparently want the Jewish vote," he said, "without taking in more Jews, because if they allow more Jews in they would lose the Roman Catholic vote." It was not, in Massey's view, the job of the Dominions to pull Democratic Party chestnuts out of the political fires.[82] A few days later Massey was in his seat as Canadian representative to the Intergovernmental Committee on Refugees.

The Dominions proved no more amenable to British chestnuts than they were to those of American origin. The British had become entangled in the Hungarian Jewish business and now, External Affairs believed, because of Palestine, they wanted the Dominions to come to their rescue. The further Canada stayed away from this business, the better. Nor were the Americans any more deserving. They had insisted on giving the Nazis in Hungary carte blanche to dump their Jews on the United Nations, and now they too wanted Canada to help clean up the mess. Better, many felt, to let the Americans and British sort it out themselves. Whatever their feelings, External Affairs argued that Canada was still required to respond to the American and British requests. The Hungarian problem was placed on the agenda for the next cabinet meeting.

Hume Wrong, who had been Canadian representative at Evian, pulled together a memorandum recommending the best Hungarian options open to the cabinet. In a conciliatory move designed to placate the Americans, he recommended that the cabinet agree to allow Jewish children in Hungary to fill the unused quota left for refugee children in France. The fine print, however, was far from conciliatory. All the guarantees demanded in the French program, guarantees that effectively undermined its application, were declared essential and transferable to the Hungarian situation. And adults were even a bigger problem. As a smoke screen Wrong suggested the cabinet agree "in principle to find temporary asylum for some adult Hungarian Jews." The number of Jews and conditions of asylum could be decided later.[83]

Once again Wrong's proposal intended to give less than what appeared at first blush. In a secret accompanying memorandum to the cabinet, Wrong explained that nothing he suggested need commit Canada to admit any adult refugees into Canada. Far from it. Obscure wording and vague references to refugee relief might, later and in less stressful times, be interpreted as a promise "to finance the maintenance of 500 to 1,000 of these refugees in some European country such as Turkey or Switzerland or, perhaps, French North Africa."[84] Wrong correctly reasoned that the American and British requests were precautionary—designed not to fill an immediate need but to allow for contingency planning lest anything actually materialize. External

Affairs believed, Wrong explained, that in spite of the current Hungarian uproar, the release offer would eventually come to nothing. The cabinet was advised that "it did not appear likely that any substantial number of Jewish refugees would be able to leave Hungary." If Wrong proved correct, an apparently liberal offer would score points with both the Americans and British at no cost to Canada. If External Affairs proved wrong and Jews got out of Hungary, little harm would have been done. All that Canada would be committed to do was financially support some refugees abroad, likely through the IGC, which Canada would probably do in the end anyway.

The cabinet debated the international situation in general and Hungary in particular, and they finally drew different conclusions than had Wrong. Any suggestion of Canadian participation in any refugee relief scheme, beyond that in Spain and Portugal, the cabinet concluded, was dangerous. No matter how cleverly worded any offer might be, it could be used at some later date by the Allies, desperate to find a home for refugees, to push Canada into admitting Hungarian or other Jews. If, on the other hand, the Hungarian Jewish problem was fast disappearing on its own, as External Affairs suggested was the case, then there seemed no harm in stalling. Concluding that no action was positive action, the cabinet "agreed that no commitments should be made at present in view of the confusing political position in Hungary."[85]

The scheme to rescue the Jews of Hungary fell through. It may already have been a dead issue when the Canadian cabinet met to consider the question—although they certainly did not know it at the time. Two months after the Canadian cabinet agreed to do nothing the refugee committee of the British Foreign Office conducted an autopsy on the defunct Hungarian scheme. Committee members agreed it was unfortunate that nothing had come of the plan; that was better, everyone also agreed, than to be awash in a sea of Hungarian Jews without a place to put them. It was noted, in passing, that all the Dominions had refused haven, even temporarily, to Hungarian Jews—all but Canada, that is: Canada hadn't even replied. The committee knew better than to interpret Canadian silence as indecision.[86]

Ironically, the very refugee crisis that Canada had attempted to side-step when it came to offering a home to refugees presented External Affairs with an opportunity to move centre stage in the international arena—just the recognition the department coveted. In January 1944 the British and Americans moved to expand the mandate of the Intergovernmental Committee on Refugees as decided at the Bermuda Conference. Their plans necessitated an enlargement of the IGC executive, and the British Foreign Office pressed for the inclusion of a Dominion on the executive. Canada, "with large immigration possibilities" and, as one misinformed Foreign Office official assumed, a "more lively interest in refugees than the other Dominions," seemed an obvious choice.[87]

Britain's motive for promoting Canada for the IGC executive had a subtle political purpose. The British saw Canadian membership on the executive as a link in a three-part chain. It was imperative, the British felt, that the Soviet Union join the executive if any postwar program of repatriation of refugees back to their homelands had any hope of success. The Soviet Union might balk at being invited onto the executive by itself, but if Canada agreed to join for the West and Switzerland or Sweden for the neutrals, then the Soviet Union might be persuaded to represent the East. But why Canada? The answer was as simple as it was unflattering. The British were sure the Canadian appointment was "safe." They believed Canadians would never be imprudent or rock the boat. The Canadians, the British believed, always played it safe, relied on British advice and voted as they were told. The only flaw in the British scheme was the possibility that the U.S.S.R. might refuse to join the committee's executive and, as a concerned Dominions Office official pointed out, Canada might be "embarrassed" to have its invitation withdrawn.[88]

Without revealing their plan to use Canada as a lure to bait the Soviet Union, the British sent out preliminary feelers to the Canadians. Canada snapped up the opportunity.[89] Why would Canada agree to take a potentially high-profile position in a refugee agency when its own policy remained so negative regarding refugees? Once again the reason was simple and politically expedient. Not only would it bring Canada into an important inner circle of postwar international planning, but it might also give the government a weapon against those at home who might protest that Canada was not doing enough for refugees—both at little financial cost and without having to take refugees. The under-secretary of state for External Affairs, Norman Robertson, brought Jolliffe into the picture lest the direction of immigration fear the move foreshadowed a change in policy on refugees. "I doubt whether Canadian membership on the Executive Committee," Robertson said, "would make any real difference in the extent of action that will be expected to be taken by this country in dealing with the refugee problem. It would, however, probably be a useful step in placating the opinion which takes the vein that Canada should be a more active participant in refugee matters."[90]

By late summer 1944 the deal was set. At the same IGC meeting where the Hungarian Jewish situation was reviewed, Massey gratefully acknowledged Canada's election to the executive, pledged his government's commitment to assist in the planning of a postwar refugee relief plan, then took his seat.[91]

It would be incorrect to assume that the Canadian government was giving no consideration to postwar immigration—just no consideration to refugee immigration. In the spring of 1944, as the light of victory began to shine more brightly in the distance, a request from the British government that Canada consider absorbing a number of discharged United Kingdom servicemen and their dependents was given quick approval by the cabinet. Only a series of technical problems including medical inspections and transfer of pensions were left to be ironed out.[92] It was not long before immigration of British servicemen became, simply, immigration of the British. Some Canadian officials warned of the distinct possibility that the end of hostilities might well signal economic backslide into depression. The government's British immigration initiative took this into account, however. At a meeting of Dominion prime ministers in London in May 1944, King reassured London and the folks at home: it was Canadian policy that no restrictions would be imposed "on the entry of migrants from British stock provided that they were able to look after themselves and would not become a charge upon public funds."[93]

Opening the door to British settlers did nothing to pry open the door for refugees. In April 1944 Herbert Emerson, the IGC director, again visited Ottawa to discuss refugee matters. He explained that his committee was requesting official "statements from various governments as to the number of refugees they would be willing to receive after the war." In turn, External Affairs officials pointed out to Emerson that the refugee matter was one that could not and would not be acted upon until postwar conditions crystallized. And, as part of his IGC executive duties, Massey was instructed by Ottawa to avoid any suggestion that Canada could confirm its postwar immigration policy until well after the war's end.[94]

Refugees would not come to Canada, not yet at least, and postwar discussions in the Intergovernmental Committee focused on the feasibility of repatriation. It must have been tempting to officials to believe the refugee problem could be solved simply by sending refugees back where they came from. All they need do is work out the mechanics.

For Jewish leaders the very notion of repatriation, of sending Jews back to the countries of their persecution, seemed a monstrous obscenity. It was imperative to advise Allied leaders of Jewish anxiety at the very notion of forced repatriation and begin to suggest options. A. J. Freiman, a friend of King's and leader of the Canadian Zionists, aided Liberal member of Parliament Arthur David Roebuck in arranging for Nachum Goldmann, head of the World Jewish Congress, to join them in a meeting with King in Ottawa in the spring of 1944. Goldmann offered King a sombre picture of a decimated European Jewry and the heavy task awaiting the postwar world in placing its scattered remnants. His immediate appeal was for Palestine to be opened to Jews. In the afterglow of the meeting Freiman wrote Chaim Weizmann: "When we left the office I was convinced our P.M. was favourably impressed. I am sure that when Mr. King attends the Imperial Conference in London he will be well-informed and kindly disposed to our Zionist cause."[95]

King, unfortunately, was more concerned with time than with causes. Regarding this meeting, King recorded in his diary that the delegation that came "to plead for the Balfour declaration being carried out and Palestine being made a home for Jews" took too long to make its presentation. One delegate, he complained, "spoke for a straight half hour." To cut off the tiresome presentation, the prime minister pleaded a previously scheduled cabinet meeting. As consolation he promised, in passing, to raise the question of Palestine at the London meetings.* The delegation was ushered out.[96]

* The plan that refugee Jews would find a permanent home in Palestine after the war held some appeal to some Canadian non-Jews as well—not always for the most sympathetic reasons. If Jews could not or would not go back to Germany or Poland or wherever, then better Palestine than Canada. Silby Barrett, a leader of the United Mine Workers of America in Nova Scotia, for example, wrote to Pat Conroy of the Canadian Congress of Labour: "It is my opinion," he said, "that Palestine should be granted to the Jews, and they should be all kept over there. We can do without them very well in Canada." Public Archives of Canada, Canadian Labour Congress Papers, Silby Barrett to Pat Conroy, April 29, 1944.

Victory in Europe was now only a matter of time. With victory would come more refugees. It became increasingly clear that many Jews would not willingly accept repatriation. In a letter to Massey, Chaim Weizmann wrote that millions of innocent Jews had been slaughtered by the Nazis. World Jewry now expected to direct its efforts toward the resettlement of an estimated two million Jews who may have survived. "It would be idle to expect and crude to encourage resettlement of these people among the ghosts of their dead and surrounded by Anti-Semitic populations," Weizmann wrote. "In these circumstances *large scale* emigration would be unavoidable."

Nor was Weizmann unrealistic about the welcome these people would have in countries like Canada. Weizmann, the lifelong Zionist, must have unknowingly hit a responsive chord with Massey, at least in part. English-speaking countries, he explained to the Canadian high commissioner, "are unlikely to welcome Jewish mass immigration and from the Jewish point of view it is far more desirable . . . to resettle immigration on a solid national basis in a Jewish state rather than to send them where they are bound to create new problems."[97] Whatever Massey's opinion on the Palestine issue, he certainly would agree Jewish refugees were unwelcome in Canada.

It was equally clear to Canadian Jewish officials that the postwar era would not usher in a new period of openness in Canadian attitudes toward Jewish refugees. Solkin warned the Jewish Immigrant Aid Society executive in Toronto not to expect any easing of immigration restrictions. "It is obvious," the director said, "that our post-war immigration work will be hard indeed and that a concentrated effort will have to be made by Canadian Jewry to bring about some reasonable modification which could satisfy even the minimum of our pressing needs."[98]

The pressing needs of Canadian Jewry to help those in Europe would grow more pressing. The Soviet sweep westward after the Nazi defeat at Stalingrad and the Allied liberation of much of western Europe soon left only Germany itself to be subdued. But with the reality of resounding victory came other realities—the magnitude of the holocaust and the desperation of survivors. In January 1945 advancing Soviet troops overran Auschwitz. Of the millions who had entered the camp, the liberators found fewer than three thousand people still alive. A string of smaller if no less shocking discoveries culminated in early April 1945, with the American entry into Buchenwald.

What so many, including many Jews, had prayed was war propaganda, exaggerations or even hysteria now paled next to the reality. That which had seemed too horrible to be imagined was not too horrible to have happened.

During the war some had known more than others. Some had pieced together the truth while others understood what it meant. If historians debate who knew what and when, an equally critical issue is whether or how knowledge, of whatever degree, shaped attitudes or actions.[99] It is clear that by the summer of 1943, at the latest, some two years before the German surrender, Canadian officials had available to them not only authenticated accounts of Nazi barbarism, but also evidence that this barbarism was part of a systematic and scientific program of mass murder of Jews. In mid January 1944, for instance, Charles Ritchie in London attended a British Foreign Office briefing on the state of Jewish affairs in Europe, especially those concerning any possible escape of Jews from German satellites and unliberated Europe. More by way of an update than a revelation, he made his report to Ottawa. "It is not possible to add anything to what is already known about the appalling conditions in Poland," he wrote. "In France, again, the conditions of the Jews are very bad. The Germans are deporting large numbers of them to unknown destinations, sometimes with the connivance of Vichy officials, but usually as a result of the direct action of the Gestapo. Conditions are also extremely bad in Roumania. The massacres have ceased but deportations to Trans-niestria [*sic*] still continue."[100]

Nor was Canadian External Affairs in the dark as to what "deportation" meant. Just as "refugee" was then a code word for "Jew," so too "deportation" was already a code word for mass murder. In May 1944, eight months before Soviet troops entered Auschwitz, External Affairs circulated for intra-departmental consideration, a matter-of-fact British Foreign Office report entitled "The Jews of Poland," detailing the brutality of the persecution and liquidation of European Jewry. "A very large proportion of the Jews in Poland," it said,

> have been put to death by the German occupying authorities since September, 1939. Immediately on their conquest of Poland the Germans began to segregate the Jews, by forcing them to wear special marks; and to expropriate their houses, their businesses and their personal property; while their food rations were only half those allowed to the Poles. At first, in

> 1939, an attempt was made to make a part of the province of Lublin north of that city into a Jewish Reserve. This policy was soon changed, by 1940, into one of concentration in ghettoes, which were established in all the larger towns. Not only all Polish Jews, but large numbers from other occupied countries were moved into the ghettoes, or into special areas in the smaller towns. The only Jews not so moved were those able-bodied men and women who were placed in labour gangs or forced to work in factories.
>
> After the German attack on the U.S.S.R. in June 1941, the German authorities began to carry out a policy of gradual annihilation of all Jews except for some of those employed in gangs or factory work. In 1942 this process was systematised, and special camps are believed to have been built, notably at Chelmno, Belzec, and Treblinka, for mass murder by suffocation. The population of the Warsaw Ghetto is said to have been reduced in August, 1942, alone from 400,000 to about 23,000. The total number of Jews who have been scientifically put to death, or have died under torture, or from starvation, disease or exposure, in German camps in Poland, is estimated at from two-thirds to nine-tenths of the Jewish population, including those brought from other countries. It is generally believed that about 300,000 are still alive in Poland, including those who are fighting among the Polish underground forces; that as many or rather more are now in the U.S.S.R. and that some probably lesser number are working in Germany in gangs or factories.[101]

Nor were the British the only source of Canadian information on the final solution. In a file simply labelled "German Atrocities," Canadian External Affairs collected official communications on the persecution of Jews. These included reports from the American, Soviet and several Allied governments-in-exile. All were circulated.

In 1944 intelligence reports, compiled from the reliable accounts of escapees, were made redundant by the ultimate evidence—the discovery and liberation of the concentration camps. Eyewitness accounts of the camps and testimony from captured guards and surviving inmates seared the pages of official reports. New form and dimension were given to terms such as "mass murder." A joint Polish-Soviet commission moved into Majdanek concentration camp near Lublin, Poland, on the heels of the Red Army. The investigating team did not try to make sense of what they found or moralize on man's inhumanity to man. It was enough to chronicle events as they had happened. Their report was the only memorial for hundreds of thousands whose death agony might have no other mark.

> The massacre of 20,000 prisoners by shooting took place on November 3, 1943. The people were shot in the ditches where they were buried to the accompaniment of the radio loudspeakers which played waltzes and fox-trots. The shooting went on from morning until six in the evening. Children were thrown into the graves alive. Witness Budzen stated that even on the next day cries came from the graves. A few days later the bodies were dug up and burned. For a number of days 1,000 to 1,500 bodies a day were burned.[102]

Any doubts Canadian officials might have harboured as to the reliability of reports of Soviet origin were soon set aside when American observer teams also entered Auschwitz and its sister camp, Birkenau. The Americans began taking sworn evidence from the few survivors, perhaps in anticipation of war crimes trials.[103] Several copies of the American findings, a report that the Canadian ambassador in Washington, Lester Pearson, called "the most appalling document ever published on the perpetration of organized atrocities," were sent to Ottawa for consideration.[104] To the report Pearson appended a clipping from the *Washington Post*. This article grappled, perhaps as Pearson did himself, with a problem of finding words in English with the necessary scope—which neither "organized atrocities" nor "mass murder" seem to have—to encompass the totality of horror: "It is a mistake, perhaps, to call these killings 'atrocities.' An atrocity is a wanton brutality. There were unspeakable atrocities at Auschwitz and Birkenau. But the point about these killings is that they were systematic and purposeful. The gas chambers and furnaces were not improvisations; they were scientifically designed instruments for the extermination of an entire ethnic group."[105]

The article argued that this crime, "which human beings find so difficult to believe or understand," remains alone in the annals of history and, as such, must have its own name—genocide. With the discovery of the camps, the public, including the Canadian public, now knew what its governments had long known about events in Europe. But if the press offered descriptions and impressions, was it possible for readers to make sense of the information? Even when confronted by the actuality that their worst nightmares were true millions of times over, could even the Canadian Jewish community grasp the enormity of the Jewish catastrophe? It is hard to know. In August 1944 Raymond Davies reported to the *Jewish Eagle* in Montreal from the recently liberated Majdanek concentration camp. His cable spoke not of the mass murders of Jews but the murders of individuals, perhaps family or friends of those in Canada:

> Men, women and children taken to Majdanek into bath houses were immediately gassed. Things left by victims fill huge warehouses in Lublin and I saw with my own eyes pile shoes numbering at least eight hundred thousand, whole boxes eyeglasses, whole shelves *tsitsim* prayer books.
> I saw mountains children's toys. And in Kolanpitsky forest I saw scores little bodies taken out from graves. These are children who left toys. I . . . never forget this dried out body mother holding her hands little child its head smashed. Mother showed no wounds and was there buried alive.

The horror of mass death, according to Davies, was juxtaposed with the bravery of the few survivors. And knowledge of the former, he cabled, carried with it responsibility to the latter. Davies made an impassioned plea to Canadian Jewry on behalf of a tattered remnant:

> You are able to cause their resurrection. You can save and return to life all these who half dead survived this general disorder.
>
> Jew! Do you understand what you are able to do? Do you understand that you are able to write a glorious page in history of all Jewish people?
>
> Do you understand what a responsibility will lie upon you if you who are lucky will not use all your possibilities to save these few remainders of your brothers? Jewish hearts where are you? Jewish mothers remember orphans left behind.
>
> You and strong people remember old and weak and lonely those who have survived.
>
> Unite all your thoughts and all your feeling in one fine universal complete immediate aid for Jewish victims of Hitlerism.
>
> I require of you in name those who still live and with whom I am. They ask of you to remember the millions of those who were killed only because they were Jews.[106]

If Davies hoped to see any of these survivors immediately resettled in Canada, he would be disappointed. Canada was not about to open its doors. In a February 1945 memorandum to the prime minister discussing the unfolding refugee problem and Canada's role in the Intergovernmental Committee, the scope of the genocide was pointed out to the prime minister. "The number of Jewish people who have been done away with must be enormous," it read. "The problem with regard to Jewish refugees," the note continued, "may not be too large and may not present 'any insurmountable difficulties'." The problem of survivors was not Canada's problem.[107]

7

ONE WAILING CRY

One morning in early May 1945 work at Globe Bedding, a mattress manufacturer in Winnipeg, came to an abrupt halt. As the company owner looked on sympathetically, women in the plant gathered around a fellow worker. They comforted her, shared her grief and perhaps anticipated their own. The worker, a fifteen-year employee at Globe Bedding, had just received a letter from her sister in Russian-liberated Poland. This was the first word she had had since the German invasion of Poland in the autumn of 1939. The sister explained simply that, "from her family of 85 people, everyone was killed with the exception of the sister and her child." The company owner appealed to the Canadian Jewish Congress on behalf of his employee to bring her sister and niece to Canada. "I don't possess the ability," he wrote, "to describe to you the picture I faced when all the girls in the plant stood around her and all that could be heard was one wailing cry." And a Congress official responded to this letter as he would to so many others. Immigration prospects out of Poland were poor. "At the moment I would say that it is out of the question. . . . I fully realize your feeling in this case. Unfortunately, there are millions of this kind."[1]

There may not have been millions of this kind, but there were many. Almost daily lists of known survivors were posted outside Congress and Jewish Immigrant Aid Society offices across Canada, and hundreds lined up awaiting their turn to see if someone they knew, someone they loved, had survived. For some patience was rewarded with a name; for most there was only disappointment. Before long more letters from survivors reached relatives and friends in Canada. Too many were the tales of horror, too few the avenues of help. Rare was the Jewish family in Canada that did not suffer losses in the catastrophe.

On October 30, 1945, Sarah Szklarska wrote from Europe to her brother in Toronto: "After many years of suffering I have been freed by the British. Dear, dear brother, I alone survive. My husband was taken by the Gestapo and I don't know how he perished. I am all alone and have nobody except you. Our dear mother was shot before my very eyes and you can imagine my suffering. When I was liberated I was a living corpse but now I look much better."[2]

These letters must be seen not just as pleas for aid and assistance—which of course they were—but also as the first steps taken by survivors to reorder shattered lives. Children, their parents dead, now sought out family in Canada they had never known, family members who had left Europe years earlier. The letters from orphaned children to faceless relatives implored an uncle or a cousin to fill the boundless void left by murdered parents. Two children in Bergen-Belsen displaced persons camp, so recently the site of a Nazi death camp, responded to a newfound aunt in Toronto: "I received your letter for which I thank you very much. I have read it with great joy. You cannot imagine how we think and worry about you, because you now are our parents, our entire family. The murderers have destroyed my parents and everything."[3] A sixteen-year-old boy, invoking raw images of the living nightmare through which he had just passed, begged relatives in Canada for rescue.

> I, your sister's son Szolek Goldrich write you a letter. I have already written a few words and now am writing a second time. You cannot imagine my happiness knowing that you know about me and I about you. I am together with my uncle Hershel Lejb. We were together in camp and with God's help we survived the tragic time about which we cannot fully account for. I am one of the children and what they have done to children you know well. I fought for my life daily and finally survived.
>
> I, therefore, beg you dear uncle not to forget me now. I am now 16 years of age, I still can have a future in life. I beg you my dear ones that you try and take me out of the cursed land where every piece of ground is soaked with blood. I conclude my writing and beg you to answer me so that I can rejoice again in receiving a letter from you. At present when I receive a letter I feel that I am no longer lonely that you will be my father and mother.[4]

And some survivors had an even more hopeless tale to tell

those in Canada. "You don't know me and you don't know you are now the only relative from my wife's family to whom I can write," a stranger wrote to a Toronto man, reaching out with a claim to his aid.

> I am the husband of your sister Sonia. We have married 1942. During four years from 1940 till 1944 have we passed through the dark tragic life in the ghetto hand by hand having our love with us, which makes the burden easier to bear. Sonia had always dreamed that our first step after the war will be a journey to you. But all turned in a way we have not expected. In September 1944 when the Russians were near the German gestapo took all Jews from the getto and send us to the most famous of the concentration camps, to Auschwitz.
>
> We came there all together: Sonia, I, my parents and sister, you sister Rozia with her three children Hesiek, Bela and Salusia. (Rozia's husband Godel died in getto 1941, so as your parents and your brother Herszel.) Believe me that I would like that my parents would have died also in getto! In Auschwitz were we separated men and women and then all elder people and children till 13–14 years have been burned in crematorium. Can you understand this?! The younger men and women after some selections have been transported to various K.L. in Germany. From our arrival to Auschwitz till to-day I have heard nothing about Sonia. I was transported to Braunschweig and till the end of the war I was in five concentration camps. It's impossible for me to describe and for you to understand what I have survived in the K.L. Enough that when the American troops came and liberated us I was lying so sick and weak that I couldn't already neither move nor speak and when the help would come a few days after it would be too late. From that day I am still lying in hospitals and now I am slowly recovering to health in Sweden. My first step here is to write to you. I have in Germany meet several girls and women from Lodz but nobody have heard about Sonia. I get crazy when I think that I can Sonia seen no more. She was so delicate and subtle and the life in camps was so hard. I become mad when I think about this all. My last hope is that she is also lying in some hospital in Germany and cannot herself go to the few centers in Germany where are coming these which seeks their relatives. I am sure that if she is alive her first step will be also to write to you. Oh, it wouldn't be a happier pair in the world as I and Sonia if we can meet

again. You cannot imagine how deep and beautiful was our love.

I have you so much to write that I don't know what to write first. I am to be in Sweden for six months. What will be with me after this time—I don't know. I will not go back to Poland. I have there no home anymore and there is no place for Jews. I would like to emigrate to America. Europe is a damned earthpart. Here will be still wars.

I must finish my letter because the person who is sending the letter to you is waiting impatiently.

Dear Moritz?! I mustn't write how impatiently I shall expect an answer from you. I will believe that perhaps you would have a sign of life from Sonia. Oh, when you can come to Europe and help me to find out her.[5]

In the spring of 1945 war in Europe came to an end. Allied troops stamped out the last pockets of resistance inside Germany and overran the bunkers in Berlin. Amid reports that Hitler had taken his own life, a caretaker German government surrendered unconditionally. But until the end, even as all else collapsed around them, Nazi leaders determined that efforts to murder the Jews would continue. Of the approximately nine million Jews in prewar Europe, fewer than three million survived the war. Among those systematically put to death were two million Jewish children.

But what of the survivors, Jewish and non-Jewish? Many were now refugees scattered outside their countries of birth, although just how many refugees there were is hard to know. Definitional problems and variations in data gathering make a mockery of statistics. Nevertheless, from the onset of the final Nazi collapse in February and March 1945 to the formal surrender of Germany in early May 1945, the number of refugees, or displaced persons as they were then being called, outside Soviet-occupied Europe grew from approximately 350,000 to 6,795,000; an estimated 6,800,000 refugees remained in Soviet-held territory. With the aid of the Allied military, the United Nations, local authorities and relief agencies, displaced persons were identified, processed and consigned to a series of displaced persons camps or reception centres, which sprang up across Germany, Austria and, in lesser numbers, other liberated territory. However, the question of what was to become of these people remained to be answered.

As far as the Soviet Union and her new allies were concerned the answer was simple. Displaced persons were displaced only as long as they did not go back to their countries of origin. The solution to the problem was therefore obvious: send them home. Ship all Soviet nationals back to the Soviet Union, all Polish nationals back to Poland, all French nationals back to France and so on. Those Germans guilty of no crimes against the Allies or local populations should also be repatriated. Those guilty of crimes, together with other culpable collaborators or quislings, should be tried.

In the late stages of the war and in the confused period immediately after, the western Allies tended to agree that simple repatriation was an obvious solution. Following the 1945 summer of victory many millions of persons were somehow processed, cared for and many eventually transported, sometimes forcibly, back to their countries of origin. But just as autumn gives way to winter, so the autumn repatriation program gave way to winter resistance. Many, especially Jews, refused to return to the eastern European heartland of anti-Semitism. Non-Jews who refused repatriation included eastern Europeans who denounced Soviet annexation or political domination of their homelands, thousands more who simply hoped for eventual resettlement in the West, and, of course, an unknown number of war criminals and pro-Nazi sympathizers and collaborators who sought to escape Allied justice. Added to these were the many Jews who, though already repatriated to Eastern Europe or liberated by the Soviets, decided to move westward. Some were escaping anti-Semitic outbreaks in Eastern Europe, while others simply and sadly discovered that the world in which they had lived, along with those they had loved, had been consumed in the fires of the Nazi genocide. They made their way westward, often illegally or with the contrivance of eastern European governments eager to rid themselves of their Jews, and found their way into the displaced persons camps of American- and British-occupied Germany and Austria. By the time the dust settled, approximately 250,000 Jewish displaced persons were being cared for in western Europe.[6] Rejecting repatriation, these Jews joined other displaced persons in awaiting new homes.

Canada, of course, was not about to offer one. When European hostilities finally ended in the spring of 1945, Canadians might agree that refugees deserved aid, sympathy and justice, but few would counsel immigration to Canada as a solution. This was not for lack of information about what had taken place in Europe and its consequences. In April 1945 Georges Vanier, Canadian ambassador to France, joined a group of American congressmen touring Buchenwald concentration camp in Germany just a week after its liberation by Allied troops. He had been assigned to gather facts about three Canadian servicemen executed in Buchenwald, together with thirty-four other Allied officers, but the ambassador learned and saw much more.

Vanier, reporting back to External Affairs in Ottawa, described the death chambers, the crematorium and the nearby lots where "naked bodies piled like so much cord wood, and on which lime was thrown" once fed the overtaxed ovens and now awaited burial in the mass graves dug by Allied bulldozers. He described his visit with the few survivors housed in an improvised hospital, many with running sores and so emaciated that their protruding bones made it difficult for them to lie for long in one position. Almost numb with shock, Vanier reported talking to several men who were still able to stand, though they were little more than skin and bones; he related his amazement at being able to see "how [their] knee and ankle joints held together." Among the survivors, Vanier informed External Affairs, were several hundred children, most of them Polish Jews. "Some had been in prison camps for years," he wrote. "Those of ten and over worked as slave labourers on munitions. Not one, so far as I know, had any idea of where his parents were; in view of the barbarous treatment inflicted on Poles and Jews by the Germans, it is possible they have all been done to death."[7]

In a report on his visit, broadcast over the trans-Canada network of the Canadian Broadcasting Corporation, Vanier described to all Canadians much of what he had already reported to Ottawa. To this mass audience, however, he confided his own sense of shame at having done nothing for the victims when something might have been done. "How deaf we were then," he lamented, "to cruelty and the cries of pain which came to our ears, grim forerunners of the mass torture and murder which were to follow."[8]

The Canadian high commissioner in London, Vincent Massey, would not be outdone by Vanier. Armed with a copy of Vanier's report, Massey too reported on Buchenwald or, more correctly, on the British public's reaction to reports from Buchenwald sent by a visiting British parliamentary team. Massey, who had previously used the power of his office to counsel Ottawa against the rescue of Jews, now described the impact of the revelations on "the people" (among whom he perhaps included himself):

> There has been a final realization that such things were done in Germany and that all tales of brutality and sadism are not merely "atrocity stories." After seeing the pictures and the news reels and reading the reports not only of reputable press correspondents, but also of a responsible parliamentary delegation, people will never again be able to close their minds and deny that the Nazis were guilty of appalling deeds. . . . There were stories published of atrocities in concentration camps before the war but the people as a whole did not believe them as they now believe the present evidence.

Massey may have set aside his personal antipathies as he reported on the public's response to Buchenwald, but he remained adamant on one point. Ultimate responsibility for these atrocities rested squarely with the Nazis. One might condemn the excesses of Nazi racial policy, express sympathy for its victims and lament the brutality of which men were capable; one might even feel guilt or shame about previous disregard and inaction. But these expressions of concern, no matter how sincere, presented Canada with no immediate obligation to the survivors, at least no obligation to offer them sanctuary. Massey, even while describing the surge of public interest generated by these events, suggested that much of this interest might be dismissed as "morbid curiosity," and he agreed that in Britain few outside the Jewish community or otherwise directly touched by these horrible revelations showed much interest in offering survivors a home.[9]

Resettlement of refugees was also far from centre stage in Canadian postwar planning. Even as the war pushed on to certain victory, the Canadian public and its government had domestic problems to worry about, and most pressing of these was the possibility of an economic depression. Indeed, Canadian postwar planners had a single recurring nightmare. With war, with its orgy of public spending, explosion in manpower demands and far-reaching technological advances, Canada had perhaps overexpanded and overspent. Now, if the experience immediately following the First World War was any measure, the Canadian economy was in for some rough jolts. Canadian leaders of the post-Second World War era were for the most part products of the Great Depression, their political or civil-service careers built on bad times. If a few, like Canada's wartime economic czar, C. D. Howe, trumpeted their confidence in business and employment prospects in the new postwar era, most warned of belt tightening, costly welfare programs and continued rationing.

The litany of woe would of course be proven wrong. The Canada of 1945 was not the Canada of 1918, and the country emerged from the Second World War a major economic force in primary and secondary industry as well as in resource development. Canada, a willing partner in the enormous task of western European reconstruction, soon found ready consumer markets at home and well beyond its own national boundaries.[10] Yet, even while the country was in fact entering upon an unprecedented economic upswing, many Canadians and their leaders, anticipating the worst, could not heed the signs of coming prosperity. Naturally enough, their misplaced fears overrode any sense of responsibility to European refugees, including Jews. Further, in the mood of economic caution that dogged the heels of victory, Ottawa was especially concerned with the smooth and gradual reabsorption of the Canadian military into civilian life. Keeping men in uniform for long after the fighting had ended would surely be unpopular at home. The Canadian public wanted the boys home, and demands for general demobilization from within the ranks grew ever louder. The government, however, wanted to forestall any economic dislocation that immediate mass demobilization might produce. It lived with visions of unemployed servicemen standing in the bread lines or, even worse, resorting to violence when jobs and new homes were not forthcoming. On the one hand, it seemed better to keep men in uniform, and yet the social or political consequences of delay were untenable. Thus, the government, juggling demands for demobilization with its possible adverse effects, finally assumed resettlement of military personnel as a national priority. Eventually, Canadian economic expansion made this resettlement easier than had been envisioned, but who could have known that at the time. And again, with the necessity to reabsorb soldiers, even to consider accepting refugees was precluded.*

* The two issues had been linked at least once before. As early as the spring of 1944, when postwar planning was officially made a government priority, the prime minister explained to a Jewish visitor that Canada could only "fill many of her large waste spaces with population once our own men have returned from the front." "I must say," King wrote later that day, "when one listens to accounts of their persecutions, one cannot have any human sympathies without being prepared to do much on their behalf." Human sympathies were all right in their place, it seems, but resettlement of troops came first; refugees would have to wait. Public Archives of Canada, King Diary, June 11, 1944, 579.

Economic fears aside, lurking hostility to "foreign" immigrants, particularly eastern Europeans and, most particularly, Jews, insured that action on refugee matters would remain for a time outside the circle of government concerns. When Canadian officials considered prospects for some renewed immigration, refugees had no part in their discussion. As far as officials were concerned, the best way to forestall any effort on behalf of refugee immigration was to leave the whole business to the Immigration Branch. Still a backwash of government activity, the Immigration Branch would seal off Canada from refugees. And this was not difficult. Officials were armed with an Immigration Act unchanged (except when made more rigid) since the onset of the Great Depression. If government wanted refugee matters buried, Immigration authorities would be glad to oblige.

The beauty of standing pat on prewar immigration legislation was obvious: it kept "undesirables" out. It was, however, predicated on an anachronism. The Immigration Act and the patchwork of regulations used to administer the act were products of a different time, a long-gone era of agricultural expansion. The surge of industrial development that Canada underwent during the war made this central pillar of Canadian immigration law obsolete. Both the systematic encouragement of rural immigration to complement (now non-existent) policies of wholesale land settlement on the prairies and the effort to attract unskilled workers for the labour-intensive extractive industries of the mining, lumbering and railroad frontiers now made no sense. The mechanization of agriculture and the extractive industries, the private ownership of most prime agricultural lands in the west, the gradual unionization of the resource industry and the massive growth of the manufacturing sector—all begged for a new immigration policy. The old law was, however, in place, and the government found it convenient. With the end of the war the reimposition of prewar immigration regulations barred all but a few, notably: "Agriculturalists having sufficient means to farm in Canada."

Out of step with the times though they might be, immigration regulations complemented government economic and social priorities. Canadian authorities understood well the value of an immigration act that excluded "undesirables" without spelling this out in potentially embarrassing detail. Almost by definition any immigration act or policy permits the entry of some groups at the expense of others. Selectivity is the raison d'être for a policy. Three months after the war's end Canada's director of immigration, A. L. Jolliffe, presented the cabinet with a confidential memorandum on the state of Canadian immigration which underscored this very point. "The claim is sometimes made," he began,

> that Canada's immigration laws reflect class and race discrimination: they do, and necessarily so. Some form of discrimination cannot be avoided if immigration is to be effectively controlled in order to prevent the creation in Canada of expanding non-assimilable racial groups, the prohibiting of entry to immigrants of non-assimilable races is necessary. Many organizations have passed resolutions urging "selective immigration." The term is so general that it can be applied to mean almost anything from near exclusion to an extremely wide range of immigrant classes. Certainly it is not possible to have selective immigration on the one hand and no discrimination on the other. The very act of selection results in discrimination.

The problem being faced by Immigration Branch authorities was not that the law was ineffective in discriminating between desirable and undesirable immigrants, but that, in spite of the law and regulations, the department was now confronting a stream of applications on behalf of an undesirable group: Jews. "A gradual increasing number of applications is being received from residents of Canada for the entry of relatives from Continental Europe," the director went on. "These proposed immigrants are not of the admissible classes and the applicants are being advised of this fact and further informed that there are no facilities for transportation or immigration examinations at this early date following cessation of hostilities."[11]

In fact, shipping on the North Atlantic *was* scarce, and there *was* a lack of immigration processing facilities in Europe. Neither problem was insurmountable—shipping priorities could be adjusted and the necessary offices set up—but Immigration officials found it convenient to leave these problems unresolved as a smoke screen masking the real reasons for inaction.[12] In October 1945 Jolliffe again made this very point to the undersecretary of state for External Affairs: "The Department is literally flooded with appeals from residents of Canada to arrange for the admission of relatives who are either in Switzerland, Italy or countries which were occupied by German Armies, and if we set up the machinery now for the examination of these people all kinds of pressure will be brought to bear on various organizations to get them to Canada."[13] To preclude any such threat, Jolliffe formally recommended that the cabinet endorse the existing immigration status quo and agree that the procedures "not be changed until the country is well advanced toward normal conditions and its immigration absorption possibilities can be accurately determined." But how long would that take? With the European refugee crisis growing worse by the day and many Canadians with relatives in Europe pressing government for permission to bring family, the director of immigration had few words of comfort as the autumn of 1945 foreshadowed a cold winter. He would have no action taken for two years, and: "Immigration policy for the years beyond 1947 should be subject of further review by Cabinet in the early months of that year."[14]

Jolliffe's recommendations were a little too rigid for the cabinet, which would affirm "that present policy should be maintained until existing conditions had changed sufficiently to warrant alterations," but could not accept that consideration of change await 1947. Instead, a politically sensitive cabinet wanted any delay open-ended; a review of immigration would be authorized when and if the cabinet wanted it.[15]

In the meantime only special cases were to be considered, again, through orders-in-council. Nor were these orders easily come by, at least not by most Canadians. If anything, Immigration officials seemed irritated at the persistent requests for such orders from concerned relatives. In one instance, a refugee admitted to Canada during the war on a temporary visa was denied permission to bring his family from Europe by Jolliffe himself, who personally monitored the case. "The members of this family [in Europe] are no worse off than hundreds of others," Jolliffe explained to External Affairs. "In fact, they are better off than most, and I do not think they should receive special treatment just because the head of the family in Canada is continually pressing for preferred treatment. As a matter of fact, he is really fortunate that he is not being returned to Europe for reunion with his family."[16] If he was not being removed, it was not for lack of government preparation. Immigration officials and the RCMP had previously prepared the mechanisms necessary to deport all refugees on temporary visas. With everything in place, a decision by the cabinet could initiate the roundup of refugees and their quick deportation.

In late May 1945, just before the official surrender of Germany, the Canadian Jewish Congress director was on the phone to Ottawa seeking clarification of the status of refugees on temporary visas. Jolliffe confided to Saul Hayes that the fate of these refugees was out of his hands, that the cabinet alone would decide when or if their removal to Europe would take place. Jolliffe volunteered, however, that neither the cabinet nor his own office would likely take action before a federal election scheduled for June 11, 1945, and that pressing the refugee case on the cabinet during an election might just turn the political spotlight on these refugees. In the troubled times nobody could guarantee a positive result. "Publicity at the present time on these matters may be harmful in that it will afford fuel for a political fire which better be left unlit."[17] Hayes took this advice to heart.

In early September Hayes again contacted Jolliffe regarding the matter of temporary visas. The Liberals had been victorious at the polls and the Allies victorious over the Axis. Jolliffe again reassured Hayes that no action one way or the other was imminent, but what he did not tell Hayes was that these refugees were quickly becoming an administrative headache. Nearly all the Jewish refugees admitted from Japan, Spain and Portugal, approximately six hundred persons, were badgering the Immigration Branch with special requests to have their visas extended or status changed to that of permanent residents. Jolliffe suspected Hayes personally orchestrated this flood of requests as a means of focusing attention on the issue. He was probably correct, but, orchestrated or not, it worked. Jolliffe discussed the temporary visa situation several times with his newly appointed minister, J. Allison Glen, and both agreed that the question should be resolved once and for all.[18]

The two also agreed that public sentiment would oppose wholesale deportation. One could just imagine news photos of the young and the elderly being herded aboard ship by armed Canadian military personnel. There was no point. A case-by-case approach was a waste of time, and the best way to handle the situation was to regularize all temporary visas by a single order-in-council. It was evident, Glen explained to the cabinet, that many of the refugees had lost everything in Europe, so "rehabilitation in Europe would be impractical at present and for some years to come." The majority had integrated well within the larger community and some had knowledge and experience that would be of "material value to Canadian trade and industry."[19]

The cabinet was not opposed to regularization, but requested that a special cabinet committee on immigration, including ministers responsible for Immigration, External Affairs, Labour, the Privy Council and the Secretary of State, or their representatives, make a formal joint recommendation to the cabinet. The committee met quickly to rehash the arguments in favour of regularizing the refugees' status. Jolliffe lent his weight for the affirmative. As far as he was concerned, just unloading the paperwork and ending special pleading on behalf of these refugees were reasons enough to support the move. The cabinet was duly advised of the committee's recommendations and on October 25, 1945, during the meeting at which the cabinet resolved to maintain Canada's harsh immigration regulations in spite of, or because of, the European refugee crisis, approval was given to the regularization of temporary visa holders.[20]

Among those routinely advised of the cabinet's decision regarding this small group of refugees was Vincent Massey. More important to the senior Canadian diplomat than the final disposition of a few Jews was an accompanying note from External Affairs cautioning that this single act must not be understood as foreshadowing any change in policy on Canada's part with respect to potential immigrants. "It is not likely," Massey was advised, "that any large scale movement of immigrants to this country will be authorized in the near future." To emphasize its point, External Affairs repeated the arguments about the shortage of trans-Atlantic passenger accommodation, the need to re-establish Canadian armed forces into peacetime occupations and the uncertainty over the postwar economy.[21]

For Massey this directive was crucially important. As Canadian representative in London, he confronted a British government eager to resolve the refugee crisis in Europe before it upset postwar reconstruction. At stake for the British were both the delicate and already strained East–West alliance and, perhaps most of all, the country's success in withstanding pressure from the Americans to ease up on restrictions against Jewish, including displaced persons', immigration into Palestine.* Since

* The British had turned to Canada once before, during the abortive Hungarian rescue fiasco, when Canada was asked how many Jewish refugees it would offer sanctuary. Canada didn't reply. As part of the Hungarian deliberations the Americans requested of the British a statistical accounting of what the British and the British Commonwealth had done for refugees. The British, in turn, officially requested this information from the Dominions, including Canada. The Canadian reply was dissembling—perhaps deliberately so. At first glance the Canadians claimed to have "provided asylum" for more than 39,000 refugees. Only on closer examination of

the end of the war and the Allies' partition of occupied Europe into administrative zones, the question of displaced persons had grown more acute for the British who, with thousands of displaced persons on their hands, fought efforts to entangle the refugee and the Palestine questions. Indeed, the British, for their part, were still refusing to acknowledge officially that the refugee issue was in any way a Jewish one, while they sought privately to relocate Jews as quickly as possible elsewhere.* To do otherwise, they feared, would only encourage discussion of a Zionist alternative and leave Britain vulnerable to more American pressure to open Palestine's gates. Accordingly, the British, unlike the Americans, refused to register Jewish displaced persons as Jews in their zone of occupation. While administrative necessity forced the British to maintain separate camps for Jewish refugees, all were classified by country of last citizenship. If there were no Jews on paper, there could be, at least on paper, no Jewish problem.[22]

In spite of this ruse, the question of Jewish displaced persons refused to go away. (In fact, the issue was aggravated by the infiltration, usually illegally, of still thousands more Jews into the British and American zones of occupation. They were coming

---

Canadian statistics does one discover that among the 39,000 refugees Canada claimed to have given aid to were 8,000 British evacuees from the wartime bombing who intended to go home, 4,500 German civilian internees from Britain who were shipped to Canada against their will and, strangest of all, 25,000 Axis prisoners of war, in Canada under Canadian military guard. In the end, only a handful of actual refugees, including diplomats from Nazi-overrun countries and the Dutch Royal Family, stood as Canada's contribution. After sending this strange accounting to the British, Canadian authorities had second thoughts on its propriety. They officially requested these statistics be withheld from distribution or publication. The British, for their part, were quite pleased to oblige the Canadians. They took "the opportunity of the Canadian Government's refusal to drop the whole project." Americans were advised the information they requested was unavailable. Public Records Office, London, Prime Minister's Office Records, 4/52/5, pt. 1, "Measures Taken by the British Commonwealth to Provide Asylum for Refugees," 815; ibid., Memorandum, Anthony Eden to Cabinet, March 25, 1945, 807.

* In May 1945 a British cabinet committee on the Reception and Accommodation of Refugees expressed concern that Jewish refugees entering Britain might unleash an anti-Semitic backlash. They also sensed little prospect of other countries accepting them. As the parliamentary under-secretary of state for the Dominions pointed out, this was no less true of the Commonwealth. Palestine remained out of the question. Thus, the only solution at the time seemed repatriation. On this the chancellor of the exchequer, the home secretary and colonial secretary were agreed. As the chancellor put it, "As regards the refusal of certain classes of displaced persons to return to their own country is concerned, this attitude was quite intolerable and ought not to be accepted as reason for non-repatriation." Public Records Office, London, Cabinet Records, 95/15, War Cabinet Committee on Reception and Accommodation of Refugees, May 16, 1945, 53.

out of hiding in Eastern Europe or out of their precarious sanctuary in Soviet-occupied countries.) In July 1946 a hard-pressed British government was again turning to the Commonwealth, including Canada, for aid. In their appeal to Canada, in part made through Massey, the British explained their dilemma over Palestine and hinted that Arab intransigence to the arrival of some European Jews in Palestine might be lessened if Arabs could be guaranteed that any refugee movement would be kept small. This could only be achieved if other countries also agreed to take Jews, and to encourage others to come forward and receive a share of the Jews, some country had to get the ball rolling. This, the British suggested, might be Canada's role, and, thanking Canada in advance, they suggested Canada could best assist if it immediately issued a declaration "setting forth the intention of the Canadian Government to take positive steps to secure a satisfactory international agreement on the general problem of displaced persons, especially if such a declaration were to contain a definite offer to accept in Canada a specific number of displaced persons, including Jews."[23]

The Canadians, however, did not see it as their business to save the British in Palestine and certainly not if it involved any guarantee to take Jews. The cabinet was not about to solve British problems by creating Canadian ones. Canada responded instead with a pledge to support "the establishment of effective international machinery to deal with the problems of displaced persons and refugees." Left unsaid was how international organizations could deal with the problem if no members of the international community would accept refugees for resettlement.[24]

It well suited the Canadian agenda to deflect responsibility for refugees away from possible receiving states and into the international arena. One Canadian diplomat in London dutifully advised the British Dominions Office that for Canada "the problem of refugees [was] an international one and should, therefore, be dealt with on a wide international basis, with the participation of as many countries as possible."[25] But if this kept Canada off the British hook, how could Canada avoid similar appeals on behalf of displaced persons' resettlement from these same international bodies? In a confidential memorandum to the cabinet in January 1946, External Affairs warned that, although this demand had "not yet been made on a significant scale," once international refugee aid officials identified and processed "permanent exiles, . . . the question of finding homes for refugees in the American hemisphere [would] almost certainly confront Canadian representatives on international humanitarian bodies."[26]

Canada was a member of two international bodies that concerned themselves in whole or in part with the care and resettlement of refugees—the United Nations Relief and Rehabilitation Administration (UNRRA) and the old Intergovernmental Committee on Refugees. UNRRA, established during the war as the stepchild of the Bermuda Conference, was responsible for immediate refugee care, processing and support, and its internationally seconded staff followed directly on the heels of Allied troops in Europe. Canada had joined the organization soon after its founding and was a member of its Standing Committee of the Council for Europe, which oversaw all European operations. The Intergovernmental Committee still assumed responsibility for long-term resettlement planning and coordination. Canada paid its fair share to these agencies (though protested that its share was too high), but Canadian membership in and support of them was, of course, never meant by government to be read as Canadian acceptance of refugees. During the war this was never at issue. Both the nascent UNRRA and the ineffectual IGC made repatriation the cornerstone of postwar refugee planning. Repatriation was faltering. Now they, not Canada, were looking to resettlement.

In the spring of 1946 the director general of UNRRA (at one time the popular mayor of New York and an intimate of the Democratic administration), Fiorello LaGuardia, stated publicly what most already knew. In a meeting of the refugee agency's council in Washington, at which Canadian ambassador to Washington, Lester Pearson, represented Canada, LaGuardia finally dismissed repatriation as a dead issue. Although the UNRRA mandate had made repatriation its priority, it now had to look to overseas resettlement as the only viable option.[27] In a follow-up letter to all the agency's delegates, LaGuardia officially asked each member state, including Canada, how far it was prepared to go in alleviating the displaced persons' problem. The director general was personally frustrated. "All nations are sympathetic to this problem," he wrote Pearson, "but . . . more than sympathy is needed and specific proposals need to be developed for actually moving people to new lands." Pearson, passing along LaGuardia's request to External Affairs, noted that the Americans had already taken steps to process as many refugees as possible under their limited-quota system. But this, Pearson knew, would neither satisfy LaGuardia nor meet the critical need of displaced persons for new homes. "Certainly, he [LaGuardia] will argue that countries such as Canada and the United States, which have been so generous in forwarding food and supplies out from their countries, should be at least a half or quarter as generous in receiving into their countries the persons who have been most tragically dealt with by the war."[28] Ottawa advised Pearson to be cautious in his reply—conciliatory but noncommittal. He should respond that, although Canada was aware and concerned about the refugee issue (witness Canada's willingness to participate in international forums designed to solve the problem), nothing could be done until a study was conducted to determine "the relationship between immigration policy and the absorptive capacity of the Canadian economy." And Pearson was doubly forearmed—the ever-handy problem of shipping could be hauled out in a pinch to preclude any possible action on Canada's part.[29]

Pearson agreed to the strategy, but was doubtful about its effectiveness. LaGuardia, he warned, might not be satisfied with this stand as he might expect Canada at least to match the token effort by the United States in admitting some refugees; in addition, LaGuardia would not be taken in by the tired shipping argument and might use it instead as a means to kick open the back door to Canada for Jews. "I do not think we should mention the shipping difficulty to Mr. LaGuardia," Pearson cautioned, "because I feel certain he will reply with an offer to get ships from the [American] War Shipping Board." Ottawa disagreed. There was no point in avoiding mention of the supposed shipping problem—LaGuardia was surely familiar with other Canadian statements on the refugee issue that made so much of it, and consistency was advisable. In any event, if shipping was no longer the problem, another could be found.[30]

What LaGuardia personally thought of Pearson's reply is not recorded; yet he could not help but conclude that Canada, like other New World countries, was avoiding the critical problem in European reconstruction—resettlement of displaced persons abroad. On June 13, 1946, LaGuardia addressed the UNRRA council again, meeting this time in New York. He was plainly disheartened. The agency's mandate would run out on New Year's Eve, 1946, and it would be remembered as having done little if it did not aggressively tackle the resettlement issue.

Canada was listed by LaGuardia with other countries that could and should, but did not, do more.[31]

At the same time that LaGuardia and his agency were making their appeal the Intergovernmental Committee on Refugees met in London. External Affairs forewarned the Canadian delegate to the meeting, J. G. Turgeon, to avoid committing Canada to anything. Turgeon, who was new both to the committee and the refugee issue, was cautioned by Ottawa on one point—others tended to overestimate the absorptive capacity of Canada. "To European eyes it is a huge, wealthy and half-empty land—the logical target for all refugee planners." To avoid making Canada the target of "refugee planners," Turgeon was instructed to press for the strongest "international machinery" to deal with the refugee problem—again, avoiding specific national commitments of any kind. The Canadian determination to have the refugee issue remain an international cause rather than a national concern underscored its preference for the status quo, and it won the day. The Intergovernmental Committee rejected recommending action by individual states in favour of uniting with the Relief and Rehabilitation Administration to establish yet another United Nations agency, the International Refugee Organization (IRO), that would, then, encompass both groups' refugee functions.

But Canada, which had championed the international approach in an effort to keep the refugee issue at arm's length, was again concerned lest it be assessed too much money in support of the new fledgling international body. In July 1946 External Affairs cautioned Turgeon, now chairman of the IRO's financial subcommittee, to guard Canadians from being overtaxed. It was suggested confidentially to Turgeon that, if poorer Latin American countries and Eastern bloc countries were assessed very heavily by the organization and were therefore unable to pay, perhaps they could be induced to pay off their assessment in kind, that is, to accept refugees on some prorated basis in lieu of cash contributions to the agency. If a value, equivalent to cash, was given each refugee accepted by a poorer country, the total amount might then be subtracted from that country's cash assessment, and this might aid in resettling refugees at relatively little pain to Canada. Civil servants might not like the amount of Canada's assessment, but they would agree that it was better to pay out dollars than to take in refugees.[32]

The cabinet, however, was a little less cavalier with Canadian dollars. When the question reached its members in the prime minister's absence in the late summer of 1946, the ministers approved Canadian participation in the scheme, but with something less than enthusiasm.* It appeared that Canada's initial contribution to the International Refugee Organization would be almost $10.5 million. A subsequent cabinet meeting in September reaffirmed Canada's agreement to join the organization, but reserved "the Canadian position as to the scale and amount of financial contributions."[33]

To Canadian Jewry, it was not Canadian participation in international agencies that mattered, but a commitment by the government to allow refugees into Canada. The refugee question was not a distant international dilemma; it was an immediate and emotional one that touched the very core of Canadian Jews' self-perception. If not all victims of the Nazis were Jews, the Nazis had marked all Jews everywhere as victims. Survivors in Canada could not deny those abroad. The application from any one individual to bring a relative into Canada became, therefore, part of the collective battle by Canadian Jewry to open Canada to refugees. Inquiries and applications addressed to the Immigration Branch with the aid of Jewish organizations were more than the sum of their parts; they were a challenge to Canadian inaction in the face of need. In June 1945 the national director of the Jewish Immigrant Aid Society explained the need for action to his Toronto office. "The more applications we have," said Solkin, "the sooner we may be able to prevail upon our government to take action. If we are to sit and wait passively until possibilities arise by themselves, we will have to wait a long time indeed." Thus, applications were encouraged by Jewish leaders, but each applicant advised to expect little or nothing. Sending an application was a symbolic act; each repre-

* Canadian willingness to participate and support international efforts to resolve the refugee issue, if the cost was right, was obviously self-serving. By keeping the refugee question a matter for international agencies to resolve, Canada hoped to avoid having to make any specific commitment that might be forced on it if the problem was thrown into the lap of western receiving countries. There was a drawback, however. What would prevent international agencies, in their own right, from becoming lobbies for resettlement of refugees by the agency's member states. If Canada could avoid that, however, the financial costs, if kept in check, would be well worth it. Furthermore, if international pressure could be weathered as it arose, then membership in refugee bodies had an important secondary benefit. It was useful domestically. Who could dare say that Canada was not doing its part to solve the refugee crisis when it was an active member of the IGC, UNRRA and their successor, the IRO? Would Canada participate if it did not actively wish to work for an end to this human misery?

sented "a lever in prying open the stone wall" that the government seemed as determined to erect after the war as it had before.[34] In late August 1945 alone, 150 applications were forwarded to Ottawa.

To flood Ottawa with applications was a desperate, as well as a tactical, manoeuvre, born of diminishing options. It seemed to the Jewish community that it could do neither more nor less. As in the years preceding the war, Jewish leaders probed for a soft spot in immigration policy; they sought an argument to which government might prove vulnerable. They found neither, however, and the flow of applications that continued to reach Ottawa were dutifully processed and filed away as ineligible under existing regulations. As Jewish leaders knew, it was for the prime minister and his cabinet, not the Immigration authorities, ultimately to determine admissions. Therefore, when it came to appeals for policy change, Hayes concluded "that it would be wise to by-pass the Department of Immigration . . . and bring the matter directly to the Prime Minister." In the late summer of 1945 the Congress requested yet another Jewish delegation be allowed to meet with King.[35]

King was not in the mood to hear any more Jewish appeals. They made him feel uneasy, even guilty—he did not want to have to say no. The Prime Minister's Office redirected Hayes to External Affairs and Immigration Branch officials, assuring him that this path was the politically wise one to follow, that keeping these officials "formally and officially" advised of Jewish concerns would avoid policy confusion later on.[36] One suspects, however, that King simply wished to detour any appeal on behalf of Jewish refugees around the political arena and into the unsympathetic hands of the public service. Once again, the Jewish community was effectively locked out.

To earlier requests from the United Jewish Refugee Agency for the admission of immediate relatives who, Jolliffe informed his minister, were "said to be the sole survivors of whole families murdered in cold blood," the answer was still no. In a memorandum of advice to Glen, Jolliffe made this rejection a matter of what he termed "principle." "I think in dealing with this application," the director explained, "it should be kept in mind that the plight of the group in question is really only a small part of the general problem of displaced persons in Europe and that the solution to the problem can only be found through international action. The question thus arises as to the wisdom of Canada taking individual action with regard to special groups." Overriding this principle by granting concessions to "special groups" was fraught with practical difficulties. If any concession was offered the Jews in this instance, it would, Jolliffe warned, only lead to more and inflated requests from other Jews and non-Jews in similar conditions. Furthermore, there was no telling what the mental and physical condition of these displaced persons might be. In view of high Canadian immigration medical standards, an exemption might need to be granted, and as a result Canada would "invite many risks and subsequent problems." Jolliffe ruled out allowing medical inspection to be conducted in Europe. Ignoring the usual excuses offered for inaction, he mentioned to his minister neither a shipping shortage nor the resettlement of Canadian forces as a priority. The director of immigration knew when to hide behind a smoke screen. This time it was unnecessary.[37] Jolliffe's letter to Hayes, however, explaining the blanket rejection covered all the appropriate ground. The letter advised the Jewish leader that the government was not "unmindful of the difficulties and hardships of the cases." "But apart from the impracticability of arranging examinations and transfers to ports of embarkation," it concluded, "there is no shipping available for any such movement."[38]

Hayes knew the truth of course, but he was also a civil servant, a civil servant to the Jewish community and accountable to that community through the Dominion Council of the Canadian Jewish Congress. Accordingly, when challenged at a council meeting for having not been forceful enough in dealings with the government on the refugee issue and after listening to council members dismiss the government's excuses as a sham, Hayes was trapped into legitimizing these very excuses:

> In the light of conditions on the continent, we have pressed the government by letter, memorandum and delegation to admit at least the relatives of Canadian Jews who survived in Europe. We offered to make all the usual guarantees etc. Our application was taken to the very highest authorities of the government but we are sorry to state that it was not granted. The review of the immigration problem conveyed to us by the Department emphasizes the absence of shipping for civilians at this time. In addition, there exists no facilities for examination by officials at ports of embarkation. What is even more important, we are informed, albeit less formally, that in the light of the looming problems of the rehabilitation of ser-

> vicemen, the repatriation of the soldiers who are not destined to form part of the occupation army in Europe, the transport of war brides, the employment situation and the unrest in the industrial labour field, it is not likely that the question of immigration into the country as a matter of policy will be favourably taken up for some time.[39]

Barring any sudden changes of heart on the part of government, the Jewish community had few tactical options; the stream of applications to Ottawa continued.

The director of immigration already considered this stream a torrent, and complained to the under-secretary of state for External Affairs that the Immigration Branch was "literally flooded with applications." But, as the Jewish community had already discovered, if these applications kept the refugee question on the desks of civil servants and consumed the time of Immigration authorities, they were not sufficient to force the problem out of civil service offices and into Parliament. The prime minister kept himself out of sight, forcing the Congress to deal with lesser lights. Senator Wilson, president of the Canadian National Committee on Refugees, again arranged for Hayes and Samuel Bronfman, president of the Congress, to meet with Glen. A joint UJRA–CNCR brief was presented to the minister responsible for immigration, pleading for a general concession to all refugees rather than solely to Jewish refugees. The thrust of the Jewish appeal centred on relatives of those in displaced persons camps, "relatives anxious to bring their kith and kin to their homes." Glen again promised nothing.[40]

Unknown to Jewish leaders, cracks were beginning to appear in the solid wall that was immigration policy, with pressure brought to bear especially by External Affairs. The department was not only home to a core of young, progressive and well-educated personnel, often more open-minded on the refugee issue than those in the Immigration Branch, but it was also confronted with the refugee issue in a way that neither Immigration authorities nor the cabinet was. In newly reopened Canadian diplomatic missions in Europe and in international forums, External Affairs had to defend the Canadian position, such as it was. For some it was an unpleasant task. Vanier was admittedly soft on refugees. His embassy in Paris was besieged by appeals from refugees and displaced persons requesting permission to join relatives in Canada, and he repeatedly appealed to Ottawa for an easing of restrictions. The ambassador was personally disappointed that he could not act favourably on these requests. "The officers of this Embassy who are concerned for this problem," he explained, "have often been favourably impressed by the character, appearance and personal histories of the applicants."[41] Others in External Affairs were more pragmatic. In late January 1946 Herbert Emerson, still director of the Intergovernmental Committee, informed Canada of a newly approved British scheme for the reunification of families: first-degree relatives of those in Britain would be admitted; Emerson respectfully suggested that Canada follow suit. Sensing that Canada needed to do something, the under-secretary of state for External Affairs wrote to Jolliffe, noting "that the demands upon Canada to make further contributions to the solution of this problem [would] increase in the near future."

It was obvious, at least to External Affairs, that Canada might wisely wish to declare itself and declare itself sooner than either Immigration authorities or the cabinet had intended, rather than suffer an international black eye. The under-secretary suggested to Jolliffe that it would be best if their respective departments were ready when the inevitable concessions were made. Accordingly, he recommended that a "small interdepartmental committee might usefully be established to consider the refugee problem in greater detail, possibly with a view to making recommendations to the Government." And others endorsed the External Affairs initiative. Lieutenant-General Maurice Pope, head of the Canadian military mission in Germany, suggested to Ottawa that it should make some concessions to refugees in view of the obvious plight of surviving Nazi war victims and those displaced by the war's aftermath. Ever practical, however, he also suggested Canada should do so while the pickings were good. "I am reminded," he informed Ottawa, "of the wisdom of Talleyrand's aphorism—To yield before one is compelled to do so and while one can still make mint by it."[42]

Attached to Pope's letter was a memorandum drawn up by Colonel S. Morley Scott that reviewed the scope of British and American efforts on behalf of refugees, both small in comparison to need, and assessed, in a general way, the various groups of displaced persons available to Canada should it decide to admit refugees in bulk. Jews were, Scott pointed out, in a special class. The Americans, for instance, accepted German-born Jews still in Germany as refugees: "While presumably safe from physical violence, Jews who had been victims of German persecution, for example, in concentration camps, could no longer expect to be spiritually at home in Germany, or to live normal lives here." Scott, reasoning that eventually Canada would be forced to accept some refugees, cautioned that the "Jew–Gentile proportion" would have to be determined and underscored the need for haste before the cream of Gentile displaced persons were skimmed off by others. This was being self-serving and practical. However, there was, he contended, another principle on which the admission of refugees to Canada could be based. Scott allowed Canada could act out of humanitarian concern. If it accepted a hard core of elderly, sick or poor, the country's contribution might be all the more meaningful. "The value of the Canadian contribution depends more upon the proportion of this hard core we can digest than upon how much of the sweet fruit we can bite off."[43] Nobody in Ottawa took this latter proposition seriously.

Massey too was becoming bullish, if selectively so, about displaced persons. His feelings about Jews and eastern or southern Europeans were well known in Ottawa. But at least one group found favour in his eyes. On an inspection tour of Canadian military installations on the Continent, the Canadian high commissioner visited a displaced persons camp in Germany under the control of Canadian army authorities. "In this camp there were about 1,500 Balts of all ages and of both sexes, most of them from Latvia," Massey wrote. "I am deeply impressed by the quality of these people who appeared to be industrious, clean, resourceful and well-mannered. The camp itself was a model of self-help, and I could not help feeling that of all the Europeans I have seen these Balts would make the most admirable settlers."[44]

In mid March 1946 an interdepartmental committee instituted by External Affairs met with representatives from that department, Immigration, Labour and Health and Welfare. The committee reviewed pro-refugee pressure from "foreign-language groups,"' including Canadian Jews, for the admission of relatives or group settlements. It also explored the ramifications of Canadian inaction in the face of mounting international pressure and the growing chorus of concern from within External Affairs. With prodding from External Affairs, it was agreed to recommend to the cabinet that Canada should move to admit some of these unfortunate people. It was also agreed that any such recommendation be couched in the form of a special program not meant to imply any change in policy or the Immigration Act. The pace of any admissions, if approved, should be tightly controlled. This could be done by falling back on ever-reliable shipping difficulties and, to add a new wrinkle, by judiciously under-staffing Canadian immigration inspection teams eventually assigned to the European operations.

The rules of admission were less important to Immigration Branch officials than the total number of refugees any program would actually admit. These officials assumed that nobody, not even External Affairs, actually wanted to see refugees admitted. From the point of view of the Immigration Branch, the real challenge for the interdepartmental committee was to devise a high-profile, low-commitment program to take External Affairs off the hook at international gatherings and split, if not pacify, pro-refugee forces in Canada. It was not, the department believed, to facilitate undesirable admissions.

Whatever their misunderstanding of External Affairs' intent, Immigration officials were not prepared to give much. Jolliffe agreed to a plan along lines already in place in Britain. "It was suggested, therefore, that permission to enter Canada should be considered only for persons among the displaced, to displaced groups who had immediate relatives in Canada, who came within the general immigration regulations in regard to health and for whom shelter, maintenance and transportation could be provided." (Unlike the British scheme, however, the committee recommended that religious, benevolent and ethnic fraternal organizations not be allowed to act as sponsors or guarantors, at least for the time being.) Thus, if the government could concoct its own definition of a refugee, perhaps of a so-called "distressed person," the immigration door could be opened wide enough to include a desirable class of settlers. They might not technically be displaced persons or refugees, but this hardly mattered. If this was not done, "migration to Canada from amongst this official refugee group might be unbalanced as to racial composition, and . . . deserving persons from countries such as the Netherlands and Norway might thereby be excluded." It was agreed that a subcommittee, with a representative from External Affairs and Jolliffe, look into definitions of "refugee" used by various agencies and conduct an analysis of "the racial and national" composition of those in refugee camps.[45]

The question of definition proved as problematic as that of "racial and national" composition proved potentially volatile.

As a result, the interdepartmental committee finally washed its hands of the whole business, recommending to the cabinet a deceptively simple immigration package—admit first-degree relatives of persons in Canada irrespective of their status in Europe. Displaced persons were included but given no administrative priority. After little discussion the cabinet gave its approval. An Order-in-Council was drawn up, and it awaited only an auspicious moment to announce the scheme.[46]

Before the government's decision on first-degree relatives was officially announced in Parliament, hints and assurances that something was afoot began to percolate down through the pro-refugee lobby—and government did little to discourage them. In reply to a routine CNCR resolution calling for government action sent to King on April 30, 1946, the prime minister took the unusual step of responding personally. "The problem of refugees," he said, "is one which is continually before the Canadian Government, which shares the concern of many citizens of Canada over the fate of thousands of people now homeless in Western Europe. . . . I can assure you that the Canadian Government will be prepared to bear its proper share of the responsibility for solving the refugee problem." King claimed that any Canadian move must be coordinated with other countries on "a broad international basis" and that any decision must await the decision, if there was one, of the United Nations Economic and Social Council then meeting in London. King was about to leave for a conference of Commonwealth leaders in London and a rumour was also making the rounds that King might address the United Nations meetings. What better time to announce a Canadian initiative of some sort on the issue of displaced persons? Hayes, who spoke to Glen, was also privately reassured that something was up. "The stage is set but . . . the opening night is being delayed until Mackenzie King and his closest colleagues give assent."[47]

Exactly what the government plan involved was difficult for outsiders to pin down, although rumours ran rampant. For fear that advance publicity might upset the government and cause it to change its plans, Jewish leaders, who knew something of the government's timetable, cautioned one another to remain patient.[48] Then on May 29, 1946, the government revealed its hand. The minister responsible for immigration, J. A. Glen, stood in the House of Commons to announce the signing of an Order-in-Council. On the surface, and for public consumption, the order seemed generous indeed, but, in effect, the fine print proved anything but. All existing immigration regulations were to apply to all applicants; these included examination of documentation, health and mental state. If this wasn't enough, a first-degree relative was very narrowly defined—father, mother, unmarried son or daughter under eighteen, unmarried brother or sister, and an orphan niece or nephew under sixteen "bereaved of both parents." The sponsoring Canadian relative must prove ability to pay for all transportation and care and, of course, guarantee the arrival would not prove a public charge. Also, in spite of Jewish hopes, the formal order made no special mention of refugees or displaced persons. Why should it? It was geared to reactivating the immigration process halted in 1931 by permitting residents of Canada to bring a limited class of first-degree relatives to Canada if they passed the medical and other hurdles of existing immigration regulations.[49] It was more a reopening of limited immigration than a settlement scheme.

Furthermore, Glen's accompanying statement in Parliament was strangely contradictory. On the one hand, he explained to a hushed Commons, the government plan to allow immediate, or first-degree, relatives into Canada was "intended as a short term measure . . . to meet in some measure the pressing demands being made on behalf of refugees or displaced persons having relatives in Canada anxious to provide them with homes." On the other hand, lest anyone assume that "a short term measure" implied some haste in its implementation, Glen explained that this would not be the case—he did not set any date for beginning the program, falling back on the well-worn problem of shipping and lack of processing facilities in Europe: "The amending of the regulations does not mean immediate action will be taken to admit immigrants from overseas." Opening Canada to select relatives was a concession of sorts to displaced persons, and so the United Nations would be told. It was not, however, a concession that should encourage anyone to start packing a suitcase.

The long-awaited Order-in-Council on which Canadian Jewry had pinned so much hope was a cruel disappointment, not just for its limited scope, but for its cynical application. "Only a relatively small number of Jews," Hayes wrote to prominent members of the Jewish community, "will find it possible to enter Canada under the broad regulations, and even these will not be able to come into the country for some time." And the government had no intention of making transport available for refugees or establishing facilities in Europe for their processing. In an accurate analysis Hayes noted that this Order-in-Council was not really innovative at all. Rather, it just removed restrictions imposed on immigration in 1931 that effectively barred family members. In addition, the Jewish community was still barred from acting as a corporate body in sponsoring the admission of refugees.[50]

Among those who could or would not be repatriated after the cessation of hostilities were many in the Polish army, the army that had fought alongside the British, notably, in the Mediterranean theatre of operations. The British were prepared to absorb some of these Poles, called General Anders' Army after the name of their Polish commander, but did not want them all. At a meeting of high commissioners in London on April 12, 1946, each commissioner was requested to refer the Polish matter to his home government.[51] Massey did so, although with somewhat less enthusiasm than he had shown in the case of Balts.[52] Indeed, during the meeting in London an uncharacteristically jovial Massey surprised some of those present with the vehemence of his anti-Polish remarks. Poles were, he allowed, only slightly better than Jews. "Mr. Massey snickered that when three Poles get together there was always a political party and a newspaper; they do not easily assimilate themselves and 'one did not want too many of them about'."[53]

In spite of Massey's misgivings Canada did find it advantageous to admit four thousand Polish war veterans. In accepting those who had fought gallantly side by side with Allied troops in North Africa and Italy, self-interest overshadowed generosity. With the formal surrender of Germany in the late spring of 1945, preparations had been made to send home thousands of German prisoners of war interned in Canada, and by August 1946 the last of these prisoners would be on their way home. These Germans would be missed, for many had served their time in Canada working in lumber camps or on farms. To Canada's good fortune, just as "a supply of heavy labour of a type which [was] in considerable demand" was leaving, the British offered Canada a replacement—Anders' Army.

Pending the cabinet's agreement, the prime minister approved a proposal "to take demobilized Polish soldiers, man for man, in return for German prisoners of war being returned to the United Kingdom." The cabinet acted with dispatch, perhaps because the coming harvest was jeopardized by lack of agricultural labour. No problems of shipping, processing facilities or reintegrating Canadian servicemen stood in the way. The scheme was approved in May 1946; negotiations were soon concluded with the British government, Polish military and Canadian agricultural officials, and the program was in place by mid July.*

Of course there would be controls on who could come. The cabinet instructed that security screening be conducted on all Polish applicants to insure no "subversives" slipped into Canada. However, Canadian Immigration and Labour personnel, working with the Polish military, stepped beyond the letter of the cabinet's instructions further to insure the acceptability of those Poles who would come. To the surprise of agreeable Polish authorities, Jewish members of the Polish army were to be carefully screened out and under no circumstance was Jewish participation in the proposed movement to be more than a token one. The Jewish chaplain serving Anders' Army was instructed to dissuade Jewish servicemen from attempting to apply.[54] Efforts to keep Jews from entering Canada under the Polish labour scheme were largely successful. Of the first 1,700 Polish veterans to arrive in Canada it was reported that only one was a Jew, a private in the Polish army, "a native of Warsaw, who [had] fought with the underground in Poland and participated in Allied campaigns from El Alamein to Italy."[55]

Unlike the sense of urgency surrounding the movement of Poles to Canada, the scheme allowing Canadian residents to sponsor their first-degree relatives, a scheme approved in the cabinet and announced in Parliament in April 1946, was still going nowhere. In July 1946 the United Nations Relief and Rehabilitation Administration incorrectly reported that the Canadian Military Mission in Berlin had established an office "for the purpose of assisting certain classes of emigrants to Canada." This report proved both premature and embarrassing. To forestall any unwanted applications the Canadian mission issued a corrective statement in August: "There are at present

* As soon as the cabinet agreed, these Allied soldiers were processed for Canada under terms reminiscent of the indentured servants of an earlier era. This scheme involved, as much as possible, only single men who waived their right to bring their families to Canada later. They were contracted out as agricultural or other labour at a rate of $45 per month for two years. After two years they were eligible for immigrant status in Canada. Each Pole was responsible for his own transportation costs to Canada, although, as anticipated, the British would cover the costs of the trans-Atlantic movement in the very ships being used to take German prisoners of war home. To underscore the labourer status accorded these Allied servicemen, the program was the responsibility of the Department of Labour working in cooperation with Canadian Immigration authorities.

no facilities for emigration from Germany to Canada. . . . Intending immigrants belonging to the admissible class may be advised to write to their relatives in Canada *by the civil mail* asking them to approach the nearest immigration office on their behalf. When Canadian immigration officers arrive in Germany, which will certainly not be during the present year [1946] the fact will be advertised and persons within the categories mentioned above will then be able to apply to the officers named in the announcement."[56]

Immigration officials in Ottawa and at the Canadian High Commission in London took the further precaution of warning refugee agencies against raising false expectations among refugees. Jolliffe wrote to UNRRA headquarters in Germany. While it was true, he acknowledged, that Canada would allow Canadian residents to apply to bring first-degree relatives, applications were not approvals. Each would-be immigrant would need to be assessed by a Canadian immigration officer in Europe, and: "We do not know when circumstances will permit the reopening of our immigration offices on the continent." P. T. Molson, posted with the High Commission office, meanwhile apprised the Intergovernmental Committee on Refugees of "the true situation." The regulations were in place—but nothing else. With no chance of refugees coming to Canada for some time, Molson explained, it "seems a pity that these unfortunate people should be allowed to remain under the illusion that steps are being taken to arrange for them to live in Canada."[57]

These explanations could not mask the actual intent of the government, and Canadian External Affairs was soon under renewed pressure at the United Nations to indicate its government's intent. External Affairs, in turn, again lobbied for action at home. It charged Glen and his department officials, especially Jolliffe, with deliberately dragging their feet—buying time in an effort to forestall the inevitable. Ambassador Vanier, unflagging in his personal concern for refugees, protested to Ottawa that few took Canadian excuses for inaction seriously. "It is simply not true that no transport is available," he said.

> This is immigration's stock reply to any question of urgency in the opening of continental inspection offices. . . . There is little doubt . . . space will shortly be available for people such as immigrants. As far as North West Europe, some space is available now. The real bottleneck in getting immigrants

> from the continent of Europe to Canada is the lack of inspection offices, not the lack of transport. This will become increasingly true each month as more ships become available on the continental lines. . . . We cannot continue to have our officers in Berlin, the Hague and Brussels answer all immigration inquiries with the flat statement that transport is not available when both the officers concerned and the applicants know this is not the case.[58]

Encouraged by his senior staff and fearing the prospects of attending the upcoming session of the United Nations without a refugee program to present, Hume Wrong, now replacing Norman Robertson as acting under-secretary of state for External Affairs, again suggested Jolliffe send inspection teams to visit displaced persons camps and begin processing eligible refugees.[59] Jolliffe again refused. He believed External Affairs could justify at least one more year's delay at the United Nations on the basis of the recent Order-in-Council—even without implementation. It was, he felt, External Affairs' duty to take the heat if necessary.

Seeing no hope of a change of heart by Immigration authorities, External Affairs carried its concerns to the cabinet. The department argued that the gulf between Canadian statements of sympathy for refugees and its actual commitment to their relief was so wide that it might undermine the Canadian position at the UN. Even worse, it might force countries inundated with refugees to press for an immediate solution through the UN that Canada would find very disagreeable indeed—in short, a quota system.

> Delegations at the Assembly will be under considerable pressure to make known their intentions in regard to the acceptance of refugees, and proposals will probably be put forward for the admission of refugees on a quota basis by receiving countries. The [Canadian] delegation might find itself in an embarrassing position if, in a discussion on the eventual disposition of refugees, it could refer only to Canada's action in the past in admitting a few refugees or in revising the immigration regulations so as to admit the relations of residents in Canada. On the other hand, if it were possible to announce a practical plan for the resettlement of even a small number of refugees, the delegation might be able to influence in a very constructive way the consideration of the refugee question.

First in order of importance, as far as External Affairs was concerned, was the opening of immigration inspection offices in continental Europe. "The acceptance of this plan would have an immediate practical effect on the refugee problem without altering the existing immigration regulations." And External Affairs was ready to go even further. It suggested expanding the Anders' Army scheme to include labourers of other nationalities, especially (and with a nod to Massey) Baltic refugees. It also recommended that the cabinet at least consider the offers by organizations such as the Central Mennonite Committee, the Canadian Ukrainian Committee and the Canadian Jewish Congress to sponsor limited group migration at their own expense.[60]

The cabinet was not nearly as flexible as External Affairs would have liked, however. Louis St. Laurent, having replaced King as secretary of state for External Affairs and chief spokesman in the cabinet from Quebec, disagreed with his own ministry officials, and led the fight for a more modest program. With his agreement, the cabinet tentatively approved a suggestion that immigration inspection in Europe be organized, but with St. Laurent the voice of moderation, rejected any notion of expanding the government's limited commitment. The United Nations would need to be pacified with what Canada was prepared to give.

> Mr. St. Laurent suggested that, in the matter of accepting refugees, it was proposed that the Canadian delegation might take the line that Canada had allowed 3,500, admitted during the war, to remain in this country; 4,000 Poles were being admitted under a scheme already in effect for agricultural labour; immigration regulations had recently been modified to permit entry of close relatives of persons already in Canada. . . . Until some estimate could be made of the total involved, it would be difficult for the government to make any further commitment for the admission of others.[61]

Even with final approval from the cabinet for the opening of inspection stations in Europe, it would take some time before overseas operations began. External Affairs, still under increasing international pressure, was not pacified. But if it could not get action it at least wanted the illusion of action. It proposed that the approval of inspection teams should be announced in Parliament in a high-profile statement by the prime minister. External Affairs hoped that this and the publicity it would generate might be just enough to curb criticism of Canada at the upcoming United Nations debate, while at the same time knowing that it would "be some time before immigration teams actually proceeded to the field."[62]

With all the fuss and delay over establishing stations in Europe, one might imagine that Immigration authorities expected a flood of refugees ready to strain Canadian "absorptive capacity." This was not the case and Immigration authorities knew it. Of the many applications filed for permission to bring refugees to Canada, very few were eligible under the recent Order-in-Council. Six thousand acceptable applications were received from Canadians wishing to bring near relatives from Europe. Most of these applications were not on behalf of refugees. By the Immigration Branch's own estimates, only 688 eligible applications had been received on behalf of first-degree relatives in displaced persons camps. Furthermore, since all applicants needed to be cleared by Canadian authorities, including medical inspectors, nowhere near 688 displaced persons could be expected to arrive in Canada. It was anticipated, however, that once inspection teams arrived in Europe, more applications might be forthcoming.[63]

In the Jewish community disappointment followed disappointment. The problem of Jewish refugees in Europe was little relieved by inspection facilities, because under existing regulations very few Jews were eligible for inspection. The Congress director conveyed the despair of Canadian Jews to the minister responsible for immigration:

> It is now clear that the order [-in-council] benefits only a few hundred Jews and it comes at a time when Canadians are becoming frantic in their efforts to help their kith and kin. A Canadian is not permitted to bring his married brother into the country although surely his interest and, more, right to seek his admission is as keen as when the brother is single. The desire to help orphans over 16 is as justified as when these orphans are under 16. I could go on to tell of the heartbreak of families in Canada who are unable to assist their very own, but I am convinced that you can see already that our point is well taken.
>
> I know that a line must be drawn somewhere and that wherever that line is drawn there will always be demands and requests from those on the outside. But the present line is so near the point of exclusion that it assists hardly any people at all.[64]

External Affairs, desperate to avoid both negative discussion in the UN of Canada's refugee policy and moves to distribute displaced persons in a quota system, also wanted to expand the categories of first-degree relatives allowed admission into Canada. What harm would there be, the department argued, in including widowed daughters, widowed sisters plus their unmarried children to age eighteen and orphaned nephews and nieces to age eighteen? In view of the enormity of the refugee crisis, External Affairs warned, "it seems probable that the above extensions will be regarded as inadequate." The cabinet for once agreed, but awaited the recall of Parliament before making an official announcement. In the meantime, Canadian Jewry still continued to plead for an expansion of categories, which, unknown to them, the government had in large measure already approved.[65]

The prime minister had for once a positive card to play, and welcomed a request for a meeting with a delegation of Jewish leaders. On a cold Friday afternoon in early February 1947 King set aside time to meet with several delegations visiting Ottawa. Between meetings with representatives of the Canada Temperance Federation, who commended King on his unflagging commitment to temperance—"To have done that and nothing else it was to have been worthwhile being in public life"—and an exuberant group from the Canadian Council of Churches—"Christian influence was making itself felt more strongly in the world"—King welcomed a small Jewish delegation again led by Samuel Bronfman and Saul Hayes. Hayes, convinced for once he could reach King and his other cabinet colleagues, made a special point of explaining that with the existing Order-in-Council fewer than one thousand Jewish refugees in Germany and Austria would benefit.[66] And it seems that King was truly moved by the delegation's pleas:

> I was deeply impressed by stories of distress this delegation of able bodied Jewish citizens brought out. One man, Gibben [Garber?], of a family of thirteen, was now the only one left except a sister who was a trained nurse in Europe. She could not be brought over to his home because she was over 18 years of age. I told Glen after the meeting that I thought we ought to find ways wherever there were families in Canada that could take on full responsibility for those distressed persons and their immediate relatives to make way for them to come. It is an absurdity when we are trying to get nurses that

> this woman who is in Europe should not be permitted to come to live with her brother, a leading citizen in Canada. There was real sorrow in the faces of some of these men.

Sorrow aside, King gave no hint to the delegation members that much of their appeal had already been answered, assuring them that he would take up their cause. (It seems too that King was pleased by the way he had handled the Jews: "I never recall a time when our announcements, [to be made] immediately before the beginning of a session, seemed to fit in so well with the delegations that we were receiving which have had to be postponed until today. In every way, the postponement has been of very great advantage.")[67]

In early 1947 the door into Canada stood ajar, ever so slightly. A special deal had been struck regarding Polish war veterans; limited categories of first-degree relatives might be brought from Europe to Canada. It didn't amount to much, however, and it seemed inconceivable to Canadian Jewry that so much sympathy had produced so little action. Why was the cabinet content to see Immigration authorities drag their feet for so long on the refugee question? Why did it knowingly mouth the Immigration Branch's excuses about lack of shipping when it knew this was only a problem as long as they wished it to be? The answer is of many parts. One might point to an exaggerated threat of a postwar economic backslide and the usefulness of an unyielding Immigration Act. But these certainly played only a minor role by 1947. In fact, the cabinet and Immigration officials alike were uneasy over another problem, that is, they had reason to believe that public opinion in Canada did not favour the absorption of large numbers of refugees, especially eastern Europeans and, more particularly, Jews. Once again, they reasoned, important segments of the public might be sympathetic to displaced persons, but this public was also notoriously capricious. It might momentarily favour the admission of numbers of refugees or displaced persons, then discover, once they had arrived, that they were not to their liking. And the government in power would have to face the backlash.

Would there be a backlash? The government thought so. It was the government, not the public, that analysed reports from Europe on the status, health and character of would-be settlers, and these reports were seldom flattering to Jews. Colonel Scott, of the Canadian Military Mission, visited refugee and displaced persons camps in the autumn of 1946 on behalf of External Affairs, and he ranked the groups there in descending order of preference, beginning with the Balts and ending with the Jews.

> I hardly know what to say about the Jews. They are not popular, but how far this is anti-Semitism and how far based upon practical experience is hard to say. No administrator talks like an anti-Semite, though some of them are strong against Zionists. It is universally stated that the Jews are physically lazy, and (though not so universally) they will not even do their own camp work. . . . They are great black marketeers, but whether worse, or only more patient than the Poles, is hard to say. . . . We have enough of all these peoples discussed in the report in Canada to be able to estimate their respective worth for our economic needs.[68]

Similar observations were made by a staff member at the High Commission in London, who toured the camps in British-occupied Germany at the request of Massey. In an ethnic sweepstakes where admission to Canada was the prize, the Balts again fared best: "Balts merit fully the high opinion which most observers have formed of them. Clean, hard working, conscientious and resourceful, they are very anxious to be employed in some way, and more than others they put this desire into practice." These "others" were ranked on the preferential ladder, from Ukrainians down to Poles, until, at the bottom, were Jews. If the truth be known, the official had not visited any Jewish displaced persons camps, but, as he explained, it was hard to avoid the negative appraisals of Jews made by ranking British officials who had already locked horns with Jewish refugees over Palestine. "The opinions expressed were not very flattering, with frequent references to black marketeering, dirty living habits and general slovenliness."[69]

It should not be supposed that others got off lightly. Major M. C. Bordet, second-in-command of the Eighth Army Corps' displaced camps section, found Jews only slightly more repugnant than Poles, the latter group nearly as unworthy as Jews when it came to consideration for admission into Canada.

> It is absolutely true that a great deal of sympathy is wasted on DP's. . . . We might have to take over our share of them but let us make that share as small as possible. They will make very poor settlers. . . . No Polish DP honestly refused to go home from an ideological point of view. I don't think

they ever had any—after five years spent doing as little as the Germans would let them do and two years doing absolutely nothing, their apathy is amazing. They are unwilling to face the hardships of life in a war-ravaged country.

These people might be the most worthy of our sympathy, but they certainly are the most undesirable people as immigrants. They will be a charge to the state from the very day they get in. Our police forces will have their work doubled. As for the Poles, they will be unemployed or in jail, and in either case, quite happy. . . .

The Lithuanians are as bad as the Poles. They are their close neighbours and have many points of similarity. They speak better German and have proven their superiority at the art of black marketeering.

The Latvians and Estonians are honest, ingenious and good workers. They would make good immigrants.[70]

Indeed, Canadian officers abroad seemed to delight in debating the relative standing of various groups—always with reference to their desirability to Canada. Wing Commander J. W. P. Thompson, for instance, challenged Colonel Scott's evaluation, moving Poles and Ukrainians up one notch and Russians down two. As a sports writer might give a confident and seasoned team the edge over one with enthusiastic and talented rookies, so Thompson gave alleged Polish individualism the edge over Russian group solidarity. "I am conscious," Thompson conceded, "that my criteria are anything but exact"—but, exact or not, Balts were again at the top, Jews at the bottom.[71]

Although the order was rarely reversed, Charity Grant, then assigned to a Canadian UNRRA team in Europe, did exactly that. In a January 1946 letter to Brooke Claxton, minister of health and welfare—a letter Claxton passed on to the prime minister—she appealed for the admission of Jewish refugees, especially children. Her argument was unpopular and she knew it: "Of course I know what will happen. Eventually Canada will say she will take in some of the Balts because they make good farmers." Jews, she protested, were unpopular because the world prized civility over survival. "The thing most people don't realize about this continent," she said, "is that everything is rotten. Moral standards have undergone such a change that to the old point of view there are no standards. For most people here every effort is turned to the everlasting struggle for existence and it doesn't matter what you do or how you do it just so long as you survive."[72]

Jews, more than others, had learned through experience that without the promise of tomorrow, survival today was a victory in itself. Grant noted the irony in this, that the very resourcefulness necessary to do just that—to survive—gave rise to much of the anti-Semitism even then flourishing in Europe. Yet it was this very resourcefulness, if transplanted to a friendly environment, that would make these Jews strong, independent and successful settlers:

> Where can they go and what can they do. No one wants them. They can't return home. They can't stay rotting in camps for the rest of their natural lives. They must do something. If you saw them you would realize that they are a desperate group and I know if I was one of them I would be the same. And the horror of what happened to them under the Nazis is something that even the most dreadful newspaper publicity and films can't describe. They have the feeling that somehow they must find a place in the world where they won't be persecuted ever. It is pitiful. You don't like what they do in their desperation but you can't help admiring their guts and vitality. And then you have got to remember that they have gone through the ultimate hell for so long that nothing you can do to restrain them has any influence on them.
>
> I don't know how to describe what I feel. To work with people who have no future is the most humbling thing you can imagine. One's own worries and troubles are so picayune, childish. Concentration camp survivors are a new race of human beings.[73]

What the prime minister thought of Charity Grant's appeal will never be known. His own thoughts on Jews remained confused and subject to influence. In early 1946 the defection of a minor Soviet diplomat in Ottawa, Igor Gouzenko, brought revelations of Communist spy rings in Canada that included a number of Jews, and King was made uneasy.* As he wrote,

* Of course not all of King's anxiety about Jews was a matter of state, at least, not directly. On one occasion, for instance, King recorded in his diary that the successful Ottawa Jewish businessman, A. J. Freiman, was employing moonlighting servants on their days off. Bad enough they steal another's servants, but, King recorded in anger, Jews also pay "fabulous sums . . . for short hours. . . . No wonder the Jews get disliked when they move into a community and things go wholly astray." Public Archives of Canada, King Diary, May 11, 1946, 417.

> I recall Goldwin Smith [noted University of Toronto philosopher] feeling so strongly about the Jews. He expressed it at one time as follows: that they are a poison in the veins of a community. Tom Eakin [past-principal of Knox College, University of Toronto], from whom I had a letter this morning, has a similar feeling about them. I myself have never allowed that thought to be entertained for a moment or to have any feeling which would permit prejudice to develop, but I must say that the evidence is very strong, not against all Jews, which is quite wrong, as one cannot indict a race any more than one can a nation, but that in a large percentage of the race there are tendencies and trends which are dangerous indeed.[74]

Public sentiment was unsettled and often confused—unsettled over the prospect of foreigners coming to Canada and confused by endless and tiresome debates over refugees, displaced persons, immigration policy, manpower needs and ethnic selectivity. In all, questions outnumbered answers, and a May 1946 editorial in the *London Free Press* posed yet another: "Have We a Policy?"—the paper was not sure, and time, it warned, was working against any fruitful debate. "We must," the *Free Press* demanded, "make up our minds what course we are to follow, and we must do it soon. Are we, as Prime Minister King suggested, not to consider any new immigration policy until all Canadians are employed? Can we agree on what constitutes full employment? Is there employment if there are jobs available, but at wages which are not acceptable? Must we agree on this before admitting immigrants?"[75]

For labour-intensive corporate interests the answers were self-evident. Business needed labour and needed it fast. If the government refused to believe postwar prosperity was here to stay and workers from abroad were required, business was convinced. In an address to the Rotary Club of Montreal in December 1945, J. S. Duncan, president of Massey-Harris, the farm implements giant, proclaimed: "Never was there a time since Canada was first settled which has been more favourable to selective immigration than at present." If he neither explained what he meant by "selective" nor directly argued for importing refugees, he did argue for more domestic consumers to expand the home market and open export possibilities. Other Canadian business leaders followed suit. Robert Stanley Waldie, vice-president of Canada Bread and president of the Imperial Bank of Canada, warned those present at the bank's seventy-first annual meeting that without immigration the current economic boom might not be sustained. Rather than spawning unemployment, he declared, immigration stimulated "consumption-good industries." This line was echoed by Canadian insurance magnate David Eckford Kilgour, president of the North American Life Insurance Company. "We must face the situation frontally," he said in an address to a Bank of Canada meeting, "that to hold the position we have attained during the war, to utilize our greatly expanded production capacity, to develop our ample spaces and our wealth of natural resources and meet our tremendous national commitments, we must attract to this country additional population."[76]

Business leaders were not without allies. In the Canadian Senate, top heavy with retired politicians and members of corporate boards, these appeals struck a responsive chord. Even Thomas Crerar, appointed to the Senate after a less than distinguished few years as minister responsible for immigration, sounded a new pro-immigration note. "It would be good business for Canada again to adopt a vigorous immigration policy," the senator said. "It will augment the productive power and strength of this country and its capacity to carry its financial burden. In addition to that we shall be doing a fine generous Christian act in endeavouring to make some contribution toward relieving the plight of the homeless millions in Europe."[77]

Crerar's own blend of business acumen with the humanitarian spirit reflected a new coalition in the Senate that tied the boardroom senators to a long suffering pro-immigration rump group, represented in the Senate by Cairine Wilson of the CNCR and Arthur Roebuck of Toronto, long a friend of Jewish causes.

If the Senate did not directly shape the cabinet's priorities, it could recommend legislation and review government practice. In April 1946 the new business and pro-immigration alliances reactivated the Senate's long dormant Standing Committee on Immigration and Labour. With the prodding of Senator Roebuck the committee was directed to initiate a total review of Canadian immigration policy and practices and to consider options for the future. The committee's public hearings and periodic reports received wide press coverage. In this respect, although the committee did not initiate new policy or lay out a reform legislative package, it did focus public attention on immigration and give advocates of reform an important platform from which to make their case.

On the morning of July 3, 1946, Saul Hayes and his research director, Louis Rosenberg, a widely respected demographer and authority on Jewish population change, appeared before the Senate committee. Hayes was determined to exploit the event for all the positive press he could get and Rosenberg had primed him well with background data.[78] Hayes and Rosenberg reviewed the recent history of Jewish immigration to Canada. They pointed out that Jews alone were classed by Immigration officials not by citizenship but by "race" or ethnic group, irrespective of country of origin. Jews were also designated as undesirable. In practice, this meant that non-Jews from the same country of origin and in the same economic or social circumstances as Jews were given preference. Underlining this point, Rosenberg created a stir in the committee by quoting from the 1941 *Annual Report* of the Immigration Branch a passage resonant of policy expounded in Nazi Germany. "Canada, in accordance with generally accepted practice," F. C. Blair had written, "places greater emphasis upon race than upon citizenship."

Hayes appealed for a new, non-discriminatory immigration act, an easing of regulations that in effect discriminated against Jews and other "non-preferred" immigrants, a realistic appraisal of the antiquated agricultural base of Canadian immigration policy and emergency measures to assist in the resettlement of refugees, Jews and non-Jews alike. It was, Hayes argued, not for lack of means but for lack of will that nothing was being done to assist these people. The millions of Jews who had died at the hands of the Nazis, he concluded bitterly, were also victims of this same lack of will—by the same people.

> It is my duty to say that the number of these victims would have been very much smaller and very many of their lives could have been saved if such countries as Canada would have paid heed to the requests of their kin and of Jewish citizens to grant a refuge to some of them while there was still time. It is a simple and true fact that because the applications made to the Immigration Branch on behalf of many of them were not favourably acted upon, their ashes and bones today lie in Buchenwald and soap had been made of their bodies instead of their being free and useful citizens of Canada life [*sic*] to-day.[79]

Not everyone who appeared before the committee was quite so open to the admission of displaced persons, especially if

Jewish. Lieutenant-Colonel Arthur Hicks, a Canadian officer who had recently returned from a tour of duty as director of a displaced persons settlement around Bergen-Belsen, stated bluntly that Jews were "not desirable immigrants for Canada." The witness explained to the committee that Jews came from overcrowded cities and that their behaviour as displaced persons showed that their morals were "low in comparison to Canadian standards."[80] If only before the Senate committee, Hicks and those who agreed with him were for once in a minority.

Thus, business and liberal elements of the community were receptive, with reservations, to renewed immigration, but the general public was not convinced. Not only was there division over the wisdom or need to open Canada's doors to immigration, but there was division, sharp division, among advocates of increased immigration over who should and should not be allowed into Canada under a liberalized immigration program. A Gallup Poll on immigration released in late April 1946 underscores these conflicts. Those favouring immigration from Europe or giving it qualified approval accounted for thirty-one per cent of the sample. Sixty-one per cent were opposed. As one might expect, seventy-one per cent of those polled in Quebec were opposed. But even those in favour of renewed immigration from Europe were not universal in their approval. Asked from which countries they would welcome immigrants, Scandinavian countries headed the list while countries from which Jews might come—Poland, "The Balkans," Russia and Ukraine—trailed the list in that order.[81]*

Most disturbing was a Gallup Poll in late October 1946. In this instance, the Gallup organization, sensing a growing willingness to reopen immigration, wished to test the boundaries of selectivity. It asked simply: "If Canada does allow more immigrants are there any of these nationalities [on a supplied list] you would like to keep out?" Individuals were allowed to vent their hostility. Some picked more than one group. The Japanese,

* Gallup polls conducted on the Palestine question are also revealing. When asked in February 1946 whether they favoured Jewish settlement of Palestine, sixty-nine per cent of Canadians polled supported free or limited settlement—a policy opposed by the British. Eight months later, a related poll asked whether Canadians would favour admitting into Canada Jews interned by the British for illegally attempting to enter Palestine. Public sympathy for Jewish immigration into Palestine had its limits. In this case, less than a quarter of those polled would have allowed these Jews into Canada. Canadian Institute of Public Opinion, Public Opinion News Service Release, February 9, 1946; Ibid., October 2, 1946; see also *Kitchener Daily Record*, October 2, 1946.

so recently defeated in the Pacific and the subject of a massive wartime propaganda assault, were ranked first in the list of undesirables by fully sixty per cent of all Canadians polled. Second on the list was not Canada's prime European enemy, Germans, but Jews. Almost half of those questioned, forty-nine per cent, checked off Jews as undesirable immigrants. Ukrainians and Poles fared far better than Jews, the hostility quotient against these groups only fifteen and fourteen per cent respectively. Given this result, one would seem right in concluding that earlier polls based on country of origin registered a high negative response to eastern European countries, not because of a desire to keep out Poles or Ukrainians, but because these same regions were known to be the source of Jewish immigration.[82] For many, it seems, the desirability of immigration was directly proportional to the degree to which Jews were excluded.

Throughout the immediate postwar years the press fed division on the immigration issue. Most newspapers in favour of a Canadian initiative in immigration still expressed caution regarding the "racial" origin of the would-be immigrants. Whether for or against immigration, however, all agreed that the indecision of the government's approach must end. "Canadians should know and the world should know what course the Ottawa Government proposes to pursue," Quebec's *Chronicle Telegraph* demanded. In July 1946 the influential Toronto *Globe and Mail* labelled the government's approach to immigration inadequate; it dismissed the token gestures of allowing in a few first-degree relatives as insufficient. And the Montreal *Gazette*, in an uncharacteristically blunt editorial, railed against the narrowness of government. It assaulted the government for pandering to anti-immigration interests. The paper felt the government should instead guide Canada toward a stronger economic future in which, the *Gazette* assumed, immigration would play an important role. "The government attitude on the question appears to be a masterpiece of sterile indirection . . . this country is taking no immigrants, does not want any, and is giving no encouragement to any prospect that any will be wanted or assisted to come here in the future. That is hardly a plan to induce prospective migrants to plan on coming to Canada when facilities are available."[83]

Once again, however, advocacy of a more active immigration policy cannot be confused with any openness to the origin of proposed immigrants. Just the opposite. Many who favoured increased immigration did so because they felt confident that mechanisms were in place to insure that undesirable immigrants did not slip through. In advocating increased immigration it was understood that appropriate care would be taken. For instance, briefs were presented to the Senate Standing Committee on Immigration and Labour by two major labour union organizations, the Canadian Congress of Labour and the Trades and Labor Congress. The former called for an end to discrimination in immigration with respect to race and nationality, but allowed that some groups were more desirable "because of their backgrounds, education or customs." The Trades and Labor Congress was less subtle, calling for renewed immigration with the exclusion of all races that could "not be properly assimilated into the national life of Canada." The *Vancouver Sun* pointed out that the two rival labour organizations differed only in tone. "The CCL is trying to say softly what the TLC says forthrightly. There are certain people who, though they may be admirable in their own way, do not assimilate racially or culturally with Canadians."[84]

The need for "selectivity" was also emphasized by the Ottawa *Citizen*: "Canada has to be careful . . . in opening the doors . . . after the experience of the United States with unsuitable migrants";[85] and it was left to the Brockville, Ontario, *Recorder and Times* to state bluntly what others camouflaged with code words and euphemistic references. Demanding that selectivity be the keystone in any new Canadian immigration drive, the *Recorder and Times* was specific about who should be let in and kept out. To cement its anti-immigration argument, the *Recorder and Times* explained that some groups were even then worming away at the very fabric of Canadian unity. Only the word *Jew* was missing.

> There has been a foreign, or at least a non–Anglo-Saxon flavour to a large percentage of the names associated with black marketing and similar illegal operations in this country during recent years. Even when the outlook during the war was darkest and the need for patriotism and sacrifice greatest, these people . . . took advantage of the emergency to enrich themselves wherever they could and they did not seem to care what happened to this country or its inhabitants. The recent Gouzenko espionage investigation has shed further light on how some of these people of foreign origin can behave in the matter of repaying Canada for sheltering, protecting and educating them.[86]

The French-language press was also divided. Here approval of renewed immigration was, if possible, more cautious about immigration selectivity and sceptical of business claims to need labour. As in English Canada there remained a bedrock of anti-immigration sentiment. In French Canada, however, it was both stronger than in the rest of Canada and had an overt anti-Jewish shrillness about it. Alexis Gagnon, for instance, wrote a series of articles in 1946 for Montreal's influential *Le Devoir*. His articles were picked up in other French-language dailies. As Gagnon described it, dark and powerful forces in Canada were then conducting an intensive pro-immigration campaign in alliance with ethnic groups. Once in Canada these groups would become partners of the Anglo-Canadian élite. Their goal, he declared, was to perpetuate the majority British domination of the state through immigration. This would, of course, thwart the impact of French Canada's high birth rate. The pro-immigration campaign, he concluded, had no economic motivation. It was a pure and simple conspiracy against French-Canadian survival.[87]

Others in the Quebec press were more temperate. They argued for some small immigration on either humanitarian or economic grounds. But such immigration, they warned, should be tightly controlled as to occupation and ethnic origin. When the Canadian Chamber of Commerce, meeting in Winnipeg, called for a vigorous policy of national development including immigration, the Quebec press played the story as an assault on French Canada. Montreal's *La Presse* and *La Patrie*, Quebec City's *Le Soleil*, *La Voix de L'Est* of Granby, *La Tribune* in Sherbrooke and *Le Nouvelliste* in Three Rivers united in asserting that, unless a selective system of immigration restriction was established, Canada would be "forced to accept a wave of undesirable immigrants."[88]

Government was thus pressed—pressed on the one hand for increased immigration by business, which demanded a larger labour pool and a larger Canadian market, by ethnic groups pleading for the admission of relatives or requesting special leave to sponsor groups of settlers, by concerned and often progressive Canadians seeking moral and positive leadership from the Canadian government, and by Canada's European allies and partners in the international arena which wished to see the problem of refugees solved once and for all. On the other hand, the government was also pressed by an anxious Canadian public, both inside and outside Quebec, warning of the economic and ethnic consequences of any immigration moves, by a deep-seated public hostility to Jews, which, it was feared, would make up the bulk of any European immigration, and by the government's own concern that the economic boom could turn to bust. Immigration, especially the immigration of Jews, might be a humanitarian imperative but was certainly a political minefield. One truth remained solidly in place. There were few Liberal votes to be gained from importing displaced persons.

Which way should government turn? In spite of the pressure on their respective departments, the ministers of immigration and labour remained adamant that precipitous action might be costly. With the stakes so high the deputy minister of labour, Arthur MacNamara, summed up prevailing attitudes: "We should not try to go too fast in the matter of encouraging immigration."[89] At the same time he did not intend to be caught napping. Immigration, including that of displaced persons, was increasingly seen as an issue of labour supply. MacNamara therefore proposed close departmental scrutiny of all policy issues involved and ordered his regional officers and regional advisory boards to meet and discuss immigration problems in the context of labour.

The comments and recommendations sent back to MacNamara reflected the range of opinion in the country itself. Most advocated an opening of immigration if tightly tied to Canadian social and occupational needs. Most also feared that selective immigration might be neglected in a mad rush to get labourers. This, it was generally agreed, was as undesirable as doing without the labour. The balance between Canadian labour needs and the need to insure ethnic selectivity was repeatedly stressed. "I have felt right along that we are duty bound to open this country to selected immigrants from among the ranks of the refugees," the chairman of the Pacific Regional Advisory Board wrote. "I was particularly interested in the remarks about Baltic Peoples. Two UNRRA officials, just recently returned, have told me of the excellent type of citizen material they are. I do not object to Jews as such, but do not believe that the Mongol type of Jew from Poland and Russia is very readily assimilated in Canada."[90]

While the deputy minister of labour sought departmental counsel, Canadian Jewry awaited action. In March 1946 Saul Hayes wrote to the minister responsible for immigration that knowledge of events in Europe "made silence . . . unthinkable." He again described the shocked disbelief of Canadian Jewry that so little had been done to relieve the plight of refugees. "The situation, as is well-known, is desperately bad and particularly demoralizing in that the survivors of six years of Nazi terror have no feeling of rehabilitation at all." He asked the ministry "to take such steps as are necessary to give them landing permits in this country," but Ottawa remained silent.[91] In July 1946 Canadian Jewry again pleaded for action. An outbreak of anti-Jewish pogroms in postwar Poland, especially fierce in Kielce, sent shock waves through the Canadian Jewish community. The Jewish Labor Committee was incensed. "We are fully aware," it declared, "of the apparent indifference to the fate of the remnant of European Jewry by peoples of other lands, our Canada included. It appears that as far as the Jew is concerned, his life, his fate and his rights to life have ceased to be on the conscience of men."[92]

The Canadian Jewish Congress made a direct and personal appeal to the prime minister. They telegraphed King urging him, in effect, to override Immigration authorities by issuing "emergency instructions to admit a reasonable number of these unfortunate people." Such an act, they assured King, "would place Canada in a proper light, could relieve a frightful problem overseas and would give new hope for victims of the religious and racial persecution by the Nazis at a time when they are becoming convinced that they are forgotten by the democratic allied world." King shunted off the telegram to his minister responsible for immigration for an answer.[93] Nothing happened.

Beyond the token of offering to admit a limited number of first-degree family members, the cabinet still resisted mounting pressure and, unbelievable as it seemed to Canadian Jewry, showed no inclination to act quickly. In September 1947, on the Jewish New Year, Samuel Bronfman issued a message to Canadian Jewry. It was not a message of hope and renewal as was customary at that time of year:

> With the approach of the solemn holy day which ushers in the New Year, many and solemn are the thoughts which agitate the minds of our people. Certainly Canadian Jewry would be unworthy of itself if it viewed with equanimity the tragic plight in which thousands of its brothers in Europe, fully two years after a war which was to bring the Four Freedoms to the four corners of the world, still find themselves. Displaced in camps that have no exit, misplaced in ships that have no destination, the pitiable remnant which

> miraculously survived the onslaught of Nazi terror knows today of peace only by hearsay. The great act of rectification which one expected from the world, the gestures which would in some measure atone for and correct the unspeakable ordeal to which our people have been subjected, failed to materialize. For all participants in the world wide conflict, schemes of rehabilitation are underway; even for the Germans there are the benefits of the Marshall plan; for the earliest and most ravaged of the Nazi victims there are only the iron curtains of the displaced persons camps.[94]

Fully three years after some death camps had been liberated, after refugee centres had been established, after international agencies had begun the search for new homes and after Canadian Jewry had begun to plead for some postwar concessions from their government, almost no Jewish refugees had yet entered Canada.

8

A PLEASANT VOYAGE

On April 19, 1948, the S.S. *Beaverbrae* stood prepared to depart the German port of Bremerhaven for Canada. It carried a full complement of passengers, mostly displaced persons. As many stood excitedly at the railings anticipating their last glimpse of Europe, the ship's loudspeaker system crackled to life. With the permission of the ship's captain, a statement prepared by Canadian Immigration Branch authorities was read to the passengers, first in German then in Russian.

> Attention!! Attention!! Please! I am speaking to you in the name of the Canadian Government. On ships carrying emigrants from Europe to Canada, incidents are supposed to have occurred amongst passengers, as a result of differences of opinion on political grounds, which could easily have had most unpleasant consequences.
>
> Differences of political opinions amongst so many nationalities which you represent, are, of course, unavoidable. We—the Canadian Government—however, look upon you all as equals—in other words—future Canadian citizens, *all*—and I repeat the word—*all*—with equal rights, and we want you all, in your own interests, to regard yourselves in exactly the same light.
>
> Do not spoil your journey with unnecessary quarrels of this sort. I wish you all—a pleasant voyage, a happy landing and every success in your new future home—CANADA.
>
> I thank you.[1]

The formalities of welcome complete, the *Beaverbrae* weighed anchor and slipped out of port. The displaced persons on board, now admonished to behave in a fashion befitting would-be Canadians, were there as the result of an extraordinary turnabout in government policy. At the end of 1946 Canadian Immigration authorities still sought ways to forestall any necessity to accept the displaced of Europe. When the *Beaverbrae* left Bremerhaven less than a year and a half later, its passengers represented but a tiny fraction of the tens of thousands of displaced persons they were undertaking to admit in 1948 alone.[2]

The wall of Canadian immigration restriction did not crumble in one year. It was breached—by the loose coalition of pro-immigration and pro-refugee interests, which the government could no longer withstand. Its strength had been building. Its time had come.

Business interests led the battle. With peace they heralded the possibility of a postwar economic boom and pressed for population growth both to enlarge the Canadian consumer market and supply needed labour, especially to extractive industries. Business found ready allies among those Canadian ethnic communities, especially among Jews, who pleaded for the admission of family members or the privilege of sponsoring a humanitarian resettlement effort. But these requests had been rejected before. A cabinet determined to defend the wall of immigration restrictions and backed by a phalanx of loyal and supportive public servants acting as the cutting edge of government policy had held fast for years. What changed by early 1947?

The key to change was national economic self-interest—the government became gradually convinced that Canada's postwar prosperity, as surprising to many as it was welcome, could be maintained. The prophet of prosperity was C. D. Howe, the powerful minister of reconstruction and supply. Howe, who entered Parliament in the Liberal sweep of 1935, had a reputation as an astute businessman and administrator. During the war he had held the key cabinet post of minister of munitions and supply, in which he oversaw much of Canada's domestic war effort, and as postwar planning became a priority, he was given an equally important post as minister of reconstruction. His was the task of insuring a smooth and, if possible, prosperous transition to a peacetime economy.

Howe had long been bullish on the economy and soon became an outspoken advocate of increased immigration—including that of displaced persons. Within the cabinet he had repeatedly pressed his colleagues for a more aggressive immigration program, at first without much success. As his forecasts of labour shortages began to come true and a buoyant economy gave no sign of weakening, the minister pressed still harder. Winning over the prime minister, he moved to ease responsibility for immigration away from J. A. Glen. Glen, who all agreed was ineffectual in the cabinet and the puppet of his still restrictionist-minded civil servants, was no more an enthusiast of increasing immigration than others in his ministry.[3] As late as February 1947 J. S. McGowan, director of colonization for the Canadian National Railway, complained to officials of the International Refugee Organization: "Unfortunately, Glen has very definitely left the impression with all those applying to him that he is trying to keep people out of this society."[4] Nor was Glen a favourite of King's. "Glen is a curious conceited fellow, very vain," King wrote. "I think he just does not want it to appear he is not wholly equal to the demands of the immigration debate which is clearly the case. He is really a disappointment as a Minister. Pleasant in personal relations but really next to useless in government."[5]

When a vacancy for deputy minister opened in Glen's ministry in the winter of 1947, King, with Howe's encouragement, sought someone with pro-immigration sympathies—someone experienced in public service but independent enough of mind to challenge a tradition of immigration restriction that stretched back through the career of F. C. Blair. King chose Hugh Keenleyside. For years a tireless and progressive member of the Department of External Affairs and already in tune with the international dimensions of the refugee issue, Keenleyside was given a mandate to clean house and make immigration a priority.[6]

Earlier, in the autumn of 1945, the cabinet had agreed to delay any move to open immigration, and had postponed all discussion of changes in immigration policy to a more opportune moment.[7] By late winter 1947, steps had to be taken to organize immigration from Britain and continental Europe, including the selective admission of refugees, and to accomplish this, the existing Immigration Act had to be revised. Although the cabinet understandably wished to proceed very cautiously, King's diary entry of January 23, 1947, suggests the new consensus among its members: "All were agreed that in the long range view, Canada would certainly need to have a large population if she hoped to hold the country for herself against the ambitions of other countries and to build her strength."[8]

The cabinet's agreement to open Canada to immigration after more than fifteen years was one thing. Forging a policy on which all could agree was quite another. King, at the time more anxious to still rumours and fears about wholesale admission of Orientals to British Columbia than he was about picking from among the various groups of displaced persons, demanded that racial and ethnic discrimination remain part of any revised legislation. The prime minister, who generally relished a good fight, did not fancy one on immigration, and so though he backed immigration, he did not want to be pressed on the question of whose.

> A good deal of confusion is in the minds of all of us as to where to draw the line and how to draw it in the matter of discrimination between different races and peoples who wish to come to Canada. There should be no exclusion of any particular race. That I think has really been wiped out against the Chinese but a country should surely have the right to determine what strains of blood it wishes to have in its population and how its people coming from outside have to be selected. There is going to be a great danger of the U.N. refusing the idea of justifiable rights of selected immigration with racial and other discriminations.[9]

The ministers, unsure of whom to keep out and how, turned to their own Interdepartmental Committee on Immigration and Labour for direction. They instructed the committee to consider setting an annual maximum made up of "allotted quotas" of immigrants based on immigrants' countries of origin and Canada's "racial composition." The cabinet secretary explained the justification for such a measure as the "natural desire of the government not to effect any radical change in the racial composition while, at the same time, not adopting a 'dog in the manger' attitude in relation to overcrowded areas elsewhere in the world."[10]

A draft statement was drawn up by the committee, submitted to the cabinet, discussed, revised, then revised again. On the afternoon of May 1, 1947, King rose to address a packed House on Canada's immigration policy. As the cabinet had agreed, the statement set out the government's new long-term commitment to sustained population growth complementing the country's economic development. On the thorny issue of discrimination, it attempted to have it both ways: "We should seek to remove from our legislation," King read, "that which may appear to be objectionable discrimination," but discrimination itself should remain; "I wish to make it clear that Canada is perfectly within her rights in selecting the persons whom we regard as desirable future citizens." It was not a right but "a privilege," therefore, to enter Canada, and Canadians had a right to protect the "character of [their] population." On the issue likely to cause even more dispute—the forthcoming immigration—King announced that steps had already been taken to open Canada's doors. Displaced persons would be among those admitted. Pointing to Canada's labour shortage, the government's "active part" in international refugee work, the success of the Polish veterans scheme and the recent regulations governing family reunification, King then asserted Canada's "moral obligation to assist in meeting the problem [of refugees]."[11]

Immediate response to King's statement was restrained. The American chargé d'affaires reported to Washington that it was not an unexpected statement, but, he added, in the first few days public reaction was muted and difficult to gauge. It was the English-language press that first pointed up the problems with the, in part contradictory, new policy. In the wake of King's statement the Montreal *Gazette*'s lead editorial, "Policy Depends on Interpretation," stated that what appeared broad in intention might prove very narrow in operation. The *Montreal Star* put its finger on the key administrative hitch: "There will be general satisfaction that Canada is prepared to play a worthy part in the alleviation of the distress of the victims of war. How worthy that role will be depends very largely upon the officials of the departments of Mines and Resources and of Labour. . . . Officials who have devoted many years to a policy designed to keep people out will not find it easy to adapt themselves to a policy designed to let people in."[12] The *Star* would be proved both right and wrong—but only right as far as Jews were concerned. Even before King read his statement, the newly appointed deputy minister, Keenleyside, had moved to open the door to displaced persons, and he soon found unexpectedly firm support at the ministerial level, when Glen fell ill and C. D. Howe stepped in as acting minister responsible for immigration. Howe, the main cabinet voice in favour of immigration, saw it as the simplest, cheapest and quickest way to find labour, skilled and unskilled. If the admission of Jews could be shown to satisfy this need, it might be acceptable. If their admission would erode public support for that of other displaced persons, particularly because of Quebec's hostility, it must be severely restricted. Others might address humanitarian considerations, but not Howe. He saw his duty: to reconstruct, not rescue.[13]

One of the first tests of the new policy's—and new administration's—attitude to Jews was the first-degree relative scheme. With Howe's indirect support, Keenleyside had begun to implement the Order-in-Council—for the most part dormant since its creation in May 1946—allowing Canadian residents to sponsor the admission of first-degree relatives.* The order included a revision, made in February 1947, that expanded the categories of first-degree relatives acceptable, but Canadian Jewry still protested that the definition of first-degree relatives was so narrow as to eliminate all but a handful of holocaust survivors.[14] In the second of two appearances before the Senate Standing Committee on Immigration and Labour, Saul Hayes commended the government for introducing the scheme, but pointed out how few Canadian Jews could bring surviving family to Canada under it: "We would contend that until legislation provides for immediate relatives up to and including first cousins and their children, the regulations will be bereft of true meaning for many Canadians who wish to aid their close kin."[15]

During these years, while comparatively few applications were filed with Ottawa on behalf of displaced persons and only a fraction of these were on behalf of Jews, many Canadians came forward with applications to bring other first-degree relatives from Europe. By October 1946 Immigration authorities reportedly had some ten thousand requests from Canadian residents. In the hope that the Canadian government might "eventually broaden the narrow limitations of [its] close relative categories," officials working with displaced persons continued to take note of individuals who reported family in Canada of whatever degree of closeness. Similarly, the Jewish Immigrant Aid Society continued to register the names of Canadian Jews who wished to sponsor surviving family or friends still (and they hoped temporarily) outside the existing regulations.[16]

While Hayes protested that Jews were generally ineligible for

* The cabinet had cynically approved the first-degree relative scheme as a temporary smoke screen, sheltering Canada from international pressure to admit refugees. With immigration now a priority, the scheme afforded advantages. It could get immigration moving quickly and at little cost, through Canadian residents already in touch with relatives in Europe, whom they were prepared to sponsor financially. Here was immigration on the cheap as far as Canada was concerned. Not less important, a first-degree relative program, if judiciously monitored, would not dramatically alter the existing ethnic structure of Canada. After all, it applied not just to eastern European displaced persons, not just to Jews, but to all those with family in Canada. Alan G. Green, *Immigration and the Postwar Canadian Economy* (Toronto, 1976), 22–23.

the existing scheme, the newly appointed Keenleyside had his own problem—the reluctance of his Immigration Branch personnel to admit immigrants. In February 1947, nine months after the first-degree relative scheme had been approved and just before Keenleyside took up his new post, the first Canadian immigration officers arrived in Germany to process eligible applicants. But these Canadian officials were both unsure how many, if any, first-degree relatives the government truly intended to admit and conditioned, by personal inclination if not years of professional experience, to reject applicants, especially eastern Europeans and, most especially, Jews. They arrived with their files, subjected each candidate to a full battery of tests, interviews, security checks, examinations and reviews—any one of which could eliminate a candidate without appeal—and approved almost no one.

International refugee officials were quite astonished. One complained bitterly to his superiors that the Canadians were making "extravagant and unnecessary demands for detail": "The trouble procedurally and otherwise by the Canadian Mission is quite out of proportion with the number of DP's taken by them." And the chief of Field Operations for the Intergovernmental Committee on Refugees dismissed the Canadians as more intent on pushing paper than on processing people.[17] As an example of this attitude, fifty berths on the *Aquitania* had been reserved by Canada for first-degree relatives; nine hundred applications were processed; when the ship sailed in March 1947, only twelve near relatives were on board.[18]

If change was to come it could only be imposed from above. Immigration authorities, nurtured on a tradition of restrictionism, seemed incapable of grasping which way the immigration wind was blowing. In the late winter of 1947 came Keenleyside; he was followed by Howe and together they made it clear that they would brook no opposition to increased immigration—certainly not from Immigration officials. Thus, it now seemed a new spirit informed Immigration; liberal and Jewish interests were delighted. Howe had shepherded cabinet endorsement of a "liberal interpretation of settlement conditions"; Keenleyside had made it clear to his officials that there was no maximum limit to the number of first-degree relatives Canada would admit.[19]

The Intergovernmental Committee on Refugees' representative in Ottawa, James Colley, wrote to his headquarters that possibilities were at last "brighter of many DP's going to

Canada."[20] The American ambassador in Ottawa reported to Washington that Canada was moving toward an unprecedented expansion of immigration that would include displaced persons:

> Minister Howe declared, "The economic future of Canada lies in an expanded population" and that no ceiling has been set on the number of immigrants Canada will admit. This is the most outspoken public statement favourable to an active policy of increased immigration yet made by a high government official directly concerned with the question. . . . Mr. Howe's statement is of particular interest since it is considered possible that Mr. Howe, now Minister of Reconstruction and Acting Minister of Mines and Resources responsible for immigration, will be named to the latter portfolio to replace Minister Glen, who is in poor health.[21]

It should not be supposed that the drive to increase immigration made the admission of Jews a simple matter of form. In opening the door to displaced persons, the cabinet was still concerned about the degree to which this movement might become a Jewish one. It was understood, it was beyond debate, that to whatever extent possible, this should be prevented; immigration preference should be given to other groups—especially British and northern Europeans. The IGC representative in Ottawa cautioned against pushing Canada on the question of Jewish refugees:

> Racial and religious prejudices are strong in Canada. The majority of Canadians cannot be convinced that all people of all races are suitable for assimilation. Raising the question [of Jews] I find only tends to develop antagonism and defeats the purpose we have in mind. . . . Complaints are heard all over the country about the delay in bringing people from the British Isles — husbands of Canadian girls, fathers, mothers, etc. . . . Besides there is the desire to see other immigrants from Britain coming to settle here. Because of this situation it is dangerous to say anything about the arrival of refugees at all, while as to Jews . . . the less that's said about them now will be better for them in the long run.[22]

T. J. Keenan, Ottawa representative of the United Nations Relief and Rehabilitation Administration, reported to his New York headquarters the results of a confidential poll on Canadian attitudes toward Jews: "They told me that they had had pretty grim returns when they investigated the welcome Jewish DP's might expect in Canada. They found that Jewish DP's [again] rated lower than the Japanese in public fancy."[23]

Public support for immigration in general was just firming up. The published portion of a Gallup Poll taken in the late summer of 1947 showed fifty-one per cent of Canadians agreeing that Canada needed immigrants, eleven per cent supporting immigration of the "right type" and thirty per cent declaring that Canada needed no immigrants. Even in Quebec, where opposition was stiffest, there was a softening of hostility—at least to the "right type." The Quebec Chamber of Commerce, for instance, realized that immigration might now be unavoidable. In a resolution to the federal government, it demanded not a stop to immigration but an increase in the number of French immigrants settling in Quebec and, as reported by the American counsel in Montreal, an end to alleged "preferential treatment given to displaced persons as against French immigrants."

Someone was listening; the cabinet approved the admission of those "born in France" on the same terms as British subjects. There was agitation, too, to relocate Dutch, Scandinavian and Baltic settlers in Canada. Howe impressed on Keenleyside a sense of urgency: "Anything that can be done to assist the movement of relatives and immigration from Holland, Belgium and the Scandinavian countries should be undertaken. Our Immigration Department will have the enthusiastic support of the [cabinet] for any steps that will contribute to the success of the movement."[24]

Prospects for the increased immigration of Jews were still clouded by public prejudice, yet that same public now at least nodded in the direction of some immigration. Too, the old immigration rules were gone, and a new spirit pervaded the Immigration Branch. Perhaps, just perhaps, once the immigration of others was in full swing, the movement of Jews might follow on its coat-tails. For one thing, the government itself was leaping over the hurdles it had built and defended. Where, one might ask, was the insoluble shipping problem now? And those staffing dilemmas? Solve them the government had to, solve them it did. C. D. Howe flew to London in the summer of 1947 in an effort to secure Canada enough passenger transport. Berths did not immediately become plentiful of course. After two years of claiming that shipping was a problem and doing everything possible to insure that that remained the case, officials truly scrambled. They even applied pressure on the

British to divert shipping from American or Australian runs, the least the British could do, Canada now argued, what with Canada taking some displaced persons off their hands. But even this did not meet the need. That same summer the cabinet approved $300,000 to subsidize refitting an older vessel, the *Huascaran*, to be made available for carriage of passengers on an "as is, where is" basis. Ironically, for the thousands of displaced persons whom this vessel would eventually carry, this ship had been awarded to Canada by Germany as part of its war reparations. It was recommissioned the *Beaverbrae*. Again, even this was not enough, and within a year the cabinet considered chartering trans-Atlantic flights to carry settlers.[25]

The absence of comprehensive immigrant processing facilities in Europe, often used as another excuse for inaction, now proved, like shipping, only a problem of will. After visiting displaced persons camps, Howe requested and received from the cabinet approval for a plan to revamp and expand the immigration organization in Europe while simplifying procedures. What seemed impossible only a few months earlier was now simply a matter of administrative reorganization. In March 1948 a press release from the Department of External Affairs outlining Canadian immigration policy noted, with pride, that in 1947 more than seven thousand displaced persons had entered Canada. "It is expected that Canada's full quota of 20,000 DP's will have reached their new homeland by mid 1948."[26]

The number of displaced persons Canada was prepared to admit, in addition to first-degree relatives, had multiplied almost overnight into the tens of thousands. In June 1947 the cabinet had approved the admission of 5,000. A month later this quota had been raised to 10,000; in October, to 20,000; and in April 1948, to 30,000.[27]

The vast majority of these people were labourers, not first-degree relatives. The 1946 scheme to admit four thousand Polish veterans as farm labourers afforded a useful model for the government, and by December 1946 the cabinet committee on immigration was discussing the merits of importing displaced persons as workers to fill vacancies in other priority sectors of the labour market. Only a few weeks later the forceful Howe overrode any cabinet reservations, winning approval for selected classes of displaced persons to be admitted into Canada for labour needs, "in particular, in the mines and forests." As if to underscore the labour, rather than immigration, interests at stake, the cabinet made clear that this program was an *exception* to existing immigration regulations, and gave ultimate responsibility for it not to the Immigration Branch but the Department of Labour. It was understood, of course, that the immigration aspects of the program would be conducted in liaison with Immigration authorities.[28]

Procedures were kept simple. Logging, lumbering and mining firms that would guarantee an individual a job under established terms could apply to the government for a portion of a total number of workers allocated for that industry. Once prospective employers signed contracts with the government, guaranteeing to abide by predetermined wage, housing and other basic conditions, selection teams made up of industry and government representatives were dispatched to Europe to select workers with appropriate skills.

In short order the original bulk-labour program was expanded to include domestic servants and agricultural workers with specialized training,[29] and among the specialized agricultural groups were sugar beet farmers. The Canadian Sugar Beet Producers Association, in cooperation with sugar processors and provincial governments in Alberta, Manitoba, Ontario and Quebec, petitioned for the admission of 1,200 families. These would replace Japanese internees and German prisoners of war who had previously supplied much of the bulk labour needed to meet the industry's needs. "As far as we can see at the moment," an industry spokesman explained, "there is little likelihood that labour conditions in the country will be remedied by the return of farm boys from overseas and from war industries in city areas because a great number of them have learned more profitable trades and will not return to their former work."

The producers association's criteria were demanding in most areas: "The prospective immigrants should be young or middle-aged, healthy—physically and mentally, have a proven background and experience in the work for which they are admitted, be no political extremists, and undertake on their part for the opportunity they are given to start a new life in a free country, to stay in the line of work for which they are admitted until they are Canadian citizens, that is, five years"; but not, to the relief of the director general of UNRRA (who monitored the progress of Canadian and other labour schemes), with respect to ethnicity.[30] "No particular racial group is designated."[31] This was not always the case.

On July 18, 1947, the cabinet approved the admission of

1,000 women as domestic servants and hospital workers, with admission of another 2,000 likely if the first batch proved "satisfactory." Ottawa cabled the acting Canadian commissioner of immigration in London that same day to ask that he immediately send a small group of domestics to Canada under the newly approved scheme. They were to be directed to select homes in Ottawa, the homes approved by Keenleyside. Also: "Protestant girls are preferred, possibly Estonians and of the best type available."[32]

The first ten domestics arrived in Canada in early October 1947. Five were assigned to serve in a hospital in Ste. Agathe, Quebec; five went to Ottawa. The latter were, indeed, well placed. One was assigned to the house of M. J. Coldwell, CCF leader in Parliament. He had approached Immigration authorities for a domestic while planning for this scheme was still in its formative stages. Coldwell later explained to the press that his wife was a paralytic requiring constant care; he had found it almost impossible to find help for her and was grateful to the government. (The domestic assigned to the Coldwell household was the only one of the five in Ottawa who could not speak English.)

Two of the remaining four were assigned to the minister of reconstruction and acting minister responsible for immigration, C. D. Howe, and one each went to Lester Pearson, then undersecretary of state for External Affairs, and Hugh Keenleyside. Press revelations of favouritism in these placements proved a small embarrassment, but a government spokesman made the best of the matter: "The women had been allocated to the houses of these four men so . . . these four could observe the working of the domestic plan at close range."[33]

Setting aside the propriety of civil servants and politicians feathering their own nests with servants, it is important to note that their notion of domestics, at least ones they were prepared to take into their homes, precluded Jews. Furthermore, as the program of bulk selection of domestics from among displaced persons went into full swing, the deputy minister of labour was cautioned by ranking women in his ministry that Jews did not make good servants. Much as Blair had earlier dismissed Jews as unfit for farming, one female consultant to the deputy minister explained: "Jews aren't willing to be domestics. It is not their forte. Few are found in this occupation in Canada." Another woman in the ministry echoed this sentiment. "Preference," she thought, should be given "to Balts as being the best group to bring in from the point of view of adaptability to hospitals and homes. Jewish women seldom accept or remain in household work." Even J. Walter Jones, premier of Prince Edward Island, got into the act. Jones explained to Ottawa that there were far fewer females than males in rural parts of his province, and so "quite a few of these girls could be absorbed into [its] economic life readily." As to ethnic selectivity, Jones preferred to put it positively: "If these girls came from points in Europe, from Germany and Holland, North, they would be most welcome in my opinion."[34]

These preferences were put into practice in displaced persons camps. In September and October 1947, for instance, a Canadian selection team screened female applicants for domestic positions at the International Refugee Organization's Amberg Resettlement Center in Germany. The organization's chief resettlement officer reported to his head office on the Canadian team's activities:

> After applicants had been called up and were being interviewed by [the Canadian] Labour Commission, we were informed that Jews could not be accepted for this scheme because they would be unacceptable as employees in domestic work. We [the IRO] agree that an employer has the right to his own decision in selection of employees by feeling strongly that any restrictions should be clearly announced before candidates are called forward.
>
> Forty Jewish candidates were interviewed. All were rejected. Four Jewish girls (the first interviewed) were accepted by Labour and cleared by Security Officer, Major Howells. The latter then withdrew security by writing "not" above the words "cleared for security" on the grounds that he had received a cable from Ottawa stating that no Jews were to be accepted.[35]

Other parts of the Canadian bulk-labour program were also *Judenrein*, or at least as *rein* as the government and some industries could keep them. For public consumption, the government declared its policy was nondiscriminatory, and it might be argued that the government stuck by its word, in part. In instructing the Canadian selection team assigned to recruit over twenty-seven hundred woodworkers, a Labour Department official stressed the need for an ethnic balance:

> No doubt the great majority of the persons selected for

> woods labour operations will be Balts and Estonians and this group should be particularly suitable from the point of view of assimilation.
>
> It is felt advisable, however, to include in this a number of Ukrainians as such action will be favourably received in some quarters here.
>
> We already have through the recruiting of Polish ex-veterans a very fair representation of Poles so that there is no particular necessity for going out of your way to include men of this nationality although this does not mean they should not be included.[36]

Even the best plans could run amok in the administrative nightmare of the camps, where many declared their nationality on the basis of perceived advantage rather than reality. In the lottery of nationalities a rash choice might mean repatriation to the East while a judicious one might grant access to the West. The team sent to select woodworkers found many Ukrainians, afraid of possible relocation in the Soviet Union, listed as Poles.

At first Jews were excluded by a little sleight-of-hand. The government, following the national designations the British used in their zone of occupation, classed individuals according to place of birth: Jews were therefore registered not as Jews, but as Poles, Latvians, Hungarians, Ukrainians or whatever. On paper, Jews no longer existed, and because most immigrants were selected by occupation, Jews could be rejected without reference to their ethnicity.

There was, however, a problem for Canadians in appearing equitable while carefully excluding Jews. Canadian selection teams had to ward off "dissatisfaction" among either the rejected or their guardians—the IGC, UNRRA and, later, the IRO. One Canadian team member was mindful that they might be open to the embarrassing charge of religious discrimination: "What I have said about regulating the nationality complexion of the selectees is even more true in regard to religion. And then there is grave danger any rules in this regard would get out and be published at home." But he then reported that "for wood work, few Jews applied—only 3 or 4 were passed." "I'm told," he explained, "Jews are not applying for overseas, but want to go to Palestine."

But were Jews waiting to go to Palestine? Or had they been forewarned that applying to Canada was a futile gesture? Perhaps the answer to both questions is yes. In any event, it did not take long before the truth of Canada's selectivity in the woodworkers scheme was known. Refugee officials had brought many Jewish woodworkers forward for interviews, and the Canadian government had advised its team to accept a few Jews in order to maintain the fiction of nondiscrimination. One had to give a little to get a lot. Forest-industry representatives, whose labour needs the teams were filling, disagreed, however. They stalled selections and requested help from industry leaders at home on the Jewish issue. The latter were not ambivalent. "The industry," its spokesman told Immigration officials, "advised their overseas representatives that such a class of labour is not acceptable and is not to be chosen." Immigration and Labour Department authorities, wishing to jeopardize neither their relationship with the forest industry nor the woodworkers scheme, fell in line behind the industry. A solicitous commissioner of immigration assured industry leaders that any effort to force Jews on the industry would "be investigated fully and nipped in the bud." The manager of the Ontario Forest Industries Association declared the industry satisfied and assumed the matter closed.[37]

The industry spokesman was precipitous. In Amberg, the International Refugee Organization found itself participating in the Canadian ruse.* The problem it presented to organization officials there seems less one of conscience and more one of efficacy. As the chief resettlement officer explained to her superior, "It has been extremely difficult to carry on the Canadian operation because specifications, restrictions and medical requirements have not been made clear in advance. When they have specified the way in which they wish the processing to be done, the restrictions of their schemes, or the exact nature of documentation required, we have always attempted to make the necessary corrections and adjustments." There lurked a fear, however, that too close a relationship could backfire, at least on

* The Canadian selection team at Amberg Processing Center originally requested that the IRO bring forward a selection of men—"single men ages 18 to 35, good physical condition, lumber experience." "Non-Jews only" was not a prerequisite of the program as far as the IRO was informed. "After Labour Selection teams started processing they announced that Jews could not be taken for the scheme as they were unemployable as lumbermen. Of the 40 men rejected by the Labour Commission, 27 were Jews; 11 Jews were returned to camps without interviewing the commission. Of the 100 visas granted 4 went to Jews." During a second series of interviews for the woodworkers scheme in the same camp several months later, the IRO personnel were fully aware of Canadian prerequisites. In this instance 292 woodworkers were accepted. "Of the acceptees 19 were Jews—as Jews were again presented to the selection team by the IRO in order that discrimination could not be charged."

the IRO. This official did not object to participating in Canadian anti-Jewish screening, but neither did she wish to get caught at it.[38]

And it would appear that the major indiscretion of the IRO's personnel was not in cooperating with Canadian teams, but, worried as they were, in detailing this relationship in written reports to their headquarters. In late July 1947 one such report, from the Ludwigsburg Processing Center, fell into the hands of the director of the Joint Distribution Committee office in Paris. He, in turn, conveyed the gist of the report to Saul Hayes.[39] And in late October 1947 Hayes was in Ottawa to take up the matter of discrimination in bulk-labour selection with Keenleyside. Keenleyside agreed problems had existed, but they had been solved. According to Hayes, the deputy minister had assured him that there were now no anti-Jewish restrictions. Indeed, Keenleyside had claimed that the department would tolerate "no discriminatory practices."[40]

Hayes was sceptical and well he might have been. Less than a month after his visit, Immigration officials in Ottawa were advised that prospective textile workers had been assembled for the Empire Cottons Division of Woods Manufacturing in Welland, Ontario. Woods Manufacturing demanded no absolute prohibitions against Jews, but had confided to the government that it did not then have any Jews in its employ; its preference was clear. The first group of textile workers would be coming to Canada "by air in the nature of an experiment," and local publicity would be unavoidable. Rather than distress the Welland community, the firm said, "it would be advisable not to include any persons of the Jewish faith." Jolliffe cabled Canadian immigration officers in Europe that the bulk movement of textile workers, not just those coming by air, "should be non-Jewish."[41]

With denials of discrimination against Jews flying in the face of evidence, it would be only a short while before Jewish community leaders discovered what was going on. Ben Nobleman, a young political activist in Toronto, was enraged at the rumours. Through labour programs, he charged, it seemed easier for war criminals to get into Canada than for Jews. "Why, Martin Bormann could come to Canada under such an arrangement."[42]

Hayes, in spite of mounting concern, remained reluctant to press the government too hard. Several Jewish community refugee proposals still hung fire and Jewish leaders dared not risk alienating cabinet, Labour or Immigration authorities. Yet, a protest had to be registered if only to allow government again to go on record, again to deny it endorsed discrimination. Hayes wrote a confidential letter to Jolliffe in which he alleged that Jews who put themselves forward as Balts or Ukrainians were selected, but that those who came forward as Jews were not.[43] Hayes's letter was passed on to the Department of Labour. It went unanswered.

There seemed little prospect of change. In December 1947 Joe Salsberg, then a Communist member of the Ontario legislature on a fact-finding tour in Europe, wrote to Hayes from Germany. Salsberg's relationship with the anti-Communist Canadian Jewish Congress leadership was strained at best. He would normally have thought twice before confiding his concerns to the Congress; but in this case the Jewish immigration crisis transcended political divisions. And Salsberg was appalled by what he found. From his "contacts, observations and discussions," he concluded: "There is a very definite anti-Jewish bias in the Canadian Immigration policies and in their application on the spot in Germany. This opinion is practically universal. Top IRO people share it with Jewish organizational representatives. While in some cases it is concealed, discrimination is brazen and unashamed in others."[44] In one case, eleven Jewish lumber workers were approved only to have the approval withdrawn at the last minute. The only Jewish woman accepted for the Canadian domestics scheme from one camp had been classed as a Pole not a Jew. Jewish workers were rejected from other bulk-labour plans after the designation "white" under race on their application forms was "scratched out" and "Hebrew" written in.

Salsberg also reported that RCMP security officers were far from even-handed with those few Jews approved at other levels. "For example," he reported, "they screened and approved for security reasons about a dozen men who were stopped by the doctor before boarding the ship, because the doctor discovered the S.S. mark tattooed under their armpits." On the other hand, a Canadian security officer questioned a Jewish child. "What were your parents doing in Auschwitz—and where did you get the money to come from Auschwitz here?" Salsberg told the Congress little it did not already know—the details were different, the sense was the same.

Jewish frustration was growing. In January 1948 a wire service story out of Munich reported that the International Refugee Organization, facing an internal investigation of racial discrimination, had released documents verifying the anti-Jewish bias in Canadian bulk-labour schemes. In addition, it had confirmed allegations that its personnel colluded with Canadian officials to exclude Jews from domestic, woodworking, railroad maintenance and hardrock mining jobs.[45] These and similar revelations forced Hayes to protest again, albeit, as softly and diplomatically as possible. In a letter to the deputy minister of labour, Hayes, focusing on the issue of domestic workers, laid out the evidence of anti-Jewish bias. He cited incident after incident where Jewish women were rejected for no other reason than their Jewishness. He proved that if the department felt Jewish domestics could not be placed, it was wrong. Jewish hospitals and other institutions had made repeated application for domestics. While they were not insistent that these positions be filled by Jewish women, it was, he chided, "obvious that these institutions [would] take Jewish girls."[46]

The wire service revelations were upsetting to the Department of Labour as well. They had counted on the confidentiality of IRO officials; now exposed, they needed to placate the Jews without shifting priorities. The deputy minister of labour, fearing this time "the matter [was] of some importance," called on Keenleyside, who advised judicious honesty: the cat had been let out of the bag; there was no longer any point in denying that Jews were selectively streamed out of most approved bulk-labour schemes, including the domestics scheme. But how to justify a disagreeable truth? Under the circumstances, unless the government and cooperating industries were now prepared to accept a considerable number of Jews, options were limited. Keenleyside felt the best tack was to take the line that in no case was there a hard and fast rule excluding Jews. It just worked out that way; tough decisions had to be made. But not, he emphasized, on ethnic grounds. Rather, hard judgements were made daily on the acceptability of individuals for specific Canadian labour needs. Regrettably, Keenleyside would have Labour officials argue, Jews had previously shown little interest in those work categories then open.[47]

There seemed some truth to Keenleyside's argument, at least with respect to woodworkers. One of the five Jewish woodworkers who had slipped in with the first 300 caused "some excitement." After starting work at a lumber camp in the northern Ontario bush, he "discovered a relative living in Oshawa, Ontario, who [was] anxious to have him leave the camp and enter employment in or near Oshawa." Almost immediately the Canadian Jewish Congress's Toronto office interceded. The local Congress executive, concerned that a poor showing by the few Jews in the lumber camps would undermine efforts to bring in any additional Jewish woodworkers, quickly passed a motion to "disassociate" itself completely "from any attempt by these men to break their contract with paper and lumber companies." A Jewish delegation from the nearest centre with a Jewish population, Fort William, Ontario, was sent to visit men in the lumber camps and persuade them to meet their obligations. The visits, according to the executive director of Congress, appeared to quell the discontent—temporarily. "The men in the camps were greatly heartened by the fact that somebody was concerned with them," Hayes wrote, "and after discussing the whole situation, they agreed that they would stay as long as was necessary. I think the visit resulted in a great strengthening of morale, and I also think that there will be no further difficulties with these individuals." Further to encourage the men to stay, their employer agreed to allow them to attend religious services outside the camp on Jewish holidays. (In case this gesture be taken as licence to demand additional privileges, the Jewish workers were cautioned "not to ask for too many special favors.")[48]

This incident was not forgotten. Coached by Keenleyside, Labour Department officials were only too pleased to remind Hayes that they had already handled requests for "the transfer of Jews, brought out as loggers from Germany, to other occupations." Such requests only underscored the department's thesis—Jews were not discriminated against because of their "Jewish extraction" but because of their suitability for employment. It was not, they again assured Hayes, racial prejudice at work in the labour schemes, but job suitability: "The Department of Labour is concerned with occupational selection, and not with the determination of representation of various racial groups in its phase of selection." In other words, the department would not relent. In late April 1948, for instance, the Canadian Immigration Mission in Germany cabled Ottawa regarding a group of fifty nurses selected for Canadian positions. The mission personnel asked whether Jewish women might be included and "if so, what number." In spite of an acute shortage of nurses in Canada and unfilled applications from Jewish hospitals, the director of immigration answered no: "Will advise if Jewish girls can be included in any later applications."[49]

Meanwhile, Immigration authorities privately conceded that discrimination in the bulk-labour program would continue despite guarantees made to the Jewish community; but they denied responsibility. David Lewis, national secretary of the CCF and later head of the New Democratic Party, questioned Keenleyside in July 1948. "The Labour Department officials in Germany," Keenleyside answered him, "are very definitely discriminating against Jewish domestics." He claimed then that he had no option but to go along.[50]

Everyone, it seemed, was ready to go along. And most would also deny that any anti-Jewish bias existed. It was, if civil servants and politicians were to be believed, not really a matter of anti-Jewish prejudice but of labour selectivity. Admittedly, Jews were selectively excluded and this might seem to some like anti-Semitism, but, Jewish leaders were assured, this was actually not the case. If one followed the government's reasoning, Jewish workers were not rejected because they were Jews but because they were Jewish workers. As Jews they might be welcome; as Jewish workers they were not suitable to Canadian economic development. That Canadian Jewry somehow failed to distinguish between anti-Semitism and national economic necessity was, civil servants were ready to argue, a Jewish problem. What, then, of the government's claim when economic selectivity in fact favoured Jewish workers? When an industry did *not* object to Jewish labour? In the spring of 1947, the spring of King's immigration policy statement, this question had finally to be addressed.

Canadian Jewry, searching for a crack in the wall of restriction wide enough to bring in Jews, marvelled at the success of several labour-intensive industries in winning approval for bulk-labour schemes. They of course weighed the possible benefits such a scheme might have for Jews, and felt obligated to continue increasing those benefits. On February 7, 1947, yet another Jewish delegation arrived in Ottawa led by Samuel Bronfman and his spokesman Saul Hayes. They were received by the prime minister and several members of his cabinet, including the ministers of labour and immigration. And the Jews were there to make yet another pitch on behalf of Jewish immigration. Once the usual formalities were over, Hayes again laid out the Jewish position. Most of it had been heard before, but Hayes had one new twist. Among the points outlined in his oral brief was a plea for labour in the needle trades industry which, according to Hayes, was "threatened with lessened production solely because of a failure to obtain skilled people amongst Canada's population."[51] There was no need for Hayes to explain to King and his cabinet why a delegation of Canadian Jewry would speak on behalf of one sector of the Canadian needle trades. King was noncommittal.

The clothing manufacturing sector of the Canadian economy was, in the national context, distinguished by the extent of its Jewish involvement. Jews predominated not only among owners of clothing firms, but also among workers—sewing machine operators, cutters, pressers and pattern makers. The union locals representing these workers in Canada and the international unions to which they belonged were also largely Jewish. The common ethnicity of many owners, workers and union officials did not insure more harmonious relations between labour and management, but when it came to the survivors of Nazism, they shared one mind and one purpose. Thus, the clothing industry, labour and management for once united, formed the backbone of a scheme to receive Jews from the displaced persons camps of Europe—a scheme predicated on the government's approval of bulk-labour importation. In this, the industry hoped, a way could be found, not to import cheap labour, but to circumvent traditional immigration practice which had kept the immigration of Jews to a minimum.

Hayes was therefore not alone in looking at the government's approval of bulk-labour schemes. Quite independently of Hayes or the Congress, several clothing manufacturers in Toronto met informally with clothing union leaders to patch together an industry presentation to government on their need for immigrant labour. Although the group would point to a "serious shortage of skilled craftsmen," the hidden agenda was to secure the entry of Jews. The industry group was dissuaded from going it alone to the government, as Hayes begged for time in the hope of putting together a well-orchestrated national campaign involving manufacturers, unions and, of course, the Canadian Jewish Congress. Samuel Posluns of the Popular Cloak Company in Toronto assured Hayes that the Toronto group would defer to a national campaign. It was understood by the Toronto group that, in acceding to a coordinated national effort, the central feature of its own concern would not get lost. Posluns impressed this upon Hayes: "Most of the potential immigrants they have in mind are of the Jewish faith."[52] The reminder was hardly necessary.

Hayes called a joint meeting of Montreal manufacturers, who

spoke for almost seventy per cent of the Canadian industry, representatives of the International Ladies Garment Workers Union, the Amalgamated Clothing Workers Union and the Jewish Labor Committee. If the group could agree, the Congress would quickly assist it in preparing a formal request to the Department of Labour outlining the needle trades' need for bulk labour.[53]

The Montreal group met in early March. Hayes had taken the precaution of drafting a brief to government, which he offered to those present. There was no doubt of their commitment. Within a week the Montreal men's and women's sectors of the industry were readied and the Toronto groups were standing by; Winnipeg quickly added its forces. An initial target group of 1,500 workers and their families would be applied for, "being 800 in the men's industry, 500 in the women's industry and 200 in the hat and cap industry." Using Hayes's draft as a guide, the Montreal group pieced together a joint brief for industry approval. Official endorsement by the needle trades' unions, which would co-sponsor the program with management, would await formal ratification by a spring convention. Unofficial but binding approval was already assured.[54]

A low-key, industry-wide campaign to win approval for the scheme from individual firms could begin. Unions would not protest against importation of labour, while management would barrage government with demands for relief from alleged labour shortages.* Tip Top Tailors, for instance, which had earlier requested permission to import Italian labour, now pointed out to the minister of labour the skills which Polish Jews could bring to the industry:

> We are having tremendous difficulty securing tailors for our industry. Most of the men and women formerly in our employ have become too old to carry on and although we have carried on schools and training for the young whom

* In fact, some clothing manufacturers were claiming a shortfall in labour in the postwar years. The large, Jewish-owned Tip Top Tailors in Toronto, for instance, complained to the government about a labour shortfall and in October 1946 requested permission to import available Italian clothing workers to their plant in Toronto. Unfortunately, Italians were still excluded from Canada under provisions of the regulations excluding previous enemy nationals. The degree to which Tip Top Tailors actually needed more workers or, for that matter, the degree to which the industry as a whole needed more, is open to question. If there was a shortfall, it was not as great as the clothing industry would soon have it appear. Public Archives of Canada, Department of Labour Records, File 1-26-5-1, J. Dunkelman to A. MacNamara, December 9, 1946.

we have interested, this programme is inadequate to supply our demand for tailors. Moreover, this procedure is very costly. . . .

Our experience in the past few years has proven that it is impossible to secure sufficient young people willing to learn tailoring, and the sooner some arrangement to bring tailors from Europe can be instituted, the benefit will accrue not only to our industry, but Canada as well.[55]

In late March separate but complementary briefs were sent to the Department of Labour on behalf of the men's and women's divisions of the industry.

Meanwhile, the Canadian Jewish Congress stayed in the shadows: any appeal to government had to be an appeal for labour not Jews; it had to come from industry not Jewish communal organizations. Hayes saw the Congress's role as "a coordinating one." He could brief union and management on how best to approach Labour and Immigration authorities, he could not go to Ottawa himself. He could help put together the necessary petition to the government; it could not bear the name of the Canadian Jewish Congress. As Hayes explained of his relationship to the industry, "We gave them the ideas and submitted draft material for their briefs. Obviously, we can't make the appointment in Ottawa nor can we show our hand. The representations must be made to Government by an industry and the industry is, so to speak, accredible."[56]

A joint labour-management delegation from the needle trades met with the ministers of labour and immigration in early May. The delegation reiterated the need for labour in the industry. Its labour force, it claimed, was dwindling, with the "average age of workers over 48 years" and little possibility of attracting Canadian-born workers. The industry guaranteed that no costs for the selection, transportation or settlement of those selected would fall on the government. They further pledged that Quebec and Ontario would each absorb one thousand settlers and their families.[57] The ministers requested assurances about cooperation in the political "screening" of would-be settlers, not of Nazis but Communists, and about industry willingness to cover the possible costs of transportation to and housing in Canada. All guarantees were given, and the meetings went well. "It was felt by those present that Ministers granted the industry a favourable hearing, and we look forward to a decision favouring the submissions made."[58] What is more, nobody raised the question of ethnic composition. Whether discreetly avoided or not, the Jewish question did not come up—not yet.

In early June, a month after King's statement on immigration policy, his cabinet met. As part of a general package of bulk-labour schemes, it approved the admission of two thousand "craftsmen for the clothing industry." There was little or no discussion of this aspect of the total program. Again there was apparently no reference to Jews—not yet.[59]

Hayes contacted the Joint Distribution Committee's Paris office for information on the availability of needle trades workers. The committee responded that no exact number of those in the needle trades was available. A survey of some 240,000 displaced persons estimated that sixteen per cent were associated with the needle trades, although how many of these told the truth, how many of those who told the truth would suit the Canadian scheme and how many would choose to migrate to Canada if given the chance, it was impossible to know. In any event, if it was necessary for Hayes to have a working number to go by, 38,000 was as good as any. The JDC volunteered to assist the Canadian scheme and immediately informed its field representatives that the scheme was in the offing.[60]

For its part the industry chose a joint labour-management team to be sent to Europe to begin making the necessary selections. In addition, industry leaders began to meet with individual clothing manufacturers, virtually assigning them responsibility for accepting specific numbers of workers—whether they needed them or not. Some firms in Toronto initially balked at pressure to take so many workers they neither knew nor needed. Whatever little resistance existed was soon shamed away, however, when one firm, the principal owners of which were Gentiles, signed up for 150 workers—all of whom they could well have done without. To the industry's great relief nearly all other manufacturers fell into line, and by mid July quotas to individual firms had been agreed on, pledges signed and a final contract with the Department of Labour confirmed.[61] The green light was on—or so it seemed.

As far as the industry selection team that would process the settlers was concerned, its mandate, or at least its public mandate, was clear: they would assist in selecting "tailors, regardless of what nationality" and "without any question as to their race."[62] But if, as the team members gathered in London for final briefings and clearance for their work, they still thought they would have a free hand in selecting Jews, they would soon be disabused of that notion.

The team members, all of whom were Jewish, understood that their hidden agenda was to bring as many Jews as possible into Canada under this scheme, and they could not foresee any difficulty on this count. With a reportedly heavy concentration of Jewish displaced persons in the needle trades, an honest selection would inevitably be top heavy with Jews. Indeed, in an effort to insure at least some non-Jewish participation, the industry selection team bent over backwards to acquire from the IRO and JDC lists of non-Jewish tailors. The JDC was also advised not to refer to the needle workers scheme as the "Jewish Project" lest the term be misunderstood or misinterpreted, at least by the government.[63]

The government was already having second thoughts—not about admitting tailors, if needed, but about admitting Jewish tailors, needed or not, and their families. Some doubted the political wisdom of letting the tailors scheme do the damage so well guarded against in other schemes. C. D. Howe, then in London for meetings with British and European officials, was warned that Jewish refugee officials were already gearing up to push forward Jewish workers for selection. Howe, fearing adverse criticism, especially in Quebec, should the King government be linked with a bulk-labour scheme that was excessively Jewish, stepped in. The powerful minister for reconstruction cabled his cabinet colleague, the minister of labour: "Suggest your selection teams be advised that not more than 50% of workers should be of one racial group." The minister of labour agreed and without consultation, instructions to the industry selection team, still in London, were revised accordingly.[64]

Howe summoned Max Enkin to Canada House in London. Enkin was a Toronto clothing manufacturer and member of the industry selection team. He knew Howe personally and had worked with Howe's Wartime Prices and Trade Board. Enkin therefore arrived at Canada House on Trafalgar Square believing the invitation from Howe purely social. The immediate social niceties finished, Howe steered Enkin into a small room, bare except for a kitchen table. Here Howe laid down the law. As he later explained to Canadian Immigration officials in London: "It was not the wish of Government that Jews only be recruited for the needlework scheme. It is likely, however, that inasmuch as a considerable number of clothing firms are owned and operated by Jews, that at least 50% of clothing workers recruited will be Jews."[65]

Thus, the all-Jewish, needle trades selection team learned that the government had imposed a severe restriction on the number of Jews to be accepted. Nothing about this restriction had been said when discussions first began, nothing had been said while negotiations were underway, and no Jewish quota was built into the signed agreements between manufacturers and government. Why then did the government act as it did? Why on the very eve of departure by the industry selection team from London to the camps of Europe was this restriction imposed? Surely it would come as no surprise to the cabinet that the vast majority of needleworkers selected would be Jews. The cabinet and civil servants may have been misled about the need for labour in the industry, but they were surely well aware that this would be—despite efforts to avoid the term—a Jewish scheme. Civil servants had received no instructions to scuttle or encumber the program from either the minister of labour or immigration or the Office of the Prime Minister. On the contrary. The scheme had been greeted with general approval by the cabinet—at least until August 1947.

In August 1947 the cabinet got cold feet. C. D. Howe, who had not been party to detailed negotiations on the scheme nor present at the cabinet meeting approving it, had become worried. The rumours he had heard that Jewish refugee interests in Europe, if not their allies in Canada, were preparing to use, even abuse, the program represented too great a risk. If Howe had no overriding personal antipathy to Jews, neither was he prepared to chance a storm of protest in Canada when Jews began arriving in large numbers—a storm that might sweep away his entire bulk-labour program. The influential minister's cautionary recommendation that a ceiling on the number of Jews admissible be set at fifty per cent had the force of law. Officials in the Labour Department and Immigration Branch then read into Howe's intent restrictions even more far-reaching. If it was undesirable that the needleworkers scheme either be used or seen as a strategy to bring Jews into Canada, then it should not be given departmental priority, nor should the percentage of Jews accepted be inadvertently inflated by the selection of Jews with large families. In addition, as the deputy minister of labour, Arthur MacNamara, instructed his officer with the Canadian Military Mission in Germany, the departure for

Canada of workers selected should be stretched out over two years, lest attention be called to the Jewish component: "Two thousand (or a few more to take care of losses) can be selected. One thousand to come this year and the balance next spring. We will take the position that *shipping facilities* does not permit of more than 1,000 this year." For the same reason MacNamara suggested his officials divide needleworkers "into two or three parties for different boats." And finally, he advised his agents that needleworkers need not be men. If the wife of a man selected was also employable in the trade, then she could also be counted against the Jewish quota. Smaller families, "of not more than say one child," would be preferred to larger ones, and: "If specially skilled married men apply the number of dependents could be accepted up to maximum of wife and two children."[66]

Government officials informed the International Refugee Organization of their quota, wording it as best they could to reduce the anti-Jewish sting. The move was explained, not as a control on the number of Jews who might reach Canada, but as a control on any groups dominating any part of Canada's bulk-labour movement. The IRO was not fooled, but neither did it question the Canadians or their quota (any more than it had in cases where Jews were completely excluded). Field officers were simply advised: "Only half of Canadian scheme can be Jewish."[67]

In London, Canadian needle trades representatives, awaiting final approval for their trip to the camps of Germany and Austria, were slowly overcoming their shock. Max Enkin, who had spearheaded the drive to collect employment pledges in Toronto, felt personally betrayed by Howe. The scheme was, in part, his creation. He had appealed to the good will of fellow employers to get the project underway; he had assured the good will of the government. There now seemed nothing he could do but go along. Had he or any team member anticipated the government's reversal, he might well have thought twice about participating.[68]

Back in Canada the newly announced quota set off additional rumbles of discontent. Saul Hayes immediately rushed off to Ottawa to plead with Deputy Minister MacNamara. It was no use. Canadian Jews, who fought quotas in law schools, medical schools, hospital appointments, private clubs and business associations, were asked to swallow one in rescuing refugees.

The project had never officially been one to bring Jews. There was no way, Hayes recalled, to turn it into one now.

> I remember arguing with MacNamara until my throat was parched that the issue was one of who were in the camps and the greatest number who could qualify, and that the issue that some had to be non-Jewish was really not only artificial, but a painful index which could perpetuate the quota system, which was akin to *numerus clausus*, which bothered the Jewish community so much and which would be hard for history to justify. Mr. MacNamara, however, was not interested in history . . . and what the record would show and what academics would prove in Ph.D. theses. He was interested in the fact that he would not be able to get through this project if it was realized that 100% were Jewish refugees.[69]

The needle trades selection team finally proceeded to Germany and Austria. Travel, selection and testing facilities were primitive. In order to cover the ground, the selection team split into two groups. At the insistence of JDC officials, they moved from camp to camp selecting only a few candidates in each. (As Enkin remembered, the whole Jewish quota could have been filled in any one camp.) The Joint Distribution Committee had its own agenda. They wanted the Canadian team not only to select Jewish workers but also to be seen selecting Jewish workers. Morale in Jewish camps was low. If even a few individuals from each camp were selected for Canada, it might create a sense of momentum—a sense that the camp was not a prison but a way station.

At first, each team carried a portable sewing machine about as a tool for testing prospective applicants. The machines soon proved too cumbersome for the teams, which travelled in Volkswagens with barely enough room for their own files and personal effects. As a result, sewing machines had to be abandoned, and testing was confined to one simple hand operation: if a candidate could successfully sew a buttonhole he was deemed a needleworker. Canadian Immigration and Labour officials who monitored the selection process seemed less concerned with the issue of skill, more concerned with race. It was left to industry delegates to decide who was professionally qualified, and they attempted to exploit this small advantage as best they could in favour of Jews. Men with families were given preference over single men and, in view of the government's correlation of family size with degree of skill, the delegates declared as many men as possible to be "skilled" workers, in that a skilled worker could bring a wife and two children. In truth, however, some of those selected, even as skilled workers, could not tell one end of the needle from the other. After telegraphing ahead to the next camp that the Canadian team was on its way, the JDC organized on-the-spot buttonhole sewing classes for those who wished to go to Canada—skill and need seldom coincided, and where possible the team sacrificed the former to satisfy the latter.[70]

The two selection teams were tireless. While working through the night to process applicants at one camp, David Solomon, a team member from Montreal, unhappily rejected a widow from Rumania, the mother of a four-year-old boy, because one-parent families were barred admission to Canada under the Canadian labour schemes. This woman's "tearful pleading was of no avail. She was forcibly led aside."

> Some time later, there appeared before me, believe it or not, a handsome young man about twenty-seven years of age, whose documentation described him as being . . . unmarried, born in Bucharest, Roumania. . . . I immediately thought, here was one opportunity to bring relief and succor to the widow with the four year old son! I told the young man . . . I would process him only under one condition, that is, if he married the widow.
>
> At 6 A.M. that very morning, a Justice of the Peace, in my presence, issued the couple a civil license and pronounced them man and wife. They arrived in Montreal, together with the four year old child, in the month of February, 1948, having occupied separate berths aboard steamship.

The couple separated immediately and were eventually divorced—in Canada.[71] They had been two of the over five thousand individuals examined and tested by selection teams during the teams' thirty-day stay. Of these, the teams designated slightly more than three thousand eligible. This was not the final word. Following on their heels would come Canadian medical, security and immigration officers who would whittle down the number eligible to the two thousand or so authorized in the needlework scheme.

The anticipated problem for the selection teams was to find willing, non-Jewish applicants.[72] Everywhere the teams experienced the reluctance of non-Jews to accept this type of job when others in Canada were open to them. Team members threw over any pretext that they were judging qualifications, not to mention skills, in order to fill the non-Jewish quota (especially as the number eligible had to exceed those finally approved by thirty or forty per cent "to allow for wastage," the result of the Canadian medical and security checks to follow). Team members feared that if they could not find adequate numbers of non-Jews, the number of Jews allowed into Canada would be reduced in keeping with the fifty per cent ratio assumed by the quota. Fears on this count seemed real enough to Montreal team member David Solomon:

> Our efforts were unintentionally frustrated by prevailing conditions, which did not permit IRO Directors to bring forward sufficient numbers of non-Jews to meet our requirements.
>
> To Bucholz Camp in the Hanover area, we returned on a non-stop trip from Dusseldorf expecting to screen 200 DP's of non-Jewish persuasion. On that day, only ten were presented in the morning and ten in the afternoon.
>
> In the City of Linz, Austria, the IRO Director gave us a signed statement to the effect that he could not fill our quota of non-Jews. This condition generally prevailed throughout each area visited.[73]

Once Canadian immigration, security and medical officers began screening those selected, the lower standards for non-Jews began to take their toll. A report on Canadian screening in Amberg noted that officials were "extremely rigid" and rejections were "running up to 75% of all applicants presented." Immigration and Labour Department officials in Ottawa watched the number of non-Jews diminish as their health officers rejected without mercy. Soon Ottawa, too, confronted a dilemma. They could cut the absolute number of persons permitted into Canada under the needlework scheme to keep the fifty–fifty ratio, lower their immigration, health and security standards for non-Jews, or revise the Jewish percentage upward. The absolute number originally authorized could not be lowered without a challenge from the industry, which still demanded labour, and Immigration officials were prepared to fight any and all efforts to lower admission standards. Only one course remained open. The director of immigration reluctantly informed Canadian officials with the International Refugee Organization: "In connection with the selection of garment workers, it has been decided to raise the number which may be selected of any one persuasion from fifty to sixty per cent." The change, however, was at first kept confidential as it might in some quarters seem like too great a concession to the Jews.[74]

After returning to Canada, Max Enkin sent Ottawa a report on his European mission. He reviewed the work of his team, the problems of European operations and his concerns for the thousands of valuable persons who would come to Canada if but given the opportunity:

> After seeing how a million uprooted people live in a war torn area and listening to the experiences of hundreds of these people, we are all moved to stress the humanitarian aspect of this project and it is our greatest hope that the government will continue to look favourably on other similar projects that may be suggested to you.
>
> To each and every displaced person we bring to Canada you are offering the opportunity to rebuild a new life—now blighted by years of war and frustrations after liberation. Canada is one of their havens and anything we can do to facilitate their rehabilitation and resettlement will ever rebound to our credit as a nation.[75]

The Canadian government had resisted most such special pleading in the past, unless, of course, it could be turned to profit Canada economically. Canadian Jewry had learned that one sad lesson if nothing else. The half-a-loaf success of twinning Canadian Jewry's desire to retrieve its European brethren with national economic self-interest had succeeded in the needlework scheme where most humanitarian appeals by the Jewish community had failed. If the government's fear of Jewish immigration had initially reduced the program's impact by half, it was still a model, the only model worth duplicating—and that is exactly what was done.

Late in 1947 the Fur Trade Association of Canada, representing manufacturers of fur coats, hats and other fur clothing, approached the government for labour. The fur industry, like its sister clothing industry, was heavily representative of Jews at both the management and union levels. Again with behind-the-scenes help and encouragement from the Canadian Jewish Congress, industry lawyers approached the Department of Labour and Immigration Branch, describing an "extreme shortage of labour": "The craftsmen, the skilled workers, who have helped create this industry are gradually dying out and there has been no tendency by Canadians, even those who are children of the immigrants who came to Canada as skilled workers, to take their place in this industry."[76] They pleaded for five or six hundred "skilled fur manufacturing craftsmen in the Displaced Persons camps that could be obtained for this industry."

With surprising speed, the cabinet gave approval, in principal, to this request. A meeting between government and fur industry representatives ironed out the details, not least of which was, once again, the fifty-fifty Jewish-non-Jewish split. The fur industry scrambled, as the clothing industry had done, to collect signed undertakings from fur firms to accept workers, and a fur-workers selection team was authorized to leave for Europe in the spring of 1948. Shortly before the team left, members were advised of one change: the deputy minister of labour matter-of-factly noted that, in line with "the basis on which the clothing workers were selected," teams should be mindful to choose "not more than 60% of any persuasion."[77]

Once in Europe the selection team complained bitterly that even the forty per cent non-Jewish quota was proving very difficult to fill. The head of the team, Harris Silver, reported that it had interviewed every furrier candidate on IRO employment lists in the British and American zones of Germany, but had found only sixty non-Jews who could qualify. The International Refugee Organization confirmed this. The team's visit almost at its end, Silver became increasingly concerned that if the government held to its quota, only ninety Jews could be admitted under the scheme, and so he grasped at another straw—professional standards. The government seemed willing to admit semi-skilled non-Jews, but, Silver argued, the fur industry needed skilled workers. It was the government itself that demanded all Jews admitted be skilled workers. Could it not lift its Jewish quota, allowing more skilled Jewish fur workers to fill the empty slots?[78] But Ottawa was unalterably unwilling to increase the Jewish component. It instead pressed industry to accept a program of non-Jewish apprenticeships. Under this plan, the remaining non-Jews selected need not be skilled, or even semi-skilled, just educable.

Pressed to the wall, the industry agreed to "do [its] best to integrate these people into the fur industry" at industry expense. The quota formula remained unchanged. In Europe, Jewish refugee officials scrambled to find non-Jews willing to come to Canada as apprentices. They had only moderate success, but in the end the number of non-Jews selected fell below the limit initially set—as did the number of Jews.[79]

Despite the quota system, the unhurried pace at which government officials processed those selected and the preference given non-Jewish labour schemes,[80] a trickle of Jewish refugees began to arrive under the tailors' and furriers' auspices. They were not alone. At the same time another group of Jewish refugees, also under a special government agreement, began to arrive in Canada—one thousand orphans.

The 1941 Order-in-Council that had authorized one thousand Jewish orphans from Vichy France admission to Canada had come to nothing. In February 1947, at a meeting between the prime minister, several of his cabinet colleagues and a Jewish delegation led by Samuel Bronfman and Saul Hayes, this Order-in-Council was resurrected. Hayes, speaking for the group, pointed to the Order-in-Council, the horror that befell those children who might have been saved and the immeasurable need of those who might yet be given a home "in the wholesome atmosphere of free Canada." He requested the Order-in-Council be reactivated. The prime minister took this request under advisement.[81]

The problem of Jewish orphan children in Europe was complex. Needs seemed great and emotions ran high. For Canadian Jewry it appeared an obscenity, a black mark on the conscience of humanity, that these children or young people should remain in distress after all they had been through. A Jewish Immigrant Aid Society official seconded to the United Nations Relief and Rehabilitation Administration in Germany, Morris Kraicer, wrote the society in Toronto of his contacts with these young survivors, confined in displaced persons camps since the war:

> All of them survived by miracle, every one of them should have been dead according to all rules of medicine. They went through hell, lost everything, even their belief that human beings can be kind.
>
> They were liberated in April, 1945, over a year ago. They expected to be moved from this cursed land, where their nearest ones were burned or gassed alive. Every inch of German soil reminds them of the years they [were] tortured and bled. The armies of liberation came, gave them candles, food, but a few weeks later things had gone back to "normal," the same camps—no barbed wire but still a guard at the gate. . . .

> A year went by and they are still here. No prospect of emigrating. You must realize that they are all youngsters in age, but not mentally. The first time in my life I met here people who conquered death. For six years they played with death hide and seek, they are the victors.
>
> You find among the people here not only sole survivors of families, but sole survivors of such famous camps like Treblinka and Sobibor and others. I remember one young girl, pretty . . . this young girl is the only person who survived from a transport of 5,000 Jews who on Sept. 3, 1942 were shipped in cattle trains to the well known crematorium in Belzec. She is the only one who escaped and two months later managed to escape from a second transport. This young girl was kept one year in Auschwitz and was eventually "liberated" in Bergen-Belsen. It is too bad we Jews have no Victoria Crosses, but she certainly deserves one.
>
> More than a year went by and she is still here. She also found a young brother in another camp. They both stay together wanting to go to Canada. More than anything else do they need a home environment. It is a crime against anything that is human to keep them here any longer.[82]

For once the government seemed to agree. After some discussion between Immigration authorities and the Canadian Jewish Congress, the minister responsible for immigration gave the plan to bring one thousand Jewish orphan children to Canada approval in principle. Jolliffe was ordered to draw up the necessary papers. A new Order-in-Council was drafted and passed by the cabinet on April 29, 1947.[83]

The terms of the order were something less than the Congress would have wished. In initial conversations Hayes had hoped to convince the government to allow legal minors, those under twenty-one years of age, to enter under the definition of orphan children. "Our argument here," Hayes explained to Jewish officials in Europe, "was that the children whom we wished to take care of five years ago are now by the passage of time 18, 19, 20 and 21." In addition, it was hoped that the government would not prove so officious in demanding verifiable evidence that a given child was indeed an orphan. Some children, Hayes supposed, could never supply proof positive "due to the difficulties of actually determining which parents are alive and which are not."[84] In response, the government allowed an upper age limit of eighteen, rather than sixteen (as allowed in the abortive plan to rescue children in Vichy). The question of orphan status, or, rather, proof of status, was left vague. The order merely fell back upon the definition of orphan used in the Immigration Act and its regulations: a child bereaved of both parents. What might be acceptable evidence of orphan status was also left unstated.

As was expected, the Canadian Jewish community pledged to guarantee all costs of the scheme, to appoint and send child-care workers to Europe to coordinate the European phase of the project with Canadian Immigration personnel and to manage the placement of the children in Canada. The government instructed the Congress to contact provincial authorities in charge of child care to clear any local obstacles to foster care or adoption, an ultimate goal of the entire program. These discussions went smoothly (except for a time in Alberta, where, as Senator Cairine Wilson reported, "the 1,000 Jewish children [were] not acceptable"). All necessary financial guarantees made, a campaign was begun to cover costs and enlist foster parents, and Congress personnel were dispatched to Europe to oversee the program.[85]

The only thing now lacking was the children, and they were not easy to come by. If Congress officials had thought the collection of one thousand Jewish orphan children eighteen years of age and younger could be arranged quickly, they were wrong. Children, especially the very young, had been easy prey to the Nazis whose reign of terror knew no age discrimination. For those children who survived, priority was given to re-establishing family contacts, or, for many orphans and especially those from western Europe, to repatriating them.[86] Jewish children in Germany or Austria whose national origin could not be determined, children who refused repatriation in favour of possibly joining distant family abroad and children who preferred the care of Zionist or other Jewish refugee agencies were also off limits to the Canadian scheme.

The Joint Distribution Committee, which agreed to assist in finding children for the Canadian Jewish Congress, cautioned Hayes that few children under seven or eight years of age had survived the holocaust. Many of those who had and were "true orphans" were now being cared for in "family groups," what were called "Kibbutz groups," by the Jewish Agency for Palestine. This Zionist umbrella organization claimed to speak for all Jewish children who had lost everything because they were Jewish, and it would agree to nothing less than removing them to a Jewish homeland. The world, the Zionists argued, had forfeited their rights to these children. These orphans were and must be the children of Israel.[87]

Canadian Jewry, however, had waited too long to let this chance to receive refugee children fall by the boards, and a local Jewish official, Dr. Manfred Saalheimer, was sent to Europe by the Canadian Jewish Congress "to get the movement under way." Despite his best efforts, he was unable to secure many children cared for by Zionists in the camps of Germany. These children, he conceded, "belong to Palestine." However, with the help of JDC personnel across Europe, he pieced together a group from France, Rumania, Czechoslovakia, Hungary, Poland, Belgium, Greece, Italy, Switzerland and Sweden, as well as a group of about two hundred and fifty children from Austria and Germany, originally earmarked for an American orphan scheme. The Americans, after processing them, found their quota had been "over-subscribed." A little shuffling of papers, Saalheimer hoped, and they could be rerouted to Canada.[88]

In letters to Hayes, Saalheimer begged him to impress upon Canadian Jewish leaders, then busy recruiting volunteer Jewish foster homes, that the children would not be babes-in-arms. It even stretched the term, he explained to call them children: "For the sake of convenience I have so far always referred to 'children'. I have made it clear before that we are likely to see arrive here very few actual children. We will receive adolescents between the ages of fifteen and eighteen, predominantly boys, the girls perhaps 30%. . . . These youngsters are as fine . . . as can be found anywhere. True, some are 'tough'; though they may not look it. If they were not tough they would not be alive today." His concern was not misplaced. In Toronto, for instance, first efforts to get foster homes or adoptive parents for the children expected were rewarded by a rush of enthusiasm. Many families offered to take orphaned children—all requested children less than seven years of age.[89]

On the European side, processing those eligible went remarkably smoothly for the most part. Security clearance was generally waived; medical inspections were conducted under the watchful eye of Canadian medical officers and related paperwork was coordinated by the JDC, IRO and Canadian officials. As seemed endemic to Jewish refugee schemes, anti-Semitism was never completely absent. The Canadian medical officer in Paris seemed especially strict in accepting these Jewish applicants. In one case, a youngster was refused a visa on medical grounds because he had flat feet, and only an appeal to the chief Canadian medical officer in London brought reason back to the Paris office and a visa for the child. The Canadian immigration officer in Rome, on the other hand, was willing to stretch the rules in favour of the orphans. He passed one orphan even though "underweight" and another "wounded by a shrapnel which had taken three fingers off his left hand": "As the boy is taking a training course as a radio technician, the consul granted him a visa." He also accepted as proof of orphan status a notarized statement from Jewish refugee officials. Each applicant who presented himself for examination was merely asked, "When and where did your mother and father die?" Visas were then granted.[90]

The first twenty orphans arrived in Halifax on the *Aquitania* on September 18, 1947. By mid November almost two hundred had come. The entire quota was eventually filled, and Ottawa granted permission for an additional group of orphan children to be brought to new homes.[91]

The orphan scheme, the needle trades and fur workers schemes, and the first-degree relative program all opened the door, however slightly and however reluctantly, for Jewish refugee immigration to Canada in the postwar years. Compared to the total number of postwar refugees admitted into Canada during this period, the 8,000 Jewish refugees pale in significance. Jews, who made up close to thirty per cent of the European refugee community, represented less than fifteen per cent of the approximately 65,000 refugees admitted into Canada through March 1948. Measured against the magnitude of the European problem —in the summer of 1947 it was estimated that approximately 250,000 Jewish survivors of Hitler awaited new homes—the number of Jews who entered Canada in 1948 seems small indeed. On the other hand, compared to prewar and wartime immigration of Jews, this figure represents a monumental growth in Jewish refugee immigration.[92]

Was the cup half full or half empty? It's hard to say. Once again the usefulness of comparisons depends on the argument one wishes to make, but it should be pointed out that Canada's contribution to resettlement of the postwar Jewish refugee community in absolute numbers between 1946 and 1950 was outdone only by Israel's and the United States'.[93] Furthermore, it must be noted that the percentage of Jews among displaced persons admitted to Canada was far in excess of the percentage of

Jews already in Canada, a prime consideration in American immigration law. In July 1948 David Lewis, national secretary of the CCF, confided his own unease at condemning Canada's role in the postwar Jewish refugee crisis—an unease that grew as much out of what the government was doing and how it was doing it, as from what could be done and was not:

> There is no doubt that there is discrimination. However, there is equally no doubt that the situation in the past year [1947–48] or more has been very much better than it had been for the previous twenty-five years. The fact is that between 15 and 20% of all DP immigrants coming to Canada today are Jewish. In view of the special hardships to which the Jewish DP's were subject for fifteen years, it certainly is not fair that so small a proportion of all immigrants should be Jews. On the other hand, justice is never complete monarch in the present immoral world. The Department of Immigration is, I think, convinced that if they attempted to increase the proportion considerably, there would be such an outcry and such opposition both in the Cabinet and outside, that even the present 15–20% might be cut off or substantially reduced. Those with prejudice and without the necessary humanity, don't look at the situation in terms in which we do. They are much more likely to demand that the proportion of Jewish immigrants to total immigration should be related to the proportion of Jewish people to the total population in Canada. This would bring the proportion down to less than 2% instead of 15–20%.[94]

For the government, Jewish refugees, and, indeed, refugees in general, remained as a case apart—that is, apart from the normal regeneration of immigration into postwar Canada. Keenleyside, in a 1948 guest lecture at Dalhousie University in Halifax, observed that arrangements made for the admission of displaced persons were "unique in Canadian history and [did] not fit readily into any of the ordinary provisions governing the admission of immigrants." That is not to say refugees did not constitute an important component of postwar immigration. They did. But at the same time the refugee crisis was also understood to be a "temporary" phenomenon of which Canada, if innovative, could take advantage even as it worked for its resolution.[95]

How long need Canada maintain these special programs,

these special allowances for refugees? By mid 1948 tens of thousands of displaced persons, including a hard-won contingent of Jews, had been approved for admission. Would it not make more sense, some now argued, to subsume refugees within the general framework of the newly revitalized immigration program, a program of selective encouragement of immigration reminiscent of the turn of the century? Had Canada not done its part for displaced persons?

Norman Robertson, who succeeded Massey as Canadian high commissioner in London, saw no advantage in keeping displaced persons programs alive—not for Canada and not for the displaced persons. As early as January 1947 he cabled Lester Pearson in External Affairs, recommending a simple solution to the refugee problem. Robertson would see all displaced persons, irrespective of national or ethnic origin, granted the "option of legal domicile in Germany" equivalent in all respects with German citizens. This would give displaced persons a status both different and better than that which they already held. If they held German national status, Canada would be relieved of drifting along an immigration course that, Robertson warned, promised "years of pressure groups, racial, religious and political, all trying to influence and distort [its] immigration policy." Germany caused the crisis, it should be part of its resolution. For those displaced persons who did not wish to establish themselves permanently in Germany, at least they would have a breathing space during which to enter a regular emigration stream out of Germany. For Canada and other overseas countries the plan would offer an "opportunity to develop selective immigration policies adapted to their needs, and absorptive capacities—and relatively unburdened by the special pressures which may well make it impossible for us to work out any coherent and sensible immigration policy at all."[96]

If Keenleyside, who eventually answered Robertson's cable, allowed that these suggestions were "worthy of very serious consideration," he denied Canada was subject to pressure from ethnic or religious interest groups. Replying to the Robertson suggestions almost a year after they were first made, Keenleyside, using Robertson's own words, pointed out to External Affairs that Canada's policy had matured over that year: "As at present defined, directed and administered our policy covering the admission of DP's is *not* unduly subject to 'special pressures' or to 'racial, religious and political' influences designed and applied to distort our programme. Moreover, our policy is scrupulously 'selective' and very carefully 'adapted to [our] needs'."[97]

For his part Keenleyside would, by late summer 1948, counsel the cabinet to reorganize displaced persons programs, not by changing the status of displaced persons but by closing down programs designed specifically for them.[98] Keenleyside pointed to both a declining Canadian demand for bulk labour of the type still available among displaced persons. He also noted that the acceptance of displaced persons by other countries had eased the immediate crunch (and by the way, picked off the best of the lot remaining). Except where specific industry orders were registered for labourers, Keenleyside recommended closing the immigration office assigned to oversee these admissions. First-degree relatives would, of course, continue to be processed, but in the same way as other immigrants. Rather than normalize the status of displaced persons by granting them German citizenship, Keenleyside would prefer to normalize the process by which they were selected.

With his minister's approval Keenleyside recommended this course to the cabinet in September 1948. Canada, he noted in passing, had nothing of which to be ashamed. In spite of the important contribution of other countries, Canada had still "by far the best record of any overseas countries in its handling of the DP movement." Nor had Canada sacrificed quality in doing good. Keenleyside reassured cabinet members: "Canada has been able, on the whole, to obtain the best of the groups that have gone overseas." Displaced persons should still come to Canada. Indeed, he argued, their number should be increased. However, they should come through the routine and established procedures used by other immigrants.[99]

The cabinet agreed. The Canadian mission was closed. Refugees might come, but only through regular channels. At its meeting in late September 1948 the cabinet authorized the number of displaced persons slated for admission to Canada be increased from 30,000 to 40,000. The additional 10,000 could come from outside existing camps.[100] The immigration door was now wide open, but skewed in favour of recently arrived Baltic refugees outside existing camps. Dismantling the administrative apparatus to process displaced persons who were migrants generally made little difference to Jewish refugees. Emigration out of Europe to Canada was now something Canada encouraged—and the classes that now qualified grew by leaps and bounds. But Jews, for the first time in modern history, were no longer dependent on the good will or self-interest of receiving states like Canada for a place to go. All the while that Canada had held fast in its determination to restrict the entry of Jews, the Jews of Europe stood in abject need. When Canada finally opened its doors to Europe in late 1947, the "Jewish problem" was being resolved elsewhere.

In early 1947 the British government, exhausted and exasperated, dumped its Palestine problem onto the United Nations. For Canada the paramount consideration regarding the Palestine issue was its divisive impact on the North Atlantic alliance. With Britain and the United States at loggerheads over the Palestine question, Canada feared a rupture of Allied solidarity that would leave other pressing problems, including the menacing shadow of Soviet influence, to fester. The Palestine issue, Canada believed, had to be resolved once and for all even if British interests, in this instance, had to be sacrificed for the greater good. In November 1947 Canada broke with Britain at the United Nations and voted for partition of Palestine into two states, one Jewish, one Arab.[101]

It would be wrong to say that the government voted to partition Palestine in order to redirect Jewish displaced persons to their national homeland, easing the pressure on Canada to accept them—thereby making the opening of immigration to Canada more palatable to civil servants, the cabinet, Quebec and the public in general. This was not the case. Nevertheless, it would also be incorrect to believe that the government was not aware of this potential benefit of their Palestine policy. In February 1947, just as the British were setting Palestine in the United Nations' lap, *Liberty* magazine reported that the Canadian government was still wrestling with the degree to which Canada would be open to displaced persons. Discussion of the issue in Ottawa, the magazine asserted, was "hush-hush" and for a good reason: "No spokesman will link Canada with Palestine but what everyone is going to know soon is that the displaced persons of Europe either come to Canada or go to Palestine. Politically it's a big question. Most politicians are fearful of Quebec, which wants no immigrants not of its faith." Whether this be speculation or not, the Canadian delegation at the United Nations went into the Palestine debate briefed from Ottawa on what a negative majority vote on partition would mean to future discussions of European displaced persons.[102] And Canada voted for partition.

The United Nations' affirmative vote on partition offered, for the first time in almost two thousand years, the all but tangible realization of a Jewish national homeland. To thousands of Jewish refugees this was a dream come true. As Canada selectively lifted the barriers to admission, Jews in large numbers lined up for admission elsewhere—much, one suspects, to Canada's relief.

On May 14, 1948, the state of Israel was proclaimed. That day 1,700 displaced persons entered their new homeland. Mass immigration to Israel, made up in large measure of European displaced persons, began—13,500 per month for the rest of 1948, 20,000 per month in 1949, and 14,000 per month in 1950. Also in the spring of 1948 both pressure on Canada to accept Jewish refugees and Canadian immigration barriers eased. If this was more than judicious planning on Canada's part, it was also less than coincidence. Thus, through the summer of 1948 Canada had approved or admitted more than 180,000 postwar immigrants, including 65,000 displaced persons. Included among the displaced persons were 8,000 Jews—orphans, first-degree relatives, members of the needle trades and fur workers scheme, and a smattering of others.[103] In the same year Canada created a new Immigration Act, under which immigration continued to grow apace. For the next few years the numbers of Jews admitted would be larger than at almost any other time in Canadian history. But total immigration was now so large that the Jewish component remained small, manageable and, perhaps most importantly, inconspicuous by comparison. In any event, the crisis was over.

9
CONCLUSION

> There is a story told that when Hitler was planning to conquer the world he went to seek the Devil's advice. "Great Lucifer," he asked, "Patron Father, how can I so confuse, exasperate and implicate the righteous nations that I may conquer and rule them in your name?"
>
> Lucifer drew him close but for a long time spoke no word. The ambitious German grew vexed and began to doubt his master. As he made ready to repeat his question, Satan threw back his head and began to laugh. "Offer them the Chosen People," he said.[1]

This prologue to Adele Wiseman's play, "The Lovebound," encapsulates an historical truth about the fate of European Jewry, a fate not sealed by the actions of the Nazis alone. Undeniably, the Nazis' determination to rid themselves and the world of Jews led directly to the blood lust of mass murder and eventually to the gas chambers and crematorium of Auschwitz. But the world was not unaware. The Nazis had early on signalled their intent if not their methods. Yet no nation interceded on behalf of those doomed—not for lack of opportunity but for lack of will. With no states prepared to take Jews, the Nazis could only conclude that none cared. As the world turned its back, the Nazis understood that they had a free hand to dispense with the Jews as they wished.

Like the other western liberal democracies, Canada cared little and did less. When confronted with the Jewish problem, the response of government, the civil service and, indeed, much of the public wavered somewhere between indifference and hostility. In the prewar years, as the government cemented barriers to immigration, especially of Jews, Immigration authorities barely concealed their contempt for those pleading for rescue. There was no groundswell of opposition, no humanitarian appeal for a more open policy. Even the outbreak of war and the mounting evidence of an ongoing Nazi program for the total annihilation of European Jewry did not move Canada. Its response remained legalistic and cold. Historians may today debate whether once war began rescue was possible, but at the time Canada wanted no part of any such scheme.[2] And with the Allies' victory the remnant of European Jewish survivors found no welcome, no succour in Canada. Though the holocaust was yet fresh in the public mind, the country was still attempting to barricade itself from the smoldering Jewish refugee question; when international pressure and economic self-interest compelled Canada to admit displaced persons, it took calculated steps to insure that Jewish admissions were kept within acceptable bounds—that is, that there were as few as possible.

There is a danger of leaving the wrong impression. It must be understood that the European Jewish crisis was never centre stage in Ottawa. Except for a small band of Immigration Branch officials preoccupied with keeping Jews out of Canada, few in government lost much sleep worrying about the Jews—perhaps because the civil servants did their work so well. To the degree that politicians allowed the Jewish issue to creep into their deliberations—which was not much or often—it was accorded a very low priority. The whole "Jewish business" was more a nuisance to be avoided than a problem to be resolved.

How could it be otherwise? Politicians and civil servants had read the public mood and had read it correctly. Whether in Quebec or English Canada, few saw Jews as desirable settlers. Folk wisdom understood Jews as clannish, aggressive and cosmopolitan. Jews, many concluded, "did not fit in," their political sensitivities were suspect, their loyalty forever in doubt, their religion based on the continued rejection of Christ, their sole preoccupation making and hording money. In the dark recesses of the public mind there may even have lurked the suspicion that the Nazis were not wrong in pinpointing the Jews as a particular problem—they were just carrying their anti-Semitism much too far.

Any discussion of Jewish refugee immigration must also be seen in its relation to a series of other domestic problems: the economic crisis that curtailed almost all immigration to Canada, the vocal anti-Jewish sentiment of Quebec politicians, the government's fear of Canada being made the dumping ground in any British or American scheme to resettle Jews and, most of all, the overriding sense on the part of the prime minister that whatever momentary sympathy might be stirred up for refugees, it would quickly be washed away in the wake of boatloads of Jews landing at Halifax or Montreal. The astute Mackenzie King knew there were no votes to be gained in admitting Jews; there were, however, many to be lost.

Would the Canadian people have taken revenge at the polls against any government that opened Canada to large numbers of Jewish refugees? Perhaps so. One need only recall the openly hostile reception that greeted the government's announcement of a token wartime program to grant temporary haven to Jewish refugees from Iberia and how Quebec's Maurice Duplessis easily turned this limited program into political capital. King was not about to hand his opposition, whether in Ottawa or in provincial capitals, the very issues it could use to advantage against his government.

The Canadian government, however, did not weakly surrender to the public's apparent antipathy to Jews. Rather, with some notable exceptions, official Ottawa shared it. In 1946 Joe Garner, recently appointed British high commissioner to Canada, arrived in Ottawa. Thirty-five years later he bemusedly recalled that his first impression of his new post was one of surprise that Ottawa should be such an overtly religious community. A self-confessed non-believer and, in his own mind, a non-Christian, Garner was taken aback by the number of "Christians Only" signs he confronted in the nation's capital. It was at the exclusive and élite Rideau Club, home away from home for Canada's ranking political figures and influential civil servants, that Garner was discreetly reassured that the club's "Christians Only" policy was not meant to bar *him*. Thus taught to decipher the mysterious codes of Ottawa anti-Semitism, Garner concluded that anti-Jewish feeling permeated official Ottawa even following the war to a greater degree than he had personally experienced anywhere else. It was, he observed, as his mind drifted back over the wartime refugee issue, disquieting to recall that cabinet ministers and their deputies surely discussed barring Jews from Canada in the imposing Rideau Club—which itself was barred to Jews.[3]

Supporting a more open and humane policy respecting Jewish refugees was what proved to be an all too weak coalition. There was, of course, the organized Jewish community only slowly and painfully disengaging from dependence on its three members of Parliament, who had long served as the official voice of Canadian Jewry. The members' failure to win even the smallest concession in Ottawa exploded the myth of their influence in the corridors of power. Their defeat left the pro-refugee campaign in the hands of the Canadian Jewish Congress, still binding together a community rent by long-standing fraternal frictions. But unity on the refugee cause still did not insure influence or success where it counted—in Ottawa. Jews were outsiders. They felt it themselves; they were looked upon as such by others. Canada's Jews, largely immigrant and working class, dismissed by many as less than desirable citizens, could never successfully combat the full force of anti-refugee and anti-Jewish sentiment abroad in the land. Despite their efforts, their cause was seen as parochial, their interests seldom in tune with those who set policy.

It is, therefore, a harsh but undeniable conclusion that the Jewish community—no matter what it did, what campaigns it waged, what momentary editorial support it won, what delegations it dispatched to Ottawa—could never get any more than the government, for its own reasons, was prepared to give, which was never much. The Jewish community was not an important part of the domestic power equation. It had no leverage. A few Jews, as individuals, might be indulged, but the Jewish community, for all the rightness of its cause, was to the end denied.

The blanket dismissal of the Jewish community as an important political force in Canada during the war years and their aftermath is not a negative reflection on the tactics Canadian Jewry employed in its campaign. It is tempting to argue, in retrospect, that other tactics might have been successfully employed. Admittedly, the Jewish community's refugee campaign was reserved, often low key, geared in the main to educating the public, cultivating the support of the press and the larger community, building a coalition with liberal and other pro-refugee interests, and winning the confidence of key politicians and public servants, while at the same time keeping both the disparate elements of the Jewish community in line and a lid on any activities likely to cast the community in a bad light. Was this wrong minded? Would militance and the politics of the street have succeeded where the path of respectability failed? These questions are intriguing but irrelevant. The strident political tactics of a later generation were not a feature of Canadian political life in the 1930s and 1940s—at least not a feature of political life available to Jews. Without doubt, mass demonstrations, civil disobedience, hunger strikes and protest marches to Parliament Hill, although perhaps cathartic to a Jewish community seething with the anguish of rejection, would only have confirmed what many Canadians believed—Jews were a disruptive, selfish and dangerous group. Jewish leaders understood this. As they weighed their options, believing all the while that good will existed in Ottawa if only it could be unearthed, they repeatedly rejected the path of active confrontation.

In one respect they did miscalculate. Impossible as it may have been to accept at the time and disquieting as it is to conclude years later, the major and unavoidable flaw in the Canadian Jews' campaign was their assumption that a civilized world would not permit exactly what, in the end, it did permit. Once the goodness of man was aroused, they naively believed, something would be done to relieve suffering victims of an evil beyond words. They were wrong. Canadian Jewry sought to tap the wellspring of human kindness, only to find it dry. The Western world, including Canada, was prepared to eulogize the Jews; it was not prepared to offer them a new home.[4]

Canadian Jewry had its allies—especially the Canadian National Committee on Refugees—but it also had little influence. Members of the national refugee committee, described by one participant as "élite non-conformists," were well meaning, but had no popular constituency. A handful of concerned, dedicated citizens scattered across Canada, they had little grassroots support and did little systematically to build any.[5] As long as the churches remained silent—which they did—and the provinces withheld support—which they did—the government could dismiss the committee members as well meaning but impractical idealists to be patronized but not taken seriously. Nor was the organization without its own problems. While most of its leaders stood shoulder-to-shoulder with Jewish leaders, others were discomforted by the "Jewishness" of its cause. Charlotte Whitton, who helped organize the refugee committee, repeatedly admonished its members to focus on non-Jewish refugees. Even the outspoken Claris Silcox, as a co-worker on behalf of refugees recalled, privately grumbled that Jews should "learn some manners so they would be more acceptable." The truly concerned and tolerant, such as Constance Hayward, the bulwark of the CNCR's administration, lamented the committee's reluctance to take on the fight against anti-Semitism as part of its mandate. To do so, others warned, might alienate whatever support for the committee there was in the larger community.[6]

Canada's door was closed by 1933 and opened only slightly by 1948—and, for Jews, only by a crack. As the European Jewish refugee crisis lessened after 1948 with the creation of the state of Israel, Canada began lifting its barriers against Jewish immigration. Among the early arrivals in 1948 were Zyshe Steiman, who came as part of the needle trades labour scheme, his wife and young daughter. In Toronto, Steiman built a new life for his family and continued to work in the garment industry. He did not forget what others had done to bring him from Europe, especially the role played by his union, the International Ladies Garment Workers in Toronto. Ten years after immigrating, Steiman had a new reason to celebrate. "Through the initiative and efforts of the International Ladies Garment Workers' Union of Toronto," he wrote to his union,

> my family and I have been given the opportunity in 1948, to leave behind the DP Camps of Germany and to come to Canada (Toronto) where after years of wandering we have found a permanent home and happiness.
>
> At this time I wish to express that it gives me great honor to belong to such an organization.
>
> Upon arrival to Canada my daughter was a child, now ten years later it gives me great pleasure to announce her forthcoming marriage, which occurs January 11, 1959, to which I would like you all to come and join me in my happiness.[7]

Steiman likely did not know fully what a political and moral victory his immigration to Canada represented. He may not have known that the path he had followed had been barred to countless thousands. In 1940 the Canadian Pacific Railway immigration agent, Mark Sorensen, wrote to his superior: "The day will come when Immigration will be under debate, and then the Ottawa Immigration Service shall be judged by [its] records. For us it will not be unimportant to have these records at our fingertips. They shall then find us as their bad conscience."[8]

EPILOGUE

(*Toronto, June 1991*)

The telephone broke the night silence. *None Is Too Many* co-author, Harold Troper, stumbled out of bed. Almost certainly, anyone telephoning at 3 a.m. was not going to be delivering good news. He picked up the receiver mid-ring. As he said hello, he remembered how difficult it had been to fall asleep after the excitement of the day. *None Is Too Many* had just officially been released and a party at a local bookstore turned into a celebration after a positive review of the book appeared in that day's *Globe and Mail*.

It was more with relief than annoyance that Troper discovered the call was neither bad news nor a wrong number. But, still half asleep, he was unprepared for what came next. A woman with a European accent asked if she was speaking with one of the authors of *None Is Too Many*. Satisfied she did not have a wrong number, she explained that she began reading the book early that afternoon and had just finished it. Compelled to talk to one of the writers, she simply looked up the number and dialed.

None Is Too Many, she continued, was her story. Puzzled, Troper tried to place her name. Could it have been misspelled? Was she in the book under a maiden name? No. She was not actually mentioned in the book itself. Rather, the book echoed her own experience. As Troper listened, she recounted her story. She came to Canada from Poland as a young woman in the late 1920s, leaving behind her mother and two younger sisters. She married and soon had a daughter of her own. As the Depression deepened, she and her husband struggled to put food on their table; but there was never so little that she did not send something home every week to her mother and sisters. At the same time, she and her husband applied to bring them to Canada. The application was rejected. Frantic, they sought help, but every door they tried was shut. Jewish agencies could do nothing; a lawyer sent them away empty-handed; direct appeals to Ottawa went nowhere. Her family never came.

"Let me understand," she pleaded. "What you are saying in your book is that there was nothing more we could have done — no other lawyer we could have hired, no politician we could have paid off, no other forms to fill out or officials to see — nothing that might have brought my mother and sisters to Canada?"

"That's right. Nothing. You did all you could."

There was a long silence, then she said, "You don't know what it's like. Every night when I go to sleep I still have a picture of my mother and sisters in my head. I think that if we had gone to a different lawyer or politician, or given money to somebody somewhere, my family would be with me today. Now you tell me we couldn't do anything more. If what your book is telling me is right, the pain I feel will still never go away, but maybe the guilt will be a little less."

Perhaps suddenly realizing what time it was, she began to apologize for the phone call. "I just wanted to thank you for writing this book," she said. "It's the only monument my mother and sisters will have. They were gassed in Auschwitz." She hung up.

It's almost ten years since that call was made and ten years since *None Is Too Many* was first published. Yet its impact remains, not because of anything we as authors intended when writing the book, but because the historical narrative detailed in *None Is Too Many* holds meaning beyond the events it records. Obviously the book has special significance for Canadians Jews, particularly those who endured the Holocaust. We can barely know what they will never forget. But the book also speaks to the larger Canadian civic culture of issues still very much centre stage in Canada today: immigration and refugee policy, systemic racism, the power of the bureaucracy to chart the course of government and, perhaps most of all, the values of a society beset by crisis. Let us not overstate the case; *None Is Too Many* offers no answers to today's questions. It was not meant to. Nevertheless, to the degree that the experience of the past can serve as a litmus test for how critical issues are dealt with today or might be dealt with tomorrow, *None Is Too Many* may serve to inform debate.

For all that, *None Is Too Many* remains a work of history. And since the book's original publication, Canada is a decade further removed from the historical events the book recalls. The ranks of those, like the early morning caller, whose life experience stands as a testament to these events, are thinning. That which they know to be true, not because it is written in books like ours but because it is their life and their pain, is today under assault. Beyond the margins of scholarship, Holocaust deniers assert that the Holocaust is a tissue of lies, a conspiratorial fraud concocted to serve the ends of a world Jewish cabal. These hateful historical charlatans claim to seek truth. In reality, they seek nothing less than to distort the past as part of an attempt to rehabilitate Hitler and the Nazi ideology.

Sadly, one must acknowledge that the same Canada that refused to give sanctuary to the victims of Nazi terror did little to prevent itself from becoming a postwar sanctuary to some of those who were the agents of that terror. Only in the late 1980s, after more than forty years of inaction, did the government move, slowly and cautiously, to deal with accused Nazi war criminals living in Canada. Laws to prosecute war criminals are now in place. The government claims the political will to act, a will sorely lacking during the preceding four decades. But it may all prove too little, too late. Most of those who should have stood trial for war crimes and crimes against humanity have either died, secure in the knowledge that their Canadian sanctuary remained undisturbed, or are now too old or infirm to stand trial. The entire enterprise remains a quagmire of legal uncertainty; time may have run out for justice.

We know that no scholarly history, not *None Is Too Many* nor any other, can substitute for justice denied or ease the pain of Holocaust survivors who see their suffering defiled by Holocaust deniers. Far from it. But scholarship does have its place in dealing with these obscenities, if only as a corrective to the wilful denial or calculated distortion of past events. Today, as the Holocaust survivors pass from our midst, scholarly historical research becomes all the more important in keeping hate-mongers from successfully distorting the past to fit their own dangerous political agenda. Without the protection of historical truth the victims of the Nazis will have died twice—once in the ghettos, gas chambers and killing fields of Nazi Europe, and again in the memory of humankind.

But *None Is Too Many* is not just about the Holocaust. It is also about Canada and, in particular, the history of Canada's immigration and refugee policies in the 1930s and 1940s. It chronicles the ability of otherwise good and caring men and women, Canadians, to avert their eyes from the sight of refugees begging sanctuary from almost certain death at the hands of the Nazis and their allies. Sheltered behind a wall of racist assumptions, administrative regulations and political calculations, Canadians were content that those for whom they felt no kinship, no sympathy and no responsibility would get no entry either.

But even as *None Is Too Many* was published in 1982, the terrible legacy of those events seemed a relic of the past. In 1982 Canada stood as a champion of the refugee cause. The national effort on behalf of the Vietnamese boat people seemed the harbinger of a new era. Unfortunately, things have been changing slowly. Of late, Canadians seem to be turning inward, as if exhausted or bedevilled by their short-lived humanitarian effort. Even as the United Nations awarded Canada a humanitarian medal for its initiatives on behalf of refugees, new regulations were being set in place to make it harder for legitimate refugees to find asylum in Canada. Not to oversimplify the issue, a key problem seemed to be Canada's unwillingness to serve as a country of first asylum, a country to which those with a legitimate fear of persecution might turn directly. A change in Canadian immigration law in 1978 designated refugees as a class of immigrant for the first time. Previously, all refugee admissions to Canada were made on a special case-by-case basis, more as exceptions to the immigration regulations than as part of them. Even under the new law, Canadian officials preferred to select refugee candidates from among the pool of applicants situated in other countries that offered them a temporary harbour from the storm. In this way, officials could select those refugees as close to the existing profile of a desirable immigrant as possible, refugees who were judged best able to adapt to life in Canada.

But the 1978 change in law opened the door to refugees who side-stepped an intermediate country and, instead, turned to Canada as a first asylum. They claimed refugee status on Canadian soil. In a world awash in refugees, the idea that they could choose Canada rather than Canada choosing only those refugees it wanted was, for many Canadians, bad enough. That Canada would also be saddled with the cost and uncomfortable burden of determining who was or was not a legitimate refugee, and then the dilemma of what to do with those denied refugee status, only made matters worse. The clamour to stem the tide of Third World refugees and retake command of who gets into Canada is proving irresistible. The battle to keep Canada's door from closing on those who need sanctuary is not going well. In the ten years since *None Is Too Many* was first published, the generosity of Canadian spirit is not on the mat, but it is on the ropes.

We do not pretend to possess any magical formula that will resolve the deepening refugee crisis or Canada's role therein. But if the story told in *None Is Too Many* has any moral, it is that Canada should never again turn its back on those in such need. We can only hope that Canadians again affirm their commitment to those for whom we are the only sanctuary. That commitment can also become part of the monument to the 3 a.m. caller's mother and sisters.

They were gassed in Auschwitz.

Irving Abella
Harold Troper

NOTE ON SOURCES

This book was based almost exclusively on primary historical materials. Every effort was made to locate and examine all relevant manuscript sources in archives and private hands and to interview as many of the individuals involved with events described in this book as possible. These sources now speak for themselves. If not all manuscript collections proved equally valuable and time blurred some memories, each piece of information gathered brought Canada's role in the crisis of European Jewry into clearer focus.

Manuscript Sources

Agudath Israel Archives, New York
  Michael G. Tress Collection

American Jewish Historical Society, Boston
  Cecelia Razovsky Papers
  Rabbi Stephen Wise Papers

Anglican Church Archives, Toronto
  Council of Social Services Files

C. H. A. Armstrong Papers, Toronto

Leo Baeck Institute, New York
  Konzentration-lager Frankreich Papers, 1939–44

Bund Archives of the Jewish Labor Movement, New York
  Canadian Correspondence Files

Canadian Institute for Public Opinion, Toronto

Canadian Jewish Congress Archives, Montreal
  Canadian Jewish Congress Papers
  Jewish Colonization Association Collection
  Louis Rosenberg Papers
  United Jewish Refugee Agency Collection

Canadian Jewish Congress Archives, Toronto
  Clipping Files to September, 1939

Central Archives for the History of the Jewish People, Jerusalem
  Auswanderung Files, 1938–45

Central Zionist Archives, Jerusalem
  Canadian Zionist Papers
  Jewish Agency for Palestine–American Section, New York Files

Department of External Affairs Archives, Ottawa

Department of Manpower and Immigration, Ottawa
  Block 500, Assession 73–23

French National Archives, Paris
  International Refugee Organization Records

Holy Blossom Temple Archives, Toronto
  Board Minutes

International Labor Organization Archives, Geneva
  Refugee Files

International Ladies Garment Workers Union Archives, New York
  Correspondence of Canadian Locals
  David Dubinsky Papers

Jewish Colonization Association, London
  Correspondence Files

Jewish Immigrant Aid Society, Montreal

Jewish Immigrant Aid Society, Toronto

Jewish Labor Committee, New York
  Canadian Correspondence

Jewish Public Library, Montreal

Joint Distribution Committee, New York

League of Nations Archives, Geneva
  High Commissioner for Refugees Records
  League of Nations Registry Files, 1933–47
  Nansen International Refugee Office Files, 1920–47

Herbert H. Lehman Papers, New York
  Flexner Files
  Senate Research Files

Multicultural History Society of Ontario, Toronto
  Burton Family Papers
  Consul of Poland (Montreal) Files
  Joshua Gershman Papers

National Archives, Washington, D.C.
  Foreign Service Posts (Canada) Records
  State Department Records

Polish Research Institute and Sikorski Museum, London
  Military Records, 1946

Public Archives of Canada, Ottawa
  Archie Bennett Papers
  Richard Bedford Bennett Papers

Peter Bercovich Papers
Canadian Labour Congress Papers
Canadian National Committee on Refugees Files
Canadian National Railway Records
Civil Service Historical Personnel Records
Brooke Claxton Papers
Cooperative Commonwealth Federation Papers
Department of Citizenship and Immigration Records
Department of Defence Records
Department of External Affairs Records
Department of Labour Records
A. A. Heaps Papers
C. D. Howe Papers
Immigration Branch Records
Samuel Jacobs Papers
Jewish Labor Committee Papers
League of Nations of Canada Society Papers
William Lyon Mackenzie King Papers
Ernest Lapointe Papers
Robert James Manion Papers
Privy Council Office Records
James Ralston Papers
Louis Rosenberg Papers
Western Canadian Jewish Historical Society Collection (copies)
Cairine Wilson Papers
Samuel Jacob Zacks Papers
Zionist Organization of Canada Papers

Public Records Office, London
Cabinet Records
Colonial Office Records
Dominions Office Records
Foreign Office Records
Prime Minister's Office Records

Queen's University Archives, Kingston
Thomas Crerar Papers

Franklin D. Roosevelt Library, New York
Franklin D. Roosevelt Papers
Myron C. Taylor Papers
U.S. War Refugee Board File, 1944–45

Mark B. Sorensen Papers, Kingston

United Church Archives, Toronto
Claris E. Silcox Papers

United Nations Archives, New York
International Refugee Organization (Washington Office) Files
United Nations Relief and Refugee Administration Headquarters Files

University of British Columbia Archives, Vancouver
German Consul and German Consulate at Montreal Files, 1909–39

YIVO Archives, New York
Hebrew Immigrant Aid Society Papers

Interviews

Monroe Abbey	Toronto	May 2, 1980
Lavy M. Becker	Toronto	May 2, 1980
Tadeusz Brzezinski	Montreal	August 29, 1980
Susan Burton	Toronto	July 2, 1979
Oscar Cohen	New York	November 29, 1978
		March 8, 1979
Elizabeth Edwards	London, England	November 14, 1979
Max Enkin	Toronto	September 19, 1979
Lord Joe Garner	London, England	November 14, 1979
James Gibson	Vineland	June 26, 1978
	Toronto	November 7, 1981
Senator H. Carl Goldenberg	Montreal	May 9, 1979
Saul Hayes	Montreal	June 20, 1978
		May 9, 1979
Constance Hayward	Toronto	June 7, 1978
Rabbi Pinchas Hirschprung	Montreal	October 4, 1979
Marius M. Holmgren	Toronto	October 28, 1981
Simon Kahane	San Francisco	January 2, 1982
Kalman Kaplansky	Ottawa	January 24, 1980
Hugh Keenleyside	Victoria	October 9, 1979
Ben Lappin	Toronto	July 29, 1981
Arthur Lermer	Montreal	October 4, 1979
David Lewis	Ottawa	January 23, 1980
Malcolm John MacDonald	London, England	November 8, 1979
Paul Martin	London, England	July 11, 1979
Nicholas Monk	Toronto	August 3, 1978
Oscar Morawetz	Toronto	September 19, 1979
Jack Pickersgill	Ottawa	January 22, 1980
Escott Reid	Ottawa	May 12, 1979
Lola Reiss	Toronto	February 19, 1980
David Rome	Montreal	June 20, 1978
		June 18, 1979
Mal Scobie	Kemptville	April 26, 1979
Nachman Shemen	Toronto	September 9, 1978
Mark B. Sorensen	Kingston	December 15, 1978
Tobie Taback	Toronto	February 22, 1980

NOTES

The following abbreviations have been used throughout the notes:

CCF	Cooperative Commonwealth Federation
CJC	Canadian Jewish Congress Archives, Montreal
CJCP	Canadian Jewish Congress Papers
CJC(T)	Canadian Jewish Congress Archives, Toronto
CNCR	Canadian National Committee on Refugees Files
DCER	*Documents on Canadian External Relations*
DCI	Department of Citizenship and Immigration Records
DEA	Department of External Affairs Archives, Ottawa
DOD	Department of Defence Records
DOL	Department of Labour Records
EA	Department of External Affairs Records
FNA	National Archives of France, Paris
FO	Foreign Office Records
FRUS	*Foreign Relations of the United States*
HIAS	Hebrew Immigrant Aid Society Papers
ILGWU	International Ladies Garment Workers Union Archives, New York
IR	Immigration Branch Records
IRO	International Refugee Organization Records
JCA	Jewish Colonization Association Collection
JCA(L)	Jewish Colonization Association, London
JDC	Joint Distribution Committee, New York
JIAS	Jewish Immigrant Aid Society, Montreal
JIAS(T)	Jewish Immigrant Aid Society, Toronto
KP	William Lyon Mackenzie King Papers (Correspondence)
KPC	William Lyon Mackenzie King Papers (Cabinet documents and minutes)
LON	League of Nations Archives, Geneva
LONC	League of Nations of Canada Society Papers
MBS	Mark B. Sorensen Papers

MP	Robert James Manion Papers
NA	National Archives, Washington, D.C.
PAC	Public Archives of Canada, Ottawa
PCO	Privy Council Office Records
PREM	Prime Minister's Office Records
PRO	Public Records Office, London
UJRA	United Jewish Refugee Agency Collection
WCJH	Western Canadian Jewish Historical Society Collection
YIVO	YIVO Archives, New York

1/Where They Could Not Enter

1. Interviews with several members of this group. All names, with the exception of Potvin's, have been changed at the interviewees' request.

2. J. Hope Simpson, *The Refugee Problem: Report of Survey* (London, 1934), 44–66; Lucy S. Dawidowicz, *The War Against the Jews, 1933–1945* (New York, 1975).

3. Quoted in A. J. Sherman, *Island Refuge: Britain and Refugees from the Third Reich, 1933–1939* (London, 1973), 112.

4. See, for example, *Canada Year Book, 1939*, 158.

5. PAC, IR, File 644452, Blair to Mrs. I. Grenovsky, December 5, 1938; PAC, MP, Blair to R. A. Bell, February 29, 1938.

6. *Canadian Annual Review, 1928–29*, 153–9.

7. LON, High Commissioner for Refugees Records, Box 5, McDonald to Bennett, March 25, 1934; JIAS(T), File 10A, B. Robinson to A. Brodey, June 11, 1934; ibid., A. J. Paull to Brodey, March 27, 1934.

8. High Commissioner for Refugees Records, Box 5, Bennett to McDonald, November 3, 1934.

9. See Gerald Dirks, *Canada's Refugee Policy: Indifference or Opportunism ?* (Montreal, 1977), 44–97; Robert Domanski, "While Six Million Cried: Canada and the Refugee Question, 1938–41" (Master's research essay, Institute of Canadian Studies, Carleton University, 1975), 14–16.

10. PAC, Civil Service Historical Personnel Records, File on F. C. Blair; Austin Cross in the *Family Herald and Weekly Star*, June 16, 1943.

11. Civil Service Historical Personnel Records, File on F. C. Blair; interview with James Gibson.

12. IR, File 54782/5, Blair to Crerar, October 12, 1938; ibid., Blair to F. N. Sclanders, September 13, 1938; ibid., Blair to Crerar, March 28, 1938; IR, File 644452, Blair to H. R. L. Henry, January 30, 1939; IR, File 54782/5, Blair to W. Baird, May 4, 1938.

13. IR, File 209160, Blair to Morris Saxe, January 17, 1934.

14. IR, File 54782/5, Blair to F. N. Sclanders, September 13, 1938.

15. Statistics cited in the Royal Commission on Bilingualism and Biculturalism, *The Cultural Contribution of the Other Ethnic Groups* (Ottawa, 1969), 247–8.

16. Interview with David Rome.

17. Interview with Oscar Cohen.

18. JIAS(T), File 164, A. J. Paull to A. Brodey, September 25, 1935. For histories of the Jewish Colonization Association in Canada and the Jewish Immigrant Aid Society, see Joseph Kage, *With Faith and Thanksgiving* (Montreal, 1962), and Simon Belkin, *Through Narrow Gates: A Review of Jewish Immigration, Colonization and Immigrant Aid in Canada* (Montreal, 1966).

19. JIAS(T), File 164, A. Brodey to A. J. Paull, October 22, 1936.

20. Interview with Oscar Cohen.

21. JIAS(T), File 10A, A. J. Paull to Solkin, April 4, 1935; PAC, CCF Papers, Heaps to M. A. Gray, May 25, 1938.

22. YIVO, HIAS, S. Belkin to HICEM, January 9, 1936. *Shtadlonim* is Yiddish, from the Hebrew *shtadlonat*, meaning intercession with higher authorities on behalf of an individual or a community. The tradition of "Shtadlones" is prevalent throughout Jewish history.

23. Belkin, *Through Narrow Gates*, 66–9; IR, File 54782/4, Blair, Memorandum for file, January 20, 1936.

24. HIAS, Report of JIAS, Montreal, February 18, 1937; interview with Saul Hayes; see, also, Leo Heaps, *The Rebel in the House: The Life and Times of A. A. Heaps, M.P.* (London, 1970), 155.

25. PAC, KP, Skelton to King, January 7, 1936, c122614.

26. IR, File 54782/5, Blair, Memorandum for file, April 19, 1938; CJC, CJCP, CPR to H. Heinemann, May 8, 1938. Heinemann sent a copy of this telegram to the Canadian Jewish Congress with a plea that the Congress help him save his family from the Nazis.

27. IR, File 641782, Blair, Memorandum for file, May 4, 1938; ibid., J. W. Black to Blair, September 2, 1938; HIAS, B. Robinson to Herman Bernstein, May 1, 1938.

28. CJCP, Caiserman to Wise, February 4, 1938.

29. *NA*, State Department Records, File 900-1/2: 840–8, Memorandum on refugees, 1938.

30. John Munro, ed., *DCER VI* (Ottawa, 1972), Memorandum from the United States delegation, March 25, 1938, 790–1; King Diary, March 29, 1938; KP, Skelton to King, March 25, 1938, c122621.

31. KP, Blair to Crerar, March 26, 1938, c112628.

32. King Diary, March 29, 1938.

33. Quoted in David Rome, "A History of Anti-Semitism in Canada" (Montreal: CJC, 1978), unpaginated.

34. See, for example, Brunelle's speech in the House of Commons, *House of Commons Debates*, 1 (1939), 305.

35. See, for example, IR, File 165172.

36. *Debates*, 1 (1939), 428. For a survey of anti-Semitism in Quebec, see David Rome, *Clouds in the Thirties: On Anti-Semitism in Canada, 1929–1939*, 13 vols. (Montreal, 1977–82); Lita Rose Betcherman, *The Swastika and the Maple Leaf* (Toronto, 1975); W. D. Ker-

naghan, "Freedom of Religion in the Province of Quebec" (Ph.D. diss., Duke University, 1966).

37. King Diary, July 5, 6, 1938.

38. H. Blair Neatby, *William Lyon Mackenzie King: The Prism of Unity* (Toronto, 1976), 268. Canadian Jewish leaders were not unaware of the position of cabinet ministers from Quebec. Following the provincial Liberal party's defeat in Quebec, the president of the Jewish Immigrant Aid Society in Montreal reported to his board that "he had it on good authority that the French Canadian element in the Federal Cabinet is strongly opposed to the admission of Jews to Canada." JIAS, Minutes of the Board of Directors, December 9, 1936.

39. King Diary, July 6, 1938.

40. NA, RG 84, File 842.00PR Refugees, Simmons to Hull, April 6, 1938.

41. IR, File 644452, Blair, Draft, April 19, 1938; KP, Blair to Skelton, April 14, 1938, c122627; IR, File 644452, Blair, Memorandum for file, April 19, 1938; ibid., Blair to Crerar, March 28, 1938.

42. IR, File 644452, Blair, Memorandum for file, April 19, 1938.

43. Ibid., Blair to Skelton, April 8, 1938.

44. CJCP, Cohen to Caiserman, April 1, 1938; ibid., Caiserman to Cohen, April 4, 1938; PAC, WCJH, Caiserman to B. Sheps, April 4, 1938.

45. CJCP, Caiserman to O. B. Rogers, April 25, 1938.

46. WCJH, Caiserman to M. Averback, April 15, 1938.

47. CJCP, Jacobs, Heaps and Factor to King, April 27, 1939; ibid., King to Heaps, May 3, 1938; NA RG 84, File 842.00PR Refugees, Skelton to Simmons, June 4, 1938.

48. King Diary, April 26, 1938.

49. KP, Heaps to King, May 16, 1938, 21492.

50. CJCP, B. Robinson to O. B. Rogers, May 23, 1938; ibid., Robinson to Cohen, May 23, 1938.

51. Interview with Oscar Cohen.

52. CJC, JCA, German Jewish Refugee File, Celie to David, May 11, 1938 (our translation).

53. Ibid., M. Serlin to JCA, June 16, 1938.

54. CJCP, Cohen to O. B. Rogers, May 25, 1938.

55. Ibid., Heaps to Caiserman, May 26, 1938; ibid., M. A. Gray to Caiserman, May 26, 1938; ibid., Gray to Caiserman, May 25, 1938.

56. WCJH, Caiserman to M. A. Gray, June 2, 1938.

57. CJCP, B. Robinson to HICEM, June 2, 1938.

58. KP, E. A. Pickering to King, June 2, 1938, 214193; ibid., Pickering to King, June 6, 1938, 214914; JCA, German Jewish Refugee File, S. Belkin to HICEM, June 9, 1938.

59. CJCP, Heaps to M. A. Gray, June 13, 1938.

60. CJCP, Special memorandum on the delegation sent by the People's Committee to Ottawa, n.d.; IR, File 644452, pt. 5, Blair, Memorandum to file, June 16, 1938.

61. WJCH, Heaps to Gray, June 20, 1938.

62. HIAS, Solkin to James Bernstein, October 3, 1938.

63. PRO, FO 371, File 21748, C. Makins, Minute, April 28, 1938, 4435.

64. PRO, FO 371, File 22528, M. Stevenson, Minute, June 21, 1938.

65. NA, RG 84, File 842.00PR Refugees, King to Simmons, June 28, 1938; ibid., Simmons to Secretary of State, June 30, 1938.

66. Munro, *DCER VI*, King to Wrong, June 11, 1938, 801–5.

67. IR, File 644452, Blair to Little, June 4, 6, 1938.

68. Ibid., Blair to Jolliffe, June 13, 1938.

69. JIAS(T), File 10A, Solkin to A. Brodey, June 29, 1938.

70. JIAS(T), File 187, Solkin to T. Taback, June 24, 1938.

71. Quoted in Evan Barzel, "Zita's Odyssey," *Jewish Life*, December 1979, 14, 26.

72. JCA, M. A. Solkin Papers, Solkin to HICEM, June 23, 1938: JIAS(T), File 10A, Solkin to A. Brodey, June 29, 1938.

73. Munro, *DCER VI*, Wrong to Skelton, June 21, 1938, 806–7; KP, King to Wrong, June 30, 1938, 223086.

74. C. H. A. Armstrong Papers, Wrong to Marga Wrong, June 1, 1938 (courtesy of J. L. Granatstein).

75. IR, File 644452, Blair to Skelton, June 13, 1938; ibid., Blair, Memorandum to file, June 13, 1938; ibid., Blair to Crerar, June 14, 1938.

76. D. A. Wyman, *Paper Walls: America and the Refugee Crisis, 1938–1941* (Boston, 1968), 43–51; see, also, H. L. Feingold, *The Politics of Rescue: The Roosevelt Administration and the Holocaust, 1938–1945* (New Brunswick, N.J., 1970): PAC, EA, Box 1870, File 327-1, Wrong, Speech to Evian Conference.

77. KP, Wrong to King, July 7, 1938, 223088.

78. René Richier as quoted in Peggy Mann, "When the World Passed By on the Other Side," *Manchester Guardian Weekly*, May 7, 1978.

79. *Danzinger Vorposter* as quoted in Mann, "When the World Passed By".

80. CJCP, Solkin to HICEM, June 23, 1938; ibid., B. Robinson to Cohen, July 14, 1938; JIAS, Solkin to S. Belkin, July 20, 1938.

81. JCA, German Jewish Refugee File, Meyer Selzer to JCA, July 27, 1938 (our translation).

82. Ibid., Bertha Fugend-Witzer to JCA, July 31, 1938 (our translation); ibid., Fugend-Witzer to JCA, September 14, 1938.

83. Ibid., Leib Goldenstein to JCA, November 2, 1938.

84. H. Carl Goldenberg Papers, H. Carl Goldenberg to Crerar, June 28, 1938 (in possession of H. Carl Goldenberg).

85. Ibid., Karl Morgenstern to H. Carl Goldenberg, August 23, 1938; ibid., Goldenberg to Heaps, August 20, 1938; ibid., Goldenberg to Crerar, August 20, 1938; ibid., King to Goldenberg, August 22, 1938; ibid., Blair to Goldenberg, September 9, 1938.

86. Ibid., H. Carl Goldenberg to King, August 25, 1938.

87. IR, File 54782/5, Blair, Memorandum on meeting with Crerar, August 26, 1938.

88. Ibid., Blair to Judd, October, 1938.

89. KP, Heaps to King, September 9, 1938, 214195; ibid., H. R. L. Henry to Heaps, September 15, 1938, 214197.

90. JIAS(T), File T10, B. Robinson to A. Brodey, October 21, 1938.

91. King Diary, May 10, 1938.

92. NA, RG 84, File 842.00PR Refugees, Memorandum of interview, July 23, 1938.

93. King Diary, September 15, 1938.

2/The Line Must Be Drawn Somewhere

1. Interview with Escott Reid.

2. Escott Reid Papers, E. Reid to R. Reid, January 28, 1939 (in possession of Escott Reid).

3. Ibid., E. Reid to R. Reid, January 30, 1939.

4. Escott Reid, "The Conscience of the Diplomat: A Personal Testament," *Queen's Quarterly* LXXIV, no. 4 (1967), 13.

5. Reid Papers, E. Reid to R. Reid, March 11, 1939.

6. King Diary, November 12, 13, 1938.

7. Ibid., November 17, 20, 1938.

8. Interview with Oscar Cohen.

9. CJC, CJCP, Caiserman, Memorandum, November 15, 1938.

10. *Toronto Daily Star*, November 21, 1938.

11. CJCP, Regional reports on mass meetings, November 20, 1938.

12. King Diary, November 22, 1938; *Toronto Daily Star*, November 23, 1938.

13. Toronto *Hebrew Journal*, November 23, 1938 (our translation).

14. King Diary, November 23, 1938; PAC, KP, A. Freiman to King, November 23, 1939, 213348; interview with Oscar Cohen.

15. King Diary, November 24, 1938.

16. CJCP, Caiserman to B. Sheps, November 28, 1938; *Toronto Daily Star*, November 25, 1938.

17. PAC, WCJH, B. Sheps to Cohen, December 10, 1938.

18. CJCP, Convention proceedings, 1938, 12.

19. PAC, LONC, Executive minutes, October 15, 1938; interview with Constance Hayward; Winnipeg *Western Jewish News*, October 6, 1938; WCJH, Cohen to B. Sheps, October 30, 1938.

20. Interview with Saul Hayes; interview with Constance Hayward.

21. KP, CNCR, Memorandum on representations, December 7, 1938, c122674–8.

22. PRO, Cabinet Records 55, Cabinet meeting, November 16, 1938.

23. PAC, EA, Box 771, File 382, Norman Robertson, "Canada and the Refugee Problem," November 29, 1938; cf. J. L. Granatstein, *A Man of Influence* (Ottawa, 1981).

24. King Diary, December 1, 1938.

25. KP, Crerar to King, December 2, 1938, c122661; ibid., Heaps to King, December 2, 1938, 214110.

26. PAC, IR, File 644452, Draft statement . . . regarding refugees, December 12, 1938; ibid., J. Pickersgill to King, December 13, 1938; EA, Box 771, File 382, Skelton, Memorandum on refugees, n.d.

27. Interview with James Gibson; see, also, Vincent Massey, *What's Past is Prologue* (Toronto, 1963), 114–5; J. L. Granatstein and R. Bothwell, "A Self-Evident National Duty: Canadian Foreign Policy, 1935–9," *Journal of Imperial and Commonwealth History*, III (1975), 214; King Diary, October 5, 1935; L. B. Pearson, *Mike: The Memoirs of the Right Honourable Lester B. Pearson, 1897–1948*, vol. 1 (Toronto, 1972), 105–6. For a more sympathetic view, see Claude Bissell, *The Young Vincent Massey* (Toronto, 1981).

28. Quoted in A. J. Sherman, *Island Refuge: Britain and Refugees from the Third Reich, 1933–1939* (London, 1973), 141; see also, John Munro, ed., *DCER VI* (Ottawa, 1972), Massey to King, October 18, 1938, 828.

29. Munro, *DCER VI*, Massey to King, November 29, 1938, 837; ibid., Massey to Skelton, December 1, 1938, 844–5; EA, Box 779, File 382, Massey to King, December 2, 1938; EA, Box 1870, File 327-11, Massey to King, December 2, 1938.

30. EA, Box 1870, File 327-11, Skelton to Massey, December 2, 1938; EA, Box 1771, File 382, Robertson "Canada and the Refugee Problem"; ibid., Winterton to King, December 6, 1938.

31. EA, Box 1870, File 327-11, Massey to King, January 13, 1939; KP, Massey to King, February 3, 1939, 160710.

32. NA, RG 84, File 800, Goodyear to State Department, March 15, 1939.

33. PAC, Cairine Wilson Papers, Minutes of CNCR founding convention, December 6, 1938, 4.

34. H. Blair Neatby, *William Lyon Mackenzie King: The Prism of Unity* (Toronto, 1976), 304–5.

35. EA, Box 779, File 382, Skelton, Memorandum, January 10, 1939.

36. CJCP, Files on anti-Semitism in Canada, 1930–40.

37. Ibid.; Lita Rose Betcherman, *The Swastika and the Maple Leaf* (Toronto, 1975), 99–137.

38. NA, RG 84, File 800, Goodyear to State Department, January 9, 1939.

39. United Church Archives, Claris E. Silcox Papers, Speeches, "Canadian Post-Mortem on Refugees," Toronto, March 21, 1939.

40. Interview with Oscar Cohen.

41. CJC, JCA, J. Stein to JCA, January 8, 1939.

42. YIVO, HIAS, HICEM to JIAS, Montreal, July 19, 1939; JIAS(T), Minutes of meeting, January 26, 1939; ibid., A. Brodey to Solkin, December 28, 1938.

43. CJCP, A. Rona to CJC, March 8, 1939.

44. JCA, B. Heinman to JCA, December 15, 1938.

45. Ibid., J. Weiss to J. Rosen, February 15, 1939.

46. Ibid., S. Zuckermann to JCA, January 6, 1939; ibid., Kluger to JCA, March 6, 1939; ibid., R. Low to JCA, December 12, 1938.

47. JIAS, Solkin to Gelbard, February 19, 1939.

48. PAC, MP, Blair to Bell, November 18, 1938; NA, RG 84, File 800, Blair to Simmons, February 3, 1939.

49. Interviews with James Gibson, Hugh Keenleyside and Jack Pickersgill.

50. MP, Blair to Bell, December 27, 1938.

51. IR, File 644452, pt. 3, Blair to Little, January 7, 1939; ibid., Blair to Little, June 14, 1939; MP, Blair to Manion, February 28, 1939; ibid., Blair to Bell, May 3, 1939; EA, Box 1871, File 61, Blair to Skelton, May 24, 1939.

52. IR, File 661315, pt. 1, Blair to Smith, May 18, 1939.

53. JIAS(T), Solkin to T. Taback, December 1, 1938.

54. CJCP, M. A. Gray to Mrs. A. Ginsberg, February 28, 1939; JCA, E. Oungre, Report on immigration farming families, March 18, 1939; ibid., E. Oungre, Report on Canada, April, 1939; ibid., Colby to Abeles and Dr. Lustig, January 16, 1939.

55. JIAS, File 21130, Solkin to JEAS, Warsaw, November 7, 1938; JIAS, File 21305, Solkin to M. A. Gray, December 9, 1938; JIAS, File 21130, Solkin to Asofsky, April 14, 1938; HIAS, Solkin to HICEM, August 1, 1939.

56. IR, File 644452, pt. 3, Blair to Little, January 7, 1939.

57. IR, File 673932, Little to Blair, August 15, 1939.

58. JIAS(T), File 10D, A. Brodey to Solkin, February 7, 1939.

59. *House of Commons Debates*, October 8, 1939.

60. CJCP, Solkin to Sam Factor, January 3, 1939.

61. Interview with Saul Hayes.

62. CJCP, Minutes of refugee committee, December 11, 1938.

63. WCJH, S. Belkin to B. Sheps, March 14, 1939.

64. Ibid., Cohen to B. Sheps, December 30, 1938.

65. Silcox Papers, Western Canada Tour File, January, 1939.

66. Montreal *Le Canada*, January 21, 1939; *Montreal Gazette*, January 21, 1939.

67. Toronto *Globe and Mail*, January 31, 1939.

68. *Debates*, January 29, 1939.

69. *Financial Post*, December 24, 1938.

70. *Windsor Star*, January 27, 1939.

71. *Saturday Night*, February 7, 1939; *Vancouver Province*, February 11, 1939; *Toronto Daily Star*, November 19, 1938; Toronto *Globe and Mail*, November 18, 1938.

72. G. Hambleton, "The Press and the Refugee Problem," *Canadian Jewish Chronicle*, March 10, 1939.

73. NA, RG 84, File 800, Goodyear to State Department, February 1, 1939.

74. *Toronto Telegram*, December 15, 1938.

75. CJCP, Caiserman to Mrs. Dunkelman, December 16, 1938.

76. *Saturday Night*, December 24, 1938.

77. NA, RG 84, File 842.00PR Refugees, Simmons to State Department, January 11, 1939.

78. MP, Stanley to Manion, December 29, 1938.

79. KP, Emerson to King, December 1, 1938, vol. 1871; ibid., Mount Allison Students Association to the Government of Canada, December, 1938, vol. 1871.

80. MP, Wrong to Manion, March 20, 1939.

81. Ibid., Manion to Rabbi Eisendrath, December 27, 1938; ibid., Manion to Wrong, March 21, 1938.

82. Ibid., Manion to Simons, February 6, 1939.

83. CJCP, Report on interview with Crerar, February 24, 1939; *Toronto Daily Star*, March 10, 1939. In fact, among the three thousand or so Sudentens to arrive before the war were six Jewish families who settled in the area of St. Walberg, Saskatchewan. Their reception was not propitious. Within weeks of arriving in their new home, many of them were complaining that the anti-Semitism of the older German settlers and the recently arrived Sudetens had made their situation "hopeless." CJCP, St. Walberg Refugee Settlement File, Willie Fleisher to H. Kay, July 5, 1939; ibid., S. Belkin to CJC, July 15, 1939.

84. JIAS(T), File 391, Solkin to A. Brodey, February 27, 1939.

85. Ibid., Solkin to T. Taback, March 31, 1939.

86. Ibid., A. G. McAvity to A. Garson, March 31, 1939.

87. Ibid., Blair to A. G. McAvity, March 2, 1939.

88. NA, RG 84, File 800, Simmons to Hull, February 1, 1939.

89. Toronto *Hebrew Journal*, April 30, 1939; ibid., July 24, 1939; ibid., May 2, 1939 (our translation).

90. G. Thomas and M. M. Witts, *The Voyage of the Damned* (New York, 1974), 135–217.

91. *New York Times*, June 3, 4, 5, 1939.

92. KP, Wrong et al. to King, June 7, 1939, 238579; King Diary, June 8, 1939; KP, King to Skelton, June 8, 1939, 237087; ibid., Skelton to King, June 9, 1939, 237095–6; IR, File 644452, Blair to Skelton, June 8, 1939.

93. *Winnipeg Free Press*, July 19, 1939.

94. PAC, Archie Bennett Papers, *CNCR Bulletin*, May 4, 1939; Silcox Papers, Refugee Clipping File.

95. MP, Birks to Manion, June 12, 1939; ibid., Birks to Crerar, June 12, 1939.

96. KP, Woodsworth to Wilson, May 10, 1939, 238438.

97. IR, File 644452, pt. 3, Blair to Little, June 14, 1939.

98. Ibid., Blair to Skelton, November 16, 1939.

3 / Der Feter Yiuv ist bei uns

1. JIAS(T), File on undated and anonymous letters from Europe, 1939–40.

2. Ibid. Yom Kippur is a day of fast, and Purim is the celebration of the Feast of Esther, during which revellers masquerade in outlandish costumes.

3. JIAS(T), Minutes of board meeting, October 22, 26, 1939.

4. FNA, IRO, Box 36, AJ43, T. Achille; ibid., British Foreign Office to Emerson, September 29, 1939; PRO, FO 371, File 24085/280, U.S. Embassy, London, to British Foreign Office, October 3, 1939.

5. PRO, FO 371, File 24085/280, Eden to King, October 12, 1939.

6. PAC, IR, File 54782/6, Blair to Little, October 24, 1939.

7. PAC, EA, Box 1871, Blair to Skelton, November 16, 1939; IR, File 661315, pt. 1, Blair, Memorandum to file, October 3, 1939.

8. CJC, CJCP, Caiserman to M. Averback, September 20, 1939.

9. CJCP, CNCR, Report of activities, September 20, 1939.

10. CJCP, Cohen to Bronfman, September 17, 1939.

11. PAC, MP, Blair to Bell, November 24, 1939.

12. IR, File 661315, pt. 1, Memorandum to file, November 25, 1939; IR, File 673931, Blair to Wynn, November 23, 1939.

13. JIAS, Solkin to Kraicer, December 13, 1939.

14. PRO, Cabinet Records 67, #3, Report of refugee committee, December 12, 1939.

15. JIAS(T), Board meetings, November–December, 1939, January –February, 1940; ibid., Refugee Files, 1939–40; CJCP, Hayes to national offices, January 2, 1940; JIAS(T), Report on activities, January–June, 1940.

16. Herbert H. Lehman Papers, National refugee service report, July 19, 1940.

17. IR, File 673931, Blair to Skelton, August 22, 1940.

18. Quoted in ibid., Blair to Robertson, May 8, 1941.

19. Ibid., Chargé d'Affaires, Tokyo, to King, November 1, 1940; ibid., Blair to Skelton, November 2, 1940.

20. MBS, Notes on the application of the Edward Pree family, 1940 (in possession of Sorensen family).

21. Ibid., Sorensen to De Mey, May 22, 1939.

22. Ibid.; interview with Mark B. Sorensen.

23. MBS, Sorensen to Macalister, January 21, 1941; ibid., Notes on Heinz Engel application, 1939; ibid., Sorensen to Cresswell, July 4, 1940; Cresswell to Van Scoy, July 18, 1940, quoted in ibid., Notes on Joseph Mahler family application, 1940; Blair to Van Scoy, June 27, 1940, quoted in ibid., Notes on Gustav Barth family application, 1940.

24. Ibid., Cresswell to Little, October 6, 1939; Little to Cresswell, November 15, 1939, quoted in ibid., Paul Eisner File, 1939; Blair to Van Scoy, June 25, 1939, quoted in ibid., Joseph Mahler File, 1939; Blair to Van Scoy, January 22, 1940, quoted in ibid., Leo Bauer Family File, 1940. The Bauers were eventually admitted to Cuba and shortly thereafter made their way to the United States.

25. Ibid., Little to Cresswell, June 11, 1940; ibid., Otto Sygall File, 1940, Sorensen, Memorandum, n.d.

26. Blair to Macalister, March 18, 1940, quoted in ibid., Dr. Maximilian Wiernick File, 1939–40.

27. Ibid., Cresswell to Macalister, March 4, 1940.

28. Ibid., Note on Leiba Feingenson File, 1940.

29. Ibid., Note on J. C. M. Brentano File, 1940.

30. Ibid., Sorensen to Cresswell, July 4, 1940.

31. PAC, KPC, Vanier to King, May 22, 1940, vol. 424.

32. Ibid., Cabinet War Committee, May 24, 1940, vol. 424; King Diary, May 24, 1940. The prime minister did have some second thoughts. Although he had little use for Crerar and found him "getting more difficult every day . . . [and] losing ground rapidly," he also found many in his cabinet, particularly Lapointe, "too restrictionist in their views." It was "very difficult", he added, "to get Lapointe to take a large view of Canada opening up to other peoples." Seemingly oblivious to his own comments during the meeting of the war cabinet, the prime minister wrote: "We simply cannot refrain from sharing the burden of the democracies in Europe in taking refugees, especially children. I urged the most immediate steps or assistance be given to relieve France and England of refugees."

33. IR, File 962419, Podoski to King, July 11, 1940; EA, Box 391, External Affairs to Dominion Secretary, July 26, 1940.

34. EA, Box 391, Blair to Skelton, July 24, 1940.

35. CJCP, Report of Ignace Schwartzbard, August 12, 1940; see, also, PAC, DOD, File 39.

36. DOD, File 262802, Wise to G. Murray, September 11, 1940; CJCP, Wise to Bronfman, September 6, 1940; London *Jewish Chronicle*, November 15, 1940; CJCP, Hayes to national officers, October 16, 1940; ibid., Hayes to CNCR, October 24, 1940.

37. JIAS(T), Report, November, 1940; ibid., Solkin to Kraicer, November 6, 1940; ibid., quoted in Solkin to S. Belkin, October 30, 1940.

38. IR, File 673931, Blair, Memorandum for file, January 17, 1941.

39. Ibid., Massey to King, January 15, 1941.

40. Ibid., Blair to Crerar, June 17, 1941; IR, File 541782, Blair to Crerar, January 21, 1941.

41. KPC, Cabinet War Committee, January 21, 1941, vol. 424; IR, File 673931, Crerar to Blair, January 22, 1941; PRO, FO 371, File 29198, Balinski to Snow, April 9, 1941.

42. IR, File 673931, Podoski to Robertson, February 19, 1941; ibid., Blair to Crerar, February 11, 1941; ibid., Blair to Podoski, February 26, 1941.

43. Ibid., Blair to Crerar, February 11, 1941; PAC, PCO, Vol. 12, File C4175, Cabinet War Committee, February 11, 1941; ibid., A. D. P. Heeney to Crerar, February 11, 1941.

44. IR, File 673931, Blair, Memorandum to file, April 22, 1941.

45. Ibid.

46. PCO, Vol. 12, C4175 Cabinet War Committee, April 4, 1941;

CJC UJRA, File 174, Memorandum regarding permission to enter Canada of Polish Jewish refugees, May 6, 1941.

47. UJRA, File 174, Phillips to Brzezinski, April 29, 1941; ibid., H. Wolofsky to Brzezinski, April 30, 1941.

48. *Kanader Adler*, May 2, 1981; UJRA, File 174, Hayes, Diary of the Polish refugee scheme, April 29–May 15, 1941.

49. IR, File 673931, Blair to Crerar, April 29, 1941; ibid., Blair to Podoski, May 2, 1941; UJRA, File 174, Memorandum regarding permission to enter Canada of Polish Jewish refugees, May 6, 1941; IR, File 673931, Blair to Robertson, May 8, 1941.

50. UJRA, File 174, Podoski to FPJ, May 8, 1941.

51. Ibid., Hayes to Rosenberg, May 12, 1941; ibid., Minutes of UJRA executive, May 14, 1941.

52. CJCP, Aldoph Held to Peters, May 15, 1941; UJRA, File 174, Fasman to Hayes, May 18, 1941.

53. UJRA, File 174, Hayes to Rosenberg, May 17, 1941.

54. CJCP, Fasman to Peters, May 14, 1941; IR, File 673931, Peters to Podoski, May 14, 1941; ibid., Podoski to Peters, May 15, 1941.

55. CJCP, Peters to Podoski, May 16, 1941; UJRA, File 174, Hayes to Rosenberg, May 16, 1941.

56. UJRA, File 174, Fasman to Hayes, May 16, 1941.

57. Ibid., Hayes to Rosenberg, May 22, 1941.

58. Ibid., Hayes to Podoski, June 3, 1941.

59. Ibid., Podoski to Hayes, June 4, 1941; ibid., Hayes to Podoski, June 5, 1941.

60. CJCP, FPJ to Bronfman, June 6, 1941.

61. Ibid., H. Wolofsky to Archie Bennett, June 17, 1941.

62. Ibid., Hayes to Podoski, June 26, 1941.

63. Ibid., Blair to Podoski, May 19, 1941.

64. IR, File 673931, pt. 1, Blair to T. Stone, May 20, 1941.

65. Ibid., Blair to T. Stone, May 28, 1941.

66. Ibid., Blair to Podoski, May 28, 1941.

67. Ibid., Wrong to Robertson, May 31, 1941.

68. UJRA, File 174, Schwartzbard to WJC, May 20, 1941; ibid., A. Tartakower to Caiserman, May 15, 1941; ibid., Podoski to Hayes, June 3, 1941; CJCP, Schwartzbard to CJC, July 7, 1941.

69. IR, File 673931, F. Taylor to Jolliffe, June 19, 1941; UJRA, Blair to Podoski, July 8, 1941; CJCP, Podoski to Peters, July 9, 1941; ibid., Hayes, Memorandum, July 11, 1941. Hayes was particularly bemused by Blair's comment to Podoski. It was only logical, he told the ambassador, for these rabbis to have applied first to the United States as they were "fleeing from hell," and, therefore, could hardly be blamed if they applied "everywhere," especially as Canada was "known as a country which [was] keeping its doors closed to Jewish refugees." He also claimed that there was a genuine shortage of rabbis in Canada; because Canadian Jews were sending $750,000 each year to support these rabbis in Poland, he argued, could not this money now be used

to support them in Canada. UJRA, Hayes to Podoski, July 15, 1941.

70. CJCP, Peters to Podoski, July 24, 1941; ibid., Podoski to Keenleyside, July 24, 1941.

71. Ibid., Hayes to Phillips, July 30, 1941.

72. IR, File 673931, Secretary of State for External Affairs to Chargé d'Affaires, Tokyo, July 23, 1941; ibid., Chargé d'Affaires, Tokyo, to External Affairs, July 25, 1941; Agudath Israel Archives, Michael G. Tress Collection, Rabbi Kalisz to M. G. Tress, July 25, 1941; IR, File 673931, Bronfman to Crerar, July 31, 1941; ibid., Robertson to Blair, August 2, 1941.

73. IR, File 673931, Blair, Memorandum for file, August 5, 1941.

74. Ibid., Blair, Memorandum to file, August 9, 1941.

75. Ibid., Little (pseud. Tororus) to Immigration Branch, August 18, 1941; ibid., Blair, Memorandum to file, August 21, 1941; ibid., Blair, Memorandum to file, August 25, 1941.

76. Ibid., Blair to Strong, October 2, 1941; ibid., Strong to Blair, October 6, 1941; ibid., Blair to Podoski, October 9, 1941.

77. Ibid., Pavlasek to Blair, October 30, 1941; ibid., Pavlasek to Blair, November 1, 1941.

78. Ibid., Blair to Robertson, November 11, 1941; ibid., Blair to Pavlasek, October 31, 1941; ibid., Blair to Pavlasek, November 5, 1941; ibid., Blair to Pavlasek, November 18, 1941; IR, File 962419, Blair to Robertson, November 5, 1941.

79. Interview with Rabbi Hirschprung. The rabbi was one of the twenty-nine.

80. IR, File 673931, Blair to Podoski, November 26, 1941; ibid., Blair to Crerar, November 26, 1941; ibid., Blair to Hayes, November 28, 1941.

81. PRO, FO 371, File 29206, FPJ to Schwartzbard, November 24, 1941, 14515.

82. UJRA, File 174, Blair to Podoski, December 6, 1941.

83. IR, File 673931, Blair, Memorandum for file, December 8, 1941; ibid., Blair to Crerar, December 10, 1941.

84. Ibid., Blair to Robertson, December 13, 1941; ibid., Blair to Podoski, December 13, 1941.

85. UJRA, File 174, Podoski to Peters, December 19, 1941; ibid., Podoski to Hayes, December 24, 1941; ibid., Hayes to Phillips, December 27, 1941.

86. IR, File 673931, Blair to Pavlasek, January 20, 1942.

87. CJCP, Schwartzbard to CJC, March 4, 1942. For an excellent discussion of when the Allied governments first learned of the holocaust, see Walter Laquer, *The Terrible Secret* (London, 1980).

88. CJCP, Bronfman to King, March 28, 1942.

89. CJCP, Report of Polish National Council, June 29, 1942.

90. Ibid., B. Sheps to Bronfman, July 6, 1942.

91. Ibid., Archie Bennett to Hayes, July 16, 1942.

92. Ibid., Hayes to Archie Bennett, July 17, 1942.

93. Ibid., Hayes to Bronfman, July 20, 1942.

94. Ibid., WJC to CJC, September 15, 1942; ibid., Hayes, Memorandum, September 15, 1942.

95. Toronto *Globe and Mail*, October 13, 1942.

96. DEA, File 4637-40C-W, Dominions Office to King, December 5, 1942; ibid., King to Dominions Office, December 11, 1942.

97. Ibid., Wrong to King, December 9, 1942.

98. *Ottawa Citizen*, December 15, 1942; KP, Department of External Affairs press conference, December 17, 1942, c167444-5.

99. JIAS(T), Solkin to Kraicer, December 19, 1942.

4/The Children Who Never Came

1. PAC, IR, File 677774, Blair to G. R. Booth, July 15, 1939.

2. See Robert Domanski, "While Six Million Cried: Canada and the Refugee Question, 1938-41" (Master's research essay, Institute of Canadian Studies, Carleton University, 1975), 57-60.

3. CJC, CJCP, Cohen to S. Zacks, November 10, 1939; ibid., Cohen to Hayes, February 25, 1940; ibid., Cohen to S. Zacks, November 10, 1939.

4. IR, File 677774, Blair, Memorandum to file, October 17, 1939.

5. PAC, EA, Box 1870, File 327-6, M. Mahoney to King, May 18, 1940, quoted in Domanski, "While Six Million Cried," 62.

6. PAC, KP, Stead to CNCR, May 15, 1940; ibid., Wilson to King, May 16, 1940; ibid., King to Wilson, May 20, 1940; IR, File 694687, referred to in Blair to Fleming, October 21, 1940; CJC, JCA, Blair to C. P. Brown, May 29, 1940; KP, Massey to Crerar, June 1, 1940; ibid., Vanier to King, June 3, 1940; ibid., King to Vanier, June 8, 1940.

7. PAC, KPC, Minutes of Cabinet War Committee, June 14, 1940, vol. 424.

8. KP, Blair to Crerar, June 27, 1940, vol. 283.

9. *Montreal Gazette*, July 11, 1940.

10. CJCP, Hayes to Cohen, June 28, 1940.

11. JIAS, File 21344, Kolmer to JIAS, Montreal, June 29, 1940; ibid., S. Belkin to Kolmer, July 25, 1940.

12. KP, Massey to King, July 23, 1940, vol. 283.

13. CJCP, Podoski to King, July 11, 1940; IR, File 962419, Blair, Memorandum for file, July 24, 1940.

14. CJCP, *CNCR Bulletin*, September 12, 1940; *Toronto Daily Star*, September 9, 1940; see Domanski, "While Six Million Cried," 66-72; see, also, Charlotte Whitton, "Children on Loan," in National Conference of Social Work, *Proceedings* (New York, 1941), 219-33.

15. Leo Baeck Institute, *Konzentration-lager Frankreich* Papers, 1939-44, Brief memorandum on the condition of women and children interned in southern France, 1941-42.

16. JIAS(T), M. Berger to Family Balluk, August 9, 1942 (our translation).

17. *Konzentration-lager Frankreich,* Papers, 1939–1944, Brief memorandum on the condition of women and children.

18. *New York Times,* August 27, September 3, 1942.

19. Michael R. Marrus and Robert O. Paxton, *Vichy France and the Jews* (New York, 1981), 264.

20. *FRUS,* 1942, 11, Tuck to Hull, September 11, 1942, 712–13.

21. *New York Times,* August 26, 1942.

22. New York *Der Tag,* August 27, 1942.

23. *FRUS,* 1942, 11, Hull to Tuck, September 28, 1942.

24. IR, File 739325, Memorandum for Blair, Unsigned, September 5, 1942; CJC, UJRA, File 224A, Hayes to Schwartz, September 5, 1942; *Kanader Adler,* September 6, 1942.

25. IR, File 739325, Hayes to Pratt, September 8, 1942; UJRA, File 224A, Pratt to Hayes, September 9, 1941.

26. UJRA, File 225, Leavitt to Hayes, September 9, 1942.

27. DEA, File 4300–40c, Bronfman to King, September 10, 1942; UJRA, File 229, Bronfman to Crerar, September 10, 1942.

28. See, for example, DEA, File 4300–40C, Weekly political intelligence summary, no. 153, September 9, 1942; ibid., Wrong to King, September 12, 1942.

29. IR, File 739325, Blair to Robertson, September 14, 1942; ibid., Crerar to Bronfman, September 14, 1942.

30. DEA, File 4300–40C, Wrong to King, September 15, 1942.

31. Ibid., Canadian Minister, Washington, to King, September 16, 1942; ibid., Canadian Minister, Washington, to External Affairs, Ottawa, September 16, 1942.

32. Ibid., Podoski to Robertson, September 21, 1939; ibid., Emerson to King, September 23, 1942; IR, File 739325, Bronfman to Wrong, September 23, 1942; DEA, File 4300–40C, Wrong to Robertson, September 25, 1942.

33. PRO, FO 371, File 32680, A. W. Randall, Minute, September 20, 1942, 12687; ibid., A. W. Randall, Minute, September 24, 1942, 12853.

34. UJRA, File 229, Leavitt to Bronfman, September 25, 1942; DEA, File 4300–40C, Wrong, Note for file, September 29, 1942.

35. UJRA, File 224A, Blair to Hayes, September 26, 1942.

36. CJCP, Hayes to Blair, September 28, 1942.

37. Ibid.; DEA, File 4300–40C, Wrong to Bronfman, September 29, 1942; ibid., Bronfman to Wrong, September 30, 1942.

38. IR, File 739325, Blair to Crerar, October 1, 1942.

39. UJRA, File 224A, Blair to Hayes, October 2, 1942; IR, File 673931, Blair, memorandum for file, October 2, 1942.

40. DEA, File 4300–40C, Dominions Office to External Affairs, October 3, 1942; PRO, FO 371, File 32680, Randall to Kimber, October 23, 1942; DEA, File 4300–40C, Canadian Embassy, Washington, to King, October 16, 1942; ibid., Wrong to Pearson, October 5, 1942.

41. UJRA, File 224A, Hayes to Cohen, September 28, 1942; UJRA, File 182, Solkin to Kraicer, October 2, 1942; UJRA, A. Seligman to UJRA, September 28, 1942; ibid., Koenig to CJC, October 2, 1942.

42. DEA, File 4300-40C, Wrong, Note for file, October 5, 1942.

43. JIAS, File 22350, Hayes to Blair, October 2, 1942; ibid., Solkin to Kraicer, October 4, 1942; ibid., Solkin to Hayes, October 5, 1942; ibid., Solkin to Kraicer, October 4, 1942.

44. UJRA, File 224A, Hayes to Sadowski et al., October 7, 1942.

45. JIAS(T), File 666, Barsky to Bronfman, October 7, 1942; JIAS, File 22350, Atkins to Solkin, October 9, 1942.

46. JIAS, File 22350, Solkin to Atkins, October 9, 1942; JIAS(T), File 666, Barsky to Atkins, October 9, 1942.

47. JIAS, File 22350, Solkin to Atkins, October 14, 1942.

48. JIAS(T), File 666, Atkins to Solkin, October 16, 1942; JIAS, File 22350, Kraicer to Solkin, October 19, 1942; JIAS(T), File 666, Solkin to Hayes, October 20, 1942.

49. UJRA, File 224A, Solkin to Hayes, October 20, 1942; ibid., Hayes to Solkin, October 20, 1942.

50. CJCP, Hayes, Memorandum, October 20, 1942; JIAS, File 22350, Solkin to M. A. Gray, October 26, 1942; ibid., Gray to Solkin, October 28, 1942; ibid., Solkin to Gray, November 4, 1942.

51. DEA, File 4300-40C, Hayes to Blair, October 13, 1942; ibid., External Affairs, Ottawa, to Canadian Embassy, Washington, October 5, 1942; ibid., Blair to Wrong, October 15, 1942; IR, File 739325, Blair to Beaudry, October 21, 1942; UJRA, File 224K, Hayes, Memorandum on interview with Blair, October 22, 1942; UJRA, File 224A, Hayes to Blair, October 13, 1942.

52. JIAS(T), *JIAS Annual Report*, 1940, 1941; Agudath Israel Archives, Michael G. Tress Collection, Union of Orthodox Rabbis to FPJ, September 24, 1942; JLC, Vol. 75, Jewish Labor Committee to Crerar, October 6, 1942.

53. CJCP, Blair to Hayes, October 10, 1942.

54. DEA, File 4300-40C, Wrong to Beaudry, October 17, 1942; JIAS(T), File 680, Solkin to Kraicer, October 14, 1942; JIAS, File 22350, Solkin to Kraicer, October 15, 1942; UJRA, File 229, Hayes, Memorandum, October 20, 1942.

55. UJRA, File 229, Peters to Bronfman, November 4, 1942.

56. UJRA, File 224A, Hayes, Memorandum on interview with JDC officials, October 22, 1942; ibid., Rosenberg to Hayes, October 19, 1942; ibid., Hayes to Zacks, November 3, 1942.

57. Marrus and Paxton, *Vichy France*, 63–70.

58. UJRA, File 224A, Hayes, Memorandum on interview with JDC leaders, October 30, 1942.

59. Ibid., Hayes to Zacks, November 10, 1942; CJCP, Hayes to UJRA officers, November 14, 1942; IR, File 739325, Hayes to Blair, November 16, 1942.

60. IR, File 739325, Blair to Beaudry, November 10, 1942; DEA, File 4300-40C, Canadian Embassy, Washington, to Hull, November 25, 1942; CJCP, Schwartz to Hayes, December 20, 1942; DEA, File 4300-40C, Hayes to Wrong, December 29, 1942; ibid., Pearson to King, December 31, 1942; ibid., Beaudry to Canadian Ambassador, Washington, January 4, 1943; ibid., Beaudry to Hayes, January 6, 1943; ibid., Beaudry to Blair, January 11, 1943.

61. IR, File 739325, Jolliffe to Blair, January 6, 1943; ibid., Blair to Commissioner, London, January 6, 1943; ibid., Blair to Beaudry, January 12, 1943.

62. DEA, File 4300-40C, Wrong to Beaudry, January 12, 1943; ibid., Beaudry to Blair, January 12, 1943; ibid., Beaudry to Wrong, January 12, 1943; ibid., Blair to Beaudry, January 13, 1943; UJRA, File 224A, Blair to Hayes, January 12, 1943.

63. DEA, File 4300-40C, External Affairs, Ottawa, to Canadian Minister, Washington, January 13, 1943; ibid., Canadian Minister, Washington, to King, January 14, 1943.

64. UJRA, File 224A, Leavitt to Hayes, January 29, 1943; DEA, File 4300-40C, Canadian Minister, Washington, to External Affairs, Ottawa, January 11, 1943.

65. UJRA, File 224A, Hayes to Blair, February 3, 1943.

66. IR, File 739325, Hayes to Blair, February 4, 1943.

67. Ibid., Blair, Memorandum for file, February 4, 1943; UJRA, File 224A, Blair to Hayes, February 4, 1943.

68. UJRA, File 224A, Draft of letter to Blair and Crerar, February 5, 1943; ibid., Hayes to Phillips, February 6, 1943; ibid., Hayes to Blair, February 11, 1943; ibid., Bronfman to Crerar, February 18, 1943; IR, File 739325, Crerar to Bronfman, February 24, 1943.

69. DEA, File 4300-40C, Robertson to Blair, February 9, 1943.

70. IR, File 739325, Blair to Robertson, February 20, 1943; IR, File 673931, Blair to Crerar, February 22, 1943; DEA, File 4300-40C, Wrong to Robertson, February 24, 1943; ibid., Pearson to Robertson, March 5, 1943.

71. Franklin D. Roosevelt Library, Franklin D. Roosevelt Papers, Joseph H. Murphy, Memorandum re: children from France, February 17, 1944, 5; FNA, IRO, Box 45, AJ43, IGC, Memorandum, December 29, 1943; ibid., Fritz Lichtenstein to Linton, December 13, 1943.

72. Roosevelt Papers, Murphy, Memorandum re: children; DEA, File 4300-40C, King to Massey, January 5, 1944; ibid., Jolliffe to Wrong, January 6, 1944; ibid., Pearson to King, January 19, 1944.

73. IR, File 739325, Wrong to Jolliffe, January 20, 1944; DEA, File 4300-40C, Jolliffe to Wrong, January 21, 1944.

74. DEA, File 4300-40C, King to Massey, January 24, 1944.

75. IRO, Box 45, AJ43, Kullman, Memorandum, February 15, 1944; ibid., Report of Joseph Schwartz, March 3, 1943; ibid., British Foreign Office to Emerson, April 13, 1944; ibid., Randall to IGC, April 20, 1944.

76. DEA, File 4300-40C, Atherton to Robertson, April 17, 1944.

77. Ibid., Robertson to Jolliffe, April 20, 1944; IR, File 739325, Jolliffe to Robertson, April 27, 1944; DEA, File 4300-40C, Wrong to Atherton, May 4, 1944.

5/Ottawa or Bermuda? A Refugee Conference

1. Interview with Simon Kahane. Quoted material in documents, in possession of Simon Kahane.

2. PRO, FO 371, File 30924/121, Count Raczyniki to Eden, December 9, 1942; PRO, Cabinet Records 95/15, Cabinet Committee on the Reception and Accommodation of Refugees minutes, December 31, 1942. The committee had originally been on "Jewish Refugees," but at the insistence of the colonial secretary, the word "Jewish" was deleted at the committee's first meeting. Ibid., Cabinet committee minutes, January 9, 1943; PRO, FO 371, File 36649, Randall to Dominions Office, January 12, 1943.

3. PAC, PCO, Vol. 49, File W36, Robertson to King, January 20, 1943; PAC, IR, File 673931, Robertson to Blair, January 20, 1943; ibid., Blair to Robertson, January 21, 1943.

4. IR, File 673931, Blair to Crerar, January 21, 1943; PCO, Vol. 49, File W36, A. D. P. Heeney to Cabinet War Committee, January 26, 1943.

5. PCO, Vol. 49, File W36, Cabinet War Committee meeting minutes, January 27, 1943; Canadian Institute of Public Opinion, News release, January 27, 1943.

6. PRO, FO 371, File 607, British Foreign Office to British Ambassador, Washington, January 15, 1943; *FRUS*, 1943, 1, British Embassy, Washington, to State Department, January 20, 1943.

7. Bernard Wasserstein, *Britain and the Jews of Europe, 1934–1945* (London, 1979), 185; PCO, Vol. 49, File W36, Dominions Office to External Affairs, February 20, 1943.

8. PCO, Vol. 49, File W36, Hull to British Embassy, Washington, February 25, 1943, copy.

9. *FRUS*, 1943, 1, Wells to Matthews, March 6, 1943; PCO, Vol. 49, File W36, Pearson to Robertson, March 3, 1943; ibid., Dominions Office to External Affairs, March 4, 1943; ibid., External Affairs to Dominions Office, March 6, 1943.

10. PCO, Vol. 49, File W36, Pearson to Robertson, March 5, 1943.

11. Ibid., Dominions Office to External Affairs, March 6, 1943; PRO, FO 371, File 36654, Minute, March 7, 1943, 3661.

12. PRO, FO 371, File 36654, Randall, Minute, March 8, 1943, 3924; Toronto *Globe and Mail*, March 4, 1943; PAC, KPC, Cabinet War Committee, March 5, 1943, vol. 425; PRO, FO 371, File 36655, McDonald to Foreign Office, March 9, 1943, 4511.

13. *New York Times*, March 2, 1943.

14. DEA, File 5059-40C, Victor Odlum to Keenleyside, March 2, 1943.

15. CJC, UJRA, File 231, Hayes to Bronfman, March 5, 1943.

16. UJRA, File 237, Drafts of program, March 9, 1943.

17. CJC, CJCP, Minutes of meeting, March 9, 1943.

18. UJRA, File 231, Hayes to Robertson, March 11, 1943; ibid., March 12, 1943.

19. FNA, IRO, Box 27, AJ43, Extract of letter from Boyd-Shannon to Dominions Office, March 13, 1943.

20. New York *Der Tag*, March 9, 1943 (our translation); UJRA, File 231, Hayes to editor, *Der Tag*, March 12, 1943.

21. PCO, Vol. 49, File W36, MacDonald to Robertson, March 13, 1943; ibid., Robertson to MacDonald, March 13, 1943; ibid., Pearson to King, March 10, 1943; IRO, Box 37, AJ43, Taylor to Foreign Office, March 17, 1943.

22. IR, File 673931, Robertson to Blair, March 19, 1943; ibid., Blair to Robertson, March 22, 1943.

23. PRO, PREM, 4, 5113, British Embassy, Washington, to Foreign Office, March 22, 1943.

24. PCO, Vol. 49, File W36, Pearson to Robertson, March 22, 1943; *House of Commons Debates*, March 4, 1943, 953-4; ibid., March 9, 1947, 1076; PCO, Vol. 49, File W36, Cabinet War Committee, March 25, 1943.

25. Franklin D. Roosevelt Library, Franklin D. Roosevelt Papers, OF 3186-1, Hull to Roosevelt, March 23, 1943.

26. *FRUS*, 1943, 111, Note on communication by Harry Hopkins, 38-9.

27. UJRA, File 231, Hayes, Memorandum of phone conversation with Bennett, March 18, 1943.

28. Ibid., Wilson to Hayes, March 23, 1943; ibid., Hayes to Aronovitch, March 29, 1943; ibid., Sadowski to Hayes, March 29, 1943; ibid., Robertson to Hayes, March 30, 1943.

29. CJCP, Hayes, Memorandum, April 1, 1943.

30. Ibid., Hayes to Bronfman, March 31, 1943; UJRA, File 231, Hayes to Rosenberg, March 31, 1943.

31. *Saturday Night*, March 20, 1943.

32. *Winnipeg Free Press*, April 3, 1943.

33. CJCP, Rosenberg to Hayes, April 8, 1943.

34. UJRA, File 231, Hayes, Memorandum on interview with leaders of American Jewish organizations, April 12, 1943.

35. Ibid.

36. Ibid., Hayes to community leaders, April 12, 1943.

37. Ibid., Hayes to CNCR, April 12, 1943.

38. PAC, CNCR, Vol. 5, Memorandum to Prime Minister, April 14, 1943.

39. CJCP, Hayes to Bronfman, April 15, 1943; IR, File 673931, Bronfman to King, April 15, 1943.

40. UJRA, File 231, Sadowski to Hayes, April 17, 1943.

41. Interview with Saul Hayes; UJRA, File 231, Wilson to Hayes, April 24, 1943; CJCP, Hayes, Memorandum, April 19, 1943.

42. PRO, FO 371, File 36656, Cabinet War Committee minutes, April 1, 1943; Montreal *Le Devoir*, April 22, 1943; PCO, Vol. 49, File W36, Dominions Office to King, April 8, 1943.

43. PRO, FO, 371, File 36658, A. Randall, Minutes, April 6, 1943; see, also, Wasserstein, *Britain and the Jews*; Henry L. Feingold, *The Politics of Rescue: The Roosevelt Administration and the Holocaust* (New Brunswick, N.J., 1970); and Monty N. Penkower, "The Bermuda Conference and Its Aftermath: An Allied Quest for 'Refuge' During the Holocaust," *Prologue: Journal of the National Archives* 13, no. 3 (Fall 1981), 145–73.

44. PRO, FO 371, File 36060, Law to Eden, April 21, 1943, 6566.

45. PCO, Vol. 49, File W36, Dominions Office to King, May 11, 1943; PRO, PREM, 4/51/3, U.K. delegate to Eden, June 28, 1943; PCO, Dominions Office to King, April 27, 1943.

46. UJRA, File 231, Robertson to Bronfman, May 7, 1943; *New York Times*, May 7, 1943.

47. IR, File 623931, Blair to Gray, May 10, 1943.

48. IR, File 673931, Blair to G. Stirling, May 27, 1943.

49. UJRA, File 231, Caiserman to Hayes, May 10, 1943; see, also, ibid., Rome to Hayes, May 27, 1943; ibid., Hayes, Memorandum, May 11, 1943; ibid., Hayes to Sadowski, May 13, 1943.

50. Ibid., Sadowski to Hayes, May 14, 1943; CJCP, Meeting of Dominion Council, Eastern Division, May 19, 1943.

51. UJRA, File 231, Hayes to Sadowski, May 17, 1943.

52. Ibid., Hayes to Gurber, May 17, 1943; ibid., Draft "A", Hayes to Robertson, May 17, 1943, letter not sent.

53. Ibid., Bronfman to Robertson, May 20, 1943; CJCP, Robertson to Hayes, May 24, 1943.

54. Quoted in L. de Jong, *Het Koninkrijk der Nederlanden in de Tweede Oorlog*, deel 9, *London* (Den Haag, 1979), 546. (We are grateful to Michael Horn for bringing this reference to our attention and for translating it from Dutch.)

55. Roosevelt Papers, OF 3186–4, Roosevelt to Hull, May 14, 1943; PCO, Vol. 49, File W36, Dominions Office to King, May 29, 1943; PRO, Colonial Office Records 733/449 (76028/2), Extract from Cabinet minutes, May 10, 1943.

6 / In the Free and Civilized World

1. DEA, File 5127–40C, Robert Law to Eden, June 28, 1943.

2. PAC, IR, File 673931, Blair to Robertson, June 5, 1943.

3. "An Eye Witness Account from Poland," *Jewish Frontier*, March 1943, 15.

4. CJC, CJCP, Memorandum on Bermuda Conference, May 11, 1943; Toronto *Hebrew Journal*, April 29, 1943.

5. Toronto *Hebrew Journal*, April 17, 1943.

6. IR, File 673931, Blair, Memorandum for file, June 5, 1943; Toronto *Hebrew Journal*, June 7, 1943.

7. IR, File 673931, Blair to Robertson, June 5, 1943.

8. Ibid., Wrong to Jack Pickersgill, June 23, 1943.

9. *House of Commons Debates*, May 27, 1943, 3067; ibid., July 1, 1943, 4233.

10. CJCP, Jewish Telegraphic Agency News, June 28, 1943.

11. IR, File 673931, Memorandum for file, June 8, 1943.

12. DEA, File 5127-40C, Memorandum for Heeney, July 2, 1943.

13. Ibid., Wrong to J. Pickersgill, June 23, 1943; ibid., Wrong to Brooke Claxton, June 28, 1943.

14. PAC, KPC, Minutes of Cabinet War Committee, July 7, 1943, c4875; PAC, PCO, File W38, Memo for War Committee draft statement on refugees, July 6, 1943.

15. *Debates*, July 9, 1943, 4558-61.

16. Ibid., July 9, 1943, 4612; ibid., July 9, 1943, 4569-70; ibid., July 12, 1943, 4654-7.

17. Ibid., July 12, 1943, 4654-7.

18. CJCP, Hayes, Latest report on sphere of operations of the Joint Distribution Committee, October 8, 1943, 4.

19. CJC, UJRA, File 200, A. Leon Kubowitzski to S. Levine, August 18, 1943.

20. Ibid., Hayes to Crerar, July 26, 1943.

21. Interview with M. Scobie; interviews with Saul Hayes and Constance Hayward; *Saturday Night*, February 28, 1950.

22. IR, File 673931, Jolliffe, Memorandum for file, August 19, 1943.

23. DEA, File 5127-40C, Notes on refugees, August 28, 1943; IR, File 673931, Jolliffe, Memorandum for file, August 30, 1943; PAC, EA, Box 2112, Suggestions for Canadian aid to refugees, August 30, 1943.

24. PAC, KP, Cabinet War Committee, September 8, 1943, vol. 425; DEA, File 5127-40C, Canadian aid to refugees, September 8, 1943; IR, File 673931, Memorandum for file, Jolliffe, September 10, 1943; DEA, File 5127-40C, Wrong to Robertson, September 15, 1943; ibid., Secretary of State for External Affairs to Massey, September 28, 1943.

25. DEA, File 5127-40C, Jolliffe to Wrong, November 2, 1943.

26. King Diary, February 13, 1944.

27. PAC, Samuel Jacob Zacks Papers, Louis Rosenberg to Zacks, July 19, 1943.

28. CJCP, Hayward to CNCR, Winnipeg, July 6, 1943.

29. *Toronto Daily Star*, November 27, 1943.

30. *Winnipeg Free Press*, November 27, 1943.

31. UJRA, File 200, James H. Gray to Rosenberg, August 12, 1943.

32. Alberta *Hanna Herald*, June 10, 1943; *Sarnia Observer*, November 24, 1943; *Simcoe Reformer*, December 22, 1943.

33. UJRA, File 231A, Rosenberg to Hayes, November 22, 1943; *Toronto Telegram*, November 26, 1943; *Fort William Times-Journal*, November 26, 1943; *Victoria Colonist*, November 26, 1943; *Sault Ste. Marie Star*, November 26, 1943; *Canadian Veteran*, November 30, 1943.

34. CJCP, Hayes, Memorandum, November 25, 1943.

35. *Winnipeg Tribune*, January 27, 1943; PAC, CNCR, Vol. 6, Gallup Poll clipping; NA, Foreign Service Posts Records, RG 84, File 800, Ottawa, 1944, Political Reports, 48-9.

36. PCO, Vol. 49, File W-34-2-S, War Information Board Survey, no. 30, February 12, 1944.

37. IR, File 673931, Blair to Pratt, June 18, 1943.

38. *Montreal Star*, November 8, 1943; *L'Evénement Journal de Québec*, November 8, 1943; Montreal *Le Devoir*, November 8, 1943; *L'Action Catholique de Québec*, November 6, 1943.

39. *L'Evénement Journal de Québec*, November 9, 1943; *Montreal Herald*, November 9, 1943; *Montreal Star*, November 9, 1943; Montreal *Le Canada*, November 9, 1943; *Sherbrooke Tribune*, November 9, 1943; Montreal *La Patrie*, November 9, 1943; Toronto *Hebrew Journal*, November 10, 1943; *Jewish Post*, November 18, 1943; *Jewish Daily Eagle*, November 17, 1943.

40. Toronto *Hebrew Journal*, November 10, 1943.

41. JIAS(T), File 666, Solkin to J. L. Atkins, November 8, 1943.

42. IR, File 673931, HICEM-ICA, New York, to James Bernstein, December 4, 1943; UJRA, File 23, Roland Aubuchon to CJC, November 18, 1943.

43. Foreign Service Posts Records, RG 84, File 800, Ottawa, 1944, Political Reports, 20; *Montreal Gazette*, January 5, 1944; UJRA, File 23, Roland Aubuchon to CJC, November 18, 1943.

44. *Liberty*, November 1943; *Fort William Times-Journal*, November 19, 1943; *Montreal Star*, November 29, 1943; see, also, Watson Thomson, "Our Inhumanity to Man," *National Home Monthly* 44, no. 10 (October 1943), 13, 32, 34, 66.

45. IR, File 673931, Cormier to Michael Eveswell, October 28, 1943; JIAS, File 22380, Solkin to JIAS officers, November 4, 1943; UJRA, File 224, UJRA, Press release, November, 1943; IR, File 673931, Jolliffe, Memorandum for file, November 18, 1943; ibid., Jolliffe, Memorandum for file, November 18, 1943.

46. IR, File 673931, Cormier to Jolliffe, November 30, 1943.

47. JIAS, File 22380, Ilja Dijour to Solkin, November 19, 1943; CNCR, Vol. 6, Jolliffe to Hayward, November 22, 1943; EA, Box 2112, Jolliffe to Wrong, December 29, 1943.

48. IR, File 673931, Jolliffe, Memorandum to file, January 11, 1944; CJCP, Hayes, Memorandum, January 11, 1944; JDC, Canada Emigra-

tion File, Memorandum re: Emigration to Canada, January 12, 1944.

49. CJCP, Memorandum of telephone conversation, Hayes with Jolliffe, February 10, 1944.

50. JDC, Canada Emigration File, JDC, Lisbon, to JDC, New York, February 18, 1944; EA, Box 2112, Ritchie to Robertson, January 19, 1944.

51. JIAS, File 22380, Ilja Dijour to Solkin, November 15, 1943; JDC, Canada Emigration File, JDC, Lisbon, Memorandum to file, November 10, 1943; UJRA, File 244, Memorandum of telephone conversation, Hayes with Jolliffe, November 22, 1943; YIVO, HIAS, Solkin to Ilja Dijour, November 16, 1943.

52. CJCP, Memorandum of telephone conversation, Hayes with Jolliffe, February 10, 1944.

53. FNA, IRO, Box 45, File 102/336, Schwartz to Emerson, January 17, 1944; ibid., Emerson to Ritchie, January 17, 1944; ibid., Ritchie to Emerson, February 14, 1944; EA, Box 2112, Ritchie to Robertson, January 19, 1944; IR, File 673931, Robertson to Massey, February 7, 1944..

54. JIAS, File 22430, Schwartz to Hayes, March 24, 1944; ibid., Hayes to UJRA officers, March, 1944; ibid., Donald Hurwitz to Leavitt, March 10, 1944; IR, File 673931, Jolliffe, Memorandum to file, April 7, 1944; ibid., Jolliffe to Wrong, May 4, 1944.

55. JIAS, File 22380, Solkin to Ilja Dijour, March 8, 1944.

56. JIAS(T), File 749, Solkin to Kraicer, March 27, 1944.

57. *Montreal Gazette*, April 7, 1944.

58. IR, File 673931, Hayes to Jolliffe, April 11, 1944.

59. CJCP, Maria Lewy to Bernstein, July 9, 1944.

60. *New York Times*, June 1, 1944; *New York Herald Tribune*, June 1, 1944.

61. *Philadelphia Record*, October 2, 1944.

62. *Moncton Transcript*, March 27, 1944.

63. DEA, File 5127-40C, Wrong to Robertson, December 1, 1944; IR, File 673931, S. W. Wood to Jolliffe, December 29, 1944; ibid., Robertson to Jolliffe, January 3, 1945; ibid., Jolliffe to Robertson, January 11, 1945; ibid., Wood to Jolliffe, February 7, 1945.

64. JIAS, File 22380, Solkin to A. L. Shluger, March 28, 1944; IR, File 673931, Jolliffe to Robertson, February 23, 1944.

65. IR, File 673931, Jolliffe, Memorandum to file, August 4, 1944; ibid., Jolliffe to Cormier, August 7, 1944; JIAS(T), File 792, Solkin to Kraicer, September 6, 1944; IR, File 673931, Jolliffe to Robertson, October 4, 1944.

66. IR, File 673931, Dr. Edith Steinback-Berger to Mrs. Alex Stiel, April 14, 1944, copy of censored wartime correspondence.

67. JDC, Canada Emigration File, Rosenberg to Hyman, May 27, 1944; IR, File 673931, Sigmund Thichtal to Herman Lewy, November 3, 1944; ibid., Ilse Marle to Mrs. Adolph Hochstim, April 16, 1944.

68. JIAS, File 22380, Solkin to Ilja Dijour, May 10, 1944; JDC, Canada Emigration File, Leavitt to Rosenberg, June 12, 1944.

69. IR, File 673931, E. Bula to Mrs. P. J. Bula, November 10, 1944.

70. DEA, File 4637-40C-W, Secretary of State for Dominion Affairs to Secretary of State for External Affairs, March 13, 1944.

71. Ibid., Robertson to Pearson, March 17, 1944; ibid., Pearson to Robertson, March 22, 1944; *New York Times*, March 25, 1944; DEA, File 4637-40C-W, Secretary of State for Dominion Affairs to Secretary of State for External Affairs, March 24, 1944.

72. DEA, File 4637-40C-W, Memorandum for Prime Minister, March 23, 1944; see, also, IR, File 673931, Statement for the Prime Minister on refugees, March 22, 1944; Franklin D. Roosevelt Library, Franklin D. Roosevelt Papers, Myron Taylor, Memorandum re: Bermuda Conference and the IGC, February 22, 1944; EA, Box 2112, Ritchie to Robertson, January 19, 1944.

73. HIAS, Solkin to Ilja Dijour, March 21, 1944.

74. EA, Box 2112, Ritchie to Robertson, January 19, 1944; see, also, R.L. Braham, *The Politics of Genocide: The Holocaust in Hungary*, 2 vols. (New York, 1981).

75. CJCP, Saul Hayes to CJC and UJRA executive members, June 26, 1944; PAC, Archie Bennett Papers, Hayes to A. Bennett, August 23, 1944.

76. PCO, File W38, Secretary of State for Dominion Affairs to Secretary of State for External Affairs, June 3, 1944; ibid., June 15, 1944; ibid., July 20, 1944.

77. PRO, Cabinet Records 95/15, Cabinet War Committee to U.S. State Department, July 22, 1944, 201.

78. IR, File 673931, Secretary of State for Dominion Affairs to Secretary of State for External Affairs, August 5, 1944.

79. PCO, Secretary of State for Dominion Affairs to Secretary of State for External Affairs, August 11, 1944; ibid., August 17, 1944; IR, File 673931, Secretary of State for Dominion Affairs to Secretary of State for External Affairs, August 18, 1944.

80. IR, File 673931, Lewis Clark to King, August 14, 1944.

81. Ibid., Bronfman to Robertson, August 15, 1944.

82. PRO, Dominions Office Records, File 121/14, Minutes, High Commissioners meeting, August 10, 1944.

83. KPC, Hume Wrong for Cabinet War Committee, Memorandum re: asylum for Jews released from Hungary, August 23, 1944, vol. 427; IR, File 673931, Jolliffe, Memorandum for file, August 23, 1944.

84. PCO, Wrong to A. D. P. Heeney, August 23, 1944.

85. KPC, Cabinet War Committee Minutes, August 31, 1944, vol. 425.

86. PRO, Cabinet Records 45/15, Minutes of refugee committee, October 23, 1944, 213.

87. PRO, FO 371, File 42746, A. W. G. Randall, Minute on file, January 11, 1944, 456.

88. PRO, FO 371, File 42747, Boyd Shannon to A. W. G. Randall, March 9, 1944, 3022.

89. PRO, Dominions Office Records, File 35/1518, WF213/58, Dominions Office to British High Commissioner to Canada, January 27, 1944; ibid., British High Commissioner to Canada to Dominions Office; IR, File 673931, Malcolm MacDonald to Robertson, January 28, 1944.

90. IR, File 673931, Robertson to Jolliffe, February 11, 1944.

91. Ibid., Secretary of State for External Affairs to Massey, August 14, 1944.

92. KP, Cabinet War Committee Minutes, April 12, 1944, vol. 425; IR, Orders-in-Council, A. D. P. Heeney to Crerar, April 14, 1944; ibid., A. D. P. Heeney to Crerar, April 28, 1944.

93. KPC, A. D. P. Heeney to Cabinet War Committee, August 9, 1944, vol. 427.

94. EA, Box 2112, Wrong to Massey, May 3, 1944; ibid., Robertson to Massey, February 6, 1945.

95. Central Zionist Archives, File 24/14739, A. Freiman to Weizmann, March 31, 1944; IRO, Box 14, AJ43, J. Bernstein to Emerson, April 23, 1944.

96. King Diary, March 31, 1944.

97. Central Zionist Archives, File 24/14734, Weizmann to Massey, May 22, 1944. The Canadian embassy in Moscow also advised Ottawa that emigration by Jews in Poland, Russia or other liberated territories was not only their wish but, directly or indirectly, supported by the authorities, many of whom might want to be rid of their remaining Jews. DEA, File 58-E(S), L. D. Wilgress to Secretary of State for External Affairs, February 7, 1945.

98. JIAS, File 22427, Solkin to Kraicer, November 16, 1944.

99. See, for example, Martin Gilbert, *The Allies and Auschwitz* (London, 1981), and Walter Laquer, *The Terrible Secret* (London, 1980).

100. EA, Box 2112, Ritchie to Robertson, January 19, 1944.

101. DEA, File 58-E(S), Foreign Office Research Department, "The Jews of Poland," May 5, 1944.

102. DEA, File 4079-E-40, Report of Extraordinary Polish-Soviet Commission on German Atrocities, 8.

103. Ibid., Pearson to Secretary of State for External Affairs, December 5, 1944.

105. *Washington Post*, December 3, 1944.

106. CJCP, Raymond Davies to *Jewish Eagle*, August 29, 1944.

107. IR, File 673931, Memorandum for the Prime Minister, February 2, 1945.

7/One Wailing Cry

1. CJC, CJCP, William Keller to Caiserman, May 11, 1945; ibid., S. Levine to William Keller, May 16, 1945.
2. JIAS(T), File 1672, Sarah Szklarska to Alter Zimmerman, October 30, 1945 (our translation).
3. JIAS(T), File 1664, Icchok Lieberman to aunt, November 6, 1946 (our translation).
4. JIAS(T), File 1165, Szdek Goldrich and Hershel Lejb Blatt to Abraham Isaac, November 10, 1946 (our translation).
5. Ibid., Simon Grobman to Maurice Ezrin, July 22, 1945.
6. For a discussion of numbers of displaced persons and the initial problems of mass relief, see Malcolm J. Proudfoot, *European Refugees: 1939–1952* (Evanston, 1956), 158–88, 318–68.
7. DEA, File 1426–P–40C, Vanier to Secretary of State for External Affairs, April 20, 1945; ibid., Vanier to King, April 27, 1945.
8. Ibid., Vanier, "Buchenwald Concentration Camp," CBC transcript, May 1, 1945; Robert Speaight, *Vanier: Soldier, Diplomat and Governor General* (Toronto, 1970), 317.
9. DEA, File 1426–P–40C, Massey to Secretary of State for External Affairs, May 7, 1945.
10. For an overview of this era of economic growth, see *Royal Commission on Canada's Economic Prospects, Final Report* (Ottawa, 1958), 75–90.
11. PAC, PCO, Memorandum re: immigration, September 5, 1945.
12. Interview with James Gibson.
13. PAC, IR, File 376333, Jolliffe to Under-Secretary of State for External Affairs, October 2, 1945.
14. IR, Orders-in-Council, Memorandum to Cabinet re: immigration policy, September 5, 1945.
15. PAC, KP, Cabinet minutes, October 2, 1945, vol. 419.
16. IR, File 376333, Jolliffe to Under-Secretary of State for External Affairs, October 2, 1945.
17. CJC, UJRA, File 300, Hayes telephone interview with Jolliffe, May 21, 1945.
18. IR, File 673931, Jolliffe to Glen, July 17, 1945; IR, File 962419, Jolliffe to Glen, October 11, 1945.
19. DEA, File 4626–40, Memorandum to Cabinet on disposition of refugees in Canada, October 15, 1945.
20. IR, Orders-in-Council, Cabinet Committee on immigration policy minutes, October 18, 1945.
21. PAC, EA, Box 2112, Wrong to Massey, November 7, 1945.
22. PRO, Cabinet Records 95/15, Cabinet War Committee on Reception and Accommodation of Refugees, October 3, 1945, 64.
23. PRO, FO 371, File 57783, Aide memoire, August 19, 1946.

24. IR, File 673931, Wrong to Glen, August 19, 1946. The British Foreign Office was disappointed but not surprised by the Canadian response. A Foreign Office official summed up the Canadian position: "It is obvious . . . that Canada still intends to stick to the policy of 'selective immigration' and does not intend to admit DP's en bloc"; and in a report to the British Prime Minister's Office, an official in the German Department of the Foreign Office pointed out that approaches to the Dominions, including Canada, "to help us out of our difficulties with refugees . . . have been almost completely barren." PRO, FO 371, File 57783, A. Walsh, Minutes, September 10, 1946; PRO FO 371, File 57778, FO German Department, Southern Department, to PMO, November 29, 1946.

25. PRO, FO 371, File 57700, A. Rive to Eric Machtig, January 18, 1946, 208.

26. EA, Box 2112, Memorandum, January 3, 1946.

27. Proudfoot, *European Refugees*, 293.

28. PAC, PCO, Box 287, Pearson to Secretary of State for External Affairs, May 31, 1946.

29. Ibid., Wrong to Pearson, June 3, 1946.

30. Ibid., Pearson to Secretary of State for External Affairs, June 4, 1946; ibid., Wrong to Pearson, June 7, 1946.

31. Ibid., R. C. Riddell to Wrong, June 13, 1946.

32. Ibid., Robertson to Turgeon, April 4, 1946; ibid., Robertson to Turgeon, July 8, 1946.

33. PAC, KPC, Minutes of Cabinet, August 12, 1946, vol. 419; IR, Orders-in Council, A. D. P. Heeney to Glen, September 11, 1946.

34. JIAS(T), File 193, Solkin to Kraicer, June 19, 1945.

35. CJCP, Hayes, Memorandum of interview with Cairine Wilson and Constance Hayward, June 9, 1945.

36. UJRA, File 300, Hayes to Wilson, August 29, 1945.

37. IR, File 673931, Jolliffe to Glen, October 12, 1945.

38. Ibid., Jolliffe to Hayes, October 22, 1945.

39. CJCP, Hayes, Report on immigration of refugees into Canada, 1946.

40. IR, File 673931, Jolliffe to Wrong, November 10, 1945; JIAS, File 22672, Hayes to committee, January 25, 1946; ibid., Wilson to Glen, January 21, 1946; IR, File 673931, Bronfman to Glen, February 20, 1946.

41. IR, File 673931, Vanier to Secretary of State for External Affairs, March 9, 1946.

42. EA, Box 2112, Robertson to Jolliffe, February 6, 1946; IR, File 673931, Pope to Secretary of State for External Affairs, March 11, 1946.

43. IR, File 673931, S. Morley Scott, "The Admission of European Refugees to Canada," March 10, 1946.

44. Ibid., Massey to Secretary of State for External Affairs, April 5,

1946; see, also, FNA, IRO, Box 35, AJ43, R. Morris Wilson to Massey, March 10, 1946.

45. IR, File 673931, Interdepartmental Committee on Immigration minutes, March 13, 1946.

46. KP, Preliminary report of interdepartmental report on immigration policy, April 4, 1946, vol. 281; ibid., Memorandum to Cabinet on immigration policy, April 30, 1946, vol. 420.

47. PAC, CNCR, Vol. 5, King to Cairine Wilson, May 6, 1946; UJRA, File 300, Hayes to Hayward, May 10, 1946.

48. Hayes warned Solkin and other Jewish Immigrant Aid Society officials: "It is essential that no publicity issue on matters pertaining to the forthcoming Order-in-Council or matters in which we are mutually concerned." Solkin assured him that the society's head office would keep "the whole matter in strict confidence," although he was distressed that he had heard rumours of government plans from several other quarters: "There is," he said, "some leakage somewhere." JIAS, File 22672, Hayes to Solkin, May 20, 1946; ibid., Solkin to Hayes, May 21, 1946.

49. *House of Commons Debates*, May 28, 1946, 1978–9.

50. Multicultural History Society of Ontario, Joshua, Gershman Papers, Correspondence File 9, Hayes to friend, June 7, 1946.

51. This was not the first effort by the British to dispose of their Polish charges. In April 1945 the British consulted the Dominions on simply granting selected Polish citizens, then in Britain, British status. This would allow them access to Commonwealth countries as British subjects, and Canadian authorities estimated that between three and five hundred Poles might eventually move to Canada under this plan. Poles, the Canadian government decided, were not the problem that other groups might be: "These refugees are mostly in the professional classes and practically all Roman Catholics by religion. Some have considerable savings and might wish to remain in this country indefinitely or at least until it would be safe for them to return to Poland." KPC, A. D. P. Heeney, Memorandum re: admission to Canada of Polish refugees, April 10, 1945, vol. 427.

52. EA, File 5127-EA-40, Massey to Secretary of State for External Affairs, April 24, 1946.

53. PRO, Dominions Office Records, 121/15, Record of meeting between Secretary of State for Dominion Affairs and the High Commissioner, April 12, 1946.

54. KPC, A. D. P. Heeney, Memorandum for Cabinet re: wood and agricultural labour, May 21, 1946, vol. 420; KP, Cabinet minutes, May 29, 1946, vol. 419; KPC, A. D. P. Heeney, Memorandum, July 11, 1946, vol. 429; ibid., Cabinet minutes, July 16, 1946, vol. 419; Polish Research Institute, Military Records, Chief of Staff, Resettlement, Section, File A.XII.66/14.

55. *Jewish Post* (Indianapolis, Ind.), November 20, 1946.

56. IRO, Box 321, File 542, Director UNRRA Team 806 to Central Jewish Committee, July 27, 1946; ibid., Canadian Military Mission, Berlin, Memorandum re: emigration from Germany to Canada, August 17, 1946.

57. IRO, Box 35, File 43, Jolliffe to J. Cheetham, August 14, 1946; ibid., P. T. Molson to L. Dow, August 19, 1946.

58. EA, File 5127-EA-40, Vanier to External Affairs, August 27, 1946; see, also, Gerald Dirks, *Canada's Refugee Policy: Indifference or Opportunism?* (Montreal, 1977), 142-6.

59. IR, File 673931, Wrong to Jolliffe, August 30, 1946.

60. KPC, Memorandum to Cabinet re: refugees, October 12, 1946, vol. 420.

61. Ibid., Cabinet minutes, October 15, 1946, vol. 419.

62. Ibid., Cabinet minutes, October 29, 1946, vol. 419; IR, File 673931, External Affairs to Canadian Military Mission, Berlin, October 19, 1946.

63. IR, File 673931, Jolliffe to Robertson, October 16, 1946.

64. UJRA, File 300, Hayes to Glen, July 17, 1946; see, also, ibid., Bronfman to King, January 29, 1947.

65. KPC, R. G. Robertson to King, February 1, 1947, vol. 281; ibid., Cabinet minutes, Report from Cabinet Committee on immigration policy, January 20, 1947; vol. 420; IR, File 541782, Bronfman to Glen, February 13, 1947; UJRA, File 300, Hayes to G. H. Robertson, November, 1946, draft.

66. CJCP, Hayes to CJC national executive, February 10, 1947.

67. King Diary, February 7, 1947.

68. IR, File 673931, Col. S. M. Scott, Memorandum re: movement of displaced persons to Canada, November 4, 1946, appended to: Pope to Secretary of State for External Affairs, November 8, 1946.

69. IR, File 673931, P. T. Molson to Massey, December 3, 1946.

70. Ibid., Extract of letter by M. C. Bordest, November, 1946.

71. EA, Box 2113, J. W. P. Thompson to Scott, November 18, 1946.

72. KP, Brooke Claxton to King, April 20, 1946, c195216.

73. Ibid., Grant to Claxton, January 20, 1946, c195217-20.

74. King Diary, February 20, 1946. The continued virulence of anti-Semitism in the postwar era was equally strong in the United States. See Leonard Dinnerstein, "Anti-Semitism Exposed and Attacked, 1945-1950," *American Jewish History* LXXI, no. 1 (1981), 134-49.

75. *London Free Press*, May 31, 1946.

76. IR, File 673931, Excerpt from J. S. Duncan to Rotary Club, Montreal, December 4, 1945; ibid., Excerpt from R. S. Waldie to Imperial Bank of Canada, n.d.; ibid., Excerpt from D. E. Kligour to Bank of Canada, n.d.

77. Ibid., Excerpt from T. A. Crerar to Canadian Senate, May 4, 1946.

78. UJRA, File 300, Louis Rosenberg to Hayes, March 15, 1946.

79. *Proceedings of the Standing Committee on Immigration and Labour*, no. 6 (Ottawa, 1946), 169–83.

80. UNA, Canada File, OVIAL Series, Box 22, File 302, Jewish Telegraphic Agency News, July 7, 1946.

81. Canadian Institute of Public Opinion, Public Opinion News Service Release, April 25, 1946.

82. Canadian Institute of Public Opinion, Public Opinion News Service Release, October 30, 1946. The results in full were:

Japanese:	60%	Middle European:	16%
Jewish:	49	Ukrainian:	15
German:	34	Polish:	14
Russian:	33	Others:	3
Negro:	31	None:	18
Italian:	25	No Answer:	3
Chinese:	24		

83. Quebec City *Chronicle Telegraph*, September 3, 1946; Toronto *Globe and Mail*, July 23, 1946; *Montreal Gazette*, August 29, 1946.

84. *Vancouver Sun*, July 27, 1946.

85. *Ottawa Citizen*, August 29, 1946.

86. Brockville *Recorder and Times*, August 30, 1946.

87. Jewish Labor Committee, Vol. 16, Hayes, Memorandum re: press opinion on immigration, October 3, 1946.

88. Ibid., Hayes, Memorandum re: press opinion on immigration, November 8, 1946. The American chargé d'affaires in Ottawa, Julian Harrington, captured the spirit of French-Canadian sentiment regarding any relaxing of restraints on immigration to Canada: "The French Canadians, as might be expected, not wishing to jeopardize their hope that in the next 25 years or so they will become the majority, have not openly favored further immigration except of a small number for humanitarian reasons." NA, RG 84, File 800, J. Harrington to Secretary of State, February 8, 1947.

89. PAC, DOL, Box 275, File 1-26-3-1, MacNamara to Glen, December 9, 1946.

90. DOL, Box 272, File 1-26-1-1, F. W. Smelts to MacNamara, December 16, 1946.

91. IR, File 673931, Hayes to Glen, March 4, 1946.

92. UJRA, File 300, Jewish Labor Committee to CJC, July 11, 1946.

93. IR, File 673931, CJC to King, July 17, 1946.

94. Central Zionist Archives, Political Palestine Papers: Canada, File 24/10.186, Message from Samuel Bronfman, 1947.

8/A Pleasant Voyage

1. PAC, IR, File 673937, pt. 17, Text of talk, April 19, 1948.
2. PAC, KPC, Cabinet Conclusions, April 21, 1948, vol. 419.

3. Interview with Hugh Keenleyside.

4. FNA, IRO, Box 76, AJ1765, McGowan to R. Innes, February 17, 1947.

5. King Diary, February 12, 1947.

6. Interview with Hugh Keenleyside.

7. KPC, Cabinet Minutes, October 2, 1945, vol. 419.

8. King Diary, January 23, 1947.

9. Ibid., February 13, 1947.

10. PAC, PCO, A. D. P. Heeney to R. G. Robertson, February 13, 1947; ibid., A. D. P. Heeney to Glen, February 14, 1947.

11. KPC, Cabinet Conclusions, March 17, 1947, vol. 419; IR, Orders-in-Council, Minutes, Cabinet Committee on Immigration Policy, March 20, 1947; KPC, Cabinet Conclusions, March 21, 1947, vol. 419; ibid., "Canadian Immigration Policy," March 20, 1947, vol. 421; ibid., Cabinet Conclusions, March 26, 1947, vol. 419; ibid., Cabinet Conclusions, April 16, 1947, vol. 419; ibid., "Canadian Immigration Policy," April 23, 1947, vol. 421; ibid., Cabinet Conclusions, May 1, 1947, vol. 419; *House of Commons Debates*, May 1, 1947, 2644–47.

12. NA, RG 84, File 800, Julian Harrington to Secretary of State, May 2, 1947.

13. *Montreal Gazette*, May 2, 1947; *Montreal Star*, May 2, 1947.

14. IR, File 541782, Bronfman to Glen, February 13, 1947; ibid., Hayes to G. H. Robertson, November, 1946, draft.

15. *Proceedings of the Standing Committee on Immigration and Labour*, no. 6 (Ottawa, 1946).

16. IRO, Box 79, AJ46, File 1529/28, IGC, Memorandum for file, October 21, 1946; ibid., Box 35, AJ43, Bickle to R. Innes, February 10, 1947; ibid., Box 79, AJ46, File 1529/28, R. Innes to IGC representatives, November 21, 1946; JCA(L), Box 947/1787, S. Belkin to JCA, New York, April 14, 1947.

17. IRO, Box 35, AJ43, M. Lush to Emerson, March 24, 1947; ibid., Box 36, AJ44, File 1519/76, Chief of Field Operations to Emerson, March 26, 1947.

18. IRO, Box 35, AJ43, File 1519/76, M. Lush to Dow, March 22, 1947; ibid., M. Lush to R. Innes, March 26, 1947.

19. KPC, Cabinet Conclusions, March 27, 1947, vol. 419; ibid., Cabinet Conclusions, April 23, 1947, vol. 419.

20. IRO, Box 35, AJ43, Colley to R. Innes, May 28, 1947.

21. NA, RG 84, File 800, Julian Harrington to Secretary of State, August 26, 1947.

22. IRO, Box 35, AJ43, Colley to R. Innes, May 9, 1947.

23. UNA, Bureau of Service, Displaced Persons Division, Tracing Series, Box 2230, UNRRA paper, T. J. Keenan to Molly Flynn, March 4, 1947.

24. Canadian Institute of Public Opinion, Public Opinion News Service Release, August 2, 1947; NA, RG 84, File 800, Montreal Con-

sular Report, 1947; Alan G. Green, *Immigration and the Postwar Canadian Economy* (Toronto, 1976), 25; PCO, H. Mitchell to Howe, August 28, 1947; ibid., Howe to Mitchell, August 29, 1947; ibid., Howe to Keenleyside, August 29, 1947.

25. Robert Bothwell and William Kilbourn, *C. D. Howe: A Biography* (Toronto, 1979), 215–6; IR, File B31627, pt. 1, Keenleyside to Pearson, April 23, 1947; KPC, Cabinet Conclusions, August 25, 1947, vol. 419; ibid., Cabinet Conclusions, June 28, 1948, vol. 420.

26. KPC, Cabinet Conclusions, August 14, 1947, vol. 419; Herbert H. Lehman Papers, Senate Research Files, Displaced Persons: Austria and Canada, "Canada's Immigration Program," March 2, 1948.

27. KPC, C. D. Howe, Memorandum for Cabinet re: displaced persons, June 2, 1947, vol. 421; ibid., Cabinet Conclusions, July 10, 1947, October 1, 1947, April 21, 1948, vol. 419.

28. IR, File 673931, Jolliffe to MacNamara, December 18, 1946; KPC, Cabinet Conclusions, January 23, 1947, vol. 419.

29. IRO, Box 35, AJ43, File 448/76, MacNamara to Jolliffe, February 25, 1947.

30. UNA, UNRRA-ERO, London, File DG25/35/1, For early immigration of experienced agricultural labor, Submission of the Canadian Sugar Beet Producers Association, January, 1947.

31. Ibid., Lowell W. Rooks to Lt. General Sir Humphrey Gale, February 10, 1947.

32. KPC, Cabinet Conclusions, July 18, 1947, vol. 419; IRO, Box 622, AJ46, C. G. Congdon to F. B. Cotsworth, July 18, 1947.

33. *Montreal Standard*, October 5, 1947.

34. PAC, DOL, Box 278, File 1-26-3-1, Mrs. Rex Eaton to MacNamara, March 28, 1947; ibid., Margaret Brier to MacNamara, April 24, 1947; ibid., J. Water Jones to MacNamara, April 17, 1947.

35. IRO, Box 622, AJ46, Isabel W. Bergman, Report of Canadian proceedings at Amberg Processing Center, December 1, 1947.

36. DOL, Box 277, File 1-26-2-1, A. H. Brown to George V. Haythorne, June 7, 1947.

37. IR, File B29300, Phelan to D. M. Lukow, as quoted in C. G. Congdon to Keenleyside, July 3, 1947; ibid., Congdon to Jolliffe, July 9, 1947; ibid., C. E. Smith to C. R. Mills, July 11, 1947; ibid., Mills to Smith, July 15, 1947.

38. IRO, Box 622, AJ46, Isabel W. Bergman, Report of Canadian proceedings at Amberg Processing Center, December 1, 1947. "It is to be noted," the report continued, "that the threat of difficulties running through the Canadian bulk labor operations seems most to involve the Jewish group. As is well known, the Jewish situation is a sticky problem. We have attempted to handle the problem as diplomatically as possible to see that our clients receive just treatment and also to protect Canada and the IRO from charges of anti-Semitism." Ibid.

39. CJC, UJRA, Robert Prochnik to Hayes, July 23, 1947.

40. CJC, CJCP, Hayes to community leaders, October 23, 1947.

41. IR, File B29300, MacNamara to Jolliffe, November 19, 1947; ibid., Jolliffe to James Colley, November 19, 1947.

42. IR, File 165172, Ben Nobleman to Howe, June 14, 1947.

43. PAC, DCI, Vol. 123, File 3-32-14, Hayes to Jolliffe, December 2, 1947.

44. UJRA, File 300, Salsberg to Hayes, December 12, 1947.

45. In the case of railway maintenance workers, it was alleged that the exclusion was ordered because: "Jewish people do not normally engage in this type of work," so could not be experienced in it. For the hardrock miners project, however, Jews were barred even though "previous experience was not necessary" for those willing to apply. Ibid., Jewish Telegraphic Agency News, "Canadian Immigration Mission's Discriminating Against Jews in Selecting D.P.s in Germany," January 9, 1948.

46. DCI, Vol. 123, File 3-32-24, Hayes to MacNamara, January 5, 1948; UJRA, File 300.

47. DCI, Vol. 123, File 3-32-14, MacNamara to Keenleyside, January 15, 1948; ibid., Keenleyside to MacNamara, January 19, 1948.

48. DOL, Box 277, File 1-26-2-1, George V. Haythorne to Soloman Grand, August 12, 1947; ibid., Grand to Haythorne, August 14, 1947; ibid., Grand to Haythorne, August 28, 1947; ibid., Haythorne to Grand, August 30, 1947.

49. DCI, Vol. 123, File 3-32-14, MacNamara to Hayes, January 23, 1948; IR, File B28865, Jolliffe to MacNamara, April 30, 1948.

50. PAC, Jewish Labor Committee Papers, Vol. 16, David Lewis to M. Lewis, July 8, 1948.

51. KP, Bronfman to King, February 14, 1947, 381898.

52. UJRA, File 300, S. Posluns to Hayes, February 14, 1947.

53. Ibid., Hayes to Posluns, February 18, 1947.

54. CJCP, Draft of brief requesting inclusion of needle trades workers among immigrants to be admitted to Canada, March 7, 1947; UJRA, File 300, Hayes to Posluns, March 12, 1947; ibid., Hayes to Max Enkin, March 12, 1947; Jewish Labor Committee Papers, Joint brief on behalf of the ladies cloak and suit industry of the Dominion of Canada, March 18, 1947; ILGWU, Toronto Joint Board Records, Box 7, File 7, Bernard Shame to S. Kraisman, March 25, 1947.

55. DOL, Box 278, File 1-26-5-1, David Dunkelman to Humphrey Mitchell, April 23, 1947.

56. IR, File B29300, pt. 1, F. M. Hereford to the Joint Immigration Labour Committee, June 2, 1947.

57. ILGWU, David Dubinsky Papers, Box 151, File 28, Joint brief, March 25, 1947.

58. UJRA, File 300, Norman Genser to Hayes, May 5, 1947.

59. KPC, Cabinet Conclusions, June 5, 1947, vol. 419.

60. JDC, Immigration of Needlepoint Workers, File 1947-51, Hayes to I. Rosen, May 9, 1947; ibid., Rosen to Hayes, May 14, 1947.

61. Interview with Max Enkin.

62. DOL, Box 278, File 1-26-5-1, Samuel Herbst to MacNamara, July 29, 1947.

63. JDC, Immigration of Needlepoint Workers, File 1947-51, Moses A. Levit to JDC, Paris, August 7, 1947; ibid., L. Stein to Irwin Rosen, August 18, 1947.

64. DOL, Box 278, File 1-26-5-1, Howe to Humphrey Mitchell, August 1, 1947; ibid., George G. Greene to MacNamara, August 2, 1947.

65. IRO, Box 622, AJ46, Memorandum by R. Innes of meeting with C. D. Howe, London, August 4, 1947.

66. DOL, Box 278, File 1-26-5-1, MacNamara to V. C. Phelan, September 8, 1947; IR, File B29300, C. G. Congdon to J. Colley, September 5, 1947; ibid., MacNamara to Phelan, September 18, 1947.

67. IRO, Box 622, AJ46, J. Colley to PCIRO, Geneva, August 25, 1947; IRO, Box 615, AJ46, PCIRO to field offices, August 25, 1947.

68. Interview with Max Enkin.

69. Hayes to David W. Ashurst, September 26, 1979 (in possession of the authors).

70. Interview with Max Enkin.

71. CJCP, Transcript of interview with David Solomon, September 28, 1966.

72. DOL, Box 278, File 1-26-5-1, Enkin to MacNamara, November 19, 1947; ibid., Samuel Herbst to MacNamara, October 8, 1947; interview with Max Enkin.

73. DOL, Box 278, File 1-26-5-1, Report by David Solomon, November 19, 1947.

74. UJRA, File 300, Robert Prochnik, Memorandum for file, November 11, 1947; IR, File B29300, Jolliffe to J. Colley, December 10, 1947.

75. DOL, Box 278, File 1-26-5-1, Enkin to MacNamara, November 19, 1947.

76. DCI, Vol. 1, File 6-1-223, Norman Genser to Keenleyside, December 1, 1947; DOL, Box 278, File 1-26-5-1, Genser to MacNamara, December 1, 1947.

77. IR, File B29300, C. E. S. Smith to N. Genser, February 5, 1945; DCI, Vol. 1, File 6-1-223, C. M. Hereford, Summary of discussion with representatives of the Canadian fur industry, February 18, 1948; IR, File B29300, R. M. Winter, Memorandum for file, February 20, 1948; DOL, Box 279, File 1-26-5-1, MacNamara to Genser, May 5, 1948; IRO, Box 622, AJ46, Immigration Branch to PCIRO, May 10, 1948.

78. DOL. Box 275, File 1-26-1-2, Harris Silver to V. C. Phelan, August 11, 1948; IRO, Box 622, AJ46, PCIRO to Immigration Branch, June 1, 1948; DOL, Box 275, File 1-26-1-2, Phelan to MacNamara, July 13, 1948; ibid., Phelan to MacNamara, July 27, 1948.

79. DOL, Box 279, File 1-26-5-2, N. Genser to MacNamara,

August 16, 1948; IRO, AJ46/622, Immigration Branch to PCIRO, October 6, 1948; CJCP, David I. Siegel, Report on Activities, November 5, 1948; IR, Orders-in-Council, Report of Interdepartmental Immigration–Labour Committee for Cabinet Committee on immigration policy, September 1, 1948.

80. DOL. Vol. 123, File 3-32-14, Hayes to Jolliffe, December 2, 1947.

81. KP, Bronfman to King, February 14, 1947, vol. 413; IR, File 739325, Bronfman to Glen, February 13, 1947; KP, R. G. Robertson to Bronfman, February 20, 1947, vol. 413.

82. JIAS(T), File 118, M. Kraicer to Solkin, June 26, 1946.

83. IR, File 739325, Jolliffe to Keenleyside, March 26, 1947; ibid., Keenleyside to Jolliffe, April 15, 1947; KPC, Cabinet Conclusions, April 29, 1947, vol. 419; IR, File 739325, Order-in-Council PC1647 re: admission of 1,000 children.

84. UJRA, File 300, Hayes to S. Grumback, April 30, 1947.

85. IR, File 739325, Memorandum, General features of planning project for immigration, reception and placement of 1,000 orphaned children; PAC, CNCR, Vol. 5, Wilson to Hayward, August 14, 1947; UJRA, File 224K, Hayes to C. E. S. Smith, July 17, 1947.

86. JDC, Canada: Immigration of Children 1946–50 File, Emilia Igel to Hayes, July 15, 1947; ibid., Emilia Igel to Jacob Jaslow, July 16, 1947.

87. IR, File 739325, Manfred Saalheimer to Hayes, September 9, 1947; CJCP, Hayes to community leaders, August 22, 1947; UJRA, File 224K, Saalheimer to Hayes, September 9, 1947.

88. UJRA, File 224K, Saalheimer to Hayes, September 9, 1947; CJCP, Hayes to community leaders, August 22, 1947; UJRA, File 224K, Saalheimer to Hayes, September 9, 1947.

89. JIAS(T), H. Latch to S. Grand, September 26, 1947.

90. UJRA, File 224K, M. Saalheimer to Hayes, September 9, 1947; ibid., Ethel Ostry to Hayes, February 14, 1948.

91. CJCP, Hayes to community leaders, September 19, 1947; B. Lappin, *Redeemed Children* (Toronto, 1963), 17.

92. Malcolm J. Proudfoot, *European Refugees: 1939–1952* (Evanston, 1956), 341; Hugh L. Keenleyside, "Canada's Immigration Policy" (Paper delivered at Dalhousie University, Halifax, November 19, 1948); Herbert H. Lehman Papers, Senate Research Files, Displaced Persons: Australia and Canada.

93. Kurt R. Grossmann, *The Jewish D.P. Problem: Its Origin, Scope and Liquidation* (New York, 1951), 26–9.

94. Jewish Labor Committee Papers, Vol. 16, David Lewis to M. Lewis, July 8, 1948.

95. Keenleyside, "Canada's Immigration Policy".

96. PAC, EA, Box 2113, Robertson to Pearson, January 23, 1947; IR, File 673931, pt. 16.

97. IR, File 673931, pt. 16, Keenleyside to R. C. Riddell, January 13, 1948.

98. DCI, Vol. 121, File 6-1-257, Memorandum of Keenleyside for Minister re: immigration of displaced persons to Canada, August 14, 1948.

99. IR, Orders-in-Council, Memorandum of Keenleyside for Cabinet Committee on Immigration Policy re: immigration of displaced persons to Canada, September 3, 1948.

100. KPC, Cabinet Conclusions, September 28, 1948, vol. 420.

101. For a review of Canadian policy on the Palestine issue see KPC, Louis St. Laurent to Cabinet, vol. 421.

102. Harold Dingman, "Liberty's Capital Report," *Liberty*, February 12, 1947; IR, File 541782, Pearson to Jolliffe, October 10, 1947; IR, File 673931, Pearson to Jolliffe, October 11, 1947; ibid., Jolliffe to Pearson, October 30, 1947.

103. Proudfoot, *European Refugees*, 357-9; ILGWU, Miscellaneous Correspondence, Toronto Joint Board Record, J. Z. Steinam to Joint Board, December 10, 1958.

9/Conclusion

1. Adele Wiseman, "The Lovebound," manuscript (Toronto, 1965).

2. See, for example, Yisrael Gutman and Efraim Zuroff, eds., *Rescue Attempts During the Holocaust* (Jerusalem, 1977); Bernard Wasserstein, *Britain and the Jews of Europe, 1934-1945* (London, 1979); Walter Laquer, *The Terrible Secret* (London, 1980); Yehuda Bauer, *American Jewry and the Holocaust* (Detroit, 1981); Lucy S. Dawidowicz, *The War Against the Jews, 1933-1945* (New York, 1976); Martin Gilbert, *The Allies and Auschwitz* (London, 1981).

3. Interview with Lord Joe Garner.

4. This point is well made in Henry Feingold, "Who Shall Bear Guilt for the Holocaust: The Human Dilemma," *American Jewish History* 68 (1979), 261-82.

5. Interview with Ben Lappin.

6. CJC, CJCP, Hayward to CNCR, Winnipeg, July 6, 1943; interview with Ben Lappin.

7. ILGWU, Miscellaneous Correspondence, Toronto Joint Board Records, Z. Steiman to Joint Board, December 10, 1958.

8. MBS, Sorensen to Cresswell, October 11, 1940 (in possession of Sorensen family).

INDEX